Best Bike Rides
Orange County, California

Help Us Keep This Guide Up to Date

Every effort has been made by the author and editors to make this guide as accurate and useful as possible. However, many things can change after a guide is published—trails are rerouted, regulations change, techniques evolve, facilities come under new management, etc.

We would appreciate hearing from you concerning your experiences with this guide and how you feel it could be improved and kept up to date. While we may not be able to respond to all comments and suggestions, we'll take them to heart, and we'll also make certain to share them with the author. Please send your comments and suggestions to the following address:

Globe Pequot
Reader Response/Editorial Department
246 Goose Lane
Guilford, CT 06437

Or you may e-mail us at: editorial@falcon.com.

Thanks for your input, and happy cycling!

BEST BIKE RIDES® SERIES

Best Bike Rides
Orange County, California

The Greatest Recreational Rides in the Metro Area

WAYNE D. COTTRELL

GUILFORD, CONNECTICUT

An imprint of Globe Pequot
Falcon and FalconGuides are registered trademarks and Make Adventure Your Story is a trademark of Rowman & Littlefield.

Distributed by NATIONAL BOOK NETWORK

All photos by Wayne Cottrell unless otherwise noted

British Library Cataloguing in Publication Information available

Library of Congress Cataloging-in-Publication Data available

ISBN 978-1-4930-2219-9 (paperback)
ISBN 978-1-4930-2220-5 (e-book)

∞™ The paper used in this publication meets the minimum requirements of American National Standard for Information Sciences—Permanence of Paper for Printed Library Materials, ANSI/NISO Z39.48-1992.

To my son Tyler, to Nancy, and to the memory of my mother Barbara and my grandmother Louella

A duo—great helmets, eh? —pedals along Aliso Creek Bikeway, with the Santa Ana Mountains' saddleback in the frame.

Contents

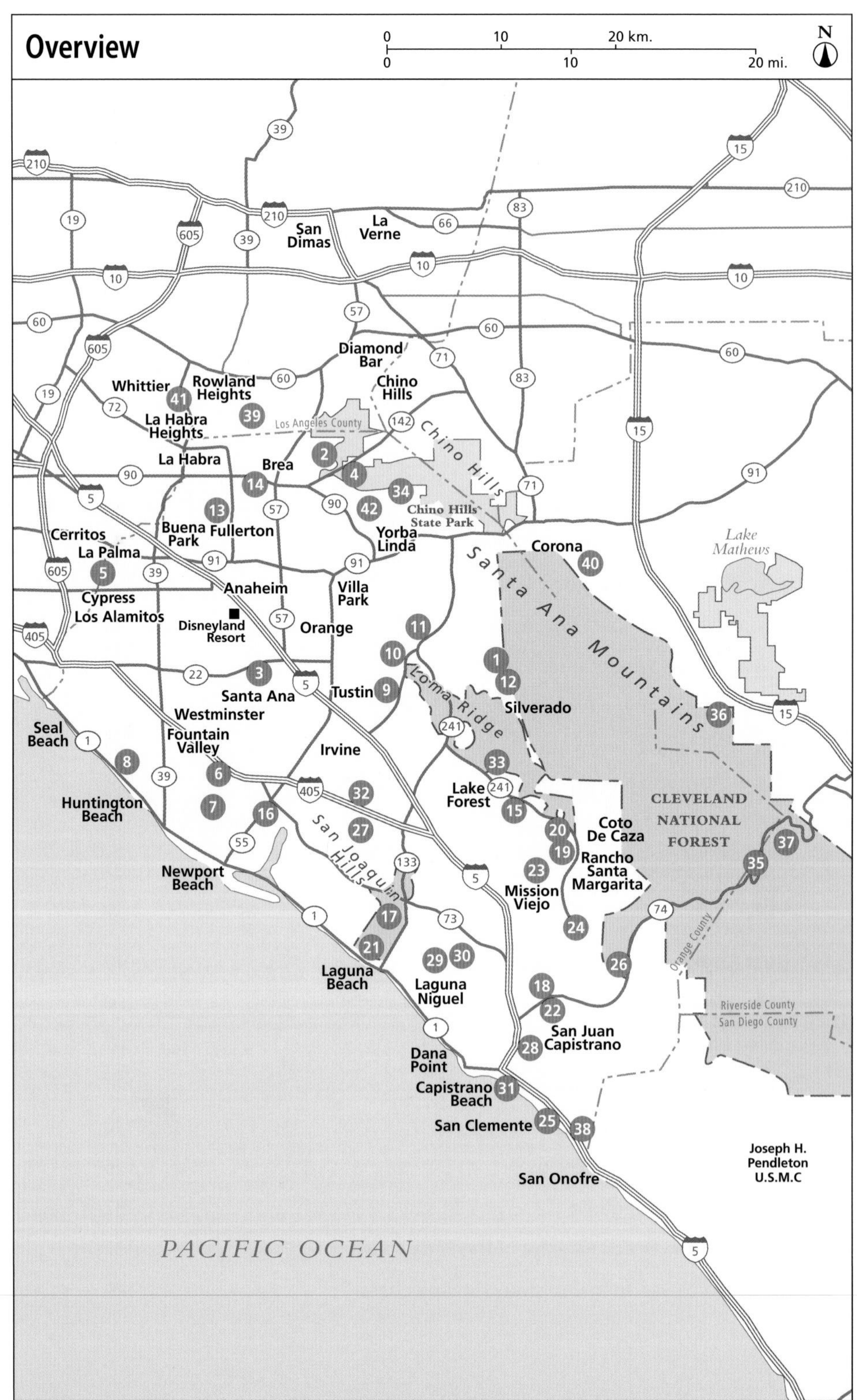
Overview
0
10
20 km.
0
10
20 mi.
N
San Dimas
La Verne
Diamond Bar
Chino Hills
Whittier
Rowland Heights
La Habra Heights
Los Angeles County
La Habra
Brea
Chino Hills
Chino Hills State Park
Cerritos
La Palma
Buena Park
Fullerton
Yorba Linda
Corona
Lake Mathews
Santa Ana Mountains
Cypress
Los Alamitos
Anaheim
Disneyland Resort
Villa Park
Orange
Tustin
Santa Ana
Westminster
Loma Ridge
Silverado
Seal Beach
Fountain Valley
Irvine
Huntington Beach
Lake Forest
San Joaquin Hills
Coto De Caza
CLEVELAND NATIONAL FOREST
Rancho Santa Margarita
Mission Viejo
Newport Beach
Orange County
Laguna Beach
Laguna Niguel
Riverside County
San Diego County
San Juan Capistrano
Dana Point
Capistrano Beach
San Clemente
San Onofre
Joseph H. Pendleton U.S.M.C
PACIFIC OCEAN

Abstract

This book offers rides of various lengths and terrain to cover a wide range of abilities, from short, flat treks for beginners, families, and recreational cyclists to long, hilly adventures for experienced and even competitive riders. The Orange County region is relatively compact, with an area just under 1,000 square miles. Corey Schlom's *The Unseen O.C.* suggests, however, that there are sides of Orange County with which few are familiar, even within its relatively small space. This book exposes the popular spots and some lesser-known corners of the county, along with some rides on the county's edge. The twenty road biking routes and twenty-two mountain biking routes highlighted here show why Orange County remains one of the top US biking destinations.

Introduction

While Orange County is statistically and geographically part of the expansive Los Angeles–Long Beach–Anaheim Metropolitan Area, Orange County is large and distinct enough to be given separate consideration. Its population of just over 3 million in 2010 represented "only" 20% of the Los Angeles urbanized area's population, but Orange County was and still is the sixth most populous county in the United States. Orange County is small and compact by Southern California standards, with an area of just 948 square miles. The county's geography is characterized as an extension of the Los Angeles Basin in the north and west, and the Santa Ana Mountains in the east, the latter of which rise to 5,687 feet (Santiago Peak). In between the basin and the mountains is Loma Ridge, which runs parallel to the Santa Anas along the eastern edge of the basin, separated from the Santa Anas by Santiago Canyon. The foothills of the Santa Ana Mountains tend to dominate the southern part of the county, with Saddleback Valley being the most prominent low-lying expanse. Because there is essentially no geographic barrier between L.A. and Orange Counties, the two are effectively seamless at their border.

Development in Orange County is concentrated in the aforementioned basin, and in the foothills leading up to Loma Ridge, as well as the foothills in the south. The newest areas of development, as of this writing, were in southern Orange County, in unincorporated areas to the south of Mission Viejo, and to the east of San Juan Capistrano. Despite the extensive development, "hidden" areas of Orange County remain comparatively untouched, including the Santa Ana Mountains, most of Loma Ridge, and various enclaves and nooks. A significant amount of land has been preserved for natural habitats, including an extensive regional park system, open spaces of the Irvine Ranch Conservancy, and Cleveland National Forest.

Bicycling in Orange County is popular and thriving, in part because of the year-round Mediterranean weather that is an attraction of the entire Los Angeles region. Packs of cyclists can be seen riding the roads in Irvine and Santiago Canyon on a regular basis. There are several long, car-free bicycle paths in the county, and most of the newer roads—particularly those in the southern part of the county—feature bike lanes. Off-road cycling is permitted on nearly all of the trails in the regional parks and in Cleveland National Forest; a limited amount of off-road riding is available in the Irvine Conservancy's open spaces.

ABOUT ORANGE COUNTY

Orange County is heavily urbanized, as suggested above, but is unusual in that there is no major central city. That is, there are thirty-four incorporated cities in the county, and none of them can claim to be the county's beacon. For the purposes of this book, Anaheim—the largest city at 351,433 persons in 2015—is treated as the county's center. But the county seat, Santa Ana, is nearly as populous (335,264 in 2015). Plus, there are two other cities with populations of 200,000 or more (Huntington Beach and Irvine), and four others with populations of 100,000 or more (Costa Mesa, Fullerton, Garden Grove, and Orange).

The county's economy was originally based on cattle ranching, in the mid-19th century until the late 1880s, when silver was discovered in the Santa Ana Mountains. Soon after settlers started flocking to the area, the county

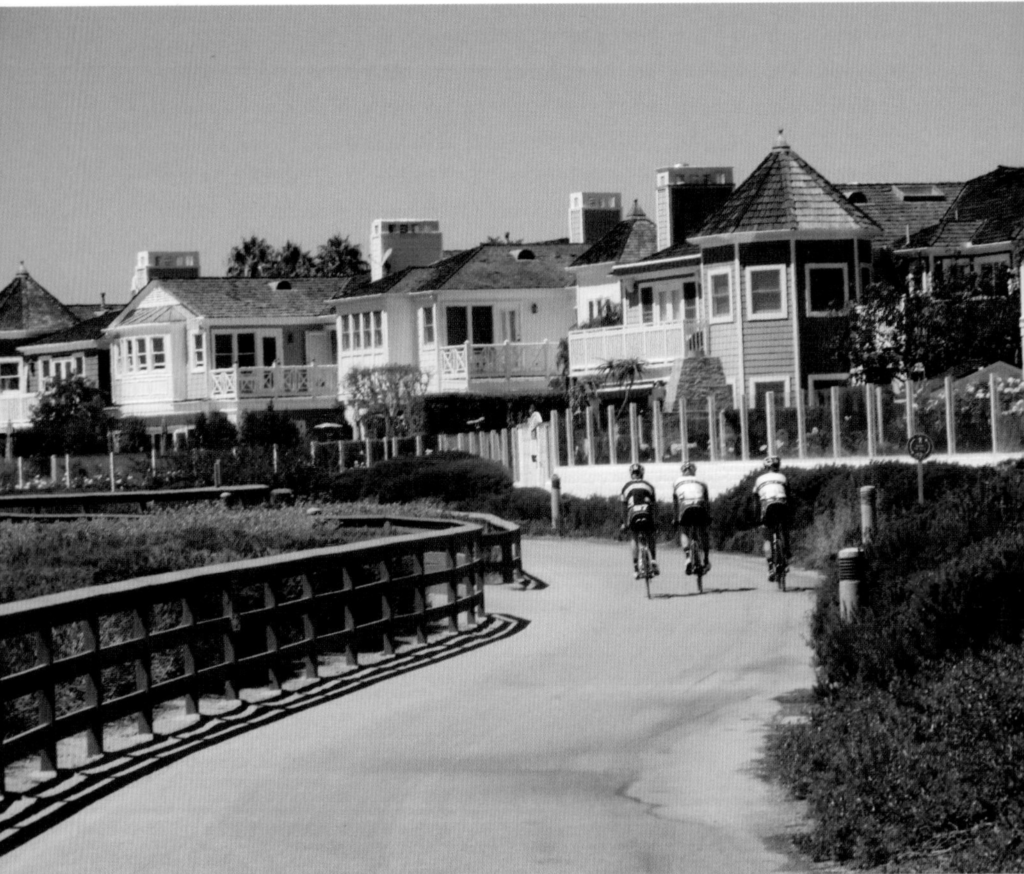

Cyclists go three abreast on a path in Westcliff, along Newport Beach's Back Bay.

was separated from Los Angeles County (1889). Agriculture also became vital to the economy, particularly citrus fruits and avocados, as well as oil extraction. With transportation improvements, which initially featured the railroad and electric trolleys, and later highways, Orange County became attractive as a Los Angeles suburb, as well as a getaway for prosperous Los Angelenos. The economy transformed after World War II with this growth, and was given a boost with the opening of Disneyland in 1955.

Today, Orange County's economy is dependent on tourism, technology, medicine, entertainment, and education. Several major companies are headquartered in the county, along with the US headquarters of several international firms. A system of toll freeways generates hundreds of millions of dollars in revenue annually. Although the county effectively declared bankruptcy in 1994, it has been able to thrive, tapping into its many resources. As for tourism, Orange County's top spots include Disneyland, Knott's Berry Farm, and the beaches, although there are plenty of "lesser" attractions, including Crystal Cathedral, Orange County Zoo, Richard M. Nixon's Birthplace and Museum, and others. Neither of the first two on the list are visited by the routes in this book, mainly because bicycle access is not favorable. But there is plenty to see in Orange County by bicycle, via the county's expansive network of trails, bikeways, and roads that are suitable for bikes. There are, in fact, so many trails, particularly in southern Orange County, that I ran out of room!

ABOUT THIS BOOK

For the purposes of the book, Orange County is divided into two regions: north and south. The cities of Newport Beach, Irvine, and Tustin mark the unofficial gateways to southern Orange County. A third region is formed on the edge of Orange County, to include routes that drift into neighboring Los Angeles, San Bernardino, and Riverside Counties. Fourteen rides are in the north, nineteen in the south, and nine are on the edge. There is a map and Miles and Directions section for each ride. Accompanying the maps and mileage logs are descriptions of each ride's main features, including road and trail conditions, traffic information, and scenery. Each ride's text also explores the history, folklore, special events, culture, flora, and fauna along the way so that the rider knows what to expect. The descriptions give each route character, helping the rider to, perhaps, relive and retrace milestones in Orange County's history. To keep the rider in the present, the descriptions also discuss demographics, urban issues, and transport infrastructure. Color photographs from the rides should entice readers to get out there and see for themselves.

Although Orange County is compact by Southern California standards, it can still be overwhelming to the uninformed cyclist who wants to go for a nice ride. Although the street systems of the cities in the northwestern part of the county are based on a rectangular grid pattern, most of the roads and routes that are great for riding are "off the grid." Thus, it is critical to have a guide offering clear descriptions of where to ride. To orient the user, the GPS coordinates of each start-finish point are included. Information on climb lengths and gradients are included as well.

RESOURCES

Bicycling in Orange County is promoted, supported, and improved by a variety of organizations, clubs, websites, and media. The key organizations are the Orange County Transportation Authority (550 South Main St., Orange, 715-560-OCTA, www.octa.net) and the Orange County Bicycle Coalition (www.ocbike.org). A number of cities have developed bike plans and/or bikeway networks, including Anaheim, Fullerton, Irvine, Lake Forest, San Juan Capistrano, Santa Ana, and Yorba Linda, while still others have developed off-road trail networks, including Laguna Niguel and San Clemente. Each of these cities may also have bicycling specialists among their planning and engineering personnel. The SoCalCycling website (http://socalcycling.com) has information on racing, clubs, bike shops, products, events, and other resources. The region is home to a host of bicycling clubs, ranging from recreational riders to serious racing teams—an excellent list is provided at http://socalcycling.com/clubs-teams. Bicycle shops are also great resources—a fine list is at http://socalcycling.com/bike-shops; also, each ride in this book is followed by information on one or more nearby bike shops. The Orange County Bicycle Coalition also has lists of clubs and shops on its website. Also, do not hesitate to treat the region's riders themselves, many of whom are quite knowledgeable, as resources.

SAFETY AND EQUIPMENT

For most of the road routes contained in this book, traffic ranges from minimal to medium heavy. In some places, the amount of traffic will depend on the time of day you are riding and the day of the week. Quiet suburban roads sometimes get swamped with traffic during the afternoon commute. In other places, traffic jams can occur on Saturday afternoons.

To be safe, it is paramount to be predictable. This means that when motorists have a good sense of what to expect from you, you'll be safer on the road. Riding with traffic, signaling turns, and generally obeying the same rules that apply to motor traffic are great habits to take up. For the novice, riding with traffic in Orange County will be easier than you think, especially if there is an adequate shoulder on the road. Riding is even easier when there is a bike lane, and easiest when there is a separated bike path. In any case, "share the road" signs are plentiful, such that drivers are aware that riders are out there.

Being predictable and eliminating bad cycling habits will go a long way in helping to minimize the chances of a collision. Avoiding bad spots caused by the ineptitude and carelessness of drivers means being able to anticipate potential problems before they happen. A couple of dangers to watch for are drivers opening car doors and drivers making left turns. The door zone—the area where car doors swing open—should be avoided, even if that requires riding farther into the traffic lane. Similarly, when avoiding potholes or other obstacles on the roadside, you have the right to take the lane. Avoid swerving; keep a level head and then move back to the right side of the road when your pathway is clear. One of the most common collisions occurs when oncoming cars turn left. Cyclists are advised to use special caution around these and other problem areas. Always assume that drivers do not see you.

Note that busy bicycle paths—such as the Santa Ana River Trail—can be hazardous when there is a mixture of path users, including pedestrians, slower cyclists, step-gliders, and others. Be prepared to act quickly and slow for children, dog walkers, and others in the path. If you are a beginning cyclist, then a bike safety class can be useful. Beginners will become more self-assured if they know basic skills such as riding predictably, being visible, and keeping a safe distance from parked cars. People who participate in a good bike safety class consistently express how much safer and more comfortable they feel riding in a variety of traffic conditions. Cycling courses also typically touch upon other topics, such as bike selection and fit, basics of bike handling, and maintenance.

What should you bring on your ride? This list varies a great deal depending on the season, the length of the ride, and how prepared you like to be. First, pack a pump and spare tube or patch kit. A small multi-tool will help with adjustments and minor repairs. Bring lights for front and back if there is even a slight chance that you'll be riding after dusk. Bring water, something to snack on, and one more layer than you think you'll need. Cell phones have proven to be handy in case help is needed; a few dollars will score you some freshly baked cookies along the way to replace your burned calories.

The weather in Orange County is perfect year-round for cycling. The higher elevations in the mountains may be the only place where you will find truly cool temperatures, and even some snowfall. Most often, a light layer of nylon or fleece is all you'll need in cooler weather; a jacket, light gloves, a thin cap, and comfortable pants will do the trick. If it's a long ride, take an extra layer. In warm weather, dress lightly, and carry plenty of fluids.

How to Use This Guide

When choosing rides in this book, observe both the length and the net elevation difference, as well as the range of ride times. The length will give you an idea of how long and doable a ride may be for you. Similarly, the net elevation difference will indicate the amount of climbing, although the indication is not exact, in that additional climbing can be concentrated between the two extremes of the net elevation differential. Road rides range from 9.8 to 46.8 miles, with more than half in the 20- to 30-mile range. The easiest rides have a high-low elevation differential of less than 250 feet—these are found along the coast, and in flatter inland areas. Much of Orange County is hilly, though, so flat rides are the exception rather than the rule. Only seven rides have an elevation differential of under 250 feet, including two mountain and five road routes. Most of the rides, mountain and road, are in the 250- to 1,000-foot high-low elevation differential range. Mountain bike rides range in length from 3.3 to 32.8 miles, with more than half in the 5- to 15-mile range. Seven of the mountain bike routes have an elevation differential of over 1,000 feet.

Taking a look at the Ride Finder section, you will see the distribution of ride distances and elevation changes. The easiest rides, and perhaps the best ones to do with children, use bike paths, have no more than a few hundred feet of elevation change, and are in the shorter-distance range. Note that rides can be improvised by turning around early on an out-and-back segment, or by concentrating on the bike path segments only. Also, longer rides can be created by doing two laps of a route rather than one. A measure that you can do—sorry, I did not do the math for this—would be to divide the elevation differential by the distance. The higher the value, the more challenging the ride.

UTM coordinates: Readers who use either a handheld or car-mounted GPS unit can punch in the UTM coordinates for each starting point, and have the GPS lead the way. The UTM coordinates are to be used with NAD 27 datum (rather than WGS83 or WGS84). All coordinates were generated using mapping software rather than taking readings in the field.

Mileage markers on the map: Do not be alarmed if the distances provided in the book do not match up with distances provided by existing trail maps or your own bike odometer. If you're using a bike odometer, keep in mind these have to be calibrated carefully; just changing to a larger tire can make a noticeable difference. While GPS devices are generally accurate, they too can lead you astray. If you backtrack or pursue a side trip and forget to subtract this distance from the total mileage covered, then of course it will

A rider heads toward San Clemente State Beach along San Clemente Beach Trail, with a retreating marine layer in the distance.

create a different mileage reading. The best policy is to use the mileage markers on the maps in this book as a rough guide that provides you with a close—but not exact—determination of distance traveled.

Traffic volumes: For many of the roads ridden in the book's routes, a recent 24-hour (1-day) traffic volume is provided. This is the average two-way volume along a specified segment of the road. Traffic volumes tend to vary by hour of the day, day of the week, and season, so the average is neither the maximum nor the minimum for the given road segment. As a general rule, a daily traffic volume of under 5,000 is light; 5,000 to 15,000 is medium; 15,000 to 25,000 is medium heavy; and 25,000 and over is heavy. Some routes use heavily trafficked roads out of necessity, for the scenery, or for the experience. Please note that traffic volumes are provided for paved roads only.

Times: To assist cyclists with ride planning, a range of estimated times (fast and leisurely) is provided for each ride. My time for the route is also provided and can be used as a benchmark. Please note that my times include all stops at traffic signals and stop signs.

HIGHWAY, STREET, PATH, AND TRAIL NAMES

Highway and street names are taken from street maps and signs. State highways are abbreviated CA. One state highway, the Pacific Coast Highway, is commonly referred to as PCH by locals. Path names are not always evident, but many of the Orange County region bike path names are painted onto the path at spaced intervals. There may also be small signs posted at entry points and junctions. Underpasses are often indicated by an overhead sign—without these, it can be difficult to tell exactly where you are relative to the outside world when on an exclusive bike path. Trails in Orange County's regional parks are well marked, as are those in the California state parks. Trails in Cleveland National Forest have sporadic signing, and sometimes the marker is that of a US Forest Service route (abbreviated FR in this book) rather than what might be indicated on a map. There are also other areas, such as the Puente Hills, where trail markers are sporadic. The mileage logs and text descriptions attempt to convey, as well as possible, proper directions, to keep you on course.

ROAD SURFACE, SHOULDER, PATH, AND TRAIL CONDITIONS

Road and path surfaces in the Orange County region are, in general, in good condition, unless otherwise noted. Similarly, shoulder widths are adequate, unless otherwise noted. Regarding trails, many of the mountain bike rides take advantage of fire roads, which are generally wide and graded. Some of the trails in the regional parks, and in Cleveland National Forest, are narrow and subject to rocky terrain. Further, some of the routes use unnamed singletrack trails to make connections—these can be overgrown, and at times rough. Erosion can occur over time, as well as fissures that are akin to small canyons on the trails. Challenging surface conditions can occur after heavy rains, after rock slides, and even after minor earth movements. Note that many of the park trails are closed for 3 days following a rainstorm. Trails can also be closed because of brush fires, construction, and even maintenance work on communications equipment.

HOW TO USE THE MAPS

Each ride map illustrates the given cycling route and starting-ending point against a backdrop of important roads, geographical features, communities, and landmarks. The maps include a limited amount of information, by intention, to emphasize the given route. Selected mile markers, along with the recommended direction of travel, are included on each map. For out-and-back segments, the mile markers generally pertain to the outbound direction of travel. The total length of the ride is listed near the starting-ending point. Note that the scale of each map may be different. If you need more detailed map and location information, then please refer to the "map" entry in each ride's header section.

Map Legend

195	Interstate Highway		Airport
6	US Highway		Bridge
6	State Highway		Building/Point of Interest
6	Featured State/Local Road		Campground
	Local Road		Elevation
	Featured Bike Route		Gate
	Bike Route	17.1	Mileage Marker
	Trail		Mountain Peak
	Railroad	P	Parking
	Airfield/Runway		Ranger Station
	State Line		Restroom
	County Line		Scenic View/Viewpoint
	Small River or Creek		School/College/University
	Body of Water		Small Park
	National Forest	1	Trailhead
	State Park/Forest/Wilderness/ Preserve/Recreational Area		Waterfall

Ride Finder

Ride	No.	Miles	Bike	Region	Elev. Differential
Aliso Creek Sneak	15	24.5	road	south	696 ft
Black Star Canyon Adventure	1	16.65	mtn	north	2,004 ft
Brea-Carbon (Free) Canyons Loop	2	22.8	road	north	783 ft
Central OC Velo	3	44.45	road	north	428 ft
Chino Hills Ridges Challenge	34	23.6	mtn	edge	1,320 ft
Chino Hills Trails Trek	4	12.3	mtn	north	1,177 ft
Circle Newport Bay	16	9.9	road	south	99 ft
Circuito Chiquito Ortega	35	12.85	mtn	edge	1,714 ft
Coyote Creek Corridor Cities	5	22.75	road	north	49 ft
Crystal Cove Mas Moro	17	15.6	mtn	south	900 ft
Cycle Surf City	6	22.55	road	north	64 ft
El Cañada Gobernadora	18	34.7	road	south	1,028 ft
El Cariso–Trabuco Peak Epic	36	32.8	mtn	edge	3,325 ft
Elsinore Mountains Divide Ride	37	45.85	road	edge	2,120 ft
Fairview-Talbert Nature Spin	7	6.2	mtn	north	76 ft
Harriett Wieder Trails Express	8	3.3	mtn	north	66 ft
Hi-Yo Arroyo Trabuco	19	12.05	mtn	south	730 ft
La Ruta Margarita	20	12.95	road	south	643 ft
Laguna Beach Pageant of the Pedals	21	23.6	road	south	656 ft
North San Juan Capistrano Steeplechase	22	12.1	mtn	south	565 ft
Olimpiada Mission Viejo	23	9.8	road	south	530 ft
Partial Pendleton Perimeter Ride	38	25.15	road	edge	173 ft

Ride	No.	Miles	Bike	Region	Elev. Differential
Peters Canyon Park and Ride	9	8.1	mtn	north	414 ft
Puente Hills Ridge Cycle	39	15.0	mtn	edge	808 ft
Riley Five Miley	24	4.65	mtn	south	320 ft
Ring around San Clemente	25	21.05	mtn	south	715 ft
Ronald Caspers Wild Ride	26	11.95	mtn	south	1,240 ft
San Joaquin Hills Expedition	27	7.45	mtn	south	761 ft
San Juan Hills Grind	28	9.85	mtn	south	686 ft
Santiago Canyon Circuit	10	30.35	road	north	1,212 ft
Santiago Oaks on Spokes	11	10.8	mtn	north	604 ft
Sierra Peak Enduro	40	24.5	mtn	edge	2,605 ft
Silverado and Modjeska Canyons Escape	12	22.3	road	north	956 ft
Soft and Hard Tails of Aliso-Wood	29	11.55	mtn	south	921 ft
South Laguna Summit-to-Sea	30	21.8	road	south	880 ft
The South OC BHC	31	28.1	road	south	604 ft
Tour of the Master Plan: Irvine Ranch	32	22.85	road	south	222 ft
Vamanos Alturas La Habra	41	29.2	road	edge	664 ft
West Fullerton Trails Survey	13	13.1	mtn	north	339 ft
Whiting Ranch Wilderness Excursion	33	5.4	mtn	south	662 ft
Yorba on Your Bike	14	24.3	road	north	384 ft
Yorba-Prado Dam Pronto	42	46.8	road	edge	808 ft

Prickly pear cacti—don't get too close—line Santiago Oaks Trail in Irvine Regional Park.

Best Northern Orange County Rides

Orange County does not feature any truly distinctive geographic barriers, other than the Santa Ana River, which runs from the northeast to the southwest through the county, and Loma Ridge and the Santa Ana Mountains, both in the eastern part of the county. The Santa Anas effectively form the border between Orange and Riverside Counties. Yet none of these geographic features suitably divide Orange County into subregions. One loose form of subregion division, which I ultimately used, was to look at when Orange County's cities incorporated. The older cities tended to be in the northwest, with a few exceptions, while the newer cities tended to be in the southeast. Only two of the cities in the south, Laguna Beach and San Clemente, incorporated before 1929. The rest of the "old" cities—Anaheim (1870—the oldest), Brea (1917), Fullerton (1904), Huntington Beach (1909), La Habra (1925), Newport Beach (1906), Orange (1888), Santa Ana (1886), Seal Beach (1915), and Tustin (1927)—are in the northwest, or north. Adding in cities that were incorporated between 1953 and 1967 (Buena Park, Costa Mesa, Cypress, Fountain Valley, Garden Grove, La Palma, Los Alamitas, Stanton, Villa Park, Westminster, and Yorba Linda) produces an area of 300 square miles, and a 2014 population of 2,126,000. So two-thirds of Orange County's population lives in just under one-third of its area!

Although northern Orange County is heavily urbanized, there are a few nice open spaces, such as the Bolsa Chica Ecological Reserve in Huntington Beach, Santiago Oaks, and Irvine Regional Park in Orange. The eastern edge of Orange is the gateway to Santiago Canyon, with Loma Ridge on the right (mostly protected and inaccessible) and the Santa Ana Mountains on the left (mostly but not entirely accessible) when heading south. Paved bike paths serve the area, including ones along Coyote Creek, near the Los Angeles County border, and Santiago Creek, which is central. There is also the well-known Santa Ana River Trail, which extends across the entire county. Further, the city of Fullerton has a nifty network of unpaved trails that connect parks and small open spaces. Thus, despite the high population density (over 7,000 persons per square mile!), there are ample opportunities for road and mountain bike riding.

Those who are drawn to northern Orange County for its attractions—notably Disneyland—might be disappointed to find that bicycle accessibility to the amusement park is limited. The bordering streets do not feature bike lanes or route signing. Yet northern Orange County has plenty to offer, in terms of the seven road and seven mountain bike rides described below.

1

Black Star Canyon Adventure

Start: Black Star Canyon Road trailhead, end of Black Star Canyon Road, near Silverado

Length: 16.65 miles (out-and-back)

Riding time: 1.5 to 4 hours (my time: 2H03:30)

Terrain and surface: 92% dirt trails and fire roads; 8% paved

Elevations: Low—858 feet at the transition from pavement to dirt along Black Star Canyon Road; high—2,862 feet at mile 8.0, just south of Skyline Road on Black Star Canyon Road

Traffic and hazards: 100% of the ride is on trails and fire roads that are not frequented by motor vehicles.

Map: *The Thomas Guide by Rand McNally—Street Guide: Los Angeles and Orange Counties* (any recent year), page 801

Getting there by car: From central Anaheim, head south on I-5 to Chapman Avenue, in Orange. Head east on Chapman. At Jamboree Road, Chapman becomes Santiago Canyon Road, heading southeast. Turn left at Silverado Canyon Road, and then turn left onto Black Star Canyon Road. Follow Black Star Canyon Road to its end; park here, near the gate.

Getting there by public transit: Black Star Canyon is comparatively remote, and is not served by public transit. The closest bus stop is at Santiago Canyon College (please see Ride 10, Santiago Canyon Circuit), located on Santiago Canyon Road, just under 8 miles from the Black Star Canyon gate. From the college, on your bike, head east on Chapman Avenue, which becomes Santiago Canyon Road at Jamboree Road. After riding on Santiago Canyon Road for a stretch, turn left onto Silverado Canyon Road, and then left again onto Black Star Canyon Road. Follow the road 1.1 miles to the gate, as above.

Starting point coordinates: 33.764408°N / 117.678061°W

THE RIDE

The Black Star Canyon Adventure is, as the name implies, an adventurous 16.65-mile mountain bike ride in the Santa Ana Mountains of northeastern Orange County. The net elevation gain of the out-and-back ride is 2,004 feet, in 8 miles. The return trip features a rapid descent. Black Star Canyon has a rich history and folklore; the canyon and surrounding lands have multiple layers of preservation, including the Irvine Ranch National Natural Landmarks, Cleveland National Forest, the Wildlands Conservancy (through the Mariposa Reserve), and some private land ownership. Artifacts from the era of the ancient Tongva-Gabrielino peoples have been found in the canyon. Mining operations in the canyon area started during the early 19th century, and continued well into the 20th before ceasing. Some old mining equipment, infrastructure, and shafts can still be seen. A brutal massacre of the Tongva, who were accused of stealing horses, occurred in the canyon in 1831, when a militia of armed fur trappers mowed them down. Some of the natives escaped, but many were slaughtered. Yet another killing occurred in the canyon in 1899, when James Gregg was murdered by Henry Hungerford in an argument over a $10 debt.

During the 1920s, the US Forest Service constructed Black Star Canyon Road to facilitate access from Orange County, through the forest, up and over the mountains, into Corona, in Riverside County. The "road" was always intended for hikers, as opposed to motor vehicles, for the purpose of forest access. A number of canyon legends have endured, such as haunted pieces of farming equipment, ghosts of those who lost their lives in canyon incidents, a homeless man (Black Star Bill) who occasionally shoots at trespassers, and even phantasmal dwarf-life creatures. I tested the suppositions by hiking down the canyon at night—alone—and encountered none of the legends. (Although this is not recommended. I had my bike, but ditched it after a rainstorm turned the trails into mush.)

Bike Shops

Sho-Air Cyclery, 8530 East Chapman Ave., Orange, (844) 722-9253, http://shoaircyclinggroup.com

Presuming that the folklore and legends have not frightened you away, begin the ride at the end of Black Star Canyon Road (motor vehicle portion), 1.1 miles north of Silverado Canyon Road. There is a gate here, marking the entrance to the backcountry. Navigate the gate, and head north on the road, which descends gradually for the next 0.6 mile. The road turns sharply to the right here, entering the canyon. To your left is private property—Irvine Lake (private) is just over the horizon. Stay to the left at the trail junction at mile 1.1. From here, the dirt road climbs at a moderate gradient of 2.8%. There are

"You're not very aerodynamic in those shorts"—two riders head toward the mouth of Black Star Canyon.

some private lands and facilities adjacent the road. There are three bridged crossings of Black Star Creek—these are great to use as markers of progress.

At mile 2.45, Black Star Canyon Road curves sharply to the left, and the gradient of the climb increases markedly. To your right, at the curve, is a hiking trail that eventually leads to Black Star Canyon Falls, a seasonal waterfall that features upper and lower falls. The two segments are connected by a man-made tunnel (dug to serve mining operations), such that the lower falls appear to be emanating from a cliff, with no apparent source. The hiking trail is not rideable, even deteriorating to bouldering and rock-scaling. Back to the road, the near-hairpin curve is at an elevation of 1,133 feet. From here, the road climbs at an average grade of 7.9% for the next 2 miles. The road twists and winds its way up the mountain, with spectacular views of the surrounding lands, as well as the urbanization off in the distance. At an elevation of 2,001 feet, a sign marks the entrance to Mariposa Reserve. The sign, upon first glance, seems to say "no trespassing." But the fine print indicates that the trail is open for public use. The gradient eases through the reserve, even turning downhill for a while. You will also notice short segments of pavement in the vicinity of the reserve—these are, apparently, remnants of the original US Forest Service road.

Mariposa Reserve features native habitats of coastal sage scrub, valley needlegrass, sycamore riparian woodland, coast live oak riparian forests, chaparral, and spring wildflowers, including Mariposa lilies (hence the reserve's name). There are plenty of birds, some of which are imperiled species, and even a couple of mountain lions who wear tracking devices. Consider the passage through the reserve as a break from the canyon's otherwise arduous terrain. Leave the reserve around mile 6, at an elevation of 2,074 feet. Resume climbing! Black Star Canyon Road continues up the mountain at an average grade of 7.8% over the next 1.8 miles. Some segments of the road were eroded when I rode it; I also noticed that the number of surface rocks increased with elevation.

Navigate the gate at mile 7.75—seasoned mountain bikers take 1 hour or less to make it this far. Continue the short distance to Main Divide Road North (US Forest Road 3S04). To your left, off the trail, is Beek's Place. Main Divide Road runs from the northwest to the southeast along the spine of the range. Turn left here; you are at an elevation of 2,803 feet, with a bit more climbing yet to come. Continue uphill at a gentler 4.4% grade to the maximum elevation of the ride, 2,862 feet, at mile 8. From here, it is a rapid descent at a 9.1% grade to the junction with Skyline Road. Turn around here; transmission equipment for a regional radio station is in the pasture to your left. Sierra Peak is in the distance—in case you are intrigued, Ride 40, Sierra Peak Enduro, takes you there. The elevation at the turnaround is 2,704 feet.

Begin the descent of Black Star Canyon (the return ride is the reverse of the way you came) with the steepest climb of the entire ride! Head up Main Divide Road North, to the crest. After a short downhill, veer off of Main Divide, to the right, onto Black Star Canyon Road. Navigate the gate, and then let 'er coast. Choose your speed here, but be aware of other trail users, eroded segments, rocks in the road, and potentially slippery turns. Enjoy the spectacular views of the canyon. The only real break on the descent is through Mariposa

Beek's Place

The ruins of Beek's Place are well known among the Santa Ana Mountains' hikers and bikers. One large and one small cabin served as Beek's Place, the weekend residence of Joseph Beek (1880–1968) and his family. Mr. Beek was an accomplished man who served as the Newport Beach harbormaster, owner of the Balboa Island Ferry, and secretary of the California State Senate. The Beek family still owns the ferry. The construction of the cabins dates from the 1930s. The family planted coniferous trees on the property, using a system of cisterns for water storage and swimming(!). Despite the family's use of a caretaker who would live on the property for lengths of time, the residence fell into disrepair. Vandalism and theft over the years contributed to the place's demise, rendering the residence uninhabitable. Members of the Beek family still visit the place, though, perhaps reliving the heydays of Joseph Beek.

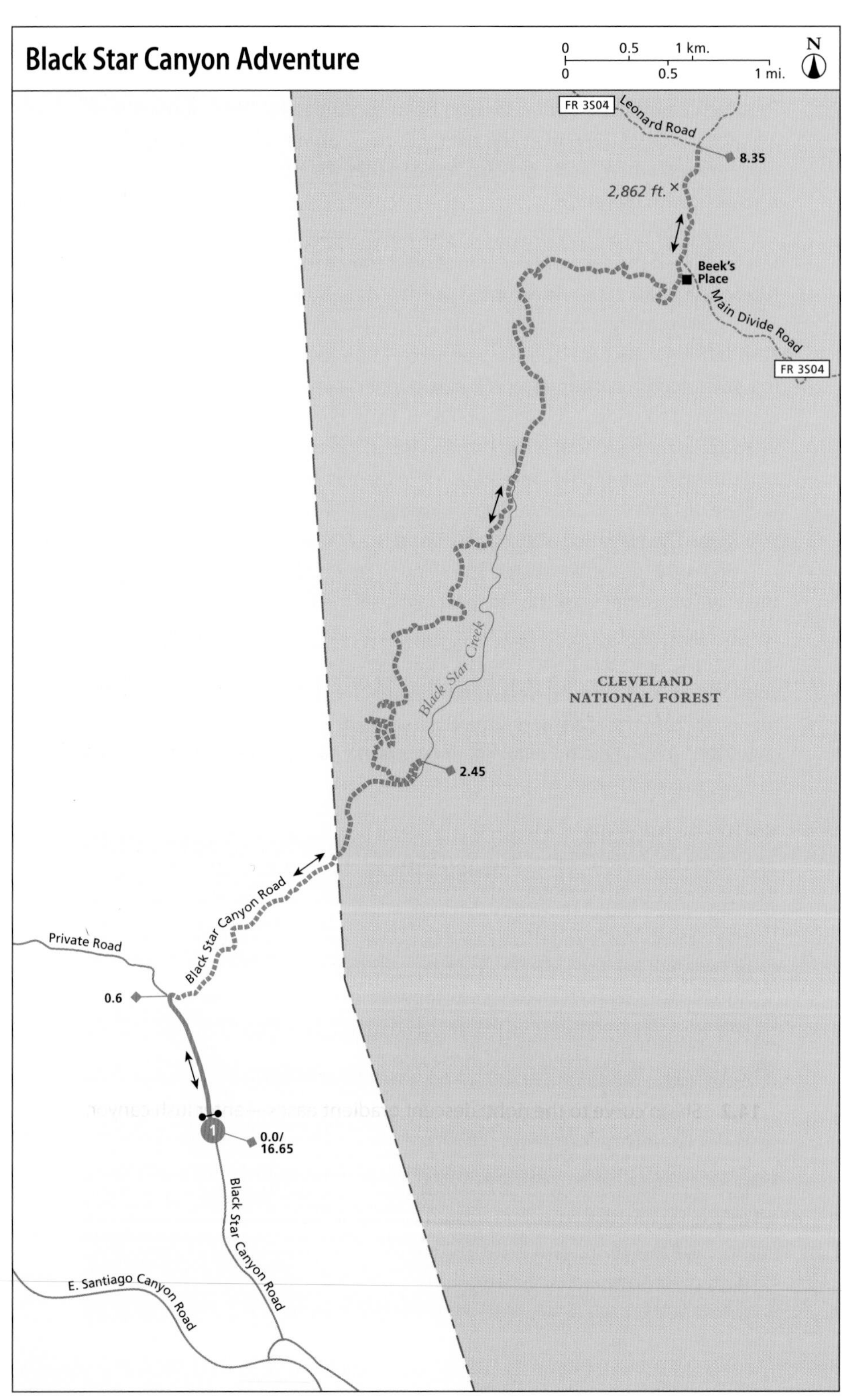
Black Star Canyon Adventure
0
0.5
1 km.
0
0.5
1 mi.
N
FR 3S04
Leonard Road
8.35
2,862 ft.
Beek's Place
Main Divide Road
FR 3S04
Black Star Creek
CLEVELAND NATIONAL FOREST
2.45
Black Star Canyon Road
Private Road
0.6
0.0/ 16.65
Black Star Canyon Road
E. Santiago Canyon Road

Reserve. After you make that final hairpin curve at mile 14.2, and start crossing the bridges over Black Star Creek, you may need to check your speed, as the lower segment of Black Star Canyon Road is heavily used by hikers. The road makes a 90-degree bend to the left at mile 16.05, and the surface returns to pavement. Signs indicate how far it is to the gate at which you started; end the ride there.

MILES AND DIRECTIONS

0.0 Start just beyond the gate at the end of Black Star Canyon Road north of Silverado Canyon Road (motor vehicles are allowed up to the gate). Head north on Black Star Canyon.

0.6 Black Star Canyon Road curves to the right (private property to the left). Pavement transitions to dirt; begin gradual climb (2.8% gradient).

1.1 Trail junction—keep straight.

2.45 Sharp curve to the left; remain on Black Star Canyon Road—gradient increases (7.9%).

4.5 Enter Mariposa Reserve (elevation 2,001 feet)—gradient eases.

5.95 Leave Mariposa Reserve (elevation 2,074 feet)—resume steep climbing (7.8% grade).

7.75 Gate near Main Divide Road; go around gate and bear left onto Main Divide.

8.0 High elevation of ride (2,862 feet).

8.35 Turn around at junction with Skyline Road, adjacent pasture with radio transmission equipment (elevation 2,704 feet). Begin climb (8.5% grade).

8.7 Return to high elevation mark (2,862 feet); begin descent.

8.95 Bear right onto Black Star Canyon Road; go around gate.

10.7 Enter Mariposa Reserve—gradient of descent eases.

12.15 Leave Mariposa Reserve—resume steep descent.

14.2 Sharp curve to the right; descent gradient eases—enter lush canyon segment.

15.55 Trail junction—keep straight.

16.05 Sharp curve to the left—continue on Black Star Canyon Road (paved).

16.65 Gate marking end of ride.

2

Brea-Carbon (Free) Canyons Loop

Start: Carbon Canyon Regional Park, 4442 Carbon Canyon Rd., Brea

Length: 22.8 miles (clockwise loop)

Riding time: 1.25 to 3.5 hours (my time: 1H28:05)

Terrain and surface: Paved roads

Elevations: Low—381 feet at Central Avenue and Brea Boulevard in Brea; high—1,164 feet at Grand Avenue and Shotgun Lane in Diamond Bar

Traffic and hazards: Daily traffic volumes in Diamond Bar were 10,940 on Brea Canyon Road south of Diamond Bar Boulevard, 44,350 on Diamond Bar Boulevard at Mountain Laurel Way, and 26,530 on Grand Avenue east of Longview Avenue; and 24,900 on Chino Hills Parkway south of Grand Avenue in Chino Hills, all counted in 2008. CA 142 carried 18,700 vehicles per day southwest of Chino Hills Parkway in 2014.

Map: *The Thomas Guide by Rand McNally—Street Guide: Los Angeles and Orange Counties* (any recent year), page 709

Getting there by car: From central Anaheim, head north on the CA 57 freeway. Exit at Lambert Road and turn right. Lambert Road becomes Carbon Canyon Road after crossing Valencia Avenue. Look for the entrance to Carbon Canyon Regional Park on the right, two-thirds of a mile after crossing Valencia.

Getting there by public transit: From central Santa Ana or Anaheim, ride Orange County Transportation Authority (OCTA) bus route 57 north on State College Boulevard to the end of the line at Brea Mall, north of Birch Street in Brea. From here, ride north on State College; turn right and head eastward on Lambert Road. Follow the above instructions from here. Bus route 57 runs every 20 minutes on weekdays, every 30 minutes on Saturdays, and every 20 to 30 minutes on Sundays and holidays.

Starting point coordinates: 33.922367°N / 117.837019°W

THE RIDE

The Brea-Carbon (Free) Canyons Loop is a 22.8-mile ride that starts and finishes at Carbon Canyon Regional Park in Brea. Besides the ride, the park is worth exploring, particularly for the grove of redwood trees. Redwoods? Yes—although these trees are not native to Southern California, these were planted in the mid-1970s and, through special care, have become the largest such grove in the region. The grove is located on the east end of the park, after a 1.1-mile walk/hike along the Carbon Canyon Nature Trail.

The ride starts in Brea and passes through the cities of Diamond Bar and Chino Hills, along with unincorporated stretches in between, before returning to Brea. The ride starts on the west end of the park (not near the redwoods), and immediately exits it, onto Carbon Canyon Road. Turn left here (there is a traffic signal), and head west. After crossing Valencia Avenue, Carbon Canyon becomes Lambert Road as you enter busier areas of Brea. Although Brea may seem fresh and new as you ride through, it is actually one of the older towns in Orange County, having incorporated in 1917.

After crossing under the CA 57 freeway, turn right onto State College Boulevard. Ride cautiously amidst the motor vehicle traffic. Next, turn right onto Brea Boulevard and head north. Brea curves to the right upon leaving

Black Gold in Brea

The city of Brea had humble beginnings as the community of Olinda, which was settled during the early 19th century primarily for the prospects of petroleum in the hills surrounding Carbon Canyon. By the late 19th century, the Union Oil Company of California had been formed, and oil-drilling towers had sprouted. The towers occupied the Brea-Olinda Oil Field, which spanned the hills between Carbon and nearby Brea Canyons. Oil workers and their families settled in the adjacent community of Randolph. The two communities eventually merged, and then were renamed Brea. Olinda was the home of baseball legend Walter Johnson (1887–1946), who lived there from age 14 until moving away to Idaho, and then on to the big leagues with the Washington Senators. He still holds a century-old record of most career shutouts by a pitcher, with 110, along with several other records. He was one of the first five major leaguers elected to the Baseball Hall of Fame. As for the oil field, production had declined by the 1950s. Yet, as of this writing, some 475 oil wells were still in operation, under the ownership of several independent oil companies.

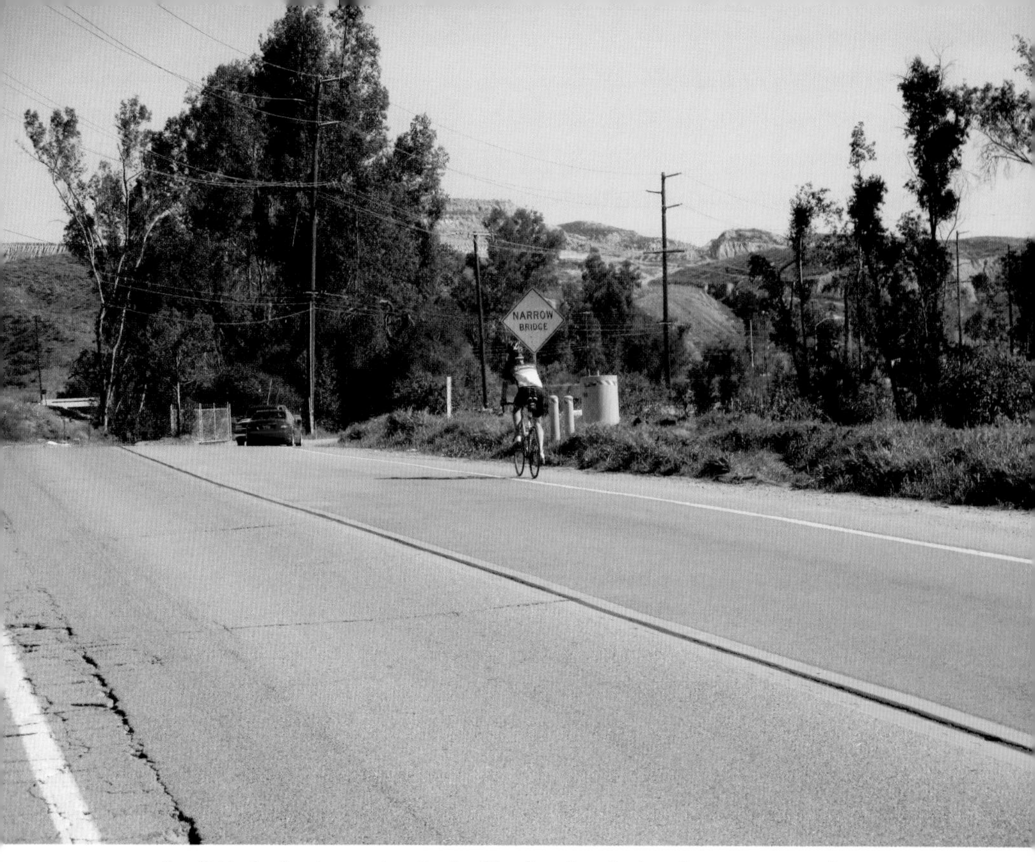

A cyclist looks ahead to see that the shoulder along Brea Boulevard continues across the upcoming narrow bridge.

the city of Brea; the road narrows and becomes Brea Canyon Road as you enter the canyon (and Los Angeles County). It is a gradual uphill, with the CA 57 freeway roaring to your right, and then to your left as you pass underneath and enter the city of Diamond Bar. In the hills to the right is the expansive Firestone Boy Scout Reservation, with numerous trails, campsites, and other facilities. While Brea has roots that date back to the early 20th century, the first significant development in Diamond Bar did not occur until the 1960s. The city incorporated in 1989; just over 50% of the population had an Asian heritage as of 2010. The city is the hometown of US women's soccer team forward Alex Morgan, who was given the Key to the City in 2016.

Turn right onto Diamond Bar Boulevard at mile 7.4. The road is gradually uphill. The boulevard is busy, but the surrounding development is predominantly residential. At mile 10.5, turn right onto Grand Avenue. This is one of the steeper climbs of the ride, at a gradient of 5.6%. Grand Avenue reaches a crest opposite Shotgun Lane and Summitridge Park; this is the high elevation of the entire ride, at 1,164 feet. From here, Grand Avenue plunges into Tonner Canyon and then climbs into the city of Chino Hills, and San Bernardino

County. After another crest, Grand Avenue descends to Chino Hills Parkway (mile 13.8)—be cautious on the intersection approach, as there is a retail development on the corner. Turn right and do the short (0.3-mile) climb to Village Center Drive. From here, the parkway descends steadily through the city.

Turn right onto Carbon Canyon Road (CA 142, at mile 15.2) to begin the final and perhaps most interesting leg of the ride. Carbon Canyon begins with a gentle climb toward the Chino Hills (the actual hills—you are still in the like-named city). After climbing 166 feet in 1.2 miles (2.6% grade), Carbon Canyon Road curves to the right at its intersection with Old Carbon Canyon Road. The canyon narrows here, commencing a twisting, winding stretch that curls its way to another crest. Hug the shoulder along here, and be aware of motor vehicles approaching from behind. After a 0.6-mile climb at a 7.8% gradient—steepest of the ride—the road reaches an elevation of 1,157 feet. You now have 5.8 miles to go, through a semi-rural environment. Most of this stretch is downhill. Enter Brea and Orange County at mile 19.1, although Brea is lightly developed out here. Enter the historic community of Olinda at mile 21.0—the road climbs for a stretch as you leave the community. The road then enters Chino Hills State Park just past Olinda—venture onto this park's trails in the Chino Hills Trails Trek (Ride 4) and Chino Hills Ridges Challenge (Ride 34).

Bike Shops

Two Wheeler Dealer, 1039 East Imperial Hwy., Brea, (714) 671-1730, www.twdcycling.com; Pro Bike Parts, 615 Berry St., Brea, (714) 255-9172

I rode this route during the afternoon commute and saw a long queue of motor vehicle traffic snaking its way up Carbon Canyon, in the opposite direction. It made coming down the canyon, in the relatively car-free reverse direction, all the sweeter! Leave the park and reenter Brea at mile 22.3. The state park, now on your left, seamlessly transitions to Carbon Canyon Regional Park. The ride ends at the entrance to the park, on your left, opposite Santa Fe Road (the intersection is signalized).

MILES AND DIRECTIONS

0.0 Start from Carbon Canyon Regional Park; enter Carbon Canyon Road (CA 142) by turning left upon exiting the park, opposite Santa Fe Road.

0.7 Traffic signal at Valencia Avenue; keep straight—now on Lambert Road.

2.55 Pass under CA 57 freeway (exercise caution).

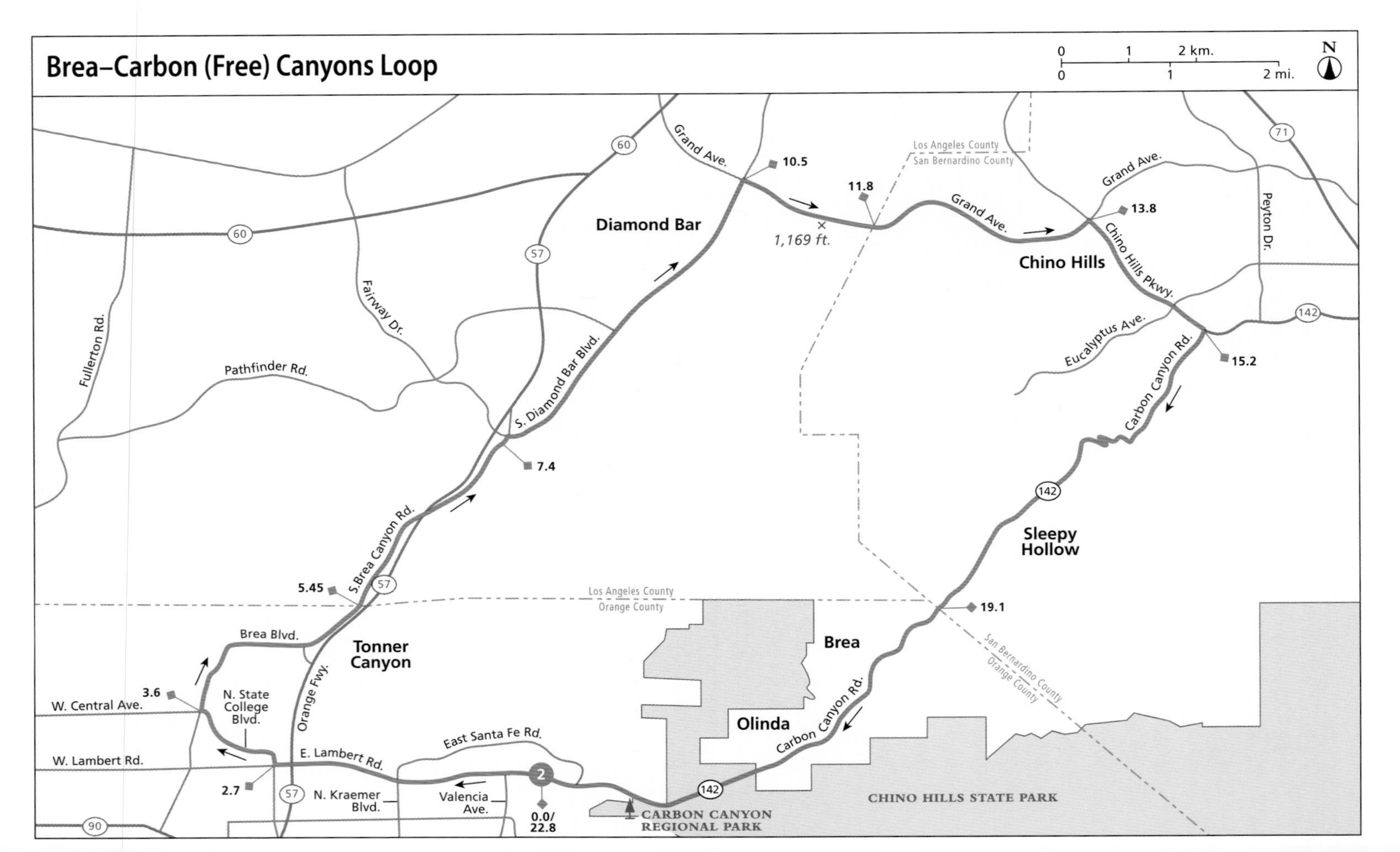

Brea–Carbon (Free) Canyons Loop
0
1
2 km.
0
1
2 mi.
N
Grand Ave.
10.5
11.8
1,169 ft.
Los Angeles County
San Bernardino County
Grand Ave.
13.8
Chino Hills
Chino Hills Pkwy.
Peyton Dr.
71
60
57
Diamond Bar
142
Eucalyptus Ave.
15.2
Carbon Canyon Rd.
Fairway Dr.
Fullerton Rd.
Pathfinder Rd.
S. Diamond Bar Blvd.
7.4
S.Brea Canyon Rd.
Sleepy
Hollow
5.45
Los Angeles County
Orange County
19.1
Brea Blvd.
Tonner
Canyon
Brea
San Bernardino County
Orange County
3.6
W. Central Ave.
N. State
College
Blvd.
Orange Fwy.
Olinda
Carbon Canyon Rd.
East Santa Fe Rd.
W. Lambert Rd.
E. Lambert Rd.
2
2.7
N. Kraemer
Blvd.
Valencia
Ave.
0.0/
22.8
CHINO HILLS STATE PARK
CARBON CANYON
REGIONAL PARK
90

2.7 Traffic signal at State College Boulevard; turn right.

3.6 Traffic signal at Brea Boulevard; turn right.

4.0 Leave Brea city limits—enter unincorporated Orange County.

5.45 Leave Orange County, enter Los Angeles County (unincorporated)—now on Brea Canyon Road.

6.8 Enter the city of Diamond Bar.

7.4 Traffic signal at Diamond Bar Boulevard; turn right.

10.5 Traffic signal at Grand Avenue; turn right.

11.4 High elevation of ride (1,164 feet), at Shotgun Lane, opposite Summitridge Park.

11.8 Leave Diamond Bar and Los Angeles County; enter the city of Chino Hills and San Bernardino County.

13.8 Traffic signal at Chino Hills Parkway; turn right.

15.2 Traffic signal at Carbon Canyon Road (CA 142); turn right.

19.1 Leave Chino Hills and San Bernardino County; enter Brea and Orange County.

21.0 Enter Olinda community of Brea.

21.2 Leave Olinda; enter Chino Hills State Park.

22.3 Reenter Brea; Chino Hills State Park is adjacent, to the left.

22.8 End of ride at entrance to Carbon Canyon Regional Park (at Santa Fe Road); turn left to enter park.

3

Central OC Velo

Start: Edna Park, 2140 West Edna Dr., Santa Ana

Length: 44.45 miles (clockwise loop)

Riding time: 2.25 to 5.5 hours (my time: 2H43:20)

Terrain and surface: 52% of ride is on car-free, grade-separated paths; 16% of the ride is on paths or walkways with at-grade crossings; and 32% is on roads shared with motor vehicles.

Elevations: Low—34 feet at MacArthur Boulevard and Susan Street in Santa Ana; high—462 feet at Santa Ana Canyon Road and Riverview Drive in Anaheim

Traffic and hazards: Counted in 2014, the busiest roads are Santa Ana Canyon Road in Anaheim (35,000 vehicles per day between Weir Canyon Road and Imperial Highway), Santiago Boulevard in Orange (20,000 vehicles per day north of Villa Park Road), and Wanda Road in Orange (15,000 vehicles per day south of Villa Park Road). Note that MacArthur Boulevard in Santa Ana carried 27,000 vehicles per day at Harbor Boulevard. There is no shoulder along MacArthur, and use of the walkway, which is a bike route, is recommended.

Map: *The Thomas Guide by Rand McNally—Street Guide: Los Angeles and Orange Counties* (any recent year), page 799

Getting there by car: From central Anaheim, head south on the I-5 freeway. Exit to the CA 22 freeway heading west. Exit at Garden Grove Boulevard; turn left onto Haster Street, followed by a left turn onto Garden Grove Boulevard. Pass under the freeway, and then turn right onto Fairview Street. Turn left onto Edna Drive; Edna Park will be on the right at 2140 West Edna Dr.

Getting there by public transit: From central Anaheim, ride Orange County Transportation Authority (OCTA) bus route 47 south, via Anaheim Boulevard, to Santa Ana. Exit at 17th Street and Edna Drive. Ride eastward on Edna Drive to Edna Park.

Starting point coordinates: 33.763325°N / 117.898606°W

THE RIDE

Central OC Velo is the consummate urban OC ride, taking the rider on a 44.45-mile trip through a diverse array of landscapes, development, and life in central Orange County. The route makes heavy use of the Santa Ana River Trail (SART), a bike path along the Santa Ana River which has been described as a "freeway for bicycles." Plans are for the path to be a true mountains-to-the-sea route, with grade separations, for some 100 miles from the foothills east of San Bernardino, to the Pacific Ocean bordering Costa Mesa. This ride covers about 20% of the proposed full length of the path. The ride visits the cities of Santa Ana, Orange, Anaheim, and Yorba Linda, and brushes by Villa Park.

Start the ride at Edna Park in Santa Ana. Navigate the small park's paths to head toward the river, and the SART. Turn left and head north. You are bound to see plenty of other cyclists along the path. The official speed limit on the SART is 10 mph; you will see numerous riders exceeding this, and perhaps you will too. Whatever the speed, always be alert to other path users, particularly near access points. The path cuts a diagonal, southwest to northeast line through Orange County, turning eastward after entering Anaheim. After passing under the I-5, CA 22, and CA 57 freeways, Angels Stadium appears on your left. After passing under Katella Avenue, adjacent the stadium, double-back to the roadway, cross over the river, and then turn left to continue heading northeast on the SART.

As for Katella Avenue, 3 miles to the west of the SART is the Disneyland Resort, one of the world's top ten destinations. Once past Katella, the SART makes a long, gradual curve to the right to head eastward, still adjacent the river. Anaheim stretches for several miles to the east along here.

The river path climbs oh-so-gradually as it moves inland. Also, the prevailing winds tend to blow toward the ocean. Once past the Imperial Highway (mile 10.35), turn left to cross over the river on a bridge. Turn right to continue heading eastward on the SART. Yorba Linda Regional Park is on the left, starting at mile 11.35. This long, linear park has water and restrooms. Soon after passing under Weir Canyon Road (mile 12.95), bear left to continue on the SART. It is a short but brisk climb (7.8% grade) to La Palma Avenue, where the path runs parallel to the street. After a short dip and uphill, the path makes an at-grade crossing of the entrance to a small retail center. Beyond the crossing,

Bike Shops

Janet's Bike Shop, 219 North Broadway, Santa Ana, (714) 953-6748; The Bicycle Tree, 811 North Main St., Santa Ana, (714) 760-4681, www.thebicycletree.org; Bicycle Wheel Warehouse (no street address), www.bicyclewheelwarehouse.com, (714) 699-2380

the path veers away from La Palma Avenue, returning to a Santa Ana River alignment, with Featherly Regional Park to your right, on the opposite side of the river. This is a pleasant segment wherein the path is depressed a few feet below the adjacent roadway but above the river.

At the end of this segment, at mile 15.7, bear left to ride up the connector to the road. Turn right at the top, onto the path that parallels Gypsum Canyon Road. Cross over the Santa Ana River here. Use caution when crossing the Featherly Regional Park entrance; return to the road. Gypsum Canyon passes under the CA 91 freeway, and there are ramps that intersect with the road. Use extra caution here, as the lighting can be poor underneath the overhead structure. Gypsum Canyon Road ends just past the freeway; turn right here to head westward on Santa Ana Canyon Road. Reenter the city of Anaheim here. The freeway roars, or perhaps stalls, to your right. Santa Ana Canyon begins to climb after it widens from two to four lanes, at mile 17.75. The high elevation of the ride, at 462 feet, is reached at Riverview Drive.

Continue to Weir Canyon Road. This is a major intersection, at which Santa Ana Canyon Road's curb lane turns right, and the adjacent lane has a through-right option. Move into this lane, and watch for motor vehicles turning right—you are going straight. Also, watch for motor vehicles turning right, from Weir Canyon Road southbound onto Santa Ana Canyon eastbound! Once you are safely through the intersection, watch for motor vehicles turning right into the retail center on your right. Phew! You may be wishing you had remained on the bicycle path, but the riding is pleasant beyond here. Santa Ana Canyon narrows, and is gradually downhill. At Imperial Highway, although not as hairy as Weir Canyon Road, again exercise caution when riding through the intersection. Beyond Lakeview Avenue, at mile 22.9, the CA 91 freeway is once again immediately to your right. Be cautious of motor vehicles turning to and from the freeway ramps in the vicinity of Lakeview. Beyond Nohl Canyon Road (mile 24.1), the road gradually curves to the left, becoming Santiago Boulevard, and entering the city of Orange. The CA 55 freeway is now roaring to your right.

Orange may be the only city in the county with "old" housing structures, dating from the 1920s. Other cities in the county destroyed older houses a while back, in favor of new construction. Continue southward on Santiago Boulevard. At Meats Boulevard, the upscale city of Villa Park is now on your left. The city is surrounded entirely by Orange. Past Arden Villa Drive (mile 26.25), Santiago turns to the left—keep straight; you are now on Wanda Road. Continue to Collins Avenue, where Wanda Road ends.

But don't turn—keep straight, onto the Tustin Ranch–Wanda Road Trail (paved bike path)! At the end of this half-mile connector, bear right, onto the Santiago Creek Bike Trail. For the next 3 miles, this paved path cuts a

Lateral tandem riding? A cyclist shows us how it's done, pulling a child's bike along the Santa Ana River Trail.

diagonal swath across Orange, heading toward its southern border with the city of Santa Ana. The path runs parallel to Santiago Creek, which is mostly dry. The creek flows upstream of this region and Villa Park Dam, though, draining the northern Santa Ana Mountains, and serving as a tributary to the Santa Ana River. Be careful to stay on the main path at the many junctions and curves. Once you are in Hart Park (mile 30.1), turn right to cross over Santiago Creek, and then turn left to remain on the path. Here, the path parallels an access road before effectively ending. Turn left onto Santiago Avenue (mile 30.7); cross the no-vehicles bridge over Santiago Creek, and enter Santa Ana.

You are now in Santa Ana's Park Santiago district. Turn left onto Grovemont Street, and then right onto Lincoln Avenue, adjacent the Metrolink railroad tracks. Head south; after crossing I-5, Lincoln narrows as the residences get tight and dense. Turn right onto Stafford Street, and then keep straight onto Civic Center Drive as the road veers to the left. You are now entering the heart of Santa Ana, although the true center city is to the west of here. Turn left onto French Street, and ride to its end, at East 3rd Street. Turn right here;

alternatively, cross the street and turn right to ride on the walkway. You will next be making two left turns; riding slowly on the walkway may be more efficient than executing two left turns in the road. The left turns take you along the perimeter of Santa Ana Downtown Plaza. Turn left onto Spurgreen Street, still on the walkway, and then turn left onto East 1st Street.

Now that you are on the other side of the plaza, carefully enter the road, and head east on East 1st Street. You are now in the predominantly Hispanic Eastside residential district. Turn right onto Maple Street and head south. Keep straight at Walnut Street and Pine Street. At Chestnut Avenue, jog to the left slightly and ride onto the Pacific Electric Bicycle Trail. This bike path follows the alignment of the old (pre-1930) Pacific Electric Interurban Railway (i.e., "Red Car") that ran between Santa Ana and Huntington Beach. The path is at-grade, with plentiful stop signs and traffic signals. The Pacific Electric Trail ends at Orange Avenue; continue across Orange (use crosswalk). Turn left and cross Adams Street (use crosswalk). Keep straight on the walkway, and then turn right onto the Union Pacific Railroad bicycle path. You may pass a squatter or two along here—all part of the urban experience (be careful not to roll

Disneyland Bicycling

While this book is indeed *Best Bike Rides Orange County*, there are no rides through or even to the Disneyland Resort. Central OC Velo comes nearest to the acclaimed amusement and resort center, passing within 3 miles of it at the Katella Avenue crossing, along the SART. As of this writing, bicycling to Disneyland was not accommodated well by the surrounding facilities. None of the streets bordering the park featured bike lanes, with the nearest stopping about 2 miles short of the resort center, on its west side. I did a site investigation, and found two bicycle racks, one on each side of the park, with space for a total of about thirty bicycles. (In comparison, the Disneyland parking structure is the largest in the United States, with space for over 10,000 motor vehicles.) One proposal, as of this writing, was to build a monorail or other rail connector from the Anaheim Regional Transportation Intermodal Center (ARTIC, bus-train station), which is adjacent Angels Stadium, to the Disneyland Resort. (The ARTIC is a stunning, arched, steel and glass frame that features air plastic pillows for letting in sunlight. At night, the arch can be illuminated with changing color lights.) The ARTIC is next to the SART, so one option might be to put one's bike on the train, for transportation directly into the resort complex. From there, it would just be a matter of finding a place to park!

over anyone's stuff). At the next crossing, which is Main Street, the path ends are offset—bear left to cross over the railroad tracks, and then bear right to continue on the path, all while (or before or after) crossing Main Street (using the crosswalk at adjacent Goetz Avenue is recommended). Use a similar strategy at the Dyer Road crossing.

The Union Pacific path turns sharply to the left just upstream of Flower Street. Follow the path, and turn then right to cross the bridge over the Santa Ana Gardens Channel. Turn right on the other side; turn right to ride along Flower Street briefly, and then turn left to cross Flower. Resume riding on the path once across. The path ends just east of Bristol Street in a small paved area; keep straight through, onto the walkway, which leads to Bristol Street. Cross here, at mile 37.15, and continue onto the Alton Avenue path. This path is sandwiched between Alton Avenue and the railroad tracks. Use caution at the bumpy street crossings. The path ends at Susan Street, in the middle of an industrial area. Turn left onto Susan, and ride on the shoulder. At MacArthur Boulevard, turn right—riding along the walkway is preferred to riding in the street, which has no shoulder. The low elevation of the entire ride (34 feet) is at this corner. Head west on MacArthur.

After just under 1 mile, and a few traffic signals, bear right off of MacArthur, and onto the SART. You are now at mile 39.7, with 4.7 miles to go, entirely on the bike path. Be sure to use the underpasses, which are often difficult to see from a distance. The path dips and then climbs at most underpasses, so watch your speed on the descents, and always check your sight distances. Cross over the Santa Ana River at mile 44.15; turn right to resume riding along the path. The ride ends at Edna Park, on your left, at mile 44.45.

MILES AND DIRECTIONS

0.0 Start in Edna Park in Santa Ana—ride through the park to access the Santa Ana River Trail (SART). Turn left and head northeast on the path.

1.3 Pass under the CA 22 freeway.

1.75 Pass under the I-5 freeway; enter the city of Orange.

2.85 Pass under the CA 57 freeway.

3.4 Pass under Katella Avenue; cross over the Santa Ana River, and resume riding northbound on the path on the other (east) side.

7.25 Pass under Tustin Avenue; enter the city of Anaheim.

7.45 Pass under the CA 91 freeway—begin a pleasantly landscaped, meandering stretch of the path.

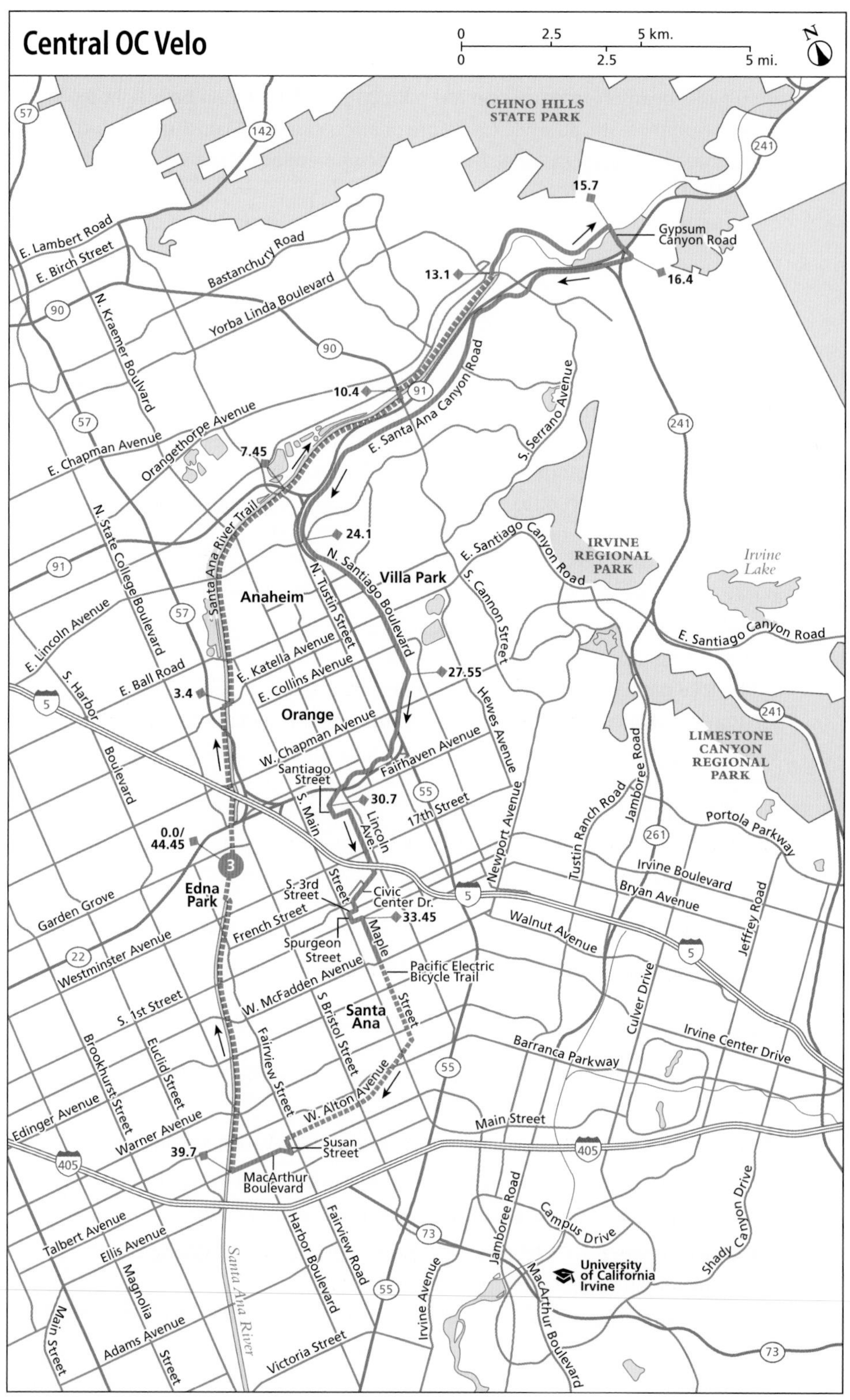

Central OC Velo
0 2.5 5 km.
0 2.5 5 mi.
N
CHINO HILLS STATE PARK
IRVINE REGIONAL PARK
LIMESTONE CANYON REGIONAL PARK
Irvine Lake
Anaheim
Villa Park
Orange
Edna Park
Santa Ana
University of California Irvine
Gypsum Canyon Road
E. Lambert Road
E. Birch Street
Bastanchury Road
Yorba Linda Boulevard
N. Kraemer Boulevard
E. Santa Ana Canyon Road
S. Serrano Avenue
Orangethorpe Avenue
E. Chapman Avenue
N. State College Boulevard
Santa Ana River Trail
N. Tustin Street
N. Santiago Boulevard
E. Santiago Canyon Road
S. Cannon Street
E. Lincoln Avenue
E. Katella Avenue
E. Collins Avenue
E. Ball Road
S. Harbor Boulevard
Hewes Avenue
W. Chapman Avenue
Fairhaven Avenue
Santiago Street
S. Main Street
Lincoln Ave.
17th Street
Newport Avenue
Tustin Ranch Road
Jamboree Road
Portola Parkway
Irvine Boulevard
Bryan Avenue
Jeffrey Road
S. 3rd Street
Civic Center Dr.
Garden Grove
French Street
Spurgeon Street
Maple Street
Walnut Avenue
Westminster Avenue
W. McFadden Avenue
Pacific Electric Bicycle Trail
Culver Drive
Irvine Center Drive
S. 1st Street
Brookhurst Street
Euclid Street
Fairview Street
S Bristol Street
Barranca Parkway
W. Alton Avenue
Edinger Avenue
Warner Avenue
Main Street
Susan Street
MacArthur Boulevard
Talbert Avenue
Ellis Avenue
Magnolia Street
Harbor Boulevard
Fairview Road
Campus Drive
Shady Canyon Drive
Jamboree Road
Irvine Avenue
MacArthur Boulevard
Adams Avenue
Victoria Street
Main Street
Santa Ana River
57
142
241
90
91
55
22
5
405
261
73
3
15.7
16.4
13.1
10.4
7.45
24.1
27.55
3.4
30.7
0.0/ 44.45
33.45
39.7

10.35 Pass under the Imperial Highway (CA 90); then turn left to cross the bridge over the Santa Ana River. Turn right after crossing to continue on the SART.

11.35 Yorba Linda Regional Park is on the left.

12.95 Pass under Weir Canyon Road; bear left at junction; begin short climb at 7.8% grade.

13.1 Crest of climb; path is now adjacent La Palma Avenue.

13.25 Dip in path, followed by short climb at 3.5% grade—path then makes an at-grade crossing of the entrance to a retail center.

13.6 Path veers right, away from roadside—now separated from motor vehicle crossings. Featherly Regional Park is to your right; enter the city of Yorba Linda.

15.7 Stay left at junction—take short connector path, then turn right to ride adjacent Gypsum Canyon Road. Cross the Santa Ana River.

16.15 Leave the path and carefully enter Gypsum Canyon Road. Watch for vehicles turning to enter Featherly Regional Park.

16.2 Pass under the CA 91 freeway—watch for vehicles entering and exiting the freeway.

16.4 End of Gypsum Canyon Road; turn right onto Santa Ana Canyon Road—CA 91 freeway is on your right. Reenter the city of Anaheim.

17.35 Begin climb at 4.0% grade.

17.75 Roadway widens.

18.2 Crest at Riverview Drive—high elevation of entire ride (462 feet).

18.35 Traffic signal at Weir Canyon Road; keep straight—busy intersection with dual right turn lanes—position yourself away from right edge of road, and use caution.

21.55 Traffic signal at Imperial Highway; keep straight. Busy intersection—use caution.

22.9 Traffic signal at Lakeview Avenue; keep straight. Use caution; watch for motor vehicles turning to enter and exit CA 91 freeway, which is on your right.

24.1 Traffic signal at Nohl Canyon Road; keep straight. Now on Santiago Boulevard.

25.6 Reenter Orange; traffic signal at Meats Avenue; keep straight.

26.25 Traffic signal at Arden Villa Drive; keep straight. Now on Wanda Road (Santiago Boulevard turns to the left here).

27.05 Traffic signal at Collins Avenue (end of Wanda Road); keep straight across, and onto the Tustin Ranch–Wanda Road Trail (bike path).

27.55 Junction with Santiago Creek Bike Trail; bear right onto path—Grijalva Community Park is on your left (across bridge).

28.25 Pass under Chapman Avenue; path crosses bridge and enters Yorba Park.

28.6 Pass under the CA 55 freeway.

29.85 Bike path curves left and enters Hart Park.

30.1 Keep straight at junction to remain on Santiago Creek Bike Trail.

30.25 Turn right to cross bridge over Santiago Creek; turn left after crossing to continue on path.

30.4 Pass under the CA 22 freeway; reenter the city of Santa Ana.

30.7 Turn left to cross extension of Santiago Street (bridge over Santiago Creek; no motor vehicles allowed), and then keep straight on Santiago Street.

30.95 Turn left onto Grovemont Street.

31.2 Stop sign at Lincoln Avenue (end of Grovemont); turn right.

32.35 Turn right onto Stafford Street.

32.5 Road turns slightly to the left; now on Civic Center Drive.

32.9 Turn left onto French Street.

33.15 Traffic signal at East 3rd Street; turn right (alternatively, cross 3rd Street, turn right, and ride slowly along walkway).

33.25 Spurgreen Street; turn left (or, if riding on walkway, turn left and continue on walkway).

33.35 East 1st Street; turn left (if riding on walkway, cross street and resume riding in road, eastbound on East 1st).

33.45 Maple Street; turn right.

33.65 Cross Chestnut Avenue; keep straight onto Pacific Electric Bicycle Trail (parallel to Maple Street). Path is not grade-separated.

35.75 End of Pacific Electric Bike Trail at Orange Avenue; cross Orange (use crosswalk), and then cross Adams Street (in crosswalk). Keep straight on walkway to Union Pacific Railroad bike path; turn right here.

35.9 South Main Street crossing—path ends are offset. Cross railroad tracks, then use crosswalk at Goetz Avenue, and then resume riding on path.

36.3 Dyer Road crossing—use crosswalk and walkway, and then resume riding on path.

36.65 Union Pacific path curves sharply to the left—turn right to cross bridge over Santa Ana Gardens Channel; then cross Flower Street in crosswalk.

36.75 Resume riding on path.

37.05 End of path—continue through paved area, and then onto walkway.

37.15 Traffic signal at Bristol Street—use crosswalk, then continue along path, parallel to Alton Avenue.

38.65 End of bike path at Susan Street (stop sign); turn left onto Susan.

38.8 Traffic signal at MacArthur Boulevard; turn right—use walkway. Low elevation of ride (34 feet).

39.7 Bear right, off of MacArthur walkway, onto connector path.

39.75 Merge with SART (watch out for bike path users)—head north.

44.15 Turn right to cross bridge over Santa Ana River; turn right after crossing to resume riding on SART.

44.45 Bike path passes by Edna Park, to your left; end the ride here.

4

Chino Hills Trails Trek

Start: Chino Hills Regional Park, Chino Hills State Park Discovery Center entrance, 4500 Carbon Canyon Rd. (CA 142), Brea

Length: 12.3 miles (clockwise loop, including a short out-and-back opening and closing segment)

Riding time: 1 to 3 hours (my time: 1H28:22)

Terrain and surface: Dirt roads and trails; one gravel segment

Elevations: Low—475 feet at Chino Hills State Park Discovery Center; high—1,652 feet on North Ridge Trail, just west of McDermont Trail

Traffic and hazards: 100% of the ride is on car-free dirt roads and trails.

Map: *The Thomas Guide by Rand McNally—Street Guide: Los Angeles and Orange Counties* (any recent year), page 710

Getting there by car: From central Anaheim, head north on the CA 57 freeway. Exit at Lambert Road and turn right. Lambert Road becomes Carbon Canyon Road after crossing Valencia Avenue. Once on Carbon Canyon Road, look for the entrance to Chino Hills State Park about a half-mile past the entrance to Carbon Canyon Regional Park, on the right.

Getting there by public transit: From central Santa Ana or Anaheim, ride Orange County Transportation Authority (OCTA) bus route 57 north on State College Boulevard to the end of the line at Brea Mall, north of Birch Street in Brea. From here, ride north on State College; turn right and head eastward on Lambert Road. Follow the above instructions from here. Bus route 57 runs every 20 minutes on weekdays, every 30 minutes on Saturdays, and every 20 to 30 minutes on Sundays and holidays.

Starting point coordinates: 33.920028°N / 117.825606°W

THE RIDE

The 12.3-mile Chino Hills Trail Trek explores the northwestern sector of Chino Hills State Park. The park is too large (14,173 acres) to be covered in a single ride (please also see Ride 34, Chino Hills Ridges Challenge). The park is nestled between restricted open spaces to the north, the city of Chino Hills to the north and east, Prado Dam and the CA 71 highway to the east, the CA 91 freeway and the city of Yorba Linda to the south, and the city of Brea to the west. The park spans Orange and San Bernardino Counties. The park is hilly, if not rugged, having a peak elevation of 1,781 feet (San Juan Hill). You will be hard-pressed to find dense foliage here, although some oak and sycamore tree groves exist in narrow canyons and other sheltered spots. But the space is primarily open, with expansive grasslands, sage scrub, and rolling vistas. The park had small beginnings, starting with 2,237 acres in 1977. With continued acquisitions from private landowners, aided by efforts from local citizens group Hills for Everyone, the park has grown sevenfold to its present-day size. Be sure to bring plenty of fluids on warm days, as the combination of dirt, dryness, warmth, and effort(!) can be dehydrating.

Start the ride in the parking lot adjacent the Chino Hills State Park Discovery Center (be sure to visit the center). Head toward the east end of the lot, emptying out onto a dirt and gravel road. Follow the road, which is Telegraph Canyon Trail, as it takes a dip to cross Carbon Canyon Creek. At the very first junction (mile 0.2), turn left onto North Ridge Trail. The opening climb may be intimidating, but do not worry—the climbing continues for several miles! North Ridge Trail is definitely the most challenging segment of the ride, with its average 6.1% grade, occasionally exposed and loose rocks, and eroded spots. In fact, North Ridge Trail was closed when I attempted to re-ride the route during the autumn of 2015—I observed that the opening portion of the trail was overgrown and presumed that the erosion was significant in places. Also, note that the *entire* park closes for several days after a rainstorm to allow for drainage, drying, and clearing. Please be sure to check park conditions (www.parks.ca.gov/?page_id=648) before venturing out.

Bike Shops

Two Wheeler Dealer, 1039 East Imperial Hwy., Brea, (714) 671-1730, www.twdcycling.com; Pro Bike Parts, 615 Berry St., Brea, (714) 255-9172

North Ridge Trail climbs nearly steadily for the next 3.5 miles, from an elevation of 483 feet at its base to 1,611 feet at a junction with an unnamed trail. You can occasionally observe Carbon Canyon Road, which is down and to your left, to crudely gauge your elevation. North Ridge Trail tends to roll

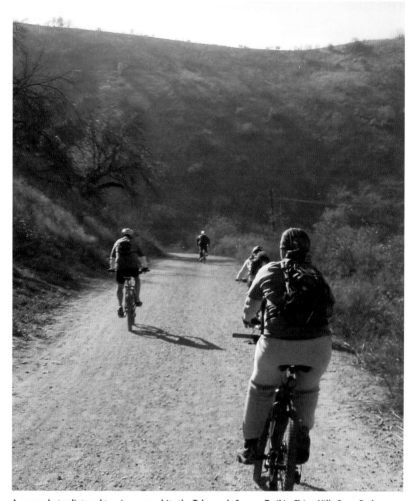

A somewhat splintered touring group hits the Telegraph Canyon Trail in Chino Hills State Park.

beyond this crest, dropping to 1,495 feet at Sycamore Trail (mile 4.6), followed by a climb at an 8.9% grade to the San Bernardino County line. From here, the trail continues through elevation changes, ultimately reaching the highest of the ride, 1,652 feet, at mile 5.95. Just beyond the crest, curve right at the T-junction, onto McDermont Trail. McDermont descends very rapidly initially, at a nearly 20% grade, to a junction with an unnamed trail. Keep control of your bike. Curve right here, to remain on McDermont. The gradient of the descent eases to 8.0%.

At the bottom of McDermont, turn right onto Telegraph Canyon Trail. This may be the most thrilling part of the ride, as Telegraph Canyon descends gradually (2.6% grade) over the next 5 miles. Although you may be inclined to cut loose and let it fly along here, please be aware that Telegraph Canyon is regularly used by bikers, hikers, and runners, as it is an artery connecting to the park's other trails. So be courteous to and cognizant of other trail users. The descent of Telegraph Canyon features a few technical segments, such as exposed rock, and a couple of minor (a few inches) drop-offs. The canyon walls on either side of the trail are nestling and protective; note that most of the connecting trails do not allow bicycles. After descending 700 feet, from an elevation of 1,210 feet at McDermont Trail, the trail curves to the right, returning you to the junction with North Ridge Trail. Keep straight here—this is the final segment of the ride. Return to the Discovery Center parking lot to conclude the ride.

MILES AND DIRECTIONS

0.0 Start the ride in the parking area of the Chino Hills State Park Discovery Center (4500 Carbon Canyon Rd., Brea). Head toward the east end of the lot, onto Telegraph Canyon Trail.

0.2 Turn left onto North Ridge Trail—begin climb at 6.1% average grade.

The Swallows of Chino Hills

The Swallows of Chino Hills? Huh? Well, many are familiar with the Swallows of San Juan Capistrano. As discussed in Ride 28, San Juan Hills Grind, the migratory American cliff swallows stopped coming back to San Juan Capistrano during the 1990s. Their new home seems to be the clubhouse of the Vellano Country Club in Chino Hills. Thousands of the swallows nest in the eaves of the building from March until October, before making their winter migratory flight to Goya, Argentina. The word is that the swallows wanted a ritzier setting than the historic mission in San Juan Capistrano, and that they wanted to work on their golf game! Seriously, the Vellano Country Club is located no more than 1.3 miles as the swallow flies from the crest of the Chino Hills Trails Trek. Thus, during the season (mid-March to mid-October), it may be possible to view the migratory swallows heading either to or from Chino Hills. To spot them, look for a small bird (5 to 6 inches in length) with a tiny bill, brown wings and tail, blue back and crown, and a square-ended tail. The bird's underparts are white, and the face is red.

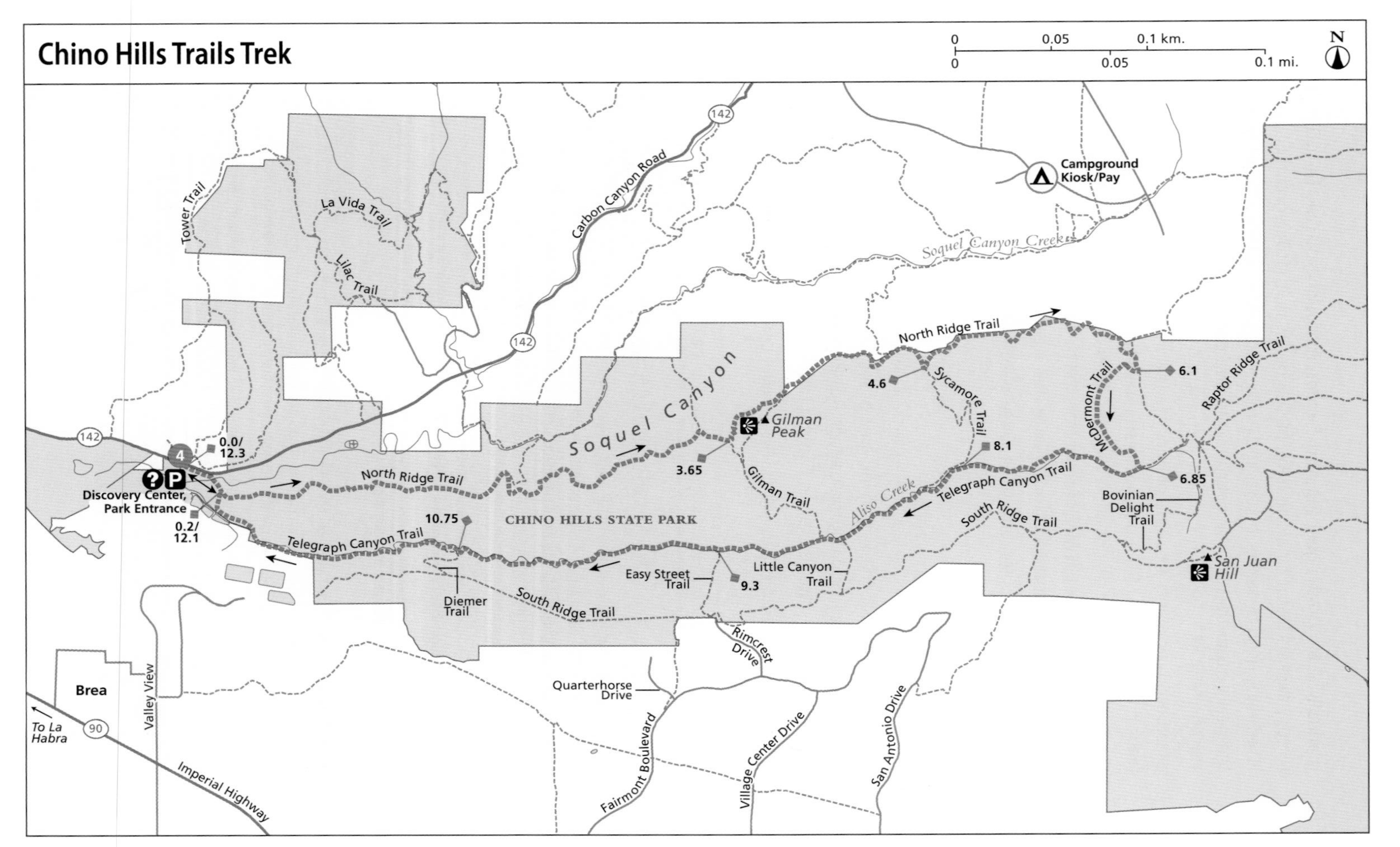

Chino Hills Trails Trek
0
0.05
0.1 km.
0
0.05
0.1 mi.
N
Campground
Kiosk/Pay
Tower Trail
La Vida Trail
Lilac Trail
Carbon Canyon Road
142
Soquel Canyon Creek
North Ridge Trail
Raptor Ridge Trail
McDermont Trail
6.1
4.6
Sycamore Trail
8.1
Soquel Canyon
Gilman Peak
3.65
Gilman Trail
6.85
0.0/
12.3
4
Discovery Center,
Park Entrance
0.2/
12.1
10.75
CHINO HILLS STATE PARK
Aliso Creek
Telegraph Canyon Trail
South Ridge Trail
Bovinian
Delight
Trail
San Juan
Hill
Easy Street
Trail
9.3
Little Canyon
Trail
Diemer
Trail
Rimcrest
Drive
Quarterhorse
Drive
Brea
Valley View
To La
Habra
90
Imperial Highway
Fairmont Boulevard
Village Center Drive
San Antonio Drive

3.65 Keep straight at junction with Gilman Trail, remaining on North Ridge Trail.

4.4 Keep straight at junction with Oil Well Road, remaining on North Ridge Trail.

4.6 Stay left at junction with Sycamore Trail to remain on North Ridge Trail.

4.8 Enter San Bernardino County.

5.2 Keep straight at junction with easement trail.

6.0 Trail curves to the right; now at McDermont Trail (high elevation of ride, at 1,652 feet, is just west of here). Begin rapid descent (19.9% grade).

6.1 McDermont Trail curves to the right—continue descent (8.0% grade).

6.85 End of McDermont Trail, and end of steep descent, at Telegraph Canyon Trail; turn right.

8.1 Keep straight at junction with Sycamore Canyon Trail, remaining on Telegraph Canyon Trail.

8.65 Keep straight at junction with Little Canyon Trail, remaining on Telegraph Canyon Trail.

9.3 Keep straight at junction with Easy Street Trail, remaining on Telegraph Canyon Trail.

10.75 Keep straight at junction with Diemer Trail, remaining on Telegraph Canyon Trail.

12.0 Telegraph Canyon Trail curves to the right.

12.1 Keep straight at junction with North Ridge Trail.

12.3 End of ride at parking area, adjacent Chino Hills State Park Discovery Center.

5

Coyote Creek Corridor Cities

Start: Central Park, 7821 Walker St., La Palma

Length: 22.75 miles (compressed figure eight)

Riding time: 1 to 3 hours (my time: 1H21:29)

Terrain and surface: 54% of the ride is on paved roads, and 46% is on paved bike paths.

Elevations: Low—4 feet, at Seal Beach Boulevard and Pacific Coast Highway (CA 1) in Seal Beach; high—56 feet, at Coyote Creek and Marquardt Street in Cerritos

Traffic and hazards: Just over half of the ride (54%) is on roads shared with motor vehicles. Using data from 2013, the heaviest traffic volumes were on Seal Beach Boulevard at I-405, at 44,000 vehicles per day. Seal Beach carried just 7,000 vehicles per day south of CA 1, however. Walker Street carried 20,000 vehicles per day north of Crescent Street in La Palma, while Crescent Street carried 12,000 vehicles per day. Lincoln Avenue carried 22,000 vehicles per day at Coyote Creek.

Map: *The Thomas Guide by Rand McNally—Street Guide: Los Angeles and Orange Counties* (any recent year), page 767

Getting there by car: From central Anaheim, head north on I-5. Exit to the CA 91 freeway heading west. Exit at Valley View Street and turn right. Turn left onto Orangethorpe Avenue, cross under CA 91, and then turn left onto Walker Street. Look for Central Park on the right, 0.75 mile south of CA 91.

Getting there by public transit: From central Anaheim, ride OCTA bus route 38 westward on La Palma Avenue to La Palma. Exit at Walker Street and head north (by bicycle). Central Park is a quarter-mile north of La Palma Avenue. Route 38 was running every 15 to 30 minutes on weekdays and every 45 minutes on weekends and holidays.

Starting point coordinates: 33.849339°N / 118.037592°W

THE RIDE

Coyote Creek Corridor Cities is a nearly entirely flat 22.75-mile ride, with a high-low elevation range of just 52 feet. The ride never strays far from Coyote Creek and the San Gabriel River Bikeway, while passing in and out of eight different Orange and Los Angeles County cities. City and/or county borders are crossed some twenty-two times in this ride, potentially filling up your passport(!). About 75% of the ride is in Orange County, with the other 25% in Los Angeles County. Scenery along the ride ranges from the bland, nondescript views along the Coyote Creek Bike Trail to a majestic view of the Pacific Ocean, at the San Gabriel River Bikeway in Seal Beach. There, you can practically dip your front wheel into the waters!

Start the ride at Central Park in La Palma. The city was originally named Dairyland, as part of a three-city conglomeration that included the adjacent Dairy City (Cypress) and Dairy Valley (Cerritos). When the milk moved eastward in the 1960s, the names of the cities were changed. Although "Dairyland" fit right in with Orange County's theme parks persona, there were never any cow-oriented attractions or rides here. Exit the parking area and head south on Walker Street. The opening portions of the ride are decidedly urban, with frequent traffic controls and plenty of motor vehicles. I have chosen relatively bike-friendly roads, however. Turn right onto Crescent Street, at mile 0.7, and head west. Leave La Palma and enter Lakewood (and Los Angeles County) at mile 1.95. Shortly thereafter, turn right, off of Crescent, and onto the Coyote Creek Bike Trail connector path. At the end of the connector make a very sharp left turn, to head southward on the bike path. Leave the path at the very next access point, and turn left onto Lincoln Avenue. Ride along the walkway to Bloomfield Street, which forms a T-intersection with Lincoln. At the traffic signal at Bloomfield, cross like a pedestrian, and then head south on Bloomfield. Cross Bloomfield when it is safe, to ride on the right. Bloomfield enters the city of Hawaiian Gardens, which is one of Los Angeles County's smallest, at just 1 square mile. Hawaiian Gardens was named for a refreshment stand that was decorated with palm fronds and bamboo.

Bike Shops

Official Stage Bicycle Shop, 12634 Del Amo Blvd., Lakewood, (562) 746-3506; Bike Land Cypress, 5530 Lincoln Ave., Cypress, (714) 995-6541

Continue through Hawaiian Gardens on Bloomfield, and enter the city of Los Alamitos (and Orange County). Bloomfield Street ends at Farquhar Avenue, at mile 4.85; turn right here and head west. Los Alamitos is known for its Armed Forces Reserve Center base. The well-known Los Alamitos (Horse) Race Course is actually in Cypress. At the end of Farquhar (mile 5.35), turn left onto busy Los

Cyclists go double-wide on the San Gabriel River Bikeway—no problem when there are no oncoming riders!

Alamitos Boulevard. To avoid being overwhelmed by this road's motor vehicle traffic, the ride detours through the unincorporated community of Rossmoor. Many of the houses in Rossmoor were designed by Earle G. Kaltenbach, who gained fame as the original designer of Disneyland's Tomorrowland. Turn right at mile 5.6 onto Orangewood Avenue to enter Rossmoor. Orangewood becomes Montecito Road, and then St. Cloud Drive, before returning to Los Alamitos Boulevard (which is now Seal Beach Boulevard—you are now in the city of Seal Beach). Though busy, riding along Seal Beach is unavoidable, as you must get to the other side of the I-405 freeway. Stay to the right, watching for freeway-bound traffic, as you climb and descend the overpass.

Seal Beach is home to the Naval Weapons Station Seal Beach, which is the largest munitions center on the West Coast. Seal Beach is also known as a surfing hotbed, and is home to Stingray Bay (at the mouth of the San Gabriel River) and surfing legend Robert August. Continue heading southward on Seal Beach Boulevard. The lowest elevation of the ride, 4 feet, is at the crossing of the busy Pacific Coast Highway. Enter Seal Beach's quaint older section after crossing the highway; the boulevard curves through here, becoming

Ocean Avenue. Ocean is parallel to the beach, which is on your left. After a scenic passage through town, turn left onto 1st Street, at the end of Ocean Avenue. 1st Street empties into a parking area—stay to the right, riding along the perimeter of the lot. Look for the access point to the San Gabriel River Bikeway, on your right. Bear right, and then turn right again, to head north on the bikeway (mile 11.8). This is the official starting point for the bikeway, which continues for about 28 miles to the north. Enter the city of Long Beach here. Your ride will veer away from the bikeway after 4 miles, at mile 15.9, onto the Coyote Creek Bike Trail.

The junction to the Coyote Creek Bike Trail is seamless: At mile 15.9, continuing on the San Gabriel River Bikeway requires a left turn onto a bridge that crosses the mouth of Coyote Creek. Nix the crossing and keep straight. The ride along Coyote Creek is speedy and uneventful, although the path makes multiple boundary crossings: from Long Beach into Seal Beach, back into Long Beach, on into Los Alamitos, a return to Long Beach, and so forth, as you pedal toward the north-northeast. At mile 17.65, the path makes an abrupt left turn to cross a bridge over Carbon Creek. At mile 18.9, at Lincoln Avenue, leave the path to cross over Coyote Creek; once across, turn right and head north to access the bike path on Coyote Creek's west bank (you were previously riding along the east bank). Cerritos Regional Park is on your left at mile 20.5—a pleasant respite on a hot day.

After passing under the CA 91 freeway at mile 21.5, leave the path, to the left, at mile 21.75. At the end of the connector, make a hard right onto Marquardt Avenue. Use caution, as the bridge across Coyote Creek is narrow, and sight distance to your left is poor. Note that the Coyote Creek Bike Trail continues for over a mile to the north; but I am having you leave the path here, as the environs become increasingly industrial. This is the highest elevation of the ride, at 56 feet above sea level. Enter La Palma after crossing Coyote Creek; you are now on Walker Street. From here, it is 1 mile southbound to Central Park, and the end of the tour.

MILES AND DIRECTIONS

0.0 Start at Central Park, 7821 Walker St., La Palma. Exit the park and head south on Walker Street.

0.7 Traffic signal at Crescent Avenue; turn right.

1.95 Enter the city of Lakewood and Los Angeles County; now on Centralia Street.

2.0 Leave Centralia Street by turning right onto connector bike path; turn 180 degrees to the left to head south on Coyote Creek Bike Trail.

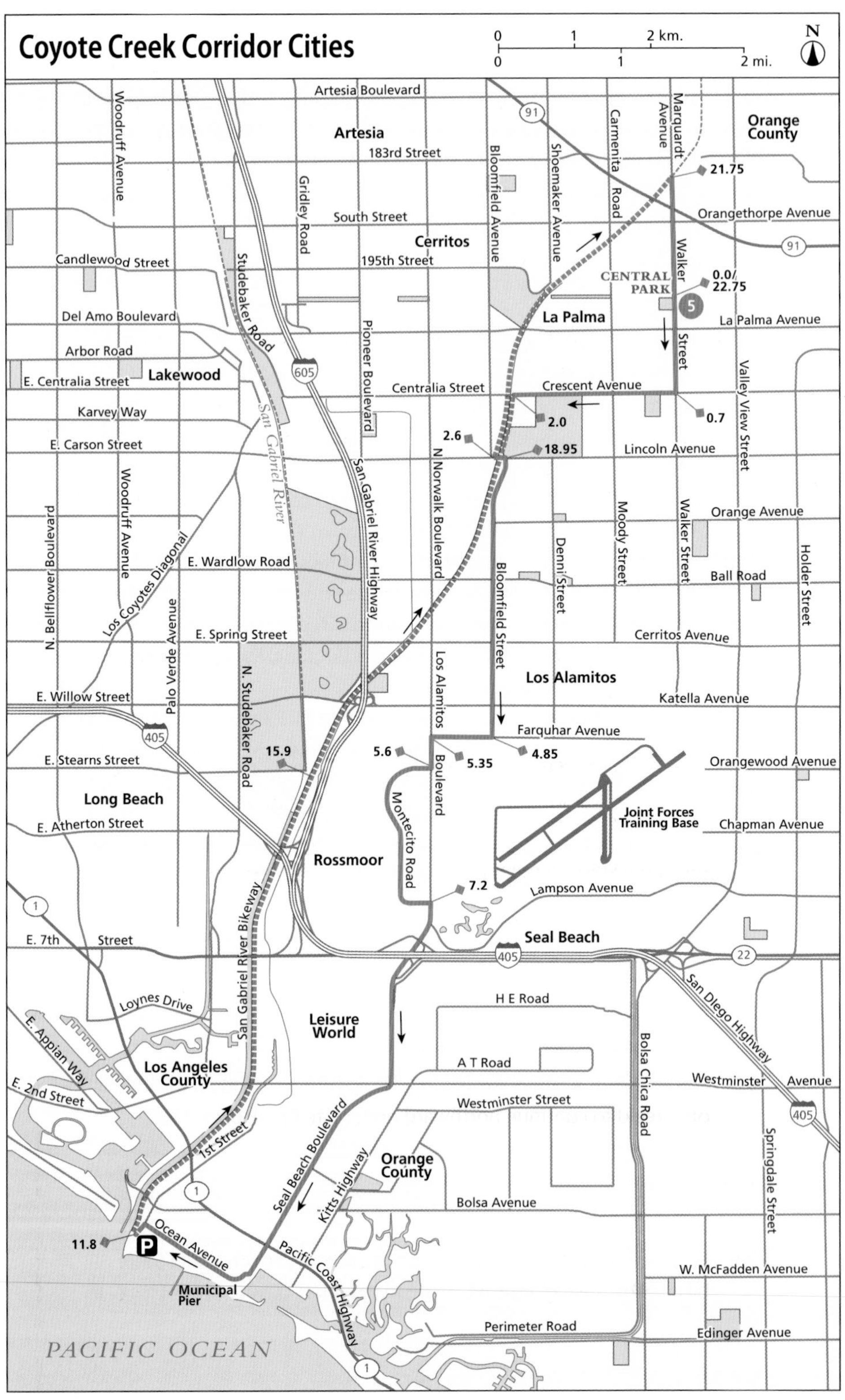
Coyote Creek Corridor Cities
0 1 2 km.
0 1 2 mi.
N
Artesia Boulevard
Artesia
183rd Street
South Street
Cerritos
195th Street
Candlewood Street
Del Amo Boulevard
Arbor Road
E. Centralia Street
Lakewood
Karvey Way
E. Carson Street
Centralia Street
Crescent Avenue
Lincoln Avenue
La Palma
La Palma Avenue
CENTRAL PARK
Orange County
Orangethorpe Avenue
Marquardt Avenue
Carmenita Road
Shoemaker Avenue
Bloomfield Avenue
Walker Street
Valley View Street
21.75
0.0/ 22.75
5
2.0
0.7
2.6
18.95
Woodruff Avenue
Gridley Road
Studebaker Road
Pioneer Boulevard
San Gabriel River
San Gabriel River Highway
N Norwalk Boulevard
Bloomfield Street
Denni Street
Moody Street
Walker Street
Holder Street
Orange Avenue
Ball Road
Cerritos Avenue
Katella Avenue
Los Alamitos
Farquhar Avenue
Orangewood Avenue
Chapman Avenue
Joint Forces Training Base
N. Bellflower Boulevard
Los Coyotes Diagonal
Palo Verde Avenue
E. Wardlow Road
E. Spring Street
E. Willow Street
E. Stearns Street
N. Studebaker Road
15.9
5.6
5.35
4.85
Los Alamitos Boulevard
Montecito Road
Long Beach
E. Atherton Street
Rossmoor
7.2
Lampson Avenue
Seal Beach
E. 7th Street
405
605
91
22
1
San Diego Highway
San Gabriel River Bikeway
Loynes Drive
Leisure World
H E Road
A T Road
Bolsa Chica Road
Westminster Avenue
Westminster Street
E. Appian Way
E. 2nd Street
Los Angeles County
1st Street
Seal Beach Boulevard
Kitts Highway
Orange County
Bolsa Avenue
Springdale Street
11.8
P
Ocean Avenue
Pacific Coast Highway
Municipal Pier
W. McFadden Avenue
Perimeter Road
Edinger Avenue
PACIFIC OCEAN

2.55 Leave bike path, to the left, to access Lincoln Avenue; turn left onto walkway (enter the city of Cypress and Orange County). Next, cross Lincoln Avenue at Bloomfield Street (traffic signal); head south on Bloomfield.

4.1 Traffic signal at Cerritos Avenue; keep straight on Bloomfield Street—enter the city of Los Alamitos.

4.85 Stop sign at Farquhar Avenue (end of Bloomfield); turn right onto Farquhar.

5.35 Traffic signal at Los Alamitos Boulevard (end of Farquhar); turn left onto Los Alamitos.

5.6 Traffic signal at Orangewood Avenue; turn right—leave Los Alamitos and enter Rossmoor (unincorporated community).

6.1 Now on Montecito Road.

7.0 Now on St. Cloud Drive.

7.2 Traffic signal at Seal Beach Boulevard (end of St. Cloud); turn right onto Seal Beach—enter the city of Seal Beach.

7.5 I-405 freeway overpass; exercise caution.

10.4 Traffic signal at Pacific Coast Highway (CA 1); keep straight—low elevation of ride (4 feet).

10.7 Now on Ocean Avenue (keep straight).

11.65 Stop sign at 1st Street (end of Ocean); turn left onto 1st—ride into parking area, and veer right to ride along lot's border.

11.8 Turn right, and then right again, to access San Gabriel River Bikeway; this is the starting point of the bike path—enter the city of Long Beach and Los Angeles County.

12.1 Stop sign at Marina Drive; cross street and keep straight to continue on bikeway.

14.35 Bikeway passes under CA 22 freeway.

15.25 Bikeway passes under I-405 freeway.

15.9 Keep straight at bikeway junction (i.e., do not take bridge over Coyote Creek) to continue northward on Coyote Creek Bike Trail.

16.75 Coyote Creek Bike Trail passes under I-605 freeway.

17.65 Bike path curves sharply to the left to cross over Carbon Creek; continue heading northward on Coyote Creek Bike Trail.

18.9 Cross under Lincoln Avenue, then turn sharply to the right to exit bike path; turn right onto Lincoln Avenue (cross over Coyote Creek),

A rider—maybe a little overdressed for a sunny spring day—cruises along the San Gabriel River Bikeway in Long Beach.

and then turn right onto connector to access Coyote Creek Bike Trail, now on west side of Coyote Creek (head north).

21.5 Bike path passes under CA 91 freeway.

21.75 Leave bike path to the left; turn right onto Marquardt Avenue—high elevation of ride (56 feet)—cross over Coyote Creek; enter Orange County and the city of La Palma—now on Walker Street.

22.0 Walker Street passes under CA 91 freeway.

22.75 End of ride at Central Park.

6

Cycle Surf City

Start: Moon Park, 3337 California St., Costa Mesa

Length: 22.55 miles (clockwise loop)

Riding time: 1 to 3 hours (my time: 1H29:15)

Terrain and surface: 74% paved roads, 26% paved bicycle paths

Elevations: Low elevation—sea level along Slater Avenue east of Graham Street in Huntington Beach; high—63 feet at Slater Avenue crossing of Santa Ana River

Traffic and hazards: The heaviest traffic volumes were along CA 1 in Huntington Beach (43,000 vehicles per day at the Santa Ana River in 2013). Warner Avenue carried 29,000 vehicles per day west of Graham Street, and Slater Avenue carried 22,000 vehicles per day west of Beach Boulevard and east of Brookhurst Street, all in 2013. Note that 26% of the ride is on a car-free bicycle path.

Map: *The Thomas Guide by Rand McNally—Street Guide: Los Angeles and Orange Counties* (any recent year), page 858

Getting there by car: From central Anaheim, head south on Harbor Boulevard. After passing over the I-405 freeway, in Costa Mesa, turn right onto Gisler Avenue. Turn right on California Street, and follow it through the residential neighborhood, all the way to its end, at Moon Park.

Getting there by public transit: OCTA bus route 43 runs north–south along Harbor Boulevard between Fullerton and Costa Mesa, every 20 minutes daily. Exit at Harbor and Gisler Avenue. Head west on Gisler, and then turn right on California Avenue. Ride to the end of California Avenue, which is where Moon Park is located.

Starting point coordinates: 33.694222°N / 117.933667°W

THE RIDE

Cycle Surf City is a 22.55-mile loop tour of the city of Huntington Beach, although the ride also passes through the cities of Fountain Valley and Costa Mesa, and a portion of Santa Ana. About one-fourth of the ride is along the Santa Ana River Trail (SART), on its southernmost segment. (Please see Ride 3, Central OC Velo, for a ride on the SART's central segment.) The route also cruises along the iconic Pacific Coast Highway (CA 1), right through the heart of Huntington Beach. You are bound to see plenty of other cyclists out here. The elevation change in the ride is minimal, with just 63 feet between the high and low points. Were it not for the numerous traffic signals encountered along the ride's "back side" (i.e., Warner and Slater Avenues), this would be a very speedy outing.

Start the ride at Moon Park in Costa Mesa, located at the end of California Street in a residential neighborhood. The park features a simulated moon landscape, created to commemorate the 1969 Apollo landing. The SART passes right by the park, and you can access the trail by navigating the park's paths. Turn left and head south on the SART. The prevailing grade is gently downhill as the Santa Ana River makes its way to the Pacific Ocean. Coming in from your left, a little over 0.1 mile into the ride, is the Banning Channel (please see Ride 7, Fairview-Talbert Nature Spin, for a brief discussion). For a while, the channel will be on the left, and the river on your left. Hold your line! Actually, neither waterway features a heavy flow, and the buffers are wide enough such that you will not feel as if one false move will find you plunging in either direction. Cross over the bridge, to your right, at mile 2.25. Cross the Santa Ana River channel to the other side; turn left and continue to head south. You may be riding against the wind, as the airflow is typically up the river.

Bike Shops

Bicycle Discovery, 8800 Warner Ave., Huntington Beach, (714) 841-1366, www.bicycle-discovery.com; Cranky's, 10625 Ellis Ave., Huntington Beach, (714) 594-3228, www.crankysonline.com; Cycletech Bike Shop, 1215 Baker St., Costa Mesa, (714) 760-4380, www.cycletechbikeservice.com; Let's Ride Bicycles, 9891 Hamilton Ave., Huntington Beach, (949) 329-3203, http://letsridebicycles.com; Performance Bicycle, 8850 Warner Ave., Fountain Valley, (714) 842-3480, www.performancebike.com/bike-shop/store/fountainvalley; Surf City Beach Cruisers, 19171 Magnolia St., Huntington Beach, (714) 321-4408, www.surfcitybeachcruisers.com; Surf City Cyclery, 7470 Edinger Ave., Huntington Beach, (714) 842-1717, http://surfcitycyclery.com

Riding along CA 1 is a rite of passage for nearly all of Orange County's cyclists—here, two riders cruise adjacent Huntington State Beach.

As you near the ocean, and CA 1, bear right onto the connector path (mile 4.65). The path takes you to CA 1; although there is a wide shoulder, use caution nonetheless when entering the highway (and watch for oncoming cyclists). Turn right and head northwest on CA 1. Although this is the busiest segment of the ride, in terms of motor vehicle traffic, it is also the most popular, in terms of bicycle traffic! Legions of cyclists are attracted to the coastal highway, using it for sightseeing, training, touring, and other purposes. I, for example, have rarely ridden along the highway alone—solo riders and small groups tend to randomly coalesce at traffic signals, transforming into pelotons and breakaway groups.

Enter the city of Huntington Beach after making the turn onto CA 1. The traffic signals become more frequent as you pass well-known cross streets such as Brookhurst, Magnolia, and Beach. By the time you reach Main Street, you are in the heart of Huntington Beach's surfside district. The Huntington Beach Pier is to your left, and the district buzzes with beachgoers, beachfront activities, beachside retail, and beach-view lodging. Jan and Dean's famous song "Surf City"—although referring to a fictional city in which there are "two girls for every boy"—had its closest fit in Huntington Beach, according to co-songwriter Jan Berry. In truth, Huntington Beach has a long surfing history, mainly because its ideal location catches ocean swells that are diffracted off of distant Santa Catalina Island. The Surf City moniker is found throughout the city.

Outside of Huntington Beach's surf legacy, the city is large, having passed the 200,000 population mark in 2014. Your pace will slow as you roll your way through the city's surfside district. At Golden West Street (mile 9.35), CA 1 opens up as you ride next to the Aera Energy facility (oil exploration and production), with the beach and the ocean off to your left. After crossing Seapoint Street (mile 10.1), CA 1 descends slightly, and then travels over an inlet to Bolsa Bay. To your right is the Bolsa Chica Ecological Reserve (please see Ride 8, Harriett Wieder Trails Express). It is a long, speedy 2.5-mile stretch along CA 1 from here to Warner Avenue, with the reserve to your right and Bolsa Chica State Beach to your left. Turn right onto Warner Avenue (mile 12.9) and head east.

Warner Avenue takes you into a residential district. While Huntington Beach may be most famous for the surfing, the city's legacy is in oil and agriculture. Oil drilling rigs are scattered throughout the city—some of the early homeowners benefited from the discovery of oil during the early 20th century. Long before the oil flowed, the city's Mediterranean climate attracted growers. Holly Sugar, a sugar processing plant, operated in the city until its

Surf's Up!

Huntington Beach's surfing history dates back just over 100 years, to the mid-1910s, when George Freeth starting riding the waves on his "surf board." He famously demonstrated the sport after the completion of the new, 1,350-foot Huntington Beach Pier in 1914. Since then, surfing has grown into a competitive sport, as well as a recreational outlet, and even a culture. In fact, 24-hour-a-day, year-round surfing was born during the 1940s and 1950s, with the advent of wetsuits, woodies, durable and lightweight boards, and other inventions.

Huntington Beach is home to the International Surfing Museum. There are also a Surfers Walk of Fame and a Surfing Hall of Fame in the same vicinity. The city is also home to the US Open of Surfing, recognized as the world's largest surfing competition. The event started in 1959 as the West Coast Surfing Championships, eventually becoming the US Open in 1994. The championships are usually held in late July or early August. As for the rest of the year, the city's calendar is filled with nearly weekly surfing events. Admission (to watch) is generally free; the only drawback is that the competitions usually start and end very early in the morning.

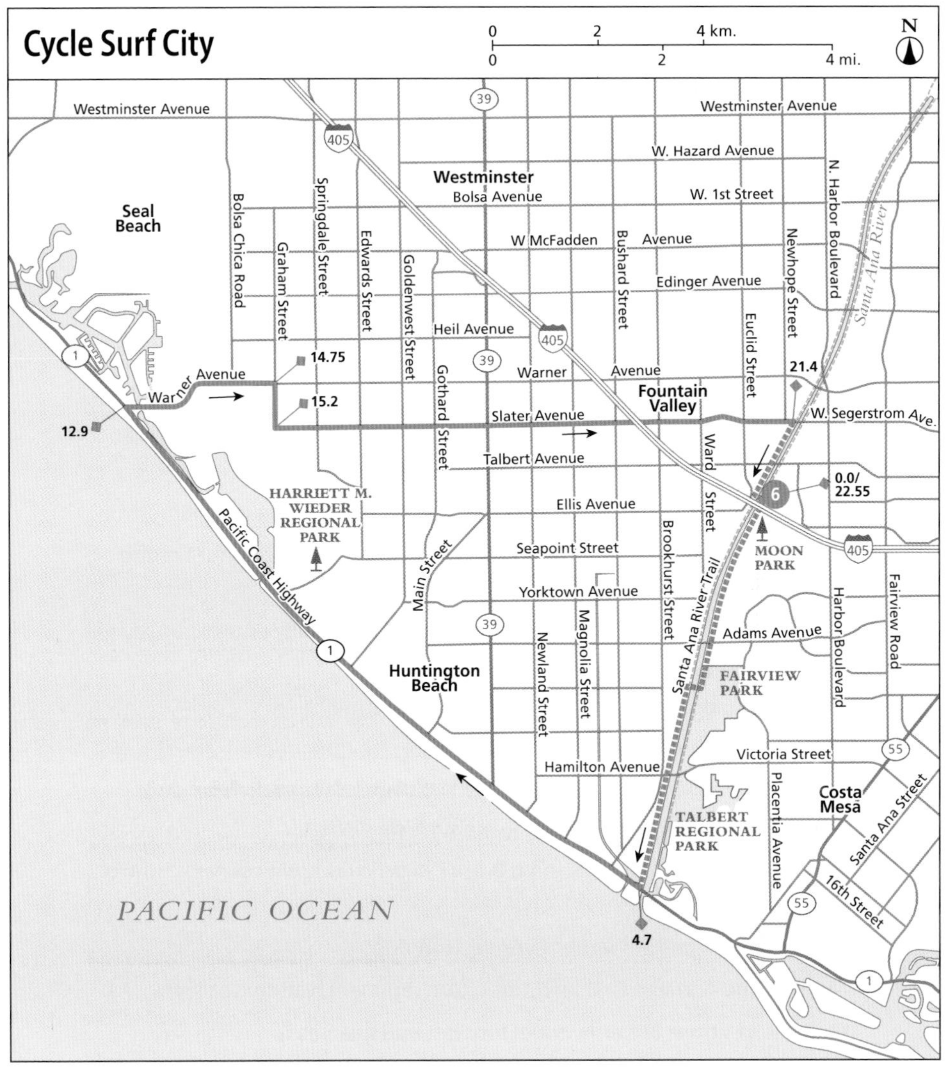

conversion into . . . an oil refinery. You may catch glimpses of history as you ride through, although the sound walls and flood-control channels tend to block one's view. Just as things are getting busy on Warner, turn right onto Graham Street and head south (mile 14.75). The elevation here is effectively sea level (i.e., 0 feet), the lowest of any ride in this book. Next, turn left onto Slater Avenue and head east (mile 15.2). Slater features a bike lane, and is more bike-friendly than Warner. Slater is mostly residential, periodically passing some retail and commercial outlets.

One mile beyond ultra-busy Beach Boulevard, Slater crosses Newland Street and enters the city of Fountain Valley. The city's claims to fame include the very first Japanese-American mayor (James Kanno, late 1950s, immediately following incorporation), a heavy influx of Vietnamese refugees following the Vietnam War, during the 1970s, and the headquarters of Hyundai Motor America. Stay on Slater until it approaches the Santa Ana River, via a bridge crossing. Cross over the river (this is the high elevation of the ride, at 63 feet above sea level), and then turn right onto the SART. From here it is just over 1 mile to Moon Park. The park is easy to target, in that it is just beyond the I-405 freeway underpass, on the left.

MILES AND DIRECTIONS

0.0 Start at Moon Park in Huntington Beach. Ride through the park, and turn left onto the Santa Ana River Trail (SART).

0.7 Banning Channel is now on the left (Santa Ana River on your right).

2.25 Turn right; cross bridge over Santa Ana River, and then turn left to continue riding southward on the SART.

4.65 Bear right onto connector path, and then carefully enter roadway (CA 1)—turn right and head northwest.

5.1 Traffic signal at Brookhurst Street; keep straight.

6.75 Traffic signal at Beach Boulevard; keep straight—enter central surfside district.

9.35 Now adjacent oil refinery; leave surfside district.

10.35 Bridge over Bolsa Bay inlet; Bolsa Chica Ecological Reserve is now on your right.

12.9 Traffic signal at Warner Avenue; turn right.

14.75 Traffic signal at Graham Street; turn right—elevation: sea level.

15.2 Stop sign at Slater Avenue; turn left and head east.

18.7 Enter the city of Fountain Valley.

19.45 Cross over I-405 freeway.

21.4 Cross over Santa Ana River; leave the road, turning right onto the SART.

22.5 Pass under I-405 freeway.

22.55 End of ride at Moon Park.

Fairview-Talbert Nature Spin

7

Start: Fairview Park, Placentia Avenue (between Adams and Victoria Avenues), Costa Mesa

Length: 6.2 miles (barbell-shaped route, with two counterclockwise loops connected by a segment)

Riding time: 25 minutes to 1.5 hours (my time: 31:47)

Terrain and surface: 71% of the ride is on graded dirt trails (7% singletrack), 23% is on paved bike paths, and 6% is on a concrete path.

Elevations: Low—7 feet, at the ride's midpoint, near the southeast corner of Talbert Regional Park; high—83 feet at the southwestern edge of Fairview Park

Traffic and hazards: 100% of the ride is on paths and trails within Fairview and Talbert Regional Parks (no motor vehicles).

Map: *The Thomas Guide by Rand McNally—Street Guide: Los Angeles & Orange Counties* (any recent year), page 858

Getting there by car: From central Anaheim, head south on I-5 (or south on CA 57 to I-5). Exit to the CA 55 freeway southbound. Exit at Victoria Avenue, turn right and head west. Turn right onto Placentia Avenue and head north. Look for the entrance to Fairview Park on the left, in advance of the overhead pedestrian bridge. Enter and park (no entrance fee).

Getting there by public transit: OCTA bus route 47A gets as close to Fairview Park as Placentia Avenue and Wilson Street. From here, it is about a half-mile north on Placentia to the park. Route 47A operates between Fullerton, Anaheim, Santa Ana, and Costa Mesa hourly, 7 days a week.

Starting point coordinates: 33.662600°N / 117.939236°W

THE RIDE

The Fairview-Talbert Nature Spin is a short mountain bike ride, suitable for beginners, in Fairview Park, Talbert Nature Preserve, and Talbert Regional Park in Costa Mesa. The two parks and one preserve are effectively adjacent to each other, and they are usefully connected by the Banning Channel Bikeway. The ride passes along the perimeter of the nature areas found in all three, without actually penetrating them. (The nature areas are most suitable for strolling and hiking.) You will be able to catch plenty of glimpses of nature, however, as you cruise through the two parks.

While Talbert Regional Park, of which Talbert Nature Preserve is a part, is an Orange County Regional Park, Fairview Park is owned by the city of Costa Mesa. Talbert has no parking—so it is sensible to start and finish in Fairview. Fairview Park's 208 acres span Placentia Avenue. The east side of the park features the Orange County Model Engineers, who offer free monthly rides on their Mackerel Flats and Goat Hill Junction Railroad. The train operates on a 7½-inch gauge, which is slightly bigger than one-eighth of full size. There are also a few trails and a walking path.

The ride starts on the larger and more expansive west side of Fairview Park. Cross over the grass adjacent the parking lot, and head north on the concrete path. Be sure to give way to other park users. Where the path curves to the right, to cross the striking pedestrian-bicycle bridge over Placentia Avenue, veer left, onto the dirt trail. And get a grip! The descent to the plant restoration area below is an 18.2% grade! Turn right beyond the base of the descent; do not take the path that heads toward the alluvial scrub area. Next, keep left and merge onto the paved bicycle path. The path parallels the Fairview Channel (which feeds into the Santa Ana River, up ahead). Continue on the path to its end, at the Banning Channel Bikeway. Turn left here and head south on the bikeway; take the next left, and then make an immediate right, to ride along the parallel dirt trail. This is a long, straight, nearly level segment in which you can switch to a bigger gear. Talbert Nature Preserve is to your left. At the end of the path, head up the short, diagonal path to reconnect with the Banning Channel Bikeway. Note the caution sign upon merging—that is, watch out for speeding road cyclists on the mainline path (although most riders use the path on the *opposite* side of the channel).

Bike Shops

The Cyclist, 1785 Newport Blvd., Costa Mesa, (949) 645-8691, www.thecyclist.com; Two Wheels One Planet Bicycle Store, 420 East 17th St., Costa Mesa, (949) 646-7717, http://twowheelsoneplanet.com.

A rider and runner share the path and the pace in Costa Mesa's Fairview Park.

Head south on the bikeway, passing under Victoria Street. The channel adjacent the bikeway is officially the Greenville-Banning Channel, designed to capture non-storm water runoff (i.e., "urban runoff") before it reaches the ocean. Thus, the water in the channel is essentially untreated wastewater—perhaps just a step up from raw sewage. Upon emerging from the underpass, turn left, and then make an immediate right onto the downhill dirt trail. This is the unceremonious entrance into Talbert Regional Park. The trails here have letters, at least on the official park map; but there are no signs or markers out on the trails. You are now on Trail A. At the next junction, turn right, putting you on Trail B. Turn right at the next junction, putting you on Trail C. As you are making the turn, look straight ahead at the somewhat unnatural formations. Those are the ramps and whoop-dee-doos of the Sheephills BMX bike area. Follow Trail C as it curves to the left and heads south, parallel to the Banning Channel Bikeway, which is at the top of the embankment above you, to your right. Follow Trail C as it curves to the left, and then left again, to become Trail D. You are now on the south side of Talbert Park. This is the lushest segment of the park, with some dense and tall vegetation on either side. Trail D curves to the left; at the next junction, turn right to remain on Trail D. This is the low elevation of the ride, at just 7 feet above sea level. This is also the ride's halfway mark, at 3.1 miles. Trail D takes you to the far eastern side of the park, where the trail turns left to head north.

Trail D bends to the left at the far northeastern corner of the park, returning you to Trail A. There is a large signboard here, with information about the park. Hidden behind the apparently minimally developed parkland is a sophisticated six-zone system of plantings. You just passed by border plantings, native grassland, a wetland zone (on the far south side), and even an alluvial woodland. The slopes and dunes that form part of the park's boundary are in a coastal strand zone, in addition to the border plants. Continue along Trail A to the park's exit, which is the same location at which you entered. Turn left and then right to return to the Banning Channel Bikeway. After passing under Victoria Street, look to the right for the paved path that drops down into the Talbert Nature Preserve. Continue on this path as it turns to dirt. At the fork, turn right, and head toward the steep bluff. Follow the path as it bends to the left, to parallel the bluff. At the next junction, turn right, to get closer to the bluff; next, turn left onto the singletrack that runs along the bluff's base. The next 0.45 mile is along the narrow trail, with a few off-camber segments. While there are a few twists and moguls, the terrain is nearly flat.

The trail narrows as a tall staircase up to Fairview Park appears on your right. Merge onto the path next to the stairs, and keep pedaling. Turn right onto the paved path, and start the climb up to Fairview Park. The park's official map humorously shows an in-line skater losing control on this path—so, yes, be mindful of other park users. The climb is at a 5.1% grade. Just when you reach the crest, bear right, onto the wide dirt trail—and keep climbing! The next segment is at a 9.9% grade, taking you to an open area planted with native grassland. Follow the wide trail as it turns southward, hugging the bluff. Don't get too close to the edge, but the singletrack trail along which you were just riding is at the bottom of the cliff. Bear left at the far southern end of the trail, which is the edge of Fairview Park. You are now 83 feet above sea level, the highest point of the ride. Trace the perimeter of the park, turning left, and then left again. Bear right and aim toward the model airplanes area, which is typically active with enthusiasts. Ride past—watch out for low-flying planes—and merge onto the concrete path. This is typically an area busy with park users (the dirt next to the path is rideable). Follow the path back to where you started to conclude the ride.

MILES AND DIRECTIONS

0.0 Start at Fairview Park in Costa Mesa, on the west side of Placentia Avenue. Cross the grass and head north on the concrete path; stay left at the fork.

0.15 Veer off path to the left, onto the dirt, in advance of pedestrian-bicycle bridge—steep downhill (18.2%).

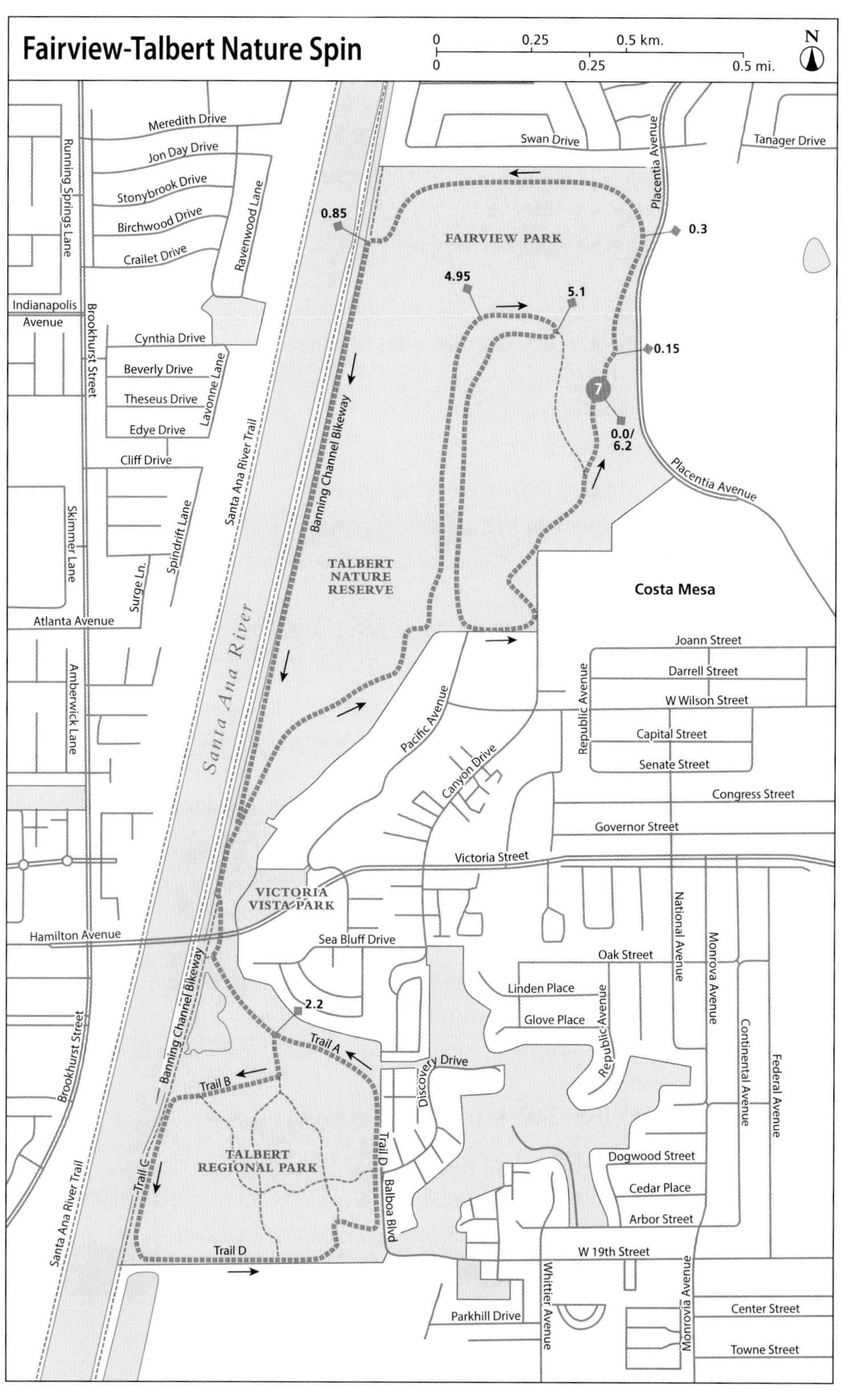
Fairview-Talbert Nature Spin
0
0.25
0.5 km.
0
0.25
0.5 mi.
N
Meredith Drive
Jon Day Drive
Stonybrook Drive
Birchwood Drive
Crailet Drive
Ravenwood Lane
Running Springs Lane
Indianapolis Avenue
Brookhurst Street
Cynthia Drive
Beverly Drive
Theseus Drive
Edye Drive
Lavonne Lane
Cliff Drive
Skimmer Lane
Spindrift Lane
Surge Ln.
Atlanta Avenue
Amberwick Lane
Santa Ana River Trail
Banning Channel Bikeway
Santa Ana River
Swan Drive
Tanager Drive
Placentia Avenue
FAIRVIEW PARK
0.85
0.3
4.95
5.1
0.15
7
0.0/
6.2
TALBERT NATURE RESERVE
Costa Mesa
Joann Street
Darrell Street
W Wilson Street
Capital Street
Senate Street
Republic Avenue
Pacific Avenue
Canyon Drive
Congress Street
Governor Street
Victoria Street
VICTORIA VISTA PARK
Hamilton Avenue
Sea Bluff Drive
Oak Street
National Avenue
Monrovia Avenue
Linden Place
Glove Place
2.2
Trail A
Trail B
Trail C
Trail D
Discovery Drive
Continental Avenue
Federal Avenue
TALBERT REGIONAL PARK
Balboa Blvd
Dogwood Street
Cedar Place
Arbor Street
W 19th Street
Whittier Avenue
Parkhill Drive
Center Street
Towne Street

0.3 Bear right onto dirt path, keep left, and then merge onto paved bike path, heading westward.

0.85 End of path; turn left onto Banning Channel Bikeway.

0.95 Turn left onto dirt trail, and then immediately turn right onto dirt trail, to parallel bikeway.

1.8 End of dirt trail—climb paved path to return to Banning Channel Bikeway.

2.0 Pass under Victoria Street, and then bear left onto path, followed by a right turn onto wide dirt road—descend into Talbert Regional Park—now on Trail A.

2.2 Turn right onto Trail B.

2.3 Turn right onto Trail C.

2.45 Trail C curves to the left; now heading south.

2.7 Trail C curves to the left; now heading east.

3.1 Turn right at the junction, onto Trail D (elevation: 7 feet); now heading east.

3.4 Curve to the left; northeast corner of park—now on Trail A, heading west.

3.6 End of Talbert Regional Park loop—keep straight.

3.75 Leave park; turn left, and then right to head north on Banning Channel Bikeway—pass under Victoria Street.

4.0 Veer off bikeway, to the right, and descend into Talbert Nature Reserve.

4.4 Turn right on junction; now heading toward bluff.

4.5 Turn right and then left onto singletrack; now heading north, parallel to bluff.

4.95 End of singletrack—merge onto path, adjacent staircase; turn right onto paved path and begin climb to Fairview Park.

5.1 Turn right, leaving path, onto dirt trail—climb at 9.9% grade to native grasslands area.

5.2 Wide dirt trail curves to the left; now heading south.

5.7 Curve to the left (edge of park); elevation 83 feet.

5.8 Turn sharply to the left onto dirt trail.

5.9 Bear right onto dirt trail, aim toward model airplanes area.

6.0 Merge onto concrete path—keep straight.

6.2 End of ride.

8

Harriett Wieder Trails Express

Start: Harriett M. Wieder Regional Park, 19251 Seapoint St., Huntington Beach

Length: 3.3 miles (clockwise loop with two "pinched" segments)

Riding time: 15 minutes to 1 hour (my time: 20:49)

Terrain and surface: 97% of the ride is on dirt trails, 2% is on a gravel road, and 1% is on a concrete sidewalk.

Elevations: Low—5 feet across a playa about halfway through the loop; high—71 feet on the far north side of the loop

Traffic and hazards: Nearly all of the ride is on trails. Just under 0.1 mile is on an oil-field access road (gravel) that may be used by vehicles.

Map: *The Thomas Guide by Rand McNally—Street Guide: Los Angeles & Orange Counties* (any recent year), page 857

Getting there by car: From central Anaheim, head south on either the I-5 or CA 57 freeway. Exit to the CA 22 freeway westbound. Exit at Knott Avenue / Golden West Street. Turn left onto Garden Grove Boulevard, and then left again onto Golden West Street. Head south on Golden West. Turn right onto Garfield Avenue and head west. At the T-intersection, turn left onto Seapoint Street. Look for the entrance to Harriett M. Wieder Regional Park on the right. As of this writing, the parking lot was free.

Getting there by public transit: OCTA bus route 25 runs between Buena Park and Huntington Beach via Golden West Street. Exit the bus at Golden West and Garfield Avenue. Head west on Garfield, and follow the instructions above to access Harriett Wieder Park.

Starting point coordinates: 33.684919°N / 118.021219°W

8

THE RIDE

The Harriett Wieder Trails Express is a nifty and quick off-road ride around the perimeter of the namesake park, which is located in Huntington Beach. Harriett M. Wieder Regional Park was still developing as of this writing, with plans to establish a full trails network. When I visited the park, the core area (4 acres) consisted of a grassy field, kids' playground, and (free!) parking lot, while the large, surrounding area contained a network of unnamed, unmarked trails. The park borders the Huntington Beach Oil Field and the Bolsa Chica Ecological Reserve, located immediately to the northwest of the field. Although navigation is challenging without any trail markers, the relatively small area of the park (33 acres), along with the plentiful landmarks, make it nearly impossible to get lost. The route is essentially a park perimeter ride. With an elevation ranging from 5 feet to just 71 feet, the length and topography are suitable for a beginner, while the occasionally rugged terrain, sharp turns, and a few short, stiff climbs, offer challenges for the experienced rider. I took about 21 minutes to complete the ride, so ambitious cyclists might choose to ride two or more laps.

Harriett M. Wieder (1920–2010) was the first female elected to the Orange County Board of Supervisors, in 1978. She served until 1995. Start the ride near the entrance to the park's parking lot, and head south, along the wide dirt trail. Seapoint Street runs parallel, to your left. Seapoint Street, in fact, is regularly used by road riders heading to and from the Pacific Coast Highway. Do not get frustrated if they are moving faster than you, while you grind along the dirt trail. Weary of being passed by road bikers? Then bear right as the dirt trail approaches Ocean Colony, an enclave of million-dollar homes which is the self-proclaimed "jewel of Huntington Beach." Ride along the edge of the property, making a sharp left at the property's corner. You may not be able to resist a glance toward the back side of these fine houses as you ride past. Follow the trail as it curves to the right and heads toward the Bolsa Chica Ecological Reserve. This 1,200-acre wetlands is home to a stunning variety of wildlife, including over 300 species of migratory birds, along with coyotes, lizards, rabbits, snakes, squirrels, guitarfish, and even sharks(!). The reserve is not open to bicycles, but there is a 1.5-mile hiking trail.

Bike Shops

Coast City Cruisers (repair shop), 7792 Connie Dr., Huntington Beach, (714) 841-6202

Where the trail starts to drop down a bluff, turn right, to ride along the edge of the bluff. Exercise caution when passing the section of the bluff that appears to have caved in—there is no barrier, and the trail is narrow. Stay to the left at the next fork, and descend toward the edge of the wetlands. Continue on this trail as it climbs back up. At the junction—wait, what is this? A

On a Harriett Wieder Park trail, with a working derrick in the background and houses beyond

ground-level pipeline? Hurdle it, and then turn left onto the adjacent, parallel trail. Turn right at the fork, adjacent the grove of trees. The trees hide a channel that flows into the wetlands. Continue along the trail, with the grove on your left, to the trail that you rode during the opening portion of the ride. Turn left here, and then turn left again when you reach the opposite side of the grove. Follow the trail as it crosses the savanna, curving to the right. As the trail narrows, there is a short "technical" section of exposed rock. You may hear the faint sounds of children to your right—that is the playground near where you started.

Continue on this trail as it descends to the low elevation of the ride. After a narrow passage on the edge of another grove of trees, the trail opens up. You are just 5 feet above sea level as you cross the small playa. Make a sharp right turn where the trail ends onto the wide gravel road. You are now 1.7 miles into the ride. As you look to your left when making the turn, you will see some fencing, protecting access to the Huntington Beach Oil Field. The gravel road is a slow uphill back to Seapoint Street. Just before reaching the street, bear left and climb the embankment (9.5% grade), onto the trail—continue climbing to where the trail levels. To your left are some of the best views of the oil field. Bear left at the next fork, 1.9 miles into the ride, and head down the narrow singletrack. Beginners, hang on! Stay with the trail as it climbs back up the other side, with fencing to your immediate left. Follow the trail as it curves to the right. Use caution as you negotiate the narrow trail adjacent the concrete abutment that protects the power plant to your right. At the end of this section, hang a sharp left, and continue.

The oil field is on your immediate left, below you, protected by fencing. At mile 2.25, rev it up for the steepest climb of the ride—it is a 13.3% grade to the top of that mound in front of you! Once up top, continue along the trail. The trail curves to the right, now at the far northern edge of the loop, passing the ride's high point (71 feet above sea level). Stay on the trail as it singletracks its way through some S-curves. Curve to the right, with a closed-off access point to your left (at Golden West Street), and start heading back. Curve left to keep the houses of Huntington Beach's Marigayle Circle on your left. Continue past the concrete abutment that you passed earlier, this time keeping to the left. Cautiously negotiate the dip in the trail, and head up the short climb to the higher, level area. You are now heading southward, with Overlook Drive to your left. Continue on the trail as it heads down the incline that you climbed earlier. Your landing is the sidewalk adjacent Overlook Street. Continue on the sidewalk for about 50 feet, and then aim for the parallel dirt trail. Continue along the trail to the park entrance. Turn right, and ride along the entry trail that leads toward the play area. Make a sharp left at the end of the trail, and head for the parking lot to conclude the ride, or take another lap.

Huntington Beach Oil Field

In an area as heavily urbanized as the Los Angeles region, oil wells and derricks seem out of place. Nonetheless, oil was a key resource in attracting folks to the region, literally fueling its growth into the mega-metropolis that it is today. One of several major oil fields in the region, the Huntington Beach one began to produce—eventually as many as 16,500 barrels of crude oil *per day*—during the 1920s. The expansion of the oil field was such that adjacent houses were uprooted and moved to the north, to a community now known as Midway City. Today, this unincorporated community is nearly completely surrounded by the city of Westminster. Also, the community of Sunset Beach, which is now part of Huntington Beach, was developed to house oil field workers. The Huntington Beach Oil Field continues to produce; having already produced over one billion barrels of crude oil, it is estimated that the value of its reserves is $37 billion.

MILES AND DIRECTIONS

(**Note:** The trails are not marked or named.)

0.0 Start in the parking lot, near the entrance to Harriett M. Wieder Regional Park in Huntington Beach. Leave the park entrance road toward the south, on the unnamed dirt trail.

0.45 Turn right to continue the ride with the Ocean Colony houses on your left.

0.5 Turn left to continue on the dirt trail; Ocean Colony houses are on your left.

0.65 Follow the trail as it curves to the right, and then turn right onto the bluffside trail (do not ride down the bluff).

0.75 Bear left at the fork in the trail.

0.85 Keep straight at the junction—begin descent.

0.95 End of trail; step over or hurdle the ground-level pipeline, and turn left.

1.05 Turn right adjacent the grove of trees.

1.15 Turn left, twice, to keep the grove on your left; follow the trail as it cuts diagonally, to the right, across the savanna.

1.35 Short climb, with some exposed rocks, followed by a descent (4.7% grade).

1.45 Keep straight across playa.

1.6 Low elevation of ride (5 feet above sea level)—continue on trail.

1.7 End of trail; turn sharply to the right, onto gravel road. Begin climb (8.0% grade).

1.75 Near end of gravel road, turn left and head up embankment (9.5% grade); continue onto trail.

1.95 Bear left at fork, and head down hill (6.6% grade), and then climb back up (6.2% grade).

2.1 Trail curves to the right; cross concrete abutment.

2.2 Turn sharply to the left; stay near fence on your left—climb steep mound (13.3% grade).

2.3 Trail curves to the right, to the high elevation of ride (71 feet above sea level); continue on twisty singletrack.

2.45 Turn right adjacent Golden West Street access point (closed).

2.5 Trail curves to the left.

2.6 Cross concrete abutment and bear left.

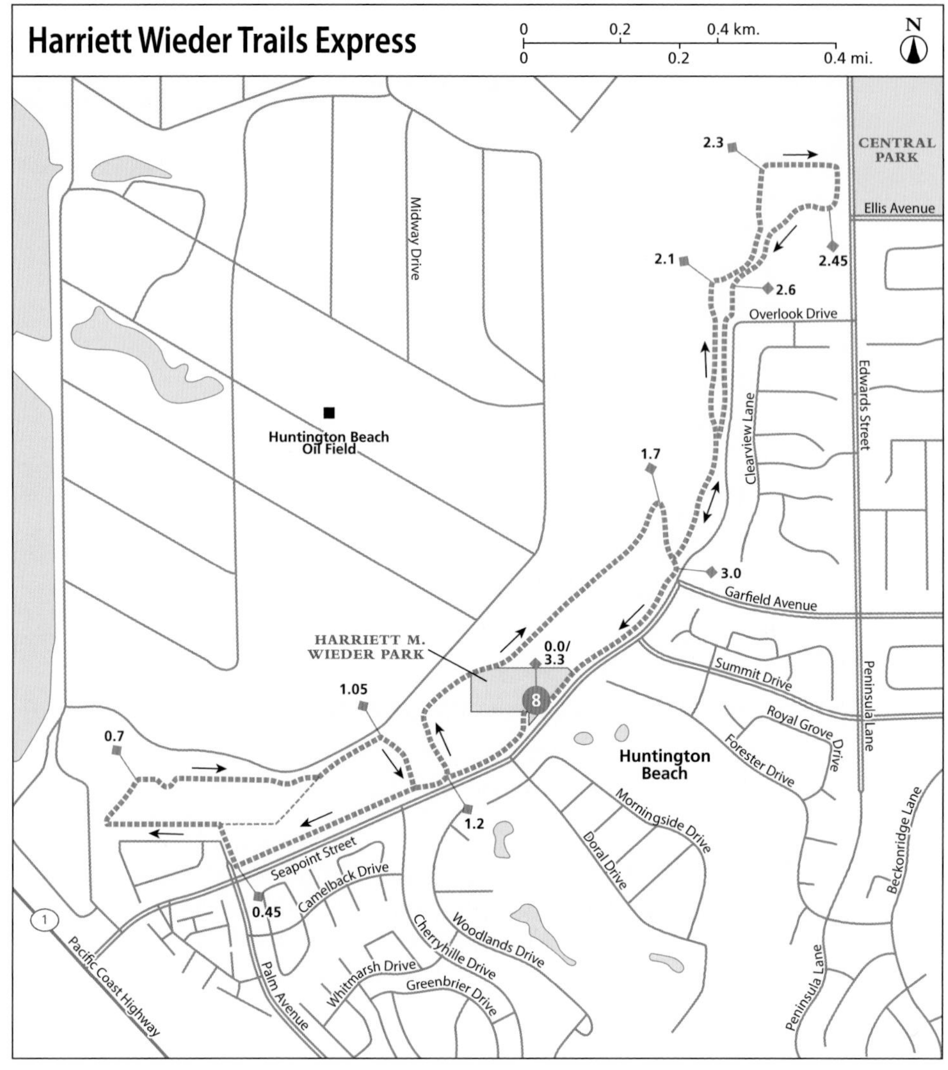

2.65 Roll over dip in trail, and head up short hill to level area; continue heading southward.

2.75 Bear left at the fork, and then right, to ride parallel to Overlook Street.

2.95 Descend to sidewalk (9.5% grade); ride along sidewalk for about 50 feet, and then veer off onto parallel dirt trail.

3.25 Turn right to enter Harriett Wieder Park's main area, on dirt path.

3.3 Turn left adjacent playground area to head toward entry road and parking lot (end of ride).

Peters Canyon Park and Ride

Start: Citrus Ranch Park, 2910 Portola Pkwy., Tustin

Length: 8.1 miles (out-and-back segment plus clockwise loop)

Riding time: 45 minutes to 2 hours (my time: 58:54)

Terrain and surface: 100% dirt trails

Elevations: Low—232 feet at the start-finish in Citrus Ranch Park; high—646 feet on East Ridge View Trail, south of Peters Canyon Trail

Traffic and hazards: 100% of the ride is on dirt trails (no motor vehicles). There are four signalized roadway crossings.

Map: *The Thomas Guide by Rand McNally—Street Guide: Los Angeles and Orange Counties* (any recent year), page 830

Getting there by car: From central Anaheim, head south on I-5. Exit at Jamboree Road, and turn left. At Portola Parkway, turn left, and then take the next left to enter Citrus Ranch Park.

Getting there by public transit: There is no public transit service to Citrus Ranch Park, but OCTA bus route 79 stops at Irvine Boulevard and Jamboree Road. From there, it is a 1.5-mile ride to Citrus Ranch Park. Route 79 connects from Larwin Square in Tustin, which is served by buses that also serve the Santa Ana Depot. Metrolink trains stop at the depot. Route 79 runs every 30 to 45 minutes Monday through Friday and every hour Saturdays, Sundays, and holidays.

Starting point coordinates: 33.745600°N / 117.728639°W

THE RIDE

Peters Canyon Park and Ride is as stated, albeit a tongue-twister: Park at the park, which is not a park and ride, and then ride the Park and Ride. The park is Peters Canyon Regional Park, which encompasses about 350 acres of a long, somewhat narrow canyon and ridge in northeastern Tustin. Although the park is a habitat of a variety of flora and fauna, you will mostly see coastal sage scrub, grassland, and some cactus. Eucalyptus Trail, ridden late in the route,

Two riders scoot, and a third chases, up East Ridge View Trail in Peters Canyon Regional Park.

features, of course, eucalyptus trees. You may also spot waterfowl overhead or nearby, as the park features wetlands and the 55-acre Peters Canyon Reservoir. James Peters was a late 19th–early 20th century farmer who purchased land from James Irvine. Peters planted a eucalyptus grove, and established a long history of cattle grazing in the canyon. The present-day park was dedicated to Orange County in 1992.

The ride is a reasonably challenging 8.1-mile route, including a 5.2-mile loop, which can be ridden clockwise or counterclockwise, and an opening and closing 1.45-mile segment. The net elevation change is "only" 414 feet, but the undulations on East Ridge View Trail, including grades that exceed 20%, may have you feeling as if there is substantially more climbing than the net elevation change suggests. The ride starts at Citrus Ranch Park, somewhat away from the hubbub of Peters Canyon Regional Park. Citrus Ranch Park features a lemon grove—bicycles are not allowed, but strolling is encouraged.

Exit the parking lot and turn left onto Peters Canyon Bikeway. South of here, the bikeway is a paved path (ridden in Tour of the Master Plan: Irvine Ranch, Ride 32); from here north, a dirt trail parallels the paved one (and then is dirt only). The ride begins with a signalized crossing of wide, busy Tustin

Ranch Road. The trail curves to the right after the crossing, and then to the left. Next cross the much-less-busy (but signalized) Pioneer Road; the trail then curves to the left adjacent Cedar Grove Park. Test your bike handling skills as you wind through a chicane, with rustic wooden rails on either side. The trail straightens as you cross a couple of quiet residential streets. Along this stretch, Peters Canyon Trail is also part of the Mountains-to-the-Sea Trail, which is an ambitious, 22-mile trail (and paved path) that stretches from Weir Canyon in the north to Newport Bay in the south. The trail climbs gradually, from the starting elevation of 232 feet at Citrus Ranch Park to over 300 feet along this segment. The trail curves sharply to the right adjacent the (dry) Lower Peters Canyon Reservoir, passing over the reservoir's dam. The reservoir was also known as Little Peters Canyon Lake, and still is when there is water in the basin. During World War II, the grounds adjacent the lake were used as a training base for the US Army, where mock battles would be staged.

Once across the dam, turn left and enter Peters Canyon Regional Park. You are now 1.45 miles into the ride, at an elevation of 324 feet. This begins a 5.2-mile loop of the park (I describe the clockwise route). The trail climbs steadily, at a 2.9% grade, up Peters Canyon. At mile 2.75, at an elevation of 525 feet, bear left onto Lake View Trail. The trail descends into a low area, with the Peters Canyon Reservoir dam looming overhead, to your right. Pray for watertight construction as you ride along here. Bear left at what appears to be the end of the trail to continue—the next segment was sandy when I rode it. Bear right at the next junction to continue on Lake View Trail. The climb up to lake level is steep (16.3% grade). The trail crests at 611 feet, then proceeds through a series of rollercoaster ups and downs, with an 8.8% gradient descent, a 10.0% climb, and then a 14.9% descent. Had enough? The trail curves right at mile 3.4 to continue a circumnavigation of Peters Canyon Reservoir. The trail is never lakeside, but is within the lake's sphere. The next stretch passes through a patch of prickly pear cactus, on gentle terrain. Keep right at all of the upcoming junctions to remain on Lake View Trail. The trail passes by a parking lot at mile 4.0—this is the northern entrance to the park (starting point for Ride 10, Santiago Canyon Circuit). Continue through the grove, and out the other side, to parallel Canyon View Avenue. The trail is right next to the road.

Bike Shops

The Path Bike Shop, 215 West First St. #102, Tustin, (714) 699-0784, www.thepathbikeshop.com; Performance Bicycle, 2745 El Camino Real, Tustin, (714) 838-0641, www.performancebike.com/tustin

Hang a sharp right adjacent Jamboree Road to continue on Lake View Trail. Stay to the left at mile 4.5—you are now back on Peters Canyon Trail, heading south. Close the loop around Peters Canyon Reservoir at mile 4.85—for a short segment, you ride in the reverse direction of the outbound route. Bear left, though, at mile 4.9, onto East Ridge View Trail. After a tame opening, over which the trail descends slightly, the most challenging segment of the ride begins. Wow! It's a 20.0% uphill grade! I admittedly had to hike this segment. The climb is thankfully short, at just 0.15 mile. The high elevation of the entire ride, 646 feet, is at the crest. You have two options at the crest: To the left, the trail actually climbs a tad more, to remain along a narrow ridge. To the right, the trail makes a steep descent (22.7% grade), and then climbs (11.4%)—the two trail options merge downstream. I took the downhill-uphill option, and was tested by the steep drop. Beyond the merge, East Ridge View proceeds through a series of short, steep descents and climbs, generally in the 10% grade range, as it rollercoasters its way along the ridge. Near the southern end of the trail, at mile 5.75, there is a 20.8% descent, followed by a 12.2% climb, and then a comparatively long (0.3-mile) 9.3% downhill grade—followed by a 17.0% downhill and a 10.7% climb!

East Ridge View Trail finally comes to an end at mile 6.3, curving to the right to become Eucalyptus Trail. This trail winds and twists its way down the hillside, with a few technical sections, while passing through a shady eucalyptus grove. Watch your speed and your line as you make your way down. The trail ends at Peters Canyon Trail to close the 5.2-mile park loop. Keep straight

Tustin

Peters Canyon Park and Ride's route is entirely within the city limits of Tustin, which had a population of 80,621 in 2014. Tustin is bordered by Santa Ana on the west, Irvine on the south, unincorporated communities of the Tustin Foothills on the north, and Loma Ridge on the east, with Peters Canyon neatly sandwiched between the Tustin Foothills and Loma Ridge. Tustin is perhaps most famous for the two airship hangars that were constructed to serve the former Naval Lighter-Than-Air Station Santa Ana, which later became Marine Corps Air Station Tustin. The base was closed in 1999. By then, the hangars had been designated National Civil Engineering Landmarks by the American Society of Civil Engineers. They are two of the largest free-standing wooden structures in the world; Hangar No. 2, for example, is 1,072 feet (327 meters) long and 292 feet (89 meters) tall. During World War II, airships, housed in the hangars when not in use, patrolled the coast. Peters Canyon Park and Ride does not pass by the hangars, but they can be glimpsed while riding the Tour of the Master Plan: Irvine Ranch, Ride 32.

across the dam (Lower Peters Canyon Reservoir) to begin the 1.45-mile trek back to Citrus Ranch Park. This segment of the ride is entirely downhill as you lose 92 feet of elevation. Use caution and patience as you cross Pioneer Road and Tustin Ranch Road (both are signalized). Please note that Peters Canyon Elementary School is located adjacent Peters Canyon Trail, just north of Cedar Grove Park. Depending on the day and time, you may encounter children along the trail (and crossing guards at the intersections). As always, be cautious and give way.

MILES AND DIRECTIONS

0.0 Start at Citrus Ranch Park in Tustin; head northeast on Peters Canyon Regional Bikeway (dirt trail).

0.1 Traffic signal at Tustin Ranch Road; cross road in crosswalk, follow trail.

0.45 Traffic signal at Pioneer Road; cross road in crosswalk, follow trail.

0.9 Cross Hannaford Drive.

1.1 Cross Silverado Terrace.

1.3 Curve right; cross Lower Peters Canyon Reservoir (dry) dam.

1.45 Bear left at junction, remaining on Peters Canyon Trail; enter Peters Canyon Regional Park—begin 5.2-mile clockwise loop around park (can also be ridden counterclockwise).

2.75 Bear left at junction, onto Lake View Trail.

2.9 Bear left at split to remain on Lake View Trail, and then bear right; begin 16.3% gradient climb.

3.05 Crest of climb, adjacent Peters Canyon Reservoir dam; begin series of steep descents and climbs.

3.4 Curve right to remain on Lake View Trail (stay to the right at all upcoming junctions).

4.0 Turn right at junction to remain on Lake View Trail, adjacent parking area.

4.1 Pass through grove and picnic area.

4.3 Lake View Trail is now parallel to Canyon View Avenue, which is to your left—curve right at Jamboree Road.

4.5 Stay left at split; now back on Peters Canyon Trail.

4.85 Keep straight at Lake View Trail junction to remain on Peters Canyon Trail, and then bear left onto East Ridge View Trail.

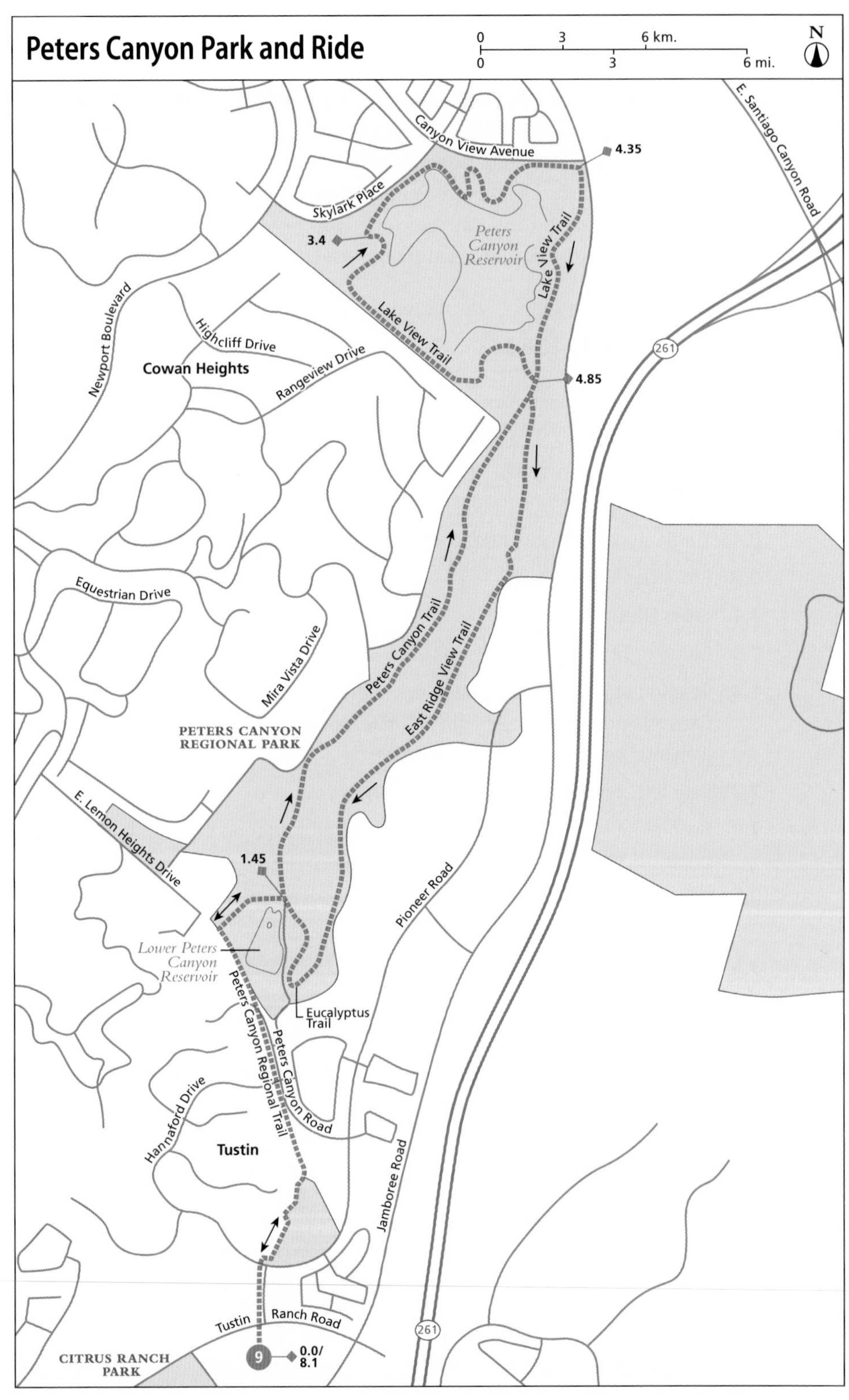

Peters Canyon Park and Ride
0
3
6 km.
0
3
6 mi.
N
Canyon View Avenue
4.35
E. Santiago Canyon Road
Skylark Place
3.4
Peters
Canyon
Reservoir
Lake View Trail
Newport Boulevard
Highcliff Drive
Lake View Trail
Cowan Heights
Rangeview Drive
261
4.85
Equestrian Drive
Mira Vista Drive
Peters Canyon Trail
East Ridge View Trail
PETERS CANYON
REGIONAL PARK
E. Lemon Heights Drive
1.45
Pioneer Road
Lower Peters
Canyon
Reservoir
Eucalyptus
Trail
Peters Canyon Regional Trail
Peters Canyon Road
Hannaford Drive
Tustin
Jamboree Road
Tustin
Ranch Road
261
CITRUS RANCH
PARK
9
0.0/
8.1

4.95 Begin steep climb (20.0% grade).

5.1 Crest of climb (elevation 646 feet); begin steep descent (22.7% grade), or take bypass trail to the left.

5.2 Continue on East Ridge View Trail, through a series of steep descents and climbs.

5.75 Begin steep descent (20.8% grade), followed by steep climb (12.2% grade).

5.85 Crest of climb; begin 0.3-mile-long descent (9.3% grade).

6.2 Descent continues, now at a 17.0% grade, then begin climb at 10.7% grade.

6.3 End of East Ridge View Trail; trail curves right, becoming Eucalyptus Trail (winding downhill).

6.65 End of Eucalyptus Trail descent, and end of Peters Canyon Regional Park loop; keep straight onto Peters Canyon Trail (cross dam).

6.8 Turn left, at end of dam, to continue on Peters Canyon Trail (Bikeway).

7.0 Cross Silverado Terrace.

7.2 Cross Hannaford Street.

7.65 Traffic signal at Pioneer Road; keep straight—remain on Peters Canyon Regional Bikeway (dirt trail).

8.0 Traffic signal at Tustin Ranch Road; keep straight, remaining on Peters Canyon Bikeway.

8.1 End of ride at entrance to Citrus Ranch Park.

10

Santiago Canyon Circuit

Start: Peters Canyon Regional Park (north entrance), 8548 East Canyon View Ave., Orange

Length: 30.35 miles (clockwise loop plus short opening-closing out-and-back)

Riding time: 1.5 to 4 hours (my time: 1H49:28)

Terrain and surface: 100% paved roads

Elevations: Low—213 feet on Jeffrey Road, north of Culver Drive; high—1,425 feet on Santiago Canyon Road, 1 mile south of Modjeska Canyon Road

Traffic and hazards: As of 2014, the heaviest traffic volumes were on Portola Parkway west of Glenn Ranch Road in Lake Forest, Irvine Boulevard east of Jeffrey Road in Irvine, and Jamboree Road north of Portola Parkway.

Map: *The Thomas Guide by Rand McNally—Street Guide: Los Angeles and Orange Counties* (any recent year), page 800

Getting there by car: From central Anaheim, head south on I-5. Exit at Katella Avenue and head east. Katella becomes Villa Park Road, and then Santiago Canyon Road, as it approaches the Santa Ana Mountains. Santiago Canyon Road bends to the right adjacent Irvine Regional Park, becoming Jamboree Road. Head southward on Jamboree. Turn right onto Canyon View Avenue; look for the entrance to Peters Canyon Regional Park on the left.

Getting there by public transit: OCTA bus route 54 runs between Garden Grove and Santiago Canyon College in Orange via Chapman Avenue. The bus was running every 20 minutes on weekdays, every 35 to 55 minutes on Saturdays, and every 40 to 65 minutes on Sundays. From the college, head east on Chapman Avenue to Jamboree Road. Turn right on Jamboree, and ride downhill to Canyon View Avenue. Turn right on Canyon View; the park entrance will be on the left. Alternatively, the ride can be started from Chapman and Jamboree—head east on Santiago Canyon Road.

Starting point coordinates: 33.785008°N / 117.761417°W

THE RIDE

The Santiago Canyon Circuit is a popular ride that incorporates one of Orange County cyclists' rites of passage: Santiago Canyon Road. Along with CA 1 (the Pacific Coast Highway) and the SART (Santa Ana River Trail), Santiago Canyon Road is probably one of the county's most-ridden roads. Its 12-mile length, with good shoulders, is not heavily traveled by motor vehicles. Plus, with the Santa Ana Mountains on the east and the Loma Ridge on the west, the canyon is sheltered from the rest of intensely developed Orange County. The clockwise loop is 30 miles in length exactly, plus 0.35 mile of out-and-back riding on the opening and closing Canyon View Avenue. The range between the low and high elevations is 1,212 feet, so there is plenty of climbing, with the steepest at a 6.0% grade.

Start the ride at Peters Canyon Regional Park in the upper northeastern corner of Orange. The ride uses the north entrance, which is actually the main entrance. Ride 9, Peters Canyon Park and Ride, enters the park from the south. Famous Orange citizens include or have included baseball pro Bert Blyleven, Grammy-nominated singer Toni Childs, actress Ruby Keeler, and mountain bike world champion Leigh Donovan. Turn right onto Canyon View Avenue upon exiting the park, and head toward Jamboree Road. Turn left here and start climbing. The starting elevation is 551 feet, and the climbing begins at a gentle 2.0% grade. At Santiago Canyon Road, turn right, and continue the climb. After a lull, the climbing resumes, this time at about a 4.0% grade.

Bike Shop

The Path Bike Shop, 215 West First St. #102, Tustin, (714) 699-0784, www.thepathbikeshop.com; Performance Bicycle, 2745 El Camino Real, Tustin, (714) 838-0641, www.performancebike.com/tustin

Santiago Canyon Road leaves Orange after crossing over the CA 261 freeway, which is one of Orange County's toll roads (not really a "free" way!). Traffic volumes drop off noticeably after crossing the last CA 261 ramp as the road heads toward its first crest. The elevation is 974 feet at the crest, 2.65 miles into the ride. Santiago Canyon Road then descends into the canyon. From the 3.5-mile mark, the road rolls until mile 5, when it starts to climb again. Irvine Lake is on the left at mile 4.1. This is a private lake that was accessible every Tuesday—during the season, as of this writing—for mountain bike racing. The race series claimed to be the largest in the United States. As for the lake, it is a man-made facility, filled with waters from Santiago Creek, which drains a large Santa Ana Mountains watershed.

The second crest of the ride is reached at mile 6.4 (elevation 1,021 feet); next, the road descends gradually to Silverado Canyon Road (please see

It's a triathlon on Portola Parkway in Irvine! A lone rider—maybe she's leading—navigates the cones and checks the signs.

Silverado and Modjeska Canyons Escape, Ride 12). From here, at mile 7.1, Santiago Canyon Road ascends gradually to Modjeska Canyon Road (elevation 1,197 feet at mile 9.95). Next, the road ascends more steeply, at a 6.0% grade, to the high elevation of the ride (1,425 feet). The road narrows through this passage, although the shoulder is adequate. The mostly undeveloped area to the right is Whiting Ranch Wilderness Park (see Ride 33, Whiting Ranch Wilderness Excursion). From the crest, Santiago Canyon Road descends at an average 3% grade for the next few miles. Cook's Corner, a popular motorcycle and mountain bike staging area, is on your left at the Live Oak Canyon Road junction (mile 12.95). Stay right—you are now on El Toro Road, on the outer limits of the city of Lake Forest.

Turn right onto Glenn Ranch Road at mile 13.95, and head up the 6.1% gradient climb. Note that just upstream of Glenn Ranch Road on El Toro was an entry to the Aliso Creek Bikeway (please see Ride 15, Aliso Creek Sneak). Glenn Ranch ascends and then descends briskly to an intersection with Portola Parkway. Turn right here; this is the busiest road of the ride. Stay to the right and be cautious. The traffic volume quickly drops off as you continue past the entrance to Whiting Ranch Wilderness Park. Turn left onto Alton Parkway (mile 16.75).

After a long, gradual descent on Alton, turn right onto Irvine Boulevard (mile 19.4). The gradual descent continues. To your left is Orange County Great Park, on the former site of the El Toro Marine Corps Air Station. After a little over 4 miles on Irvine—rather speedy, if you catch a tailwind—turn right onto Jeffrey Road (mile 23.55). Next, turn left onto Portola Parkway. Portola continues to descend gradually to the lowest elevation of the ride (213 feet) north of Culver Drive. Portola is in the annals of bike racing history, having served as the route of the 2008 USA Elite Road Race Championships. In that race, teammates James Mattis and Andy Jacques-Mayne broke away from the field with 48-year-old Thurlow Rogers, who had been a fifth-place finisher in the 1984 Olympic Games road race. Although Rogers may have been the sentimental favorite, the two teammates outnumbered him, with Mattis taking the win.

El Toro

El Toro means "the bull," which is actually the former name of the city of Lake Forest. Next to the city is Marine Corps Air Station (MCAS) El Toro, which was commissioned in 1943, during World War II, and was decommissioned in 1999. The base covers 4,682 acres and included four runways, two of which were capable of handling the US military's largest jet aircraft. Air Force One regularly landed here between World War II and 1999, carrying every US president during that period. Residential growth in the areas surrounding the base, especially during the 1980s and 1990s, presented problems for aircraft operations, particularly with flight path and noise issues. The growth, along with some environmental concerns, led to the base's closing. During its history, the base had a few incidents. In 1965, a US Air Force jet bound for Okinawa crashed just after takeoff, killing all eighty-four on board. In 1988, Colonel Jerry Cadick miraculously survived a 300-mph crash when his aircraft, performing an aerial loop maneuver, passed too close to the ground. As part of decommissioning, all of the base's operations were transferred to MCAS Miramar in San Diego. Since closure, the base has been identified as an environmental remediation site. Contamination of the site's soils resulted from the leaking of volatile organic compounds, including industrial solvents and aircraft fuel. Portions of the base have nonetheless been converted to other uses, including Orange County Great Park (playground, athletic field, merry-go-round, hot-air balloon ride). Some of the old taxiways have been used for bike racing.

You may pretend that you are vying for the elite road race title as you ride along Portola. Cross over the CA 261 freeway, and then turn right onto Jamboree Road (mile 27.15) to begin the long climb (2.0% grade) back to Peters Canyon Regional Park. The park will be on your left as you ride up Jamboree; the high ridge to your left is ridden in Ride 9, Peters Canyon Park and Ride. Turn left onto Canyon View Avenue, at the northeast corner of the park, and head west. Look for the entrance to the park on the left—this is the conclusion of the ride.

MILES AND DIRECTIONS

0.0 Start at Peters Canyon Regional Park (north entrance) in Orange; head east on Canyon View Avenue. Starting elevation: 551 feet.

0.15 Traffic signal at Jamboree Road; turn left and begin climb at 2.0% grade.

0.7 Traffic signal at Santiago Canyon Road; turn right—climbing at a 3.7% grade, increasing to 4.1% after a short dip.

1.65 Cross over CA 261 freeway; leave city of Orange, enter unincorporated Orange County.

2.65 Crest of climb (elevation 974 feet); begin descent at 3.4% grade.

4.1 Irvine Lake (private) on the left.

4.95 Begin climb at 2.5% grade.

6.4 Crest of climb (elevation 1,021 feet); begin gradual descent to Silverado Canyon.

7.1 Silverado Canyon Road intersection (keep straight); begin long, gradual climb.

9.95 Modjeska Canyon Road intersection (keep straight); climb gets steeper (6.0% grade), and roadway narrows.

11.0 Crest of climb (high elevation of ride: 1,425 feet); begin descent (average 3% grade).

12.95 Cook's Corner (Live Oak Canyon Road); stay right—now on El Toro Road.

13.25 Entrance to Aliso Creek Bikeway on the right; stay on the road.

13.95 Traffic signal at Glenn Ranch Road; turn right—begin climb at 6.1% grade.

14.3 Crest of climb (elevation: 1,078 feet); begin descent (4.0% grade).

15.55 Traffic signal at Portola Parkway; turn right.

16.5 Whiting Ranch Wilderness Park entrance on the right (keep straight).

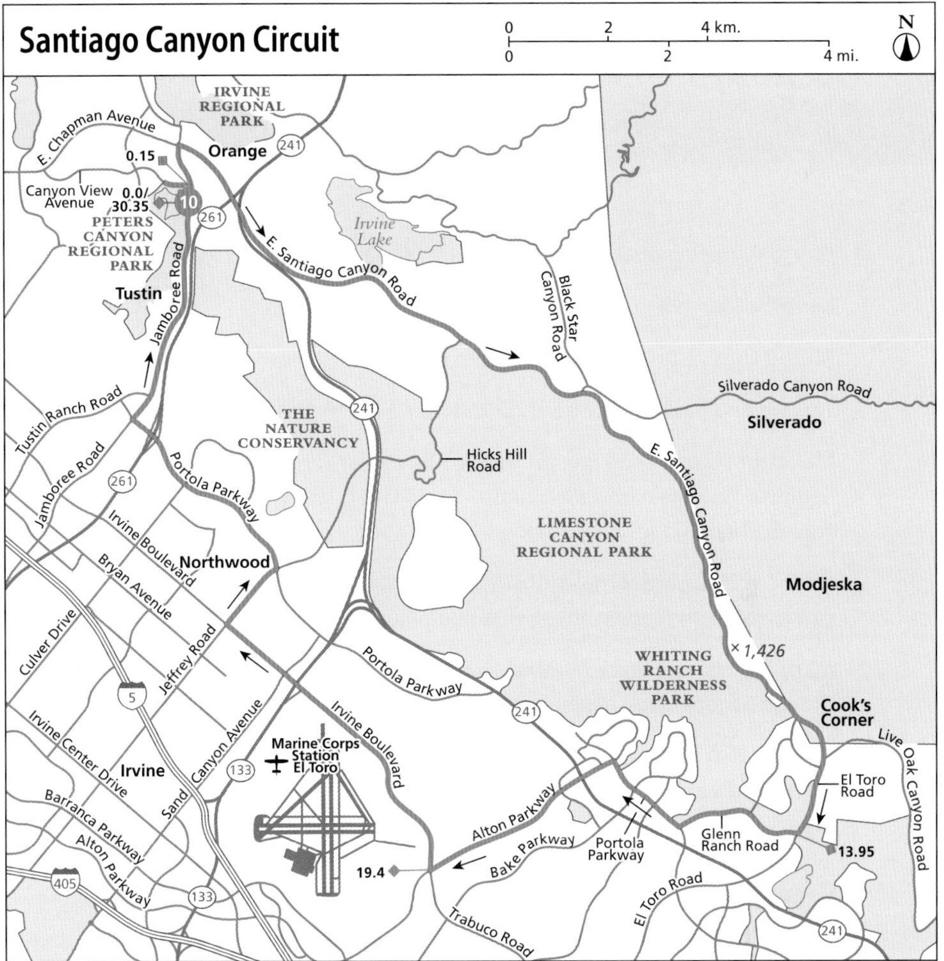

16.75 Traffic signal at Alton Parkway; turn left—begin descent (2.6% grade).

19.4 Traffic signal at Irvine Boulevard; turn right—Great Park (formerly El Toro Marine Corps Air Station) is on the left.

23.55 Traffic signal at Jeffrey Road; turn right.

24.45 Traffic signal at Portola Parkway; turn left.

26.25 Elevation 213 feet, north of Culver Drive (low elevation of the ride).

27.15 Traffic signal at Jamboree Road; turn right—begin climb at 2.0% grade.

30.2 Traffic signal at Canyon View Avenue; turn left—Peters Canyon Regional Park is on the left.

30.35 End of ride, at entrance to Peters Canyon Regional Park.

Santiago Oaks on Spokes

Start: Irvine Regional Park, 1 Irvine Park Rd., Orange

Length: 10.8 miles (figure eight)

Riding time: 1 to 3.5 hours (my time: 1H22:05)

Terrain and surface: 90% dirt trails, 10% paved roads

Elevations: Low—454 feet on Towhee Trail, near Santiago Oaks Regional Park main entrance; high—1,074 feet near the Coachwhip Trail–Barham Ridge Trail junction

Traffic and hazards: The entire ride takes place within two adjacent parks; traffic on roads within Irvine Regional Park is light.

Map: *The Thomas Guide by Rand McNally—Street Guide: Los Angeles and Orange Counties* (any recent year), page 800

Getting there by car: From central Anaheim, head south on I-5. Exit at Katella Avenue and head east. Katella becomes Villa Park Drive, and then Santiago Canyon Road. Continue on Santiago Canyon to Jamboree Road; turn left here. The road curves to the right and enters Irvine Regional Park. Once inside the park, past the entrance station (small fee on weekdays, slightly higher on weekends and holidays), turn left at the first intersection, and park in the nearest lot.

Getting there by public transit: OCTA bus route 54 runs between Garden Grove and Santiago Canyon College in Orange via Chapman Avenue. The bus was running every 20 minutes on weekdays, every 35 to 55 minutes on Saturdays, and every 40 to 65 minutes on Sundays. From there, head east on Chapman, and then turn left on Jamboree Road. Enter Irvine Regional Park at the end of Jamboree.

Starting point coordinates: 33.797031°N / 117.756856°W

THE RIDE

Santiago Oaks on Spokes is a mountain bike ride on some popular trails in two adjacent parks, Irvine Regional Park and Santiago Oaks Regional Park (RP). The ride begins in Irvine RP, continues to Santiago Oaks RP, and then returns to

A rider swerves to avoid a sizable boulder, amid cacti and other vegetation, on Barham Ridge Trail.

Irvine RP, but not after navigating a few gnarly trails that may test your bike handling. The ride is suitable for beginners, though, in that it avoids expert trails in Santiago Oaks. Start the ride in the picnic area of Irvine RP, located immediately to the left after entering the park. There were small entrance fees, slightly higher on the weekend, as of this writing (free if you bicycle in).

Start the ride on the park road that heads toward the park entrance-exit. The starting elevation is 571 feet. Keep straight across the entry-exit road, though, onto Horseshoe Loop Trail. Follow the signs to stay on Horseshoe Loop—avoid any spurs. The trail begins with an 8.8% gradient climb to a bench; bear left to continue on Horseshoe Loop. From here, the trail climbs steadily to 722 feet above sea level; after a right-hand curve, the trail descends steadily to Peters Canyon Road (mile 1.15). Bear right; from here, Horseshoe Loop Trail is concurrent with the road, although you can ride on the adjacent dirt. Follow the road as it curves to the left to cross Santiago Creek (usually dry, but can be flooded). Keep curving to the left on the paved road. Look for a dirt trail on your right—this is the continuation of Horseshoe Loop Trail. It is a steep (14.3% grade), rocky climb to the top. The plateau is busy with spur trails and connectors. In general, take a line that leads toward the north, far side of where you entered the plateau. Ultimately, the trail curves to the left, and then to the left again; finally, make a hard right and head downhill, off of the plateau. The downhill is steep (8.2% grade) and rugged, so hang on!

At the bottom, the trail curves to the left and crosses Santiago Creek (again), and then curves right. From here, keep straight at all of the junctions, until you reach the southwest side of the park, very close to the road that you took to enter the park. Turn right, onto Santiago Creek Trail (mile 3.2). This is one of a handful of trails that connect Irvine RP with Santiago Oaks RP. What a great way to transition between parks! Santiago Creek Trail is scenic, with cacti growing along the route, and a stunning mountain backdrop. The prevailing direction is north—keep heading in this direction at all junctions. As you reach the outskirts of Santiago Oaks RP, the trail empties onto Lolita Street (mile 4.6), which is a paved road that climbs steeply (15.8% grade). The road provides access to the nearby dam, although there is no water here (because of upstream damming and diversion). Follow Lolita as it descends steeply (11.0% grade), and then curves to the right. Once you have returned to dirt, you are back on Santiago Creek Trail. The trail crosses the wash, and then curves to the left to continue into Santiago Oaks.

Pay attention to the signs, as there are plenty of connecting trails; stay on Santiago Oaks Trail. The trail eventually takes you into the heart of the park, which is dense with oak trees. Turn right onto Towhee Trail, which accesses the low elevation of the ride (454 feet; mile 5.45). Next, bear left onto an unnamed "trail" that is actually a stairway—dismount and walk the stairs. Remount at the top, staying to the right and continuing onto Wilderness Trail. Wilderness begins with a brisk climb (8.9% grade). Follow Wilderness as it switches back to head southward; look for the junction to Oak Trail, on the left. Turn left here (mile 6.3); it is a challenging 9.2% grade as Oak Trail climbs from 502 to 720 feet in just under a half-mile. Bear right onto Bumble Bee Trail (mile 6.85) to continue the climb, now at a whopping 14.7% grade. Beyond the crest (813 feet elevation), Bumble Bee loses elevation quickly, in switchbacks, as it descends into the canyon.

Bike Shops

Adrenaline Bike Shop, 366 South Tustin St., Orange, (714) 288-2012, www.adrenalinebikes.com; Bike Alley, 2823 East Chapman Ave., Orange, (714) 997-3980, http://bikealleybmx.com (BMX specialist); Black Market Bikes, 280 North Sacramento St., Orange, (714) 925-9942, www.blackmarketbikes.com (bike repair shop); Performance Bicycle, 2745 El Camino Real (The Market Place), Tustin, (714) 838-0641, www.performancebike.com/bike-shop/store/tustin

At the bottom of the canyon, although a right turn may look tempting (downhill), turn left onto Yucca Ridge Trail, and then quickly bear right onto Coachwhip Trail. Prepare to be whipped, as Coachwhip climbs at a steady 7.8% grade to reach an elevation of 1,058 feet. A few outcroppings and switchbacks are thrown in to make this a memorable trail. At the crest (mile 8.25), turn right onto Barham Ridge Trail, which climbs slightly to the highest elevation of the ride (1,074 feet). The expansive view, along with the exertion, may make you feel as if you have climbed to a much higher elevation. Barham Ridge starts with a semi-technical descent—choose your line carefully. Just when it appears that the trail is heading for a precipice (actually, it is), bear left onto Chutes Trail (mile 8.75). This is the "easy" way down. Experts use Ridge Chutes Trail, which is parallel, to your left. The alternative is much more technical and challenging than Chutes.

Yet Chutes offers challenges of its own, with its somewhat narrow track, a steep drop-off on the left, and tight, switchback turns. After a little over 1 mile of tricky descending, turn left, at the end of Chutes, onto Roadrunner Loop Trail. To return to Irvine RP, Roadrunner crosses a somewhat deep but rideable gorge. There are actually a couple of options, with the westernmost one (to your right) being the most rideable. Once on the other side, bear right to access the singletrack edition of Roadrunner Loop. (The trail also has a

Fall 2007 California Firestorm

Dryness, drought, winds, and other interventions periodically contribute to the ignition of fires in California. Sometimes the burning escalates, as it did during 2007, when some 9,000(!) separate wildfires torched over 1 million acres along a path stretching from Santa Barbara County in the north to the US-Mexico border in the south. There were fifteen fatalities and 160 injuries, nearly 80% of which involved firefighters. The fires started in March, and continued until November—separate fires started in different places at different times, with some ending while others ignited or burned. The inaugural fire was in the Santiago Oaks region: the "241" Fire started on March 11 when a stolen car was set afire near a CA 241 tollbooth. It was contained by the 13th, burning 2,036 acres and destroying two structures. The fire spread in just 3 hours. High winds, low humidity, warm temperatures, and dry brush contributed to the spread. Personnel had difficulty accessing the blaze in the rugged terrain of Windy Ridge, just to the east-northeast of Santiago Oaks. The 241 Fire was only a prelude of the siege to come.

straight, wide-track edition to your left, but that would be boring!) Roadrunner Loop snakes its way through the overgrowth and groves, with its direction never fully clear. After about 0.6 mile of singletracking, the trail opens up to cross Santiago Creek (again). Continue to the park road; turn right, and follow the road back to the parking area at which you started. Did you complete the ride without putting a foot down?

MILES AND DIRECTIONS

0.0 Start in the parking area located just north of the entrance to Irvine Regional Park. Head toward the park entrance on the paved park road.

0.1 On the other side of the entrance (i.e., south side—do not exit the park), ride onto Horseshoe Loop Trail. Follow the signing to ensure that you are on the right trail.

0.15 Begin steep (8.8% grade) climb to a bench; bear left to continue on Horseshoe Loop.

0.85 Crest of Horseshoe Loop Trail (722 feet elevation); begin descent.

1.15 Trail empties onto Peters Canyon Road (paved park road); turn right—trail is now concurrent with road.

1.5 Cross Santiago Creek (usually dry, can be flooded).

1.8 Bear right, off of paved road, onto dirt trail—begin steep (14.3% grade) climb. You are still on Horseshoe Loop Trail.

1.85 Crest of climb; now on plateau—keep straight, remaining on wide trail; follow trail as it curves to the left.

2.35 Turn sharply to the right; begin downhill on rocky trail (8.2% grade).

2.55 Cross Santiago Creek (usually dry); after curving to the right, keep straight at all junctions.

3.2 Turn right onto Santiago Creek Trail.

4.6 Steep climb (15.8% grade) to Lolita Street (paved road), then a steep descent, adjacent dam; curve right at the bottom of the descent.

4.75 Still on Santiago Creek Trail (dirt); trail curves left and enters Santiago Oaks Regional Park. Watch the signs to ensure that you remain on Santiago Creek.

5.6 Bear right at junction onto Towhee Trail, then turn left—dismount and negotiate stairs; remount and keep straight (back on Santiago Creek).

5.8 Bear right onto Wilderness Trail; begin 8.9% gradient climb.

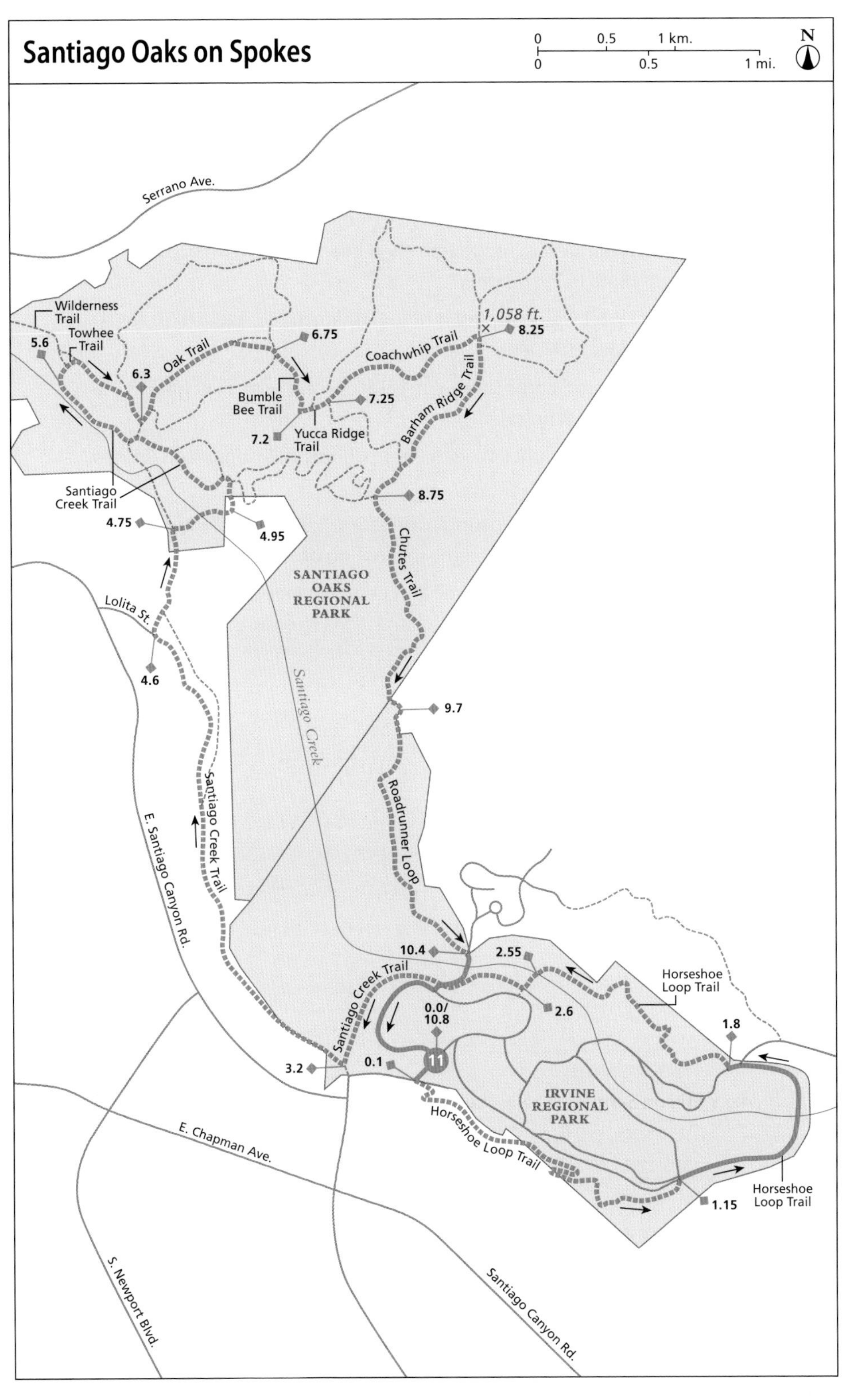
Santiago Oaks on Spokes
0
0.5
1 km.
0
0.5
1 mi.
N
Serrano Ave.
Wilderness Trail
Towhee Trail
5.6
6.3
Oak Trail
6.75
Bumble Bee Trail
Yucca Ridge Trail
7.2
7.25
Coachwhip Trail
1,058 ft.
8.25
Barham Ridge Trail
8.75
Santiago Creek Trail
4.75
4.95
Chutes Trail
SANTIAGO OAKS REGIONAL PARK
Lolita St.
4.6
Santiago Creek
9.7
Roadrunner Loop
Santiago Creek Trail
E. Santiago Canyon Rd.
10.4
2.55
Horseshoe Loop Trail
Santiago Creek Trail
2.6
0.0/ 10.8
1.8
3.2
0.1
11
IRVINE REGIONAL PARK
Horseshoe Loop Trail
E. Chapman Ave.
1.15
Horseshoe Loop Trail
S. Newport Blvd.
Santiago Canyon Rd.

6.0 Stay to the left (at two successive junctions) to continue on Wilderness Trail.

6.3 Turn left onto Oak Trail; begin climb (9.2% grade).

6.75 Bear right onto Bumble Bee Trail; continue climbing (14.7% grade).

6.85 Crest of climb (813 feet elevation); begin descent (9.6% grade).

7.2 Bear left onto Yucca Ridge Trail, then bear right onto Coachwhip Trail; begin climb (6.2% grade).

8.25 End of Coachwhip; turn right onto Barham Ridge Trail—high elevation of ride: 1,074 feet.

8.75 Bear left onto Chutes Trail—continue descent with switchbacks; occasionally technical.

9.4 Keep straight at junction with Ridge Chutes Trail; remain on Chutes Trail.

9.6 Stay to the right for crossing of deep wash; now on Roadrunner Loop Trail. Steep descent and climb in crossing of wash.

9.7 Follow Roadrunner Loop Trail as it enters Irvine Regional Park—singletrack, winding trail. Watch the signs to ensure that you remain on Roadrunner Loop.

10.4 Cross Santiago Creek (dry wash).

10.5 End of trail; turn right onto paved park road.

10.8 End of ride at parking area adjacent park road.

12

Silverado and Modjeska Canyons Escape

Start: Black Star Canyon trailhead, end of Black Star Canyon Road, unincorporated Orange County

Length: 22.3 miles (two out-and-back segments)

Riding time: 1.25 to 3.5 hours (my time: 1H21:29)

Terrain and surface: 100% paved roads

Elevations: Low—897 feet at the end of Black Star Canyon Road (at the start-finish); high—1,853 feet at the end of Silverado Canyon Road

Traffic and hazards: Santiago Canyon Road was carrying 7,000 vehicles per day in 2014. Watch out for short sight distances along the roads in Silverado and Modjeska Canyons.

Map: *The Thomas Guide by Rand McNally—Street Guide: Los Angeles and Orange Counties* (any recent year), page 801

Getting there by car: From central Anaheim, head south on I-5 to Chapman Avenue, in Orange. Head east on Chapman. At Jamboree Road, Chapman becomes Santiago Canyon Road, heading southeast. Turn left at Silverado Canyon Road, and then turn left onto Black Star Canyon Road. Follow Black Star Canyon Road to its end; park here, near the gate.

Getting there by public transit: Black Star Canyon is comparatively remote and is not served by public transit. The closest bus stop is at Santiago Canyon College (please see Ride 10, Santiago Canyon Circuit), located on Santiago Canyon Road, just under 8 miles from the Black Star Canyon gate. From the college, on your bike, head east on Chapman Avenue, which becomes Santiago Canyon Road at Jamboree Road. After riding on Santiago Canyon Road for a stretch, turn left onto Silverado Canyon Road, and then left again onto Black Star Canyon Road. Follow the road 1.1 miles to the gate, as above.

Starting point coordinates: 33.764408°N / 117.678061°W

Having dropped their companion, who would later catch up, two teammates speed along Silverado Canyon Road.

THE RIDE

The Silverado and Modjeska Canyons Escape is a rural, 22.3-mile ride in eastern Orange County. The route heads up and back down two canyons that penetrate the Santa Ana Mountains. The two out-and-back segments are connected by a ride along Santiago Canyon Road. Rural Orange County? Yes, surprisingly, densely developed Orange County still has plenty of undeveloped and natural space—enough to escape from the urban hubbub and experience a country getaway. Santiago Canyon is nestled between Loma Ridge on the west and the Santa Ana Mountains on the east. Santiago Creek, which snakes through the canyon, flows toward the northwest, emptying into the Santa Ana River.

The ride starts at the end of Black Star Canyon Road north of Silverado Canyon. Head *away* from the canyon (southward), on Black Star Canyon. The starting point is the lowest elevation of the ride (897 feet). As they say, "it's all uphill from here!" At the end of Black Star Canyon Road, turn left and head eastward on Silverado Canyon Road. Enter the community of Silverado at mile 3.1. The entire community is a California Historical Landmark. From here, the road climbs at an average gradient of 3.6%, although there are a few short, steeper segments. The canyon road is narrow, with no shoulder, so be on the lookout for motor vehicles. The narrow canyon has a cozy feel, with many residences located at the road rather than set back from the road. The canyon is actually a 2,500-foot-deep gorge, with mountains towering on either side. Silverado Creek, a year-round stream, runs the length of the canyon. Houses hug the road all the way up the canyon. The canyon is lush and dense with vegetation, providing shade along much of the route. The paved road ends at mile 6.65. For some, this is where the canyon begins, as the unpaved Silverado Canyon Trail heads up into Cleveland National Forest.

For you, however, turn around here and head back down the canyon. The elevation at the turnaround is 1,853 feet, the highest of the ride, nearly 1,000 feet above where you started. Watch your speed and the sight distances on the descent, as you may find yourself traveling as fast as the motor vehicles. The gradient of the road eases as you leave the community of Silverado. Continue to the end of Silverado Canyon Road, at Santiago Canyon Road. Carefully look to the left and right before turning left and heading southeast (mile 12.2). This portion of the ride duplicates a stretch of Ride 10, Santiago Canyon Circuit. Note that Santiago Canyon Road is a false flat, climbing gradually from 1,004 feet at Silverado Canyon to your next turn at Modjeska Canyon Road (1,196 feet).

Bike Shops

Sho-Air Cyclery, 8530 East Chapman Ave., Orange (844) 722-9253, http://shoaircyclinggroup.com

Turn left onto Modjeska Canyon Road (mile 15.15) and head up the canyon, making sure to turn left again at mile 16.05 to remain on Modjeska Canyon. This canyon is not as steep or deep as Silverado Canyon, but it nonetheless has its own history and town. The road ends at the Tucker Wildlife Sanctuary (mile 16.7), at an elevation of 1,336 feet. Turn around here, and return to base. Be sure to turn right at the bottom of the canyon to remain on Modjeska Canyon Road. Turn right onto Santiago Canyon Road (mile 18.25), and enjoy the gradual downhill to Silverado Canyon Road. Turn right here (mile 21.15), followed by an immediate left turn onto Black Star Canyon Road. Continue on Black Star Canyon to the end of the road to conclude the ride.

MILES AND DIRECTIONS

0.0 Start at the end of Black Star Canyon Road, at the gate marking the entry to Black Star Canyon. Turn around and head south on Black Star Canyon (elevation 897 feet).

1.15 Turn left onto Silverado Canyon Road.

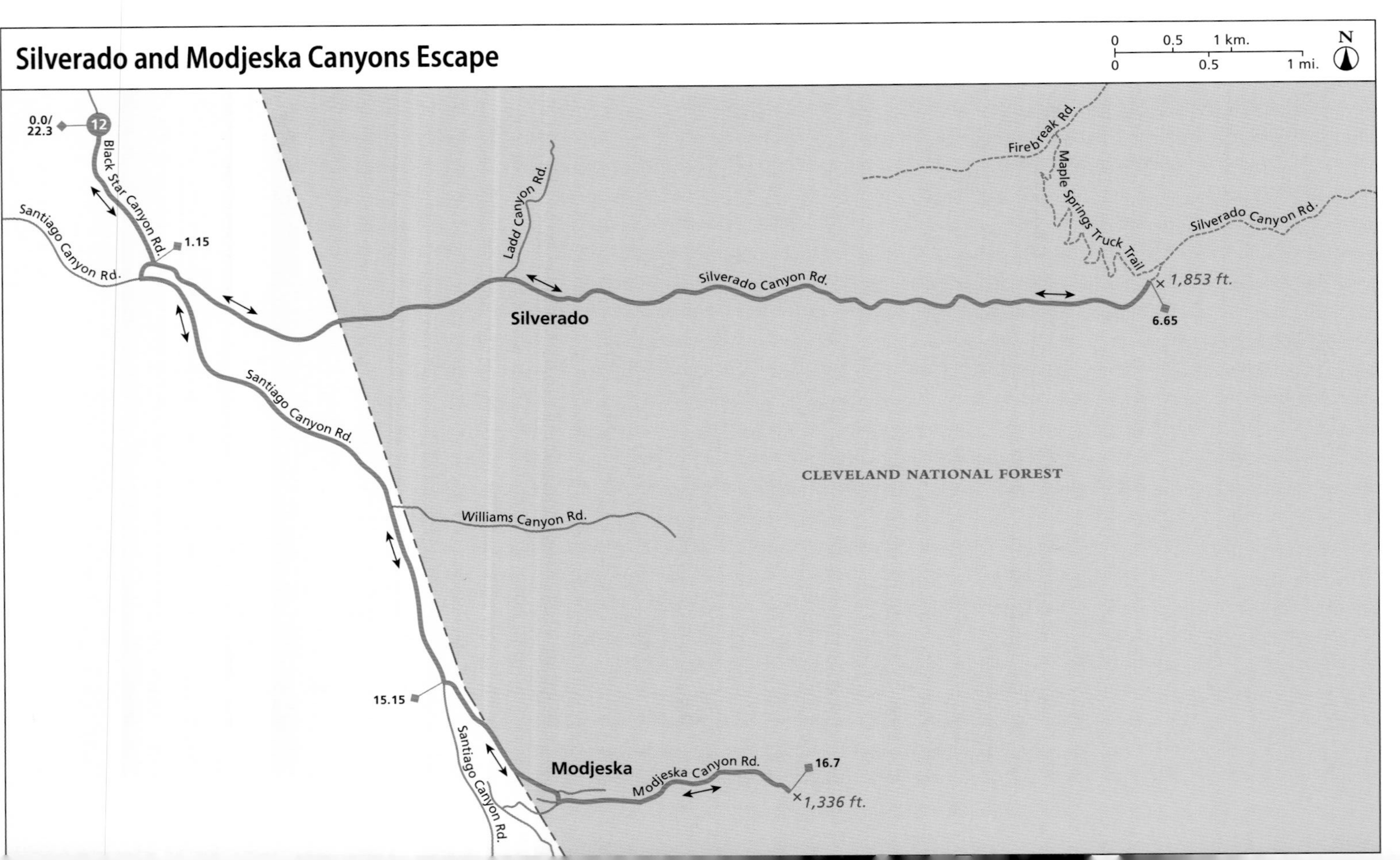
Silverado and Modjeska Canyons Escape
0
0.5
1 km.
0
0.5
1 mi.
N
0.0/
22.3
12
Black Star Canyon Rd.
1.15
Santiago Canyon Rd.
Ladd Canyon Rd.
Silverado
Silverado Canyon Rd.
Firebreak Rd.
Maple Springs Truck Trail
Silverado Canyon Rd.
1,853 ft.
6.65
Santiago Canyon Rd.
CLEVELAND NATIONAL FOREST
Williams Canyon Rd.
15.15
Santiago Canyon Rd.
Modjeska
Modjeska Canyon Rd.
16.7
1,336 ft.

3.1 Enter community of Silverado; begin 3.6% gradient climb.

6.65 End of Silverado Canyon Road; turn around (elevation 1,853 feet).

9.75 Leave Silverado community.

12.2 Stop sign at Santiago Canyon Road; turn left.

15.15 Turn left onto Modjeska Canyon Road.

Silverado and Modjeska

The community of Silverado has an illustrious history, having morphed since its early days as a mining town. The community was founded in 1878, in association with silver and coal mining and logging. The original name of the community, during Spanish rule, was Cañada de la Madera, which meant Timber Canyon. Later, a merger of English and Spanish words generated the name "Silverado." Mining activities diminished in the early 20th century. Remnants and relics of the mining operations still exist in the adjacent mountains. As mining subsided, the popularity of Silverado as a retreat increased, especially during the 1940s. Since then, a stable community of about 2,000 residents has formed, complete with a store, church, school, post office, and other amenities. While somewhat idyllic in its isolation and beauty, Silverado has seen its share of disasters. In 1939 and 1969, flooding resulting from torrential rains washed away houses, and caused general devastation. Fires, especially ones in 2007 and again in 2014, triggered canyon evacuations as firefighters fought blazes and managed to save structures. Even the old mines have been associated with disaster; in 2002, two amateur explorers drowned in a flooded passageway of the nearby Blue Light Mine.

Modjeska, a community of several hundred residents in Modjeska Canyon, is perhaps best known for its namesake, Helena Modjeska. Ms. Modjeska was a Polish actress, born in 1840 in Krakow, who emigrated to the United States in 1876 with her husband, Karol Bozenta Chlapowski. The two, along with several émigrés (one of whom was future Nobel Prize winner Henryk Sienkiewicz), purchased a ranch, with the intention of leaving the theater and living a utopian, rural life. Yet within one year, Ms. Modjeska was back on stage, reprising several of her Shakespearean roles. Her ranch home, Arden, is on the National Register of Historic Places as a National Historic Landmark. Ms. Modjeska's son by a previous relationship, Ralph Modjeski, would become a preeminent civil engineer and bridge designer of the early 20th century. His Quebec Bridge is still the world's longest cantilever bridge.

Racing the sun, enjoying the solitude of Santiago Canyon Road, with Loma Ridge to the left.

16.05 Turn left to continue on Modjeska Canyon Road.

16.7 End of Modjeska Canyon Road, at Tucker Wildlife Sanctuary; turn around (elevation 1,336 feet).

17.35 Turn right to continue on Modjeska Canyon Road.

18.25 Stop sign at Santiago Canyon Road; turn right.

21.05 Turn right onto Silverado Canyon Road.

21.15 Turn left onto Black Star Canyon Road.

22.3 End of ride at the end of Black Star Canyon Road.

13

West Fullerton Trails Survey

Start: Ford Park, 435 West Wilshire Ave., Fullerton

Length: 13.1 miles (opening and closing out-and-back segment, connecting to a counterclockwise or clockwise loop)

Riding time: 1 to 3.5 hours (my time: 1H18:49)

Terrain and surface: 88% dirt trails, 10% paved roads, 2% concrete walkways

Elevations: Low—150 feet at Ford Park; high—489 feet on Castlewood Trail

Traffic and hazards: A total of 10% (1.3 miles) of the route is ridden on city streets. Bastanchury Road was carrying 17,700 vehicles per day west of Parks Road in 2015.

Map: *The Thomas Guide by Rand McNally—Street Guide: Los Angeles and Orange Counties* (any recent year), page 738

Getting there by car: From central Anaheim, head north on Harbor Boulevard, entering Fullerton. Turn left on Wilshire Avenue, and continue for several blocks. Ford Park will be on the right, west of Ford Avenue.

Getting there by public transit: Ride OCTA bus route 47 northward on Anaheim Boulevard to Metrocenter Fullerton, which is in central Fullerton. From the station, head north on Harbor Boulevard, or any parallel side street, to Wilshire Avenue. Turn left and head west on Wilshire Avenue to Ford Park. From the region surrounding Anaheim, ride Amtrak or Metrolink (train) to Metrocenter Fullerton, and then follow the preceding instructions.

Starting point coordinates: 33.872394°N / 117.932092°W

THE RIDE

Many out-of-towners are unaware of the network of dirt trails neatly tucked into the city of Fullerton's Coyote Hills communities. The connected trails enable a nearly continuous off-road route, save a few street crossings and traffic signals. The alignments of the trails are not evident on street maps, and it may take a few exploratory rides to get oriented. The trails are very popular with those who know about them, as demonstrated by the steady stream of mountain bikers, runners, hikers, and equestrians. There is a standard Fullerton trails loop that local riders do; this book's version modifies the loop slightly. I rode the book's route counterclockwise, but the prevailing direction among local riders is clockwise. Whatever direction you choose, be courteous to the other trail users, and give way on narrow and technical sections.

Fullerton has had an intriguing history. The city was originally established for its agriculture; at one time, Fullerton boasted more orange groves than any other American city. The economy gradually diversified to include oil production, then, later, food processing. The original formula for Hawaiian Punch was developed in Fullerton during the 1930s. By the end of the 1940s, guitar-maker Leo Fender was developing his Fender Telecaster, which would later be used by musicians such as Kurt Cobain and Keith Richards. California State University, Fullerton, the city's biggest employer, was founded in the early 1960s. Famous Fullertonians include Gwen Stefani (her group, No Doubt, performed at CSU Fullerton, where she was a student, during their pre-breakout years), singer-songwriter Jackson Browne (graduate of Sunny Hills High School), four-time Olympic swimming gold medalist Janet Evans, actor Steven Seagal, and former assistant US attorney general Viet D. Dinh (George W. Bush administration).

Start the ride at Ford Park, one of Fullerton's fifty(!) city parks, located just west of Ford Avenue on West Wilshire Avenue. Head east on West Wilshire. At the first stop sign, turn left onto Ford Avenue and head north. Carefully cross busy Chapman Avenue, and continue heading north, into one of Fullerton's older neighborhoods. After crossing Malvern Avenue, it is a 9.7% climb to Brookdale Place. Turn right onto Brookdale and enjoy the short descent. After riding for 3 city blocks, turn left into the paved alley and head north. The alley is an alternative to the parallel Harbor Boulevard. Be aware that motor vehicles use this alley. Where the alley ends, at Berkeley Avenue, turn left onto the sidewalk and head west. Ride slowly here, and be sure to give way to pedestrians. After about 300 feet, turn left onto the Juanita Cooke Greenbelt Trail, the first of this ride's featured dirt trails. In the 1930s and 1940s, Juanita Cooke was a City of Fullerton liaison to the Fullerton Recreation Riders, a club of equestrians. The development of the trails in the city can be attributed to

A horse and rider and two cyclists share the Juanita Cooke Greenbelt Trail in Fullerton.

the equestrians of Cooke's era. The trail heads northwest and then north, with at-grade crossings at Valley View Avenue, Richman Avenue, and Bastanchury Road. The tree-lined trail quietly slices its way between residential areas on either side. Keep straight at the junction with Hiltscher Park Trail at mile 1.75. You will be returning to this junction later, on your way back. Prior to Bastanchury, Juanita Cooke Trail descends steeply (17.0%)—a barrier at the top of the hill warns trail users to walk down. You can ride down, but be aware that the trail comes to an abrupt end at the crossing road. You are now 2.0 miles into the ride.

Press the button and wait for the traffic signal to cross Bastanchury. Now, where is the trail? Up the road—ride along the walkway, adjacent Morelia Avenue. At Laguna Road, make a right, and then an immediate left to resume riding along the Juanita Cooke Greenbelt Trail. Next up is a long, uninterrupted stretch of nearly 1 mile. Cross Hermosa Drive and continue heading north. Note that this segment of the trail is out-and-back. About a quarter-mile beyond the underpass (West Las Palmas Drive), make a U-turn (you can actually make a triangular turn using the fork in the trail) and return. You are now 3.6 miles into the ride. At Hermosa Drive, turn right and aim for Laguna

Lake. Ride along the left (i.e., south) side of the lake, along Bud Turner Trail (Bud Turner was another Fullerton Recreation Rider from the Juanita Cooke era). The lake is usually stocked with trout, catfish, bass, and bluegill for fishermen. At the end of the lake, cross Clarion Drive and continue on Bud Turner Trail (signs indicate the locations of the trailheads). From here, the trail undulates and rolls over a few roots and off-camber segments. To your right is the Fullerton Recreation Riders Equestrian Center, which is the heart of the city's trail system.

Continue past the center, and follow the trail as it nears Euclid Street. Cross Laguna Road, and turn left, onto the dirt trail, to ride parallel to Euclid. Look for the opening in the barrier—use the crosswalk (and the pedestrian signal) to cross Euclid. You are now 5.0 miles into the ride. Negotiate the barriers and enter Nora Kuttner Trail. For the next half-mile, Nora climbs 202 feet at an average gradient of 7.5%. There were a few eroded segments when I rode this. Be watchful of riders heading in the opposite direction. The trail crests at 468 feet of elevation, then descends at 9.6% to its terminus at Castlewood Drive. While riding along Nora Kuttner, you may notice a vast open space to your right (with trails!). This area has, apparently, been slated for development for years, but the requisite approvals have yet to be finalized. Hence the fencing and No Trespassing signs. From the terminus of Nora Kuttner, turn right and ride along the (dirt) path that parallels Castlewood Drive. Wait for the traffic signal to cross Gilbert Street.

Once across Gilbert Street, head for the trailhead. You are now on Castlewood Drive Trail. Bland name, but this may be the most interesting trail of the ride! Start with a brisk climb at a 12.1% gradient to the high elevation of the entire route (489 feet). From here, the trail descends, curves, climbs, and then descends. There is some erosion along here, as well as eucalyptus and other trees. The trail ends at Rosecrans Avenue's sidewalk, 7.2 miles into the ride. Turn left here, and ride along the sidewalk or, alternatively, along the bordering dirt shoulder. Remain adjacent Rosecrans as you cross Sunny Ridge Drive and Gilbert Street (traffic signal). After a brisk downhill, the trail veers to the left, away from Rosecrans, becoming Rosecrans Trail. Follow the trail as it veers right, to parallel Coyote Hills Drive, and then away from the road, to enter West Coyote Hills Tree Park. You are now just over 8 miles into the ride. Rosecrans Trail curves to the left, through the park, and then to the right, for one of the steeper ascents of the

Bike Shops

East West Bikes, 206 North Harbor Blvd., Fullerton, (714) 525-2200, www.ewbikes.com; Fullerton Bicycles, 424 East Commonwealth Ave., Fullerton, (714) 879-8310, www.fullertonbicycle.com

route. From a park elevation of 302 feet, the trail climbs to 370 feet to cross Parks Road. The last segment of the climb is a 17.5% grade(!).

Once at the crest, cross Parks Road, and continue onto Parks Road Trail. This trail crests at 395 feet, then descends quickly, curving to the right and crossing Camino Rey (quiet residential street). Once across Camino Rey, the trail makes sweeping curves to the left and right as it passes through Virgil "Gus" Grissom Park. There is a parallel, paved path through the park, although your speed may be a bit intimidating to other park users. Cross Rosecrans Avenue (use the pedestrian signal), and continue the pleasant descent. Roger B. Chaffee Park is to your left; next enter Edward White Park. Cross Peacock Lane, now 9.5 miles into the ride—watch out for bumpy interfaces at the crossing. After a railroad crossing, Parks Road Trail comes to an abrupt end at Bastanchury Road. Turn right here, and travel along Bastanchury, either in the road or on the adjacent walkway, for the next 0.3 mile. Continue past Valencia Mesa Drive. Turn left onto Valley View Avenue, which is the next intersection. Wait for an opening in oncoming traffic; alternatively, cross like a pedestrian. From an elevation of 151 feet at the intersection, Valley View climbs at a 6.0% grade before easing to a 3.0% grade. Stay to the right where Valley View splits. Continue to the very end of Valley View; jog left onto La Mesa Drive, and then right onto Hiltscher Park Trail.

Hiltscher Park Trail, similarly to other Fullerton trails, cuts between adjacent residential communities before entering a stretch of park-space. Cross busy Euclid Street at mile 10.5; follow the trail as it curves to the left, and then into a highly visible crosswalk. Enter Hiltscher Park beyond Euclid, climbing to a junction with Juanita Cooke Greenbelt Trail. You are now 11.35 miles into the ride (elevation 270 feet), with 1.75 miles to go, reversing the opening segment. Head south on Juanita Cooke, crossing Richman Avenue, and then Valley View Drive. At the end of the trail, bear right onto the walkway to parallel Berkeley Avenue. Turn right into the alley, and head south to Brookdale Place. Turn right onto Brookdale, and climb the tree-lined street. Turn left onto Ford Avenue; it is a speedy descent (9.7% grade). Watch your speed, as you will be crossing Malvern Avenue, and then busy Chapman Avenue. Wait for an opening here, and then head south to Wilshire Avenue. Turn right on Wilshire, and return to Ford Park.

MILES AND DIRECTIONS

0.0 Start from Ford Park in Fullerton; turn left onto Wilshire Avenue and head east.

0.05 Stop sign at Ford Avenue; turn left.

0.1 Stop sign at Chapman Avenue; keep straight.

0.25 Stop sign at Malvern Avenue; keep straight.

0.35 Turn right onto Brookdale Place.

0.7 Turn left; enter alley.

0.85 Turn left onto walkway adjacent Berkeley Avenue.

0.95 Turn left onto Juanita Cooke Greenbelt Trail.

1.2 Cross Valley View Drive.

1.55 Cross Richman Avenue

1.75 Begin 9.6-mile counterclockwise loop, at junction with Hiltscher Park Trail.

2.0 17.0% descent to Bastanchury Road (signalized crossing); once across, keep straight on Morelia Avenue (or use parallel walkway).

2.25 Bear right onto Laguna Road, then cross Laguna and reenter Juanita Cooke Greenbelt Trail.

3.2 Cross Hermosa Road—begin out-and-back segment.

3.35 West Las Palmas Drive underpass.

3.6 U-turn at end of trail; return to Hermosa Drive.

4.05 Turn right onto Hermosa, then left onto Lakeside Drive, and then right onto Bud Turner Trail (Laguna Lake on the right).

4.45 Leave Laguna Lake; cross Clarion Drive (follow signs).

4.9 End of Bud Turner Trail; turn right onto Laguna Road, and then turn left onto dirt path, parallel to Euclid Street.

5.05 Cross Euclid Street at designated (signalized) pedestrian crossing; enter Nora Kuttner Trail (7.5% grade climb).

5.55 Crest of Nora Kuttner Trail; begin descent (9.6% grade).

5.75 End of Nora Kuttner Trail; turn right onto Castlewood Drive Trail (parallel to Castlewood Drive).

6.0 Traffic signal at Gilbert Street; keep straight—begin climb (Castlewood Drive Trail; 12.1% grade).

6.45 High elevation of ride (489 feet); begin long descent (4.0% grade).

7.2 End of Castlewood Drive Trail at Rosecrans Avenue; turn left to ride parallel to Rosecrans.

7.3 Cross Sunny Ridge Drive.

7.55 Traffic signal at Gilbert Street; keep straight.

7.95 Rosecrans Trail veers left, away from Rosecrans Avenue.

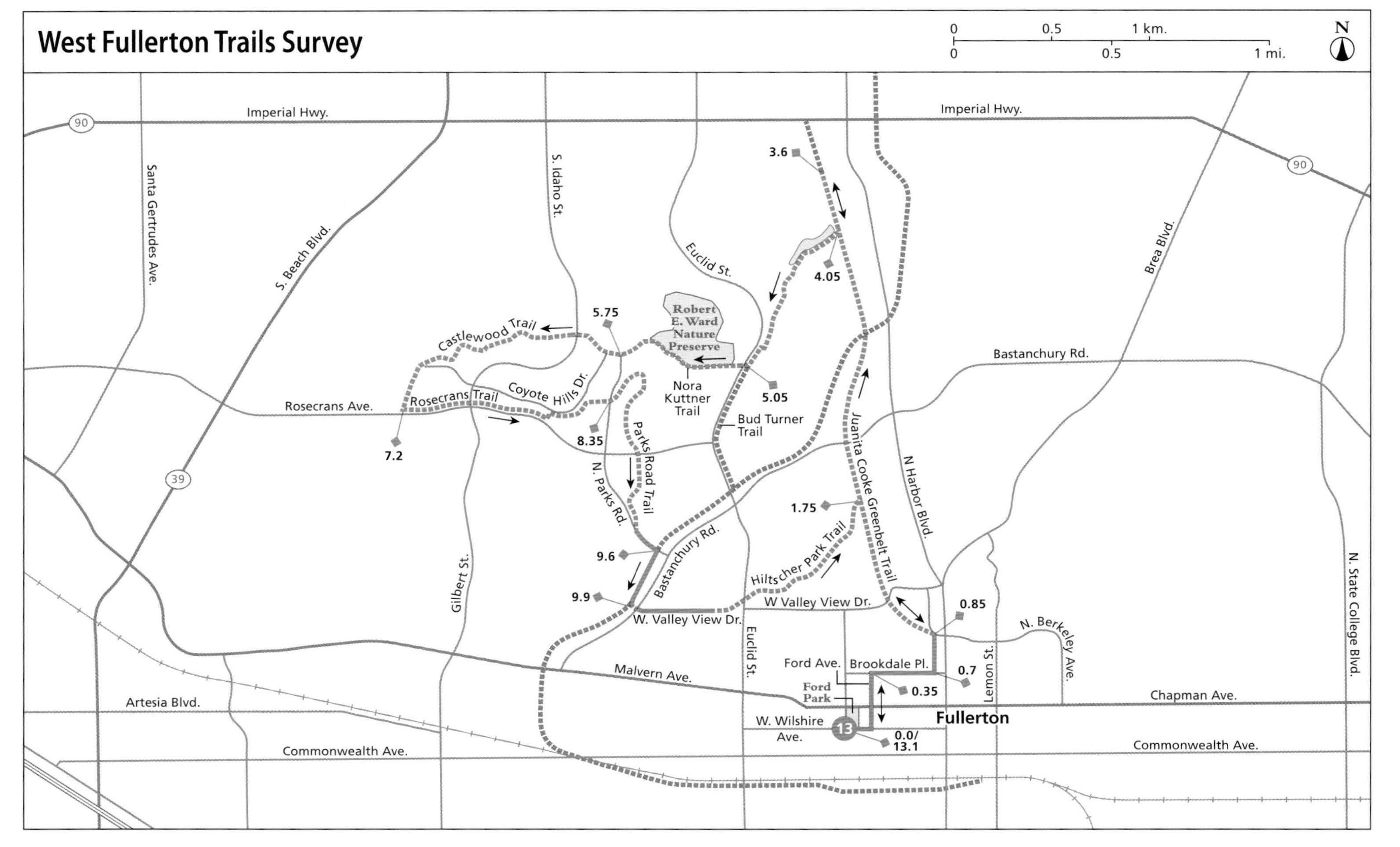
West Fullerton Trails Survey
0
0.5
1 km.
0
0.5
1 mi.
N
Imperial Hwy.
Imperial Hwy.
90
90
39
Santa Gertrudes Ave.
S. Beach Blvd.
S. Idaho St.
Euclid St.
Brea Blvd.
Bastanchury Rd.
Robert E. Ward Nature Preserve
Nora Kuttner Trail
Bud Turner Trail
Castlewood Trail
Coyote Hills Dr.
Rosecrans Trail
Rosecrans Ave.
Parks Road Trail
N. Parks Rd.
Juanita Cooke Greenbelt Trail
N Harbor Blvd.
Hiltscher Park Trail
Bastanchury Rd.
W Valley View Dr.
W. Valley View Dr.
Gilbert St.
Euclid St.
Malvern Ave.
Artesia Blvd.
Commonwealth Ave.
Commonwealth Ave.
Ford Ave.
Brookdale Pl.
Ford Park
W. Wilshire Ave.
Fullerton
Lemon St.
N. Berkeley Ave.
Chapman Ave.
N. State College Blvd.
3.6
4.05
5.05
5.75
7.2
8.35
1.75
9.6
9.9
0.85
0.7
0.35
0.0/ 13.1
13

8.05 Rosecrans Trail veers right to parallel Coyote Hills Drive, and then right, away from Coyote Hills Drive, entering West Coyote Hills Tree Park.

8.3 Steep climb (17.5% grade)—cross Parks Road; now on Parks Road Trail.

8.6 Cross Camino Rey.

9.0 Cross Rosecrans Avenue (use pedestrian signal).

9.5 Cross Peacock Lane.

9.6 End of Parks Road Trail at Bastanchury Road; turn right onto Bastanchury (use road or walkway).

9.9 Turn left onto Valley View Avenue (or cross Bastanchury, if using walkway).

10.05 Stay right at split in Valley View Avenue.

10.3 Bear left at La Mesa Drive, and then right onto Hiltscher Park Trail.

10.5 Cross Euclid Street—use pedestrian crossing.

11.1 Cross Richman Knoll (residential street).

11.35 End of Hiltscher Park Trail; turn right onto Juanita Cooke Greenbelt Trail.

11.55 Cross Richman Avenue.

11.9 Cross Valley View Avenue.

12.15 End of Juanita Cooke Trail; turn right onto walkway, adjacent Berkeley Avenue.

12.2 Turn right into alley.

12.4 Stop sign at Brookdale Place; turn right.

12.75 Stop sign at Ford Avenue; turn left.

12.85 Stop sign at Malvern Avenue; keep straight.

12.95 Stop sign at Chapman Avenue; keep straight.

13.05 Stop sign at Wilshire Avenue; turn right.

13.1 End of ride at Ford Park.

14

Yorba on Your Bike

Start: Rolling Hills Park, 1515 East Bastanchury Rd., Fullerton

Length: 24.3 miles (opening and closing out-and-back segment, connecting to a clockwise loop)

Riding time: 1.25 to 3.5 hours (my time: 1H48:31)

Terrain and surfaces: 68% paved roads; 32% paved paths

Elevations: Low—273 feet in Craig Regional Park in Fullerton; high—657 feet at Bastanchury Road and Fairmont Boulevard in Yorba Linda

Traffic and hazards: A total of 68% (16.6 miles) of the route is ridden on city streets. The heaviest traffic volumes in 2014 were on Bastanchury Road east of Lakeview Avenue (15,000 vehicles per day), Yorba Linda Boulevard southeast of San Antonio Road (23,000 vehicles per day), Esperanza Road near Fairlynn Boulevard (10,000 vehicles per day), Kellogg Drive south of Mountain View Avenue (10,000 vehicles per day), and Golden Avenue east of Craig Regional Park (5,000 vehicles per day).

Map: *The Thomas Guide by Rand McNally—Street Guide: Los Angeles and Orange Counties* (any recent year), page 739

Getting there by car: From central Anaheim, head north on the CA 57 freeway. Exit at Yorba Linda Boulevard; turn left and head west, entering Fullerton. Turn right onto State College Boulevard and head north, followed by a left onto Rolling Hills Drive (head west). At Maple Avenue, turn left—continue to the end of the road, adjacent Rolling Hills Park. Park here.

Getting there by public transit: Ride OCTA bus route 57 from central Santa Ana or Anaheim to Fullerton via State College Boulevard. Exit at Rolling Hills Drive. Head west on Rolling Hills; turn left on Maple Avenue, and ride to the end of the road (Rolling Hills Park). Bus route 57 runs every 20 minutes on weekdays, every 30 minutes on Saturdays, and every 20 to 30 minutes on Sundays and holidays.

Starting point coordinates: 33.900608°N / 117.898431°W

THE RIDE

The city of Yorba Linda is probably most famous as the birthplace of President Richard Nixon, and the home of the Richard M. Nixon Presidential Library and Museum. A less-famous feature is a series of disconnected paths that cross the city, allowing one to see Yorba Linda from a very quiet vantage point. The city has been ranked as one of the wealthiest in the country, as well as among the best places to live.

The route starts in Fullerton, and then passes through Placentia, before arriving in Yorba Linda. Start the ride at Rolling Hills Park in northeastern Fullerton, from the southern end of Maple Street, south of Rolling Hills Drive. The park's address refers to Bastanchury Road, but start from the park's "back side." Head north on Maple Avenue, and then turn right onto Rolling Hills Drive. Continue across State College Boulevard to the end of Rolling Hills, and then continue onto the bike path. The path—the Craig Regional Park Trail—descends into Craig Regional Park to the lowest elevation of the entire ride (273 feet). Turn right onto the park road, once in the park, and make left turns to create a counterclockwise loop. Do not complete the loop, though—once on the other side of the park, opposite your entrance, veer off the park road onto the path, and head up the hill to Associated Road, which borders the park. Turn right onto the walkway and ride to the signalized crossing.

Wait for the green signal, and then cross Associated, continuing onto Rolling Hills Road. Pass under the CA 57 freeway at mile 1.65. Enter Tri-City Park (welcome to Placentia) and, as you did at Craig Regional Park, head around the park's interior via a counterclockwise loop. Slow down here, as the park's lakeside path is frequented by casual strollers and children. As at Craig, do not complete the loop; veer off of the path when you reach the opposite side, onto the park road. Head toward the park's exit; cross Kraemer Boulevard, and continue heading east on Golden Avenue. The city of Placentia may be best known as the final residence of Corrie Ten Boom, the Dutch holocaust survivor and author.

At mile 3.6, turn right, off of Golden Avenue, onto McCormack Lane, for a short jaunt through a Placentia neighborhood. Turn left onto Williams Avenue, followed by a right turn onto Traynor Avenue. Traynor bears left, becoming Mathewson Avenue, which then bears right, becoming Spahn Lane. The jaunt ends at Bastanchury Road; turn left here and enter the city of Yorba Linda. When possible, ride up onto the walkway, since you will be veering off the road and onto El Cajon Trail (paved bike path), to your right; there is no curb cut at the trailhead. Continue heading southeasterly along El Cajon. This bike path does not feature grade-separated crossings. Be sure to slow down and look both ways at all street crossings. At Prospect Avenue, 4.7 miles into the

A rider enjoys a peaceful stretch along El Cajon Trail in Yorba Linda.

ride, get off the path, turn left, and head north. This marks the beginning of a clockwise loop around Yorba Linda—you will return here later. After crossing Bastanchury Road, turn right onto Brooklyn Avenue. Next, turn left onto Valley View Avenue and head north. Turn right onto Lakeview Avenue, and head uphill (2.9% grade), and then down. When you reach Bastanchury Road once again, turn left and head east.

Follow Bastanchury Road as it travels eastward across Yorba Linda, climbing to the highest elevation of the ride (657 feet) at Fairmont Boulevard (mile 8.8). From here, Bastanchury descends and then climbs again to the road's terminus at Village Center Drive. Cross Village Center Drive, and then ride up onto the walkway. Follow the walkway as it bears left onto an unnamed bike path. The path heads eastward, rolling for about three-fourths of a mile, and ending at San Antonio Road. Note that after crossing Via Gorzo, the path descends steeply (18.7% grade) for about 500 feet to San Antonio. Turn right onto San Antonio and head south, through a Yorba Linda neighborhood. Turn left onto Yorba Linda Boulevard, which heads downhill. Yorba Linda Boulevard is a busy but pleasant, tree-lined road; be sure to stay to the right, and watch for turning motor vehicles. Keep your speed in check on the descent, and look for New River Road, which comes up on your left. Turn left here (mile 11.45). New River passes by a retail center, and then descends to Esperanza Road. Turn right onto Esperanza, which passes under Yorba Linda Boulevard. Just beyond the underpass, turn right onto Avenida Barcelona. Look for the unnamed bike path on your left, just past Avenida Granada.

This bike path has several residential street crossings, including a few awkward ones (i.e., no curb cuts). Stay to the left at the junction just beyond Yorba Ranch Road. I recall the path being rough on this stretch, probably from tree roots causing pavement damage. The path ends at Paseo del Prado. Turn left here, and return to Esperanza Road. Turn right onto Esperanza—ride along this road for the next 1.1 miles. Turn right onto Fairlynn Boulevard (mile 14.5), and head into another Yorba Linda neighborhood. As Fairlynn curves to the left, look for the easy-to-miss bike path on your left. This is the beginning of the El Cajon Trail.

The El Cajon Trail is the main feature of the ride. The path winds its way across Yorba Linda, along the back sides of residences and businesses. Nearly all of the crossings are at grade, and there are a few discontinuities that require riding along a road or walkway. But all of that adds to the fun! Avoid riding the path for time, as this is a route to slow down and enjoy. The path's route is generally diagonal from the southeast to the northwest. The trail opens with a stretch between the Imperial Highway on the left, and some residences on your right. The path then borders a golf course—stay to the left at the junction. The path abruptly ends at Arroyo Cajon Drive; turn left here and head downhill to Kellogg Drive. Turn right onto Kellogg, climbing gradually (2.2% grade). Next, turn left onto Mountain View Avenue (mile 16.4) and continue climbing (3.3% grade). The El Cajon Trail is officially the walkway on your left, although you are just as well off to ride in the road. Turn left onto Grandview Avenue, now 16.6 miles into the ride. Look for the continuation of El Cajon on your right, just before Buena Vista Avenue. The trail curls around the Buena Vista Equestrian Center, which is on your left. The trail crosses Sunset Lane and Los Altos Lane before coming to a fork. Stay to the left here, and continue to another apparent endpoint, at Lakeview Avenue.

Bike Shops

Jax Bicycle Center, 2520 East Chapman Ave., Fullerton, (714) 441-1100, http://jaxbicycles.com; Road Warrior Bicycles, 337 South State College Blvd., Fullerton, (714) 270-6458, www.roadwarriorbicycles.com

Turn left onto Lakeview Avenue's walkway, and cross over the bridge (the Imperial Highway is below you). Next, look for the El Cajon Trail on your left. The path reverses course, and then turns left to pass under Lakeview Avenue (the only grade-separated crossing along the trail). Continue to the next crossing, which is Yorba Linda Boulevard. To your left, after crossing, is the Richard M. Nixon Presidential Library and Museum (mile 17.9). It is definitely worth a visit. After crossing Eureka Avenue, stay to the left at the next junction. There is a fork in the trail as it approaches Casa Loma Avenue; either way is fine. The left fork crosses Casa Loma, and then heads around the Yorba Linda Community Center. The right fork crosses Casa Loma, then rides along the Yorba Linda Boulevard walkway, bypassing the community center; turn sharply to the left, just beyond the center, to rejoin the trail. From here, the trail crosses El Cajon Avenue, and then Prospect Avenue to close the loop that you started at mile 4.7. You are now 19.6 miles into the ride. The remainder of the ride reverses the opening portion of the route.

Continue on El Cajon Trail to its terminus at Bastanchury Road. Turn left and ride along Bastanchury's walkway. Look for an opening in traffic, and cross Bastanchury when it is clear. Turn right onto Spahn Lane; follow the road as it curves to the left, becoming Mathewson Avenue, and then to the right, becoming Traynor Avenue. At the end of Traynor, turn left onto Williams Avenue, followed by a right onto McCormack Lane, and then a left onto Golden

Richard Nixon's Yorba Linda Legacy

Richard M. Nixon was elected to the presidency twice, first defeating Democrat Hubert Humphrey in 1968 and then winning a landslide victory over George McGovern in 1972. But he may be best known as the only US president to resign from office, which he did in 1974 in the midst of the Watergate scandal. Before becoming president, Mr. Nixon served in the US Congress as a representative and senator from California, and as Dwight Eisenhower's vice president during the 1950s. He had his share of defeats, including the 1960 presidential election to John F. Kennedy, and the California gubernatorial race to Pat Brown in 1962. Mr. Nixon was born in Yorba Linda in 1913, the second of four siblings. His family was considered to be poor, and their ranch failed in 1922. They moved to Whittier, where he attended school. Mr. Nixon would later move away to attend law school (Duke University) and enter the political realm (Washington, DC). Although he spent only the first nine years of his life in Yorba Linda, his family's hardships probably set the tone for a lifetime of ambition. Mr. Nixon passed away in New York in 1994; the funeral took place in Yorba Linda and was attended by five US presidents and first ladies.

The Richard M. Nixon Presidential Library and Museum opened in July 1990, with Nixon in attendance. Originally opened as a private institution, the facility later opened to the public.

Avenue. Golden Avenue continues westward to Tri-City Park. This time, once in the park, turn right to continue the counterclockwise loop that you started on the outbound trip. Again, watch your speed on the occasionally busy lakeside path. Exit Tri-City Park on the other side, and continue onto Rolling Hills Road. After passing under the CA 57 freeway and arriving at Associated Road, cross the road, turn right, and look for the path leading down into Craig Regional Park. Turn right at the bottom, and continue the counterclockwise loop that you started on the outbound trip. This park, like Tri-City Park, features a lake—you may have missed seeing it when heading outbound. Look for the Craig Regional Park Trail toward the end of your loop; turn right, and climb the hill to Rolling Hills Drive. Continue heading west, across State College Boulevard, returning to the neighborhood in which you started. Look for Maple Avenue; turn left, and ride to the end of Maple, adjacent Rolling Hills Park, to conclude the ride.

MILES AND DIRECTIONS

0.0 Start from Rolling Hills Park at the end of Maple Avenue in Fullerton; head north on Maple.

0.2 Stop sign at Rolling Hills Drive; turn right.

0.7 Traffic signal at State College Boulevard; keep straight.

0.75 End of Rolling Hills Drive; continue onto Craig Regional Park Trail (paved path).

0.95 End of path; turn right onto park road (in Craig Regional Park).

1.15 Turn left to continue loop on park roads (low elevation of ride: 273 feet).

1.4 Veer right, off of road, onto path—climb hill to Associated Road, then turn right onto walkway adjacent Associated Road.

1.5 Cross Associated Road at traffic signal; continue eastward on Rolling Hills Road.

1.65 Pass under CA 57 freeway.

2.4 Enter Tri-City Park and city of Placentia; ride through lot, and bear right onto lakeside path.

2.6 Bear right, off of path, onto park road, then stay to the right at junction and head toward park exit.

2.7 Traffic signal at Kraemer Boulevard; keep straight—now on Golden Avenue.

3.6 Turn right onto McCormack Lane.

Yorba on Your Bike

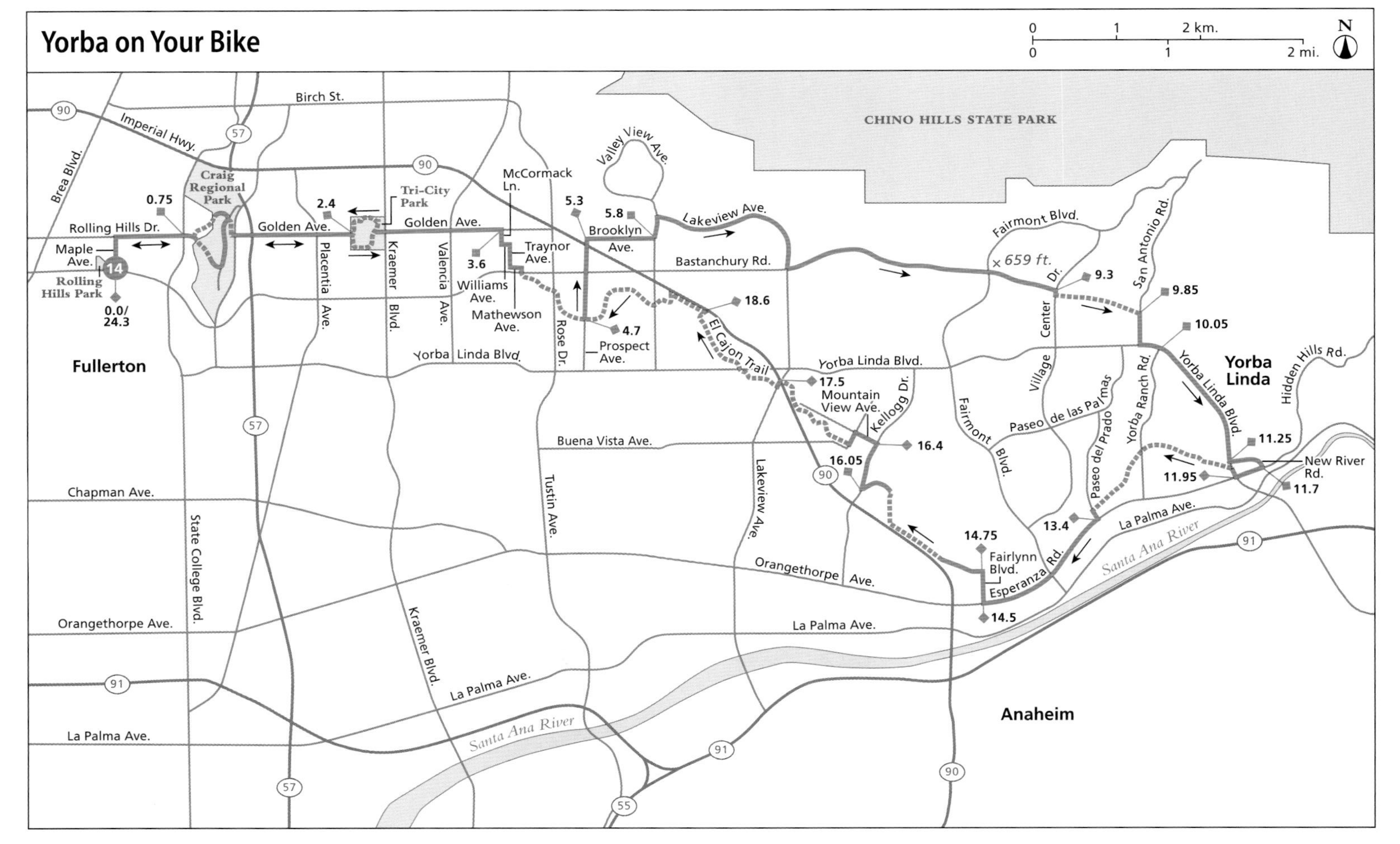

3.7 Turn left onto Williams Avenue.

3.75 Turn right onto Traynor Avenue.

3.9 Road curves to the left—now on Mathewson Avenue.

4.0 Road curves to the right—now on Spahn Lane.

4.05 Stop sign at Bastanchury Road; turn left—ride along walkway after crossing street. Enter city of Yorba Linda.

4.1 Bear right onto El Cajon Trail (paved bike path).

4.3 Cross Rose Drive—continue on trail.

4.7 Turn left onto Prospect Avenue—begin clockwise loop around Yorba Linda.

5.3 Turn right onto Brooklyn Avenue.

5.8 Stop sign at Valley View Avenue: turn left.

5.95 Traffic signal at Lakeview Avenue; turn right—begin climb (2.9% grade).

7.25 Traffic signal at Bastanchury Road; turn left.

8.8 High elevation of ride (657 feet) at Fairmont Boulevard.

9.3 Traffic signal at Village Center Drive; cross Village Center, and then turn right onto walkway—follow walkway as it curves to the left, onto a bike path.

9.7 Cross Avenida de los Arboles—keep straight.

9.95 Cross Via Gorzo—keep straight; begin steep descent (18.7% grade).

10.05 End of path at San Antonio Road; turn right.

10.25 Traffic signal at Yorba Linda Boulevard; turn left—begin descent.

11.45 Traffic signal at New River Road; turn left (watch for motor vehicles when moving left).

11.7 Traffic signal at Esperanza Road; turn right.

11.9 Pass under Yorba Linda Boulevard, then turn right onto Avenida Barcelona.

12.05 Turn left onto bike path.

12.2 Cross Avenida Antigua—keep straight, followed by crossings of Via del Bisonte, Via del Conejo, Dominguez Ranch Road, and Yorba Ranch Road.

12.9 Stay to the left at junction; begin rough pavement segment.

13.35 End of path at Paseo del Prado; turn left.

13.4 Stop sign at Esperanza Road; turn right.

13.95 Pass under Fairmont Boulevard.

14.5 Traffic signal at Fairlynn Boulevard; turn right.

14.75 Turn left onto El Cajon Trail (bike path).

15.2 Keep straight at junction within golf course.

15.8 End of path at Arroyo Cajon Drive; turn left.

16.05 Stop sign at Kellogg Drive; turn right.

16.4 Traffic signal at Mountain View Avenue; turn left—3.3% gradient climb.

16.6 Stop sign at Grandview Avenue; turn left.

16.7 Turn right onto El Cajon Trail.

17.05 Cross Sunset Lane—keep straight.

17.2 Cross Los Altos Lane—keep straight.

17.35 Fork in path; stay left.

17.5 End of path at Lakeview Avenue; turn left onto walkway and cross bridge, then turn left off of walkway, onto El Cajon Trail—reverse direction, and then pass under Lakeview Avenue.

17.85 Traffic signal at Yorba Linda Boulevard—continue across, on trail. Richard M. Nixon Presidential Library and Museum will be on your left.

18.1 Cross Eureka Avenue.

18.6 Cross Casa Loma Avenue—stay to the left at the fork, just before crossing, to ride around Yorba Linda Community Center; stay to the right at the fork, just before crossing, to ride along walkway adjacent Yorba Linda Boulevard.

18.75 Paths rejoin beyond community center (turn left, and then right if Yorba Linda route was taken).

18.9 Cross Valley View Avenue—keep straight.

19.4 Cross El Cajon Avenue—keep straight.

19.6 Cross Prospect Avenue—keep straight. End of clockwise loop.

19.95 Cross Rose Drive—keep straight.

20.15 End of path at Bastanchury Road; turn left onto walkway—cross Bastanchury when clear.

20.25 Enter city of Placentia; turn right onto Spahn Lane.

20.3 Spahn Lane curves to the left—now on Mathewson Avenue.

20.35 Mathewson Avenue curves to the right—now on Traynor Avenue.

20.55 Stop sign at Williams Avenue; turn left.

20.6 Stop sign at McCormack Lane; turn right.

20.7 Stop sign at Golden Avenue; turn left.

21.6 Traffic signal at Kraemer Boulevard; keep straight—enter Tri-City Park, and bear right onto park road, continuing onto lakeside path.

21.95 Leave path and enter parking lot, then exit Tri-City Park; enter city of Fullerton—now on Rolling Hills Road.

22.7 Pass under CA 57 freeway.

22.85 Traffic signal at Associated Road; cross street, and then turn right onto walkway.

22.9 Bear left onto path; ride down into Craig Regional Park.

23.0 End of path at park road; turn right, and then make a series of left turns to continue counterclockwise loop around park.

23.35 End of park loop; turn right onto Craig Regional Park Trail—climb 5.4% grade out of park.

23.55 End of path—continue onto Rolling Hills Drive.

24.1 Turn left onto Maple Avenue.

24.3 End of ride at end of Maple Avenue, adjacent Rolling Hills Park.

Best Southern Orange County Rides

Southern Orange County is located to the south of Costa Mesa, Santa Ana, and Tustin. The subregion includes the cities of Aliso Viejo, Dana Point, the four Lagunas (Beach, Hills, Niguel, and Woods), Lake Forest, Mission Viejo, Newport Beach, Irvine, Rancho Santa Margarita, San Clemente, and San Juan Capistrano, along with the unincorporated communities of Coto de Caza, Emerald Bay, Ladera Ranch, Las Flores, and Rancho Mission Viejo. As of 2015 the largest city in southern Orange was Irvine, at 250,384, followed by Mission Viejo at 96,652, and the region's total population was about 950,000, reflecting one-third of the county (and one-fourth the area).

In 2015 the population density of southern Orange County, at 4,000 per square mile, was substantially lower than that of northern Orange, which was at 7,000. Nineteen of the book's rides are in southern Orange County, as opposed to fourteen in northern Orange, reflecting greater opportunities for road and off-road (trail) riding. Southern Orange County's biggest attractions are its coastline (beaches, ocean), planned communities, Mission San Juan Capistrano, Irvine Spectrum, Dana Point Harbor, Balboa Island, regional and state parks, park trails, and paths and trails linking communities and parks. Many of these are visited by the rides in this section. The diversity in southern Orange County is not nearly as great as that in northern Orange, perhaps because of or contributing to the population's generally conservative political bent. But there is an intriguing mix of cultures that ranges from the "content" (wealthy, exclusive, posh) to Bohemian (surfing, art, beachcombing). You are bound to get a dose of both ends of the range when you are out and about on your bicycle.

Aliso Creek Sneak

Start: Trailhead off of El Toro Road near Marguerite Parkway, in Lake Forest

Length: 24.5 miles (out-and-back)

Riding time: 1.25 to 3.5 hours (my time: 1H30:16)

Terrain and surface: 99% paved bicycle path and limited-access roadway, 1% one-way public road

Elevations: Low—94 feet at Aliso Canyon Trail (turnaround point); high—790 feet at the start-finish point, near El Toro Road and Marguerite Parkway

Traffic and hazards: The entire ride is on paths and roads which carry only the occasional maintenance vehicle. There is one short segment on a one-way public road that facilitates access to Aliso and Wood Canyons Regional Park—watch for motor vehicles that are looking to park. There is one at-grade, double-street crossing where the path continues on the diagonally opposite street corner. Here, use the pedestrian buttons and wait for the green signals before crossing.

Map: *The Thomas Guide by Rand McNally—Street Guide: Los Angeles and Orange Counties* (any recent year), page 862

Getting there by car: From central Anaheim, head south on I-5. Exit at El Toro Road; turn left, and then left again to head northeast on El Toro. The trailhead is near the intersection with Marguerite Parkway, on the left. Use caution when entering and exiting, and when driving near the bike path.

Getting there by public transit: Ride OCTA bus route 89 from Laguna Beach or Laguna Hills to El Toro Road and Santa Margarita Parkway in Lake Forest. Exit here, and head north on El Toro Road to the trailhead, which is near Marguerite Parkway. The bus was running every 35 minutes on weekdays and every 70 minutes on weekends and holidays.

Starting point coordinates: 33.661000°N / 117.642972°W

THE RIDE

The Aliso Creek Sneak is a "sneaky" tour of the communities along Aliso Creek, in that use of the Aliso Creek Bikeway allows one to "sneak" through several cities without ever seeing much motor vehicle traffic (or, at times, not really knowing where one is relative to the outside world). The ride is 24.5 miles in length, out-and-back on a single bikeway, with an extension into Aliso and Wood Canyons Regional Park along a limited-access park road. Any portion of the ride would be suitable for children. The ride is effectively all downhill to the turnaround, and then all uphill to the finish. The path passes through the cities of Lake Forest, Laguna Hills, Aliso Viejo, and Laguna Niguel before entering Aliso and Wood Canyons Regional Park.

Start the ride at the trailhead near El Toro Road and Marguerite Parkway. The Aliso Creek Bikeway actually continues to the north of here, eventually intersecting with El Toro Road. Riders who are game can either start or finish by heading out-and-back on the northerly portion of the bikeway, adding about 3 miles total. Otherwise, head southward on the bikeway. The staging point is the highest elevation of the ride (790 feet). As they say, it's all downhill from here! The path parallels El Toro Road for the first 2 miles, passing under Portola Parkway at mile 0.6, and then Normandie Drive at mile 1.15. Despite the lure of the bikeway, you may see a number of riders using the road, particularly small groups and pelotons. The bikeway passes under El Toro at mile 2, and then continues heading southward. There is a rare, at-grade crossing at Creekside, at mile 2.5. This is a pleasant, tree-lined stretch along which the bikeway is between residences on one side and Aliso Creek on the other. Pass under Trabuco Road at mile 3.1, and then Jeronimo Road at mile 3.45. Curve to the left as the bikeway navigates Heroes Park. Beyond the park, the bikeway parallels Los Alisos Road before passing under Muirlands Boulevard (mile 4.75) and entering El Toro Park (see photo). Follow the signs, some of which are easy to miss, to ensure that you are still on the bikeway. If you find yourself descending to a channel, riding immediately adjacent Aliso Creek, then you are probably on the right path.

Bike Shops

Twohubs Cycling Boutique, 27231 Burbank #201, Foothill Ranch (Lake Forest), (877) 480-2453, www.twohubs.com; The Bike Company, 21098 Bake Pkwy. #112, Lake Forest, (949) 470-1099, www.bikeco.com

You should eventually be riding along the opposite bank of Aliso Creek, passing under Los Alisos Boulevard. Pass under I-5 at mile 5.6—leave Lake Forest, and enter the city of Laguna Hills. Two of the city's most famous natives are singer Aloe Blacc and 2000 Olympic medalist swimmer Chad Carvin. The

A rider pedals from sun to shade in El Toro Park in Lake Forest, along the Aliso Creek Bikeway.

bikeway climbs gradually after passing under I-5, curving to the left to parallel Paseo del Valencia. After a couple more street crossings, the bikeway comes to the intersection between Paseo del Valencia, Stockport Street, and Laguna Hills Drive (mile 6.8). The continuation of the bikeway is diagonally opposite the corner, so the safest approach is to cross each street in succession, waiting for the traffic signal each time. Crossing diagonally is not recommended.

After crossing, the bikeway parallels Laguna Hills Drive, and is now downhill. The path then veers to the left to enter Sheep Hills Park. Stay on the perimeter of the park, veering to the right on its opposite side to leave the park, and pass under Moulton Parkway. Enter the city of Aliso Viejo. Along the path, there is a nature trail on the right, in case you want to ditch your bicycle for a few minutes to do some hiking. The city was Orange County's newest as of this writing, having incorporated in 2001. The city gained notoriety in 2004 when officials proposed a ban on polystyrene cups for their containment of dihydrogen monoxide. Although it may have sounded toxic, the chemical was just a fancy, scientific name for water. Perhaps a drink of water would be in order as you ride through the city! The bikeway crosses a wooden bridge at mile 8.05; bear left after crossing to continue.

Pass under the CA 73 freeway at mile 8.65, and then Pacific Park Drive at mile 9.15, shortly after curving to the right, and then to the left. You may pick up some good speed after the underpass; be sure to stay to the right of the center line around the next turn. The bikeway passes by a few athletic fields and a skate park, with Aliso Creek (usually dry) on your left. Pass under Aliso Creek Road at mile 10.45. The bikeway finally ends at Awma Road, at mile 10.7. Enter the city of Laguna Niguel.

But don't turn around here! Turn right onto Awma Road. Watch for motor vehicles, many of which are looking for a parking space to access Aliso and Wood Canyons Regional Park, as you ride along this road. The ride on Awma is short; turn left at its end, onto Aliso Canyon Road. This is a lightly used park road. The road heads toward Aliso Canyon, which is on the horizon. The road ends at a gate, at mile 11.5; go around the gate by riding on the dirt trail for 20 or 30 feet. Return to the road on the other side of the gate. Continue heading into the canyon. You are now in Aliso and Wood Canyons Regional Park (please see Ride 29, Soft and Hard Tails of Aliso-Wood). Wood Canyon Trail is on the right at mile 12.25.

The road continues beyond here, but there is a gate just past the trail junction. Access beyond the gate is restricted (despite an open-gate policy). This is the ride's low elevation (94 feet). The Pacific Ocean is downstream of

Aliso Canyon—What's Down the Road?

Not to be confused with Aliso Canyon in the Santa Susana Mountains, north of Los Angeles, which was associated with a massive natural gas leak in 2015 (forcing the relocation of over 11,000 residents), this ride's Aliso Canyon is comparatively tame and safe. "Our" Aliso Canyon is located in the San Joaquin Hills, and was carved out by Aliso Creek. Access is restricted to the southernmost 3 kilometers (1.85 miles) of Aliso Canyon Road because, in 2014, the Aliso Creek Water Reclamation Facility was opened (at the end of the road). "Water Reclamation Facility" is just a fancy name for a wastewater treatment plant. Unbeknownst to most canyon users, a sewage line runs the length of Aliso Canyon. Aliso Creek absorbs plenty of urban runoff, which has only increased over the years with development in southern Orange County. The runoff has caused erosion and damage to riparian zones within the canyon. Aliso Creek flows to the ocean, passing through Aliso Beach, about 1.5 miles downstream. Thus, it is crucial to treat the water before it flows into increasingly sensitive areas. The plant cost $2.8 million to build, and produces over 700,000 gallons of recycled water per year.

here a few miles, although the surrounding mountains block your view. The return ride is fun and scenic, although mostly uphill. The average gradient on the return trip is 1.1%—just steep enough to give you a workout!

MILES AND DIRECTIONS

0.0 Start the ride at the trailhead along Aliso Creek Bikeway off of El Toro Road in Lake Forest, just south of the El Toro Road and Marguerite Parkway intersection. Head south on the bikeway.

0.6 Pass under Portola Parkway.

1.15 Pass under Normandie Drive.

2.00 Pass under El Toro Road.

2.50 Cross Creekside (road—at grade).

3.1 Pass under Trabuco Road.

3.95 Pass under Jeronimo Road.

4.2 Curve left, now in Heroes Park.

4.4 Curve right; bikeway is now adjacent Los Alisos Boulevard.

4.75 Pass under Muirlands Boulevard.

5.05 Pass under Los Alisos Boulevard.

5.6 Pass under I-5 freeway; enter city of Laguna Woods.

6.25 Bikeway curves left; now adjacent Paseo del Valencia.

6.4 Cross Kennington Street (at grade).

6.5 Cross Avenida Sevilla—Beckenham Street (at grade).

6.8 Traffic signal at Stockport Street—Laguna Hills Drive; wait for signal to cross Paseo del Valencia, and then wait for signal to cross Laguna Hills Drive.

7.35 Cross Indian Hills Lane (at grade), then veer left to enter Sheep Hills Park.

7.6 Stay right to leave Sheep Hills Park; pass under Moulton Parkway, enter city of Aliso Viejo.

8.05 Cross over wooden bridge, and then bear left.

8.65 Pass under CA 73 freeway.

9.15 Pass under Pacific Park Drive.

10.45 Pass under Aliso Creek Road.

10.7 End of path at Awma Road; turn right.

10.85 End of Awma Road; turn left onto Aliso Canyon Road.

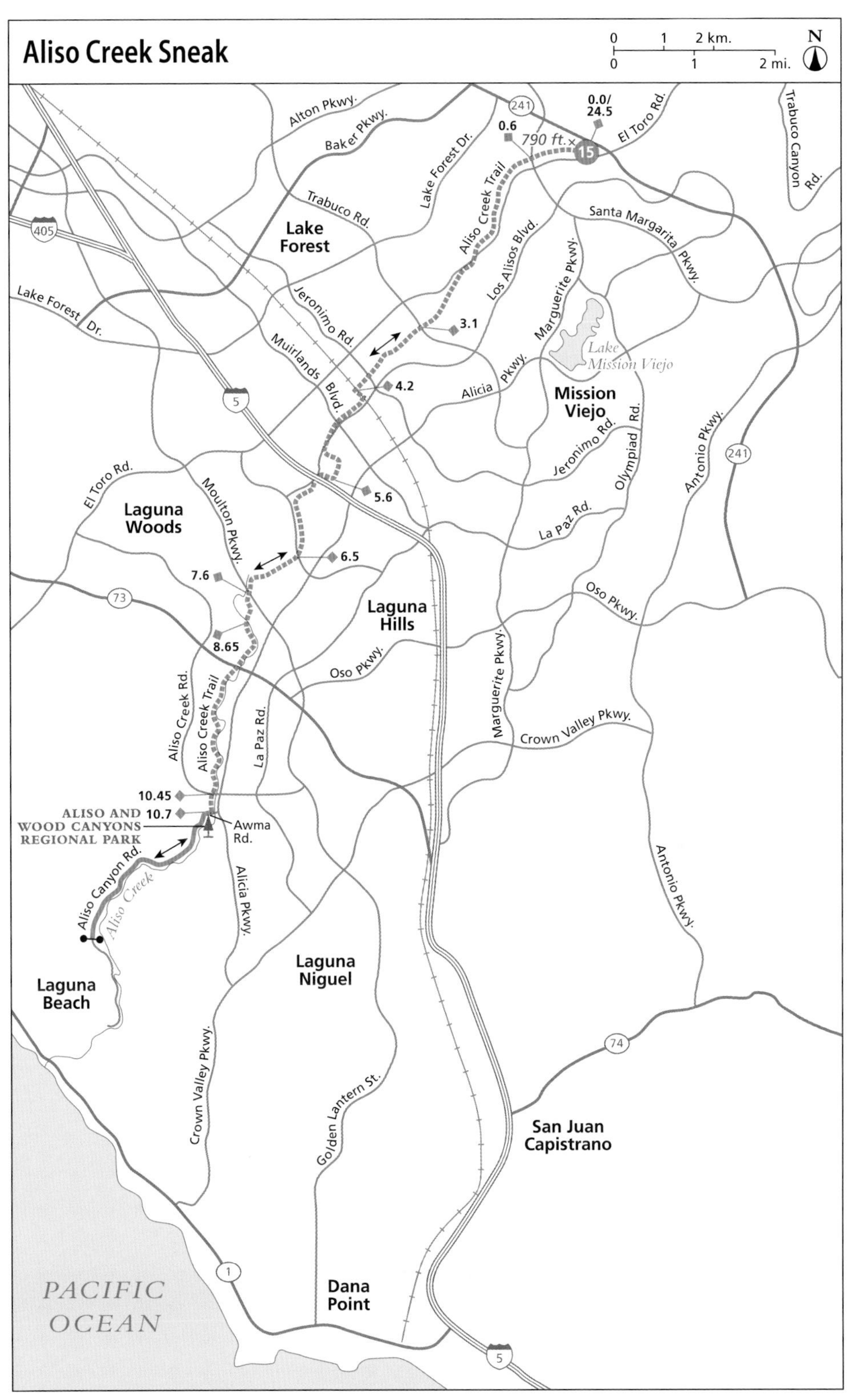

Aliso Creek Sneak
0 1 2 km.
0 1 2 mi.
N
Alton Pkwy.
Baker Pkwy.
Lake Forest Dr.
Trabuco Rd.
Lake Forest
El Toro Rd.
Trabuco Canyon Rd.
0.0/ 24.5
0.6
790 ft.
15
Aliso Creek Trail
Santa Margarita Pkwy.
Los Alisos Blvd.
Marguerite Pkwy.
Lake Mission Viejo
Mission Viejo
Lake Forest Dr.
Jeronimo Rd.
Muirlands Blvd.
3.1
4.2
Alicia Pkwy.
Jeronimo Rd.
Olympiad Rd.
Antonio Pkwy.
El Toro Rd.
Laguna Woods
Moulton Pkwy.
5.6
6.5
7.6
La Paz Rd.
Laguna Hills
Oso Pkwy.
8.65
Oso Pkwy.
Aliso Creek Rd.
Aliso Creek Trail
La Paz Rd.
Marguerite Pkwy.
Crown Valley Pkwy.
10.45
10.7
ALISO AND WOOD CANYONS REGIONAL PARK
Awma Rd.
Aliso Canyon Rd.
Aliso Creek
Alicia Pkwy.
Antonio Pkwy.
Laguna Beach
Laguna Niguel
Crown Valley Pkwy.
Golden Lantern St.
San Juan Capistrano
PACIFIC OCEAN
Dana Point

11.5 Gate; go around via dirt trail, and then return to road; enter Aliso and Wood Canyons Regional Park.

12.25 Aliso Canyon Trail on the right; turn around here.

13.0 Gate; go around via dirt trail, and then continue via Aliso Canyon Road.

13.65 Turn right onto Awma Road—watch for motor vehicle traffic.

13.8 Turn left onto Aliso Creek Bikeway; enter city of Aliso Viejo.

14.05 Pass under Aliso Creek Road.

15.4 Pass under Pacific Park Drive.

15.85 Pass under CA 73 freeway.

16.5 Cross wooden bridge, and then turn left.

16.9 Pass under Moulton Parkway; enter Sheep Hills Park and city of Laguna Hills.

17.1 Leave Sheep Hills Park; bikeway is now parallel to Laguna Hills Drive (2.6% gradient climb).

17.2 Cross Indian Hills Road (at grade).

17.7 Traffic signal at Paseo del Valencia; cross Paseo del Valencia, and then cross Stockport Street to continue on bikeway.

18.0 Cross Avenida Sevilla—Beckenham Street (at grade).

18.1 Cross Kennington Street (at grade).

18.9 Pass under I-5 freeway; enter city of Lake Forest.

19.5 Pass under Los Alisos Boulevard.

19.8 Pass under Muirlands Boulevard.

20.55 Pass under Jeronimo Road.

21.4 Pass under Trabuco Road.

22.0 Cross Creekside (street—at grade).

22.5 Pass under El Toro Road.

23.35 Pass under Normandie Drive.

23.9 Pass under Portola Parkway.

24.5 End of ride at trailhead adjacent El Toro Road, just south of Marguerite Parkway (continuing northward on the bikeway to its end is optional).

Circle Newport Bay

16

Start: Upper Newport Bay Nature Preserve and Ecological Reserve, 2301 University Dr., Newport Beach

Length: 9.9 miles (clockwise loop)

Riding time: 30 minutes to 2 hours (my time: 35:15)

Terrain and surface: 66% paved paths, 26% paved roads, and 8% walkways

Elevations: Low—5 feet along Back Bay Drive; high—104 feet along Santiago Drive

Traffic and hazards: CA 1 carried 48,600 vehicles per day south of Dover Drive in 2014; Dover Drive carried 29,000 vehicles per day near CA 1 in 2002. Traffic volumes were light along Back Bay Drive and Santiago Drive.

Map: *The Thomas Guide by Rand McNally—Street Guide: Los Angeles and Orange Counties* (any recent year), page 889

Getting there by car: From central Anaheim, head south on I-5. Exit to the CA 55 freeway southbound, and then junction to the CA 73 freeway and head southeast. Exit at Campus Drive and turn right. Campus becomes Irvine Avenue. After about 1 mile, turn left onto University Street. Look for the entrance to Upper Newport Bay Nature Preserve and Ecological Reserve on the right. Park in the dirt lot.

Getting there by public transit: OCTA bus route 178 operates between Huntington Beach and Irvine, via Newport Beach, every 45 minutes on weekdays. Exit the bus at University Street and Irvine Avenue, immediately adjacent Upper Newport Bay Nature Preserve.

Starting point coordinates: 33.654767°N / 118.885892°W

THE RIDE

Circle Newport Bay is a compact 9.9-mile road ride, suitable for families, that traces the perimeter of Upper Newport Bay, with a slight deviation at the bay's southern end. Any portion of the ride would be suitable for children. About two-thirds of the ride is on paved bike paths; of this, about 60% is along a road that is one-way for motor vehicles, and two-way for bicycles. The rest of the ride is on roads shared with motor vehicles, and on walkways shared with pedestrians. Only a short 0.33-mile segment along the Pacific Coast Highway is truly busy with motor vehicles. Elevations vary from just 5 feet above sea level, adjacent Upper Newport Bay, to 104 feet through the Westcliff community of Newport Beach. The entire route around Upper Newport Bay is also referred to as the Back Bay Loop Trail, although this book's version is slightly different from the "official" loop.

The entire ride is within the corporate limits of Newport Beach. Newport Beach is the fifth-oldest city in Orange County, having been incorporated since 1906. Incorporation was triggered by the completion of a Pacific Electric Railway line that connected Newport Beach with downtown Los Angeles. The city has thrived during its century-plus life, with the eighth-highest median home price in the country as of 2009. The city's attractions include Balboa Island, and the ferry used to reach it, Corona del Mar State Beach, The Wedge (popular surfing zone), the Orange County Museum of Art, Crystal Cove State Park (see Ride 17, Crystal Cove Mas Moro), the annual Newport to Ensenada International Yacht Race (largest in the world), and Newport Harbor (largest recreational boat harbor on the US Pacific coast).

Start the ride in the Upper Newport Bay Nature Preserve, located on University Drive, just east of Irvine Avenue. Leave the dirt parking lot, and turn right onto the paved bike path (Bayview Trail). The path heads downhill, crossing the Santa Ana Channel. After a quarter-mile, there is a wooden boardwalk on the left, probably there to facilitate drainage from the adjacent hillside. The boardwalk ends at mile 0.4. Stay to the right at mile 0.9, at the merge with a

Bike Shops

Fresh Bikes, 1995 Port Nelson Place, Newport Beach, (949) 533-4366, http://freshbikes.com (bicycle repair shop); Newport Cruisers, 2233 West Balboa Blvd. #105, Newport Beach, (949) 675-5010, www.newportcruisers.com; Pro Bike Supply, 353 Old Newport Blvd., Newport Beach, (855) 777-2454, www.probikesupply.com (parts and supplies); Two Wheels One Planet Bicycle Stores, 420 East 17th St., Costa Mesa, (949) 646-7717, http://twowheelsoneplanet.com

Riders pedal along Back Bay Drive through the Upper Newport Bay Ecological Reserve.

path from Mesa Drive. Turn right at the Jamboree Road intersection, where the path continues as a walkway along this busy arterial. Cross over San Diego Creek at mile 1.4, and then stay to the left at the merge with the San Diego Creek Bikeway. Stay on the walkway at the next intersection. Turn right here; you are now on the Eastbluff Side Path, parallel to Eastbluff Drive. There is a short but stiff climb (5.0% grade) to the next intersection. Turn right here, and ride into the street, onto Back Bay Drive. After a brisk descent (7.1% grade), Back Bay Drive levels. For the next 2.9 miles, Back Bay Drive is one-way for motor vehicles, such that cyclists have full use of half of the road. Watch out for runners, walkers, and slower cyclists, though.

Back Bay Drive dips as low as 5 feet above sea level, as you ride adjacent the Upper Newport Bay wetlands. Take a moment or two to watch the migratory bird action. Riders with an ornithological bent might be able to identify a few bird species. Also, enjoy the sweeping turns, roadside bluffs, and fabulous vistas. Leave Back Bay at mile 4.8, and enter the Newport Dunes Resort area. The resort features cottages, RV parking, and a marina. Turn right onto the Newport Dunes Resort entrance road—but turn right onto the opposite side of the entrance road, and access the walkway through the curb cut.

Ride parallel to the entrance road. The walkway veers away from the gated entrance area, becoming a continuation of the Bayview Trail! The path passes the (fenced-in) resort. The path ends at Bayside Drive; turn left and enter the road. At the traffic signal with the Pacific Coast Highway (CA 1, or PCH), turn right to ride along the busiest segment of the ride.

CA 1 lifts up and over the Upper Newport Bay inlet. Once across the bridge, turn right onto Dover Drive. At the next driveway, on your right, leave the street and ride along the walkway, for a little less than 400 feet. Bear right at the uphill path, and climb up into Castaways Park. The gradient is 7.6%. Bear left at the next junction, and continue riding on the paved path. Stay right at the next junction. The path then curves sharply to the left to head northward. You are now riding on the perimeter of the Westcliff neighborhood—also referred to as West Santa Ana Heights—with steep bluffs, leading down to Upper Newport Bay, to your right. Newport Beach and neighboring

Newport Beach

Although Newport Beach is one of Orange County's oldest cities (incorporated in 1906), the city has kept pace with the times. Not included among the city's attractions listed above is Fashion Island at Newport Center, a shopping and entertainment center. In 1930, the classic film *All Quiet on the Western Front* was shot on the site of Fashion Island, while in 1953 the National Scout Jamboree was held on the same site, long before its transformative development. Newport Beach has been a hotbed of fictional and reality shows: *The O.C.*, *Arrested Development*, MTV's *Newport Harbor: The Real Orange County*, and *The Real Housewives of Orange County* are all either based in or on Newport Beach. INXS's 1988 video for "The Devil Inside" was filmed at the Balboa Fun Zone, and the facade of the reunion venue from 1997's *Romy & Michelle's High School Reunion* was that of the Newport Beach Central Library. Beneath the high-profile, urban exterior, Newport Beach serves a critical environmental role. Upper Newport Bay, which is connected to the Pacific Ocean, and is also referred to as the Back Bay, is on the Pacific Flyway, and is an important stopover point for a large number of migratory birds. Some 35,000 birds have been counted here in one day(!). Several rare, endangered and sensitive species use the Back Bay, including the Belding's savannah sparrow, black rail, brown pelican, burrowing owl, California gnatcatcher, California least tern, and the San Diego cactus wren. The entire reserve-preserve covers 1,000 acres, of which 135 acres is the land-based nature preserve (mostly in the northwestern corner of the space).

Costa Mesa tangled for some time over the annexation of the Westcliff–West Santa Ana Heights community, with Newport Beach finally winning. There is another sharp curve to the left at mile 7.1; at the very next junction, turn right. Follow this path to its end, and then enter the street. Bear slightly to the left to continue riding northbound on Santiago Drive. This pleasant residential street passes by some of the community's fine houses. The ride's highest elevation, at 104 feet, is near the intersection with Antigua Circle. Follow Santiago as it curves to the left, eventually descending to Irvine Avenue. Turn right here, but get on the walkway, which veers to the right just 100 feet from here, resuming the Bayview Trail.

You are now on the northwest side of Upper Newport Bay, reentering the nature preserve. Bayview Trail undulates through here, with a couple of short, tough climbs, and easy descents. Follow Bayview Trail as it makes a sweeping curve to the right. The ride ends at the entrance drive to the Upper Newport Bay parking area.

MILES AND DIRECTIONS

0.0 Exit the Upper Newport Bay Nature Preserve parking lot; turn right onto the Bayview Trail bike path.

0.15 Bridge over Santa Ana Channel.

0.25 Wooden boardwalk on the left, for the next 0.15 miles.

0.9 Stay right at the merge with the Mesa Drive path.

1.25 Turn right at intersection with Jamboree Road; now on walkway (still on Bayview Trail).

1.4 Bridge over San Diego Creek; then stay left at merge with San Diego Creek Bikeway.

1.65 Turn right at intersection with Eastbluff Drive; now on Eastbluff Side Path.

1.95 Turn right onto Back Bay Drive; leave path and enter road (short 7.1% downgrade).

2.4 Lowest elevation of ride (5 feet), along Back Bay Drive.

4.8 Leave Back Bay area; still on Back Bay Drive, but motor vehicles now have full use of the road.

5.15 Turn right onto "wrong side" of Newport Dunes Resort entrance road; access walkway via curb cut—path veers away from road, continuing as Bayview Trail bike path.

5.8 End of path; turn left and enter Bayside Drive.

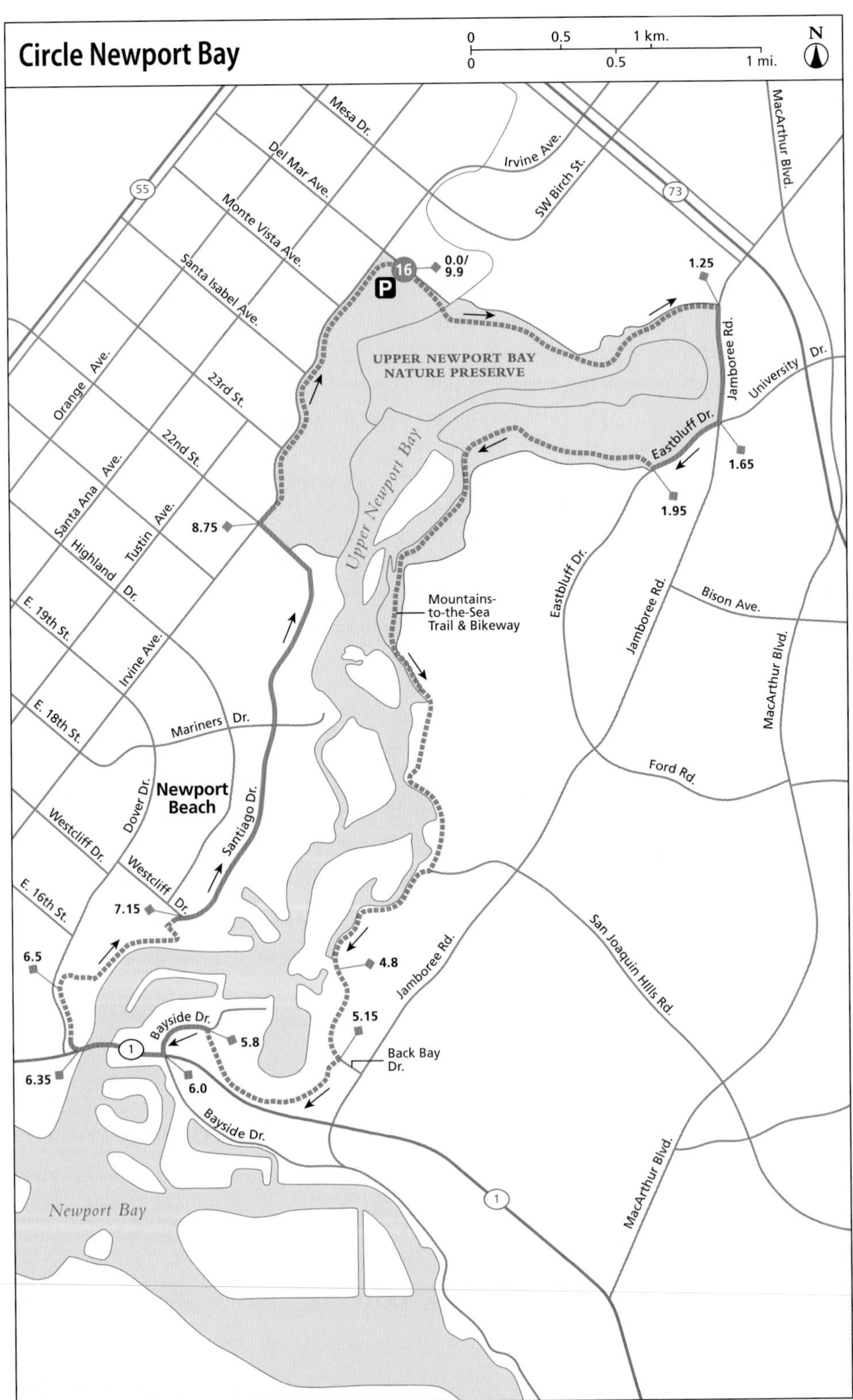

Circle Newport Bay
0
0.5
1 km.
0
0.5
1 mi.
N
Mesa Dr.
Del Mar Ave.
Monte Vista Ave.
Santa Isabel Ave.
Irvine Ave.
SW Birch St.
MacArthur Blvd.
55
73
16
0.0/
9.9
P
1.25
UPPER NEWPORT BAY
NATURE PRESERVE
Orange Ave.
23rd St.
22nd St.
Jamboree Rd.
University Dr.
Eastbluff Dr.
1.65
1.95
Upper Newport Bay
Santa Ana Ave.
Tustin Ave.
8.75
Highland Dr.
Mountains-
to-the-Sea
Trail & Bikeway
Eastbluff Dr.
Jamboree Rd.
Bison Ave.
E. 19th St.
Irvine Ave.
MacArthur Blvd.
E. 18th St.
Mariners Dr.
Newport
Beach
Dover Dr.
Santiago Dr.
Ford Rd.
Westcliff Dr.
Westcliff Dr.
E. 16th St.
7.15
San Joaquin Hills Rd.
6.5
4.8
Jamboree Rd.
5.15
Bayside Dr.
5.8
1
Back Bay
Dr.
6.35
6.0
Bayside Dr.
MacArthur Blvd.
1
Newport Bay

6.0 Traffic signal at Pacific Coast Highway (CA 1); turn right.

6.15 Bridge over inlet to Upper Newport Bay.

6.35 Turn right onto Dover Drive (off-ramp).

6.4 Leave road and ride up onto walkway.

6.5 Leave walkway and turn right onto unnamed bike path; ride up hill (7.6%) into Castaways Park.

6.65 Turn left at junction onto unnamed bike path, then stay right at merge with another path.

6.75 Sharp curve to the left.

7.1 Sharp curve to the left; then turn right onto unnamed connector path; continue into street, bearing slightly left to continue northbound on Santiago Drive.

8.15 Highest elevation of ride (104 feet) near Antigua Circle.

8.75 Turn right onto walkway at intersection with Irvine Avenue, then bear right onto Bayview Trail bike path.

9.9 End of ride at entryway to parking lot for Upper Newport Bay Nature Preserve.

Crystal Cove Mas Moro

Start: Willow Canyon trailhead, Laguna Coast Wilderness Park, 18751 Laguna Canyon Rd., Laguna Beach

Length: 15.6 miles (clockwise loop)

Riding time: 1.5 to 4.5 hours (my time: 2H22:48)

Terrain and surface: 100% of the route is on dirt trails and roads.

Elevations: Low—52 feet on BFI Trail in Crystal Cove State Park; high—952 feet on Bommer Ridge Trail north of Big Bend Trail, in Laguna Coast Wilderness Park

Traffic and hazards: 100% of the route is on dirt trails and roads (no motor vehicles)

Map: *The Thomas Guide by Rand McNally—Street Guide: Los Angeles and Orange Counties* (any recent year), page 920

Getting there by car: From central Anaheim, head south on I-5. Exit at El Toro Road; turn right, and then turn right again to head southwesterly on El Toro. At the end of El Toro, turn left onto Laguna Canyon Road. Look for the Willow Canyon trailhead on the right, shortly after making the turn.

Getting there by public transit: Ride OCTA bus route 89 from central Laguna Beach, or Laguna Hills, to the Willow Canyon trailhead on Laguna Canyon Road. The bus was running every 35 minutes on weekdays and every 70 minutes on weekends and holidays.

Starting point coordinates: 33.580078°N / 117.762278°W

THE RIDE

Crystal Cove Mas Moro is a challenging, 15.6-mile mountain bike ride through Laguna Coast Wilderness Park and Crystal Cove State Park near Laguna Beach. The main challenge is that the route climbs up to and descends from three ridges. So although the net high-low elevation difference is 900 feet, the net elevation difference of the three climbs is 2,147 feet, not including minor

Majestic view of the Pacific Ocean from Moro Ridge Trail in Crystal Cove State Park

undulations along the way. Yet the ride features perhaps the most spectacular view of any in this book—that of the Pacific Ocean as you descend from Moro Ridge in Crystal Cove State Park. I would challenge you to find a more breathtaking view of the Pacific. To enjoy this unique and exciting view, you have to get up there!

Start at the Willow Canyon trailhead located just off of Laguna Canyon Road, just south of El Toro Road. Laguna Coast Wilderness Park features an abundance of grassland and chaparral, with occasional groves of oak, sycamore, and willow trees. The park is a gateway to coastal canyons, of which only a few remain in this region because of extensive development. Begin by heading south on Stagecoach South Trail. Be sure to sign in at the (usually) unmanned tent, and to check out the framed artwork on display. A painting on the trail? Yes—Laguna Beach is well known for its annual Pageant of the Masters and Festival of the Arts. So why not place art along the trail? Stagecoach South undulates, including some singletrack, as it heads southward, parallel to Laguna Canyon Road. If you are not warmed up yet, a short 18.0% grade at mile 0.6 will certainly get your heart pumping! The short climb is followed by a short descent. Another steep (13.3% grade) climb comes at mile 1.0. Despite the short climbs, you have actually lost elevation since the start.

Bear right onto Big Bend Trail at mile 1.1—and this is where the climbing truly begins. The average grade is 21.2% for the next 0.4 mile. You may need to hike part of this—no problem, but be on the lookout for descending riders. Big Bend climbs to 687 feet at mile 1.5, takes a break for 0.3 mile, and then resumes climbing at a 10.8% grade until mile 2.2. The last quarter-mile of Big Bend features a short descent, and then another climb. Big Bend ends at mile 2.45; turn right onto Bommer Ridge Trail. Bommer Ridge continues to climb to the high elevation of the entire ride (952 feet). This wide trail offers some great views to both your left and right. After some gradual climbs and descents, riding along the ridge, turn left onto Emerald Canyon Road (dirt trail; mile 3.3). Emerald Canyon Road descends into Emerald Canyon (7.4% grade)—there are a few technical sections. Although Emerald Canyon Road continues down the length of the canyon, to a dead end, turn right onto Old Emerald Falls Trail at mile 4.35. (As an optional extension, ride to the end of Emerald Canyon Road and return.)

Old Emerald Falls Trail begins with a gradual ascent, occasionally winding and twisting. The gradient becomes noticeably steeper at mile 4.65, increasing to a whopping 18.8%. There are a few switchbacks as the trail makes it way up to Moro Ridge. Enter Crystal Cove State Park somewhere along here (no sign). The gradient eases at mile 4.9, although your legs will still feel the burn of the climb, now at a 6.8% grade. Old Emerald Falls ends at mile 5.35; turn left onto Moro Ridge Trail, now at an elevation of 897 feet. You have now conquered two of this ride's three ridges!

Moro Ridge Trail is a featured segment of the ride. Crystal Cove State Park offers many similarities to Laguna Coast Wilderness Park. One key difference, though, is that Crystal Cove extends from the hills, where you are now, all the way to the ocean. Crystal Cove includes about 3 miles of beach, as well as an underwater preserve. The park, therefore, can entertain scuba divers and mountain bikers at the same time. For the first mile, Moro Ridge descends gradually to 792 feet, and then climbs to a crest of 872 feet, at mile 6.5. From here, the trail descends at a 6.1% grade to East Cut-Across Trail (mile 7.0). Keep straight here. At mile 7.85, the trail begins to descend precipitously (8.9% grade), with a stunning ocean view in the background. You may have to stop for a moment to savor the spectacle. Moro Ridge sweeps its way down to 205 feet of elevation at mile 8.95. Turn right onto BFI Trail. The origins of the BFI moniker are unknown. The "layman's" definition is that BFI is short for "Big Fat Incline," while the "rattled hiker's" definition is unprintable. Whatever the case, the average grade of the trail's descent is 9.3%, made more challenging by a series of moguls thrown in about halfway down.

The end of BFI Trail is the low elevation of the ride (52 feet). Turn right here, onto Moro Canyon Trail. Alternatively, if you need a refresher, there are water and restrooms just to your left, across the bridge. Moro Canyon Trail begins a long, gradual climb up Moro Canyon. The average grade of the climb is 2.2% for the next 1.5 miles. The gradient increases to 11.1% at mile 10.75, coming after making a left turn to remain on Moro Canyon Trail. Rather than easing, the gradient increases to 15.4%, followed by a brisk descent, and then a gentler climb (6.2% grade) to the next junction. Turn left here, onto Slow'n'Easy Trail. The name may seem to be a misnomer, given that the opening climb is at a 9.2% grade! Yet the alternative East Loop Trail is even steeper. Keep it slow'n'easy as the trail climbs to 756 feet, eases for a short stretch, then resumes climbing (5.7% grade). The trail reaches 951 feet at a gate that marks your departure from Crystal Cove State Park. Reenter Laguna Coast Wilderness Park.

Bike Shops

KOM Cycling, 28 Argonaut St., Suite 100, Aliso Viejo, (949) 371-3795, www.kom-cycling.com; G2 Bike, 27101 Aliso Creek Rd. #146, Aliso Viejo, (949) 891-8900, www.g2bike.com

Turn right onto Bommer Ridge Road (dirt) at mile 13.5. Note that this trail passes within a few tenths of a mile of where you were earlier in this ride, near Emerald Canyon Road. Keep straight on Bommer Ridge Trail—watch the signs to ensure that you remain on the correct trail. Once past the Moro Ridge Trail junction (keep straight here), Bommer Ridge begins to descend (6.2% grade). At mile 14.15, bear left onto Willow Canyon Road (dirt). This is the ride's last hurrah as Willow Canyon sweeps to the right, and then makes a long, steady, steep (8.9% grade) descent down the canyon. The grade is steeper along one segment. Watch your speed, as the trail tends to get busy toward the bottom, which is near the Willow Canyon trailhead. Bear left at the bottom of the descent, remaining on Willow Canyon Road. From here, it is another tenth of a mile to the trailhead, and the end of the ride.

MILES AND DIRECTIONS

0.0 Start at the Willow Canyon trailhead on Laguna Canyon Road, just south of El Toro Road, in Laguna Beach. Starting elevation: 223 feet.

0.6 Short climb up 18.0% grade.

1.0 Short climb up 13.3% grade.

1.1 Bear right onto Big Bend Trail—begin climb up 21.2% grade.

1.5 Gradient eases; opportunity to recover.

1.8 Climbing resumes (10.8% grade).

2.2 False crest—gradient eases before climbing resumes (7.4% grade).

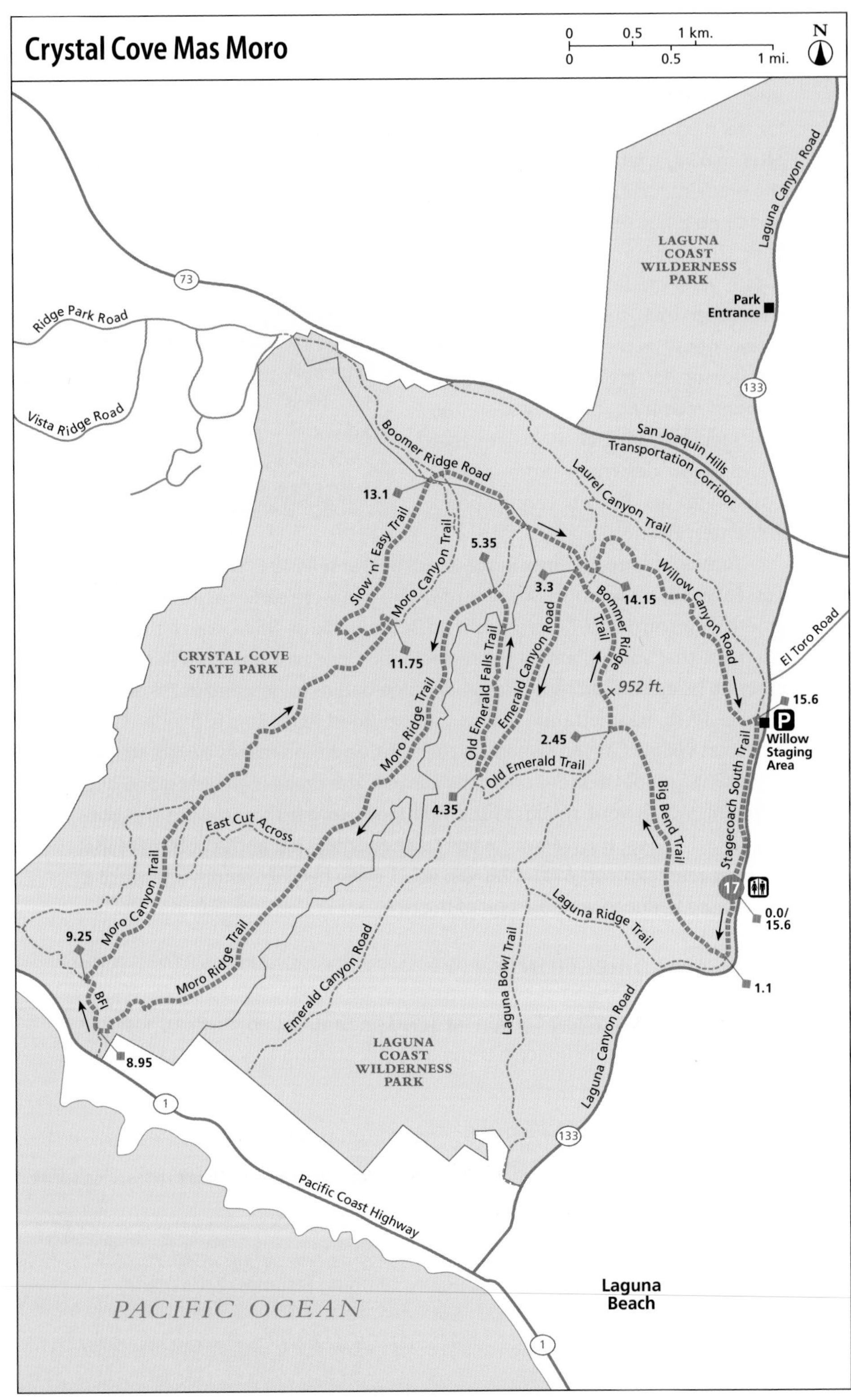
Crystal Cove Mas Moro
0
0.5
1 km.
0
0.5
1 mi.
N
LAGUNA COAST WILDERNESS PARK
Laguna Canyon Road
Park Entrance
73
Ridge Park Road
Vista Ridge Road
133
San Joaquin Hills Transportation Corridor
Boomer Ridge Road
Laurel Canyon Trail
13.1
Slow 'n' Easy Trail
Moro Canyon Trail
5.35
3.3
14.15
Willow Canyon Road
Bommer Ridge Trail
El Toro Road
CRYSTAL COVE STATE PARK
11.75
Moro Ridge Trail
Old Emerald Falls Trail
Emerald Canyon Road
952 ft.
15.6
Willow Staging Area
2.45
Old Emerald Trail
4.35
Big Bend Trail
Stagecoach South Trail
East Cut Across
Moro Canyon Trail
17
Laguna Ridge Trail
0.0/
15.6
9.25
Moro Ridge Trail
Emerald Canyon Road
Laguna Bowl Trail
1.1
BFI
Laguna Canyon Road
8.95
LAGUNA COAST WILDERNESS PARK
1
133
Pacific Coast Highway
PACIFIC OCEAN
Laguna Beach
1

2.45 End of Big Bend Trail—turn right onto Bommer Ridge Trail; continue climbing (4.4% grade).

2.6 High elevation of ride (952 feet)—rolling terrain from here.

3.3 Turn left onto Emerald Canyon Road (dirt)—begin descent (7.4% grade).

4.35 Turn right onto Old Emerald Falls Trail (elevation 443 feet)—begin gradual climb (2.3% grade).

4.65 Gradient of climb increases to 18.8%—enter Crystal Cove State Park (no sign).

4.9 Gradient of climb eases to 6.8%.

5.35 End of Old Emerald Falls Trail; turn left onto Moro Ridge Trail (elevation 897 feet).

6.5 Begin descent (6.1% grade).

7.0 Grade of descent eases at East Cut-Across Trail junction; keep straight.

7.85 Begin steep descent (8.9% grade)—Pacific Ocean in full view.

8.95 Turn right onto BFI Trail; continue steep descent (9.3% grade).

9.25 End of BFI Trail; low elevation of ride (52 feet). Turn right onto Moro Canyon Trail; begin gradual climb (2.2% grade).

10.75 Stay left at junction to continue on Moro Canyon Trail; gradient of climb increases to 11.1%, and then to 15.4%.

11.2 Short descent, followed by a climb (3.9% grade).

11.75 End of Moro Canyon Trail; turn left onto Slow'n'Easy Trail—begin climb at 9.2% grade.

12.25 Grade of climb eases; climb then continues at 5.7% grade.

13.0 Gate; leave Crystal Cove State Park, reenter Laguna Coast Wilderness Park. Elevation: 951 feet.

13.1 End of Slow'n'Easy Trail; turn right onto Bommer Ridge Road (dirt).

13.75 Keep straight at junction with Moro Ridge Trail; begin descent (6.3% grade).

14.15 Bear left onto Willow Canyon Trail; descend 8.9% grade.

15.5 Bottom of descent; bear left to continue on Willow Canyon Trail.

15.6 End of ride at Willow Canyon trailhead.

18

El Cañada Gobernadora

Start: Sendero Field, 28632 Ortega Hwy., San Juan Capistrano (Rancho Mission Viejo)

Length: 34.7 miles (two out-and-back segments—with fully constructed roads)

Riding time: 1.75 to 4.5 hours (my time: 2H06:22 without section under construction)

Terrain and surface: 100% paved roads

Elevations: Low—172 feet at Sendero Field; high—1,200 feet at Avenida de las Flores and Sarra Cenia in Rancho Santa Margarita

Traffic and hazards: As of 2014, Antonio Parkway was carrying up to 36,000 vehicles per day near Oso Parkway, near Ladera Ranch; La Pata Road carried 9,000 vehicles per day south of Avenida Pico in San Clemente. La Pata's volume of 3,000 vehicles per day south of Ortega Highway will increase with the completion of the road into San Clemente. Ortega Highway (CA 74) was carrying 27,000 vehicles per day near Sendero Field.

Map: *The Thomas Guide by Rand McNally—Street Guide: Los Angeles and Orange Counties* (any recent year), page 952

Getting there by car: From central Anaheim, head south on I-5. Exit at Ortega Highway (CA 74) in San Juan Capistrano; turn left and head east. Look for Sendero Field on the left just west of Antonio Parkway, just beyond Reata Drive.

Getting there by public transit: Ride OCTA bus route 191 from San Juan Capistrano Train Depot to Ortega Highway (CA 74) and La Novia in San Juan Capistrano. Exit and head east on CA 74. Sendero Field will be on the left, just west of Antonio Parkway. Route 191 was running every 30 to 60 minutes on weekdays and every 60 minutes on weekends and holidays.

Starting point coordinates: 33.519514°N / 117.623506°W

THE RIDE

El Cañada Gobernadora may be a strange ride title, meaning "Canyon of the Governor's Wife." It may also seem strange that this was the only ride that I could not complete, because one of the road segments, a portion of La Pata Road in San Clemente, was under construction as of this writing. The ride description anticipates the completion of the road, and your opportunity to complete the entire route. (I did the route in stages, skipping the missing link, and then estimating its length.)

Start the ride at Sendero Field in San Juan Capistrano. Cautiously cross Ortega Highway (CA 74) and turn left. Turn right at the traffic signal, onto La Pata Road. As of this writing, La Pata provided access to Rancho Mission Viejo Riding Park, San Juan Hills High School, the surrounding neighborhood, and the Prima Deshecha Landfill and adjacent green waste facility. Many of the motor vehicles on the road are destined for the landfill, including plenty of refuse trucks. La Pata Road's completion should bring increased traffic volumes to the road. La Pata climbs from Ortega Highway to the landfill (4.3% average grade), which is at 581 feet, 2.05 miles into the ride. A 2.1-mile gap in La Pata is to be completed, which will be mostly downhill from here into San Clemente. After a brisk descent to Avenida Pico (mile 5.1), La Pata climbs to 588 feet (7.4% grade) at mile 6.0, followed by a descent to the road's end adjacent Richard T. Steed Memorial Park and San Clemente Dog Park (mile 6.5). La Pata simply ends here—beyond the end of the road is San Onofre State Beach; beyond that is Marine Corps Base Camp Pendleton.

Bike Shop

Buy My Bikes, 32302 Camino Capistrano, San Juan Capistrano, (949) 493-5611, http://buymybikes.com

Turn around and start the arduous climb up La Pata (4.5% grade) to the first crest. Enjoy the descent to Avenida Pico, and then prepare for a 3-mile climb back to the Prima Deshecha Landfill. It is a rapid descent down La Pata to Ortega Highway (mile 12.8). Keep straight this time; you are now on Antonio Parkway, climbing at an average 4.2% grade, past Rancho Mission Viejo (new as of this writing) and Ladera Ranch, where construction began in 1999. The next crest is at O'Neill Drive (elevation 621 feet, mile 14.75), adjacent Ladera Ranch. Antonio Parkway rolls for the next 2.5 miles or so, roughly on the eastern edge of south Orange County's urban development. El Cañada Gobernadora is actually a waterway that flows into San Juan Creek from the Santa Ana Mountains. It formerly served as an unofficial boundary between urban development to the west and wilderness to the east. That division is only partially the case today, given the new development trends.

These two riders flew past me as if I had brake rub, on Antonio Parkway near Oso Parkway in Rancho Santa Margarita.

The Antonio Parkway—La Pata Road corridor is likely to be the easternmost through route in southern Orange County for decades to come. Enter the city of Rancho Santa Margarita just south of Oso Parkway. North of Oso Parkway (mile 17.5), Antonio begins a long, gradual climb into central Rancho Santa Margarita (average grade: 1.9%). Antonio remains busy all along here, passing by schools, stores, churches, and residences; there is a bike lane for the entire distance. After crossing Santa Margarita Parkway (mile 23.05), traffic volumes drop significantly as you enter a residential neighborhood. Turn right onto Avenida de las Flores to loop around Trabuco Mesa Park. The elevation here is 1,200 feet, the highest of the ride. Once on the other side of the park, turn right onto Vereda Laguna to close the loop and return to Antonio. Turn left onto Antonio, and begin the long southbound ride back to Rancho Mission Viejo and Reata Park.

You are at mile 24.05 after turning from Vereda Laguna onto Antonio Parkway. The next 5.8 miles or so are in Rancho Santa Margarita, which stretches as far southward as Oso Parkway. Rancho Santa Margarita has the dubious distinction of having the longest name of any city in the United States. After the long descent to Oso Parkway, Antonio rolls until the O'Neill Drive intersection, beyond which it is downhill. Enjoy the final, somewhat dramatic descent down the parkway to Ortega Highway, being wary of motor vehicle traffic. Turn right here and ride 0.2 mile to the entrance to Sendero Field, on the right, where the ride ends.

MILES AND DIRECTIONS

0.0 Start at Sendero Field in Rancho Mission Viejo, 28632 Ortega Hwy. (just outside of San Juan Capistrano). Starting elevation: 172 feet (lowest of the ride). Turn left onto Ortega Highway (CA 74) and head east.

0.2 Turn right onto La Pata Road—begin climb.

2.05 Crest of La Pata, adjacent Prima Deschecha Landfill entrance (elevation 581 feet). The next segment of La Pata was under construction as of this writing.

Canyon of the Governor's Wife

The original inhabitants of the Cañada Gobernadora valley were the Acjachemen tribe. Today, their full name is the Juaneño Band of Mission Indians, Acjachemen Nation. The band was seeking federal recognition as of this writing. Although their numbers have diminished, the tribe once occupied the region spanning from the San Joaquin Hills and Aliso Creek in Orange County to the north, to Las Pulgas Creek in San Diego County (currently Camp Pendleton) in the south, and from the Pacific Ocean in the west to the Santa Ana Mountains in the east. Aliso Creek formed a boundary between the Juaneño and the Tongva (Gabrielino) peoples. San Juan Creek was the locus of the region, wherein multiple villages of up to 300 residents in size were established. El Cañada Gobernadora flowed (and flows) into San Juan Creek, and was part of the Juaneño region. Their language, a dialect of the Luiseño, was lost by the beginning of the 20th century, although there have been attempts to revive it.

Spanish priests, who arrived in Southern California in the 19th century, and who later brought along friars, servants, soldiers, and others, set about to rename geographical features and settlements in their native tongue, occasionally borrowing from Native American terms. The origin of "Canyon of the Governor's Wife" is unknown, but it may have been a reference to the leadership of the time, possibly California's or a Mexican subregion's.

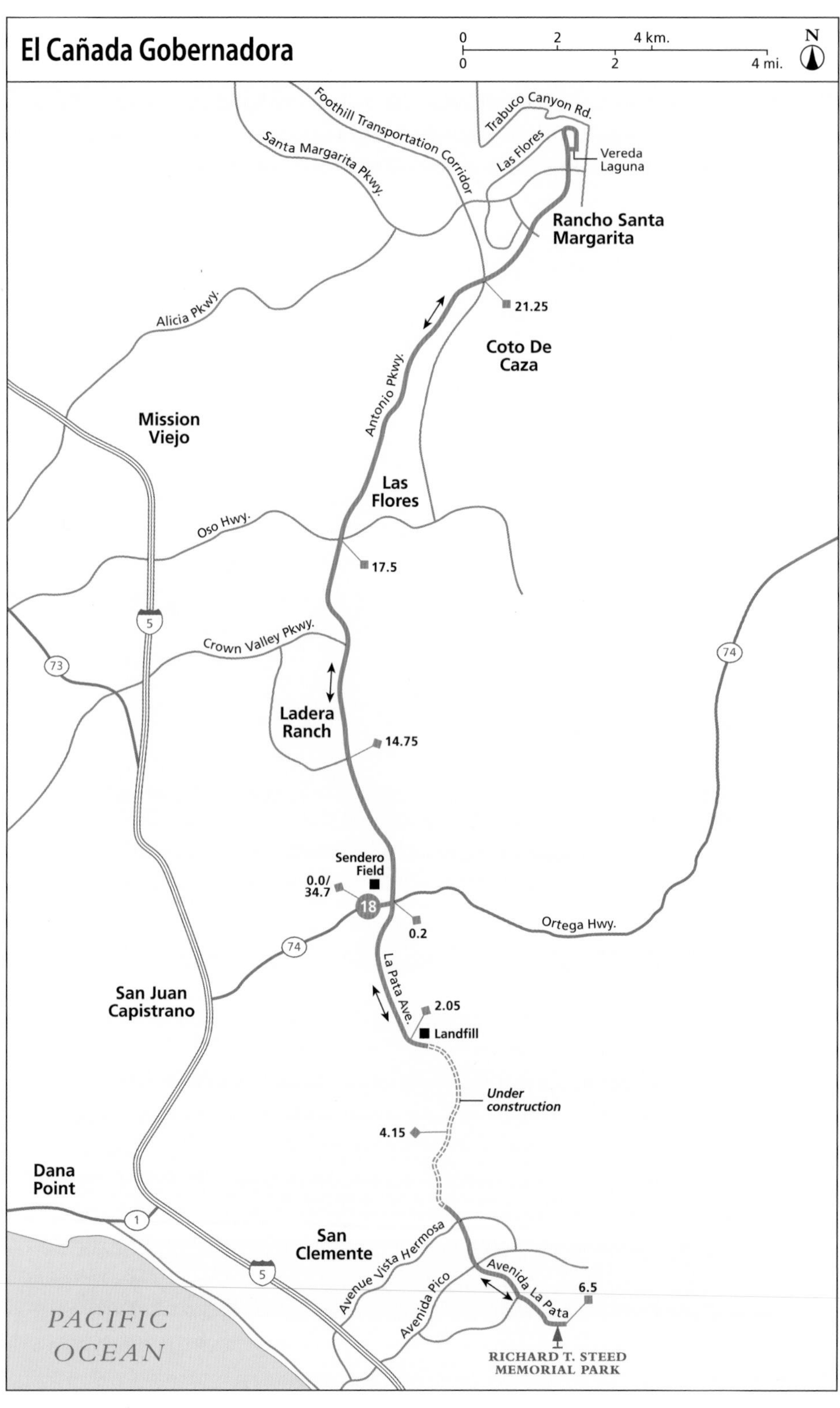
El Cañada Gobernadora
0
2
4 km.
0
2
4 mi.
N
Foothill Transportation Corridor
Trabuco Canyon Rd.
Santa Margarita Pkwy.
Las Flores
Vereda Laguna
Rancho Santa Margarita
21.25
Alicia Pkwy.
Coto De Caza
Antonio Pkwy.
Mission Viejo
Las Flores
Oso Hwy.
17.5
5
Crown Valley Pkwy.
73
74
Ladera Ranch
14.75
Sendero Field
0.0/ 34.7
18
0.2
Ortega Hwy.
74
La Pata Ave.
San Juan Capistrano
2.05
Landfill
Under construction
4.15
Dana Point
1
San Clemente
Avenue Vista Hermosa
5
Avenida La Pata
6.5
Avenida Pico
PACIFIC OCEAN
RICHARD T. STEED MEMORIAL PARK

5.1 Traffic signal at Avenida Pico—end of descent (elevation 252 feet); keep straight onto climb (7.4% grade).

6.0 Crest of climb (elevation 588 feet); begin descent.

6.5 End of La Pata Road; turn around and reverse route—climb 4.5% grade.

7.05 Crest of climb; descend (7.4% grade) to Avenida Pico.

7.9 Traffic signal at Avenida Pico; keep straight—begin climb.

10.95 Crest of climb (elevation 581 feet) adjacent Prima Deschecha Landfill; begin descent.

12.8 Traffic signal at Ortega Highway; keep straight—end of descent (elevation 197 feet); begin climb (4.2% grade).

14.75 Crest of climb at O'Neill Drive—begin rolling section.

17.5 Traffic signal at Oso Parkway; keep straight—elevation 585 feet. Begin long, gradual climb into central Rancho Santa Margarita.

23.05 Traffic signal at Santa Margarita Parkway; keep straight—elevation 1,147 feet. Enter residential neighborhood, with lower traffic volumes.

23.55 Stop sign at Avenida de las Flores; turn right to loop around Trabuco Mesa Park.

23.75 High elevation of ride (1,200 feet) at Sarra Cenia.

23.95 Turn right onto Vereda Laguna.

24.05 Stop sign at Antonio Parkway; end of loop around Trabuco Mesa Park. Turn left to head south on Antonio.

24.3 Traffic signal at Santa Margarita Parkway; keep straight—traffic volume on Antonio increases significantly. Begin long, gradual descent.

29.8 Traffic signal at Oso Parkway; keep straight—end of long descent.

32.6 Traffic signal at O'Neill Drive; keep straight; begin downhill (4.2% grade).

34.5 Traffic signal at CA 74; end of descent—turn right.

34.7 End of ride at entrance to Sendero Field.

19

Hi-Yo Arroyo Trabuco

Start: Arroyo Vista Park, 29661 Avenida de las Banderas, Rancho Santa Margarita

Length: 12.05 miles (counterclockwise loop)

Riding time: 1 to 3 hours (my time: 1H22:17)

Terrain and surface: 46% dirt trails, 36% paved roads, 18% paved paths

Elevations: Low—761 feet at along Arroyo Trabuco Trail, near Arroyo Vista trailhead; high—1,491 feet on Vista Trail near Live Oak Canyon Trail

Traffic and hazards: In 2014, Avenida de las Banderas was carrying 13,000 vehicles per day adjacent Arroyo Vista Park; Avenida Empresa was carrying 25,000 vehicles per day at Santa Margarita Parkway.

Map: *The Thomas Guide by Rand McNally—Street Guide: Los Angeles and Orange Counties* (any recent year), page 892

Getting there by car: From central Anaheim, head south on I-5. Exit to CA 133 eastbound, and then to CA 241 southbound. Note that 133 and 241 are toll freeways (the toll roads will send you a bill). Exit at Santa Margarita Parkway in Rancho Santa Margarita and turn right. Turn left onto Avenida Empresa, followed by a right turn onto Avenida de las Banderas. Look for Arroyo Vista Park on the right.

Getting there by public transit: Ride OCTA bus route 82 from Saddleback College in Mission Viejo to Arroyo Vista and Avenida de las Banderas in Rancho Santa Margarita, every 50 to 70 minutes on weekdays and every 100 minutes on Saturdays (no service on Sundays and holidays).

Starting point coordinates: 33.624308°N / 117.612961°W

THE RIDE

Hi-Yo Arroyo Trabuco crams a little bit of everything into a 12.05-mile loop in Rancho Santa Margarita. The route includes paved roads, paved paths, and dirt trails—the trails include wide-track and singletrack, both flat and steep. As suggested by the title, the ride's feature is the Arroyo Trabuco, which is a

Two riders charge along Arroyo Trabuco Trail, with the CA 241 freeway in the foreground and the Santa Ana Mountains' saddleback in the distance.

seasonal wash that contributes to draining the Santa Ana Mountains. ("Hi-Yo" was, of course, the Lone Ranger's signature shout-out to his horse, Silver—the equestrian equivalent of an ignition switch.)

Start the ride at Arroyo Vista Park in Rancho Santa Margarita, a fine neighborhood park located on Avenida de las Banderas. The starting elevation is 842 feet. Exit the park and turn left onto Banderas. Turn left onto Avenida Empresa at the traffic signal. You may be thinking, "Say, I thought this was a mountain bike ride!" Relax—the first 10% of the route is the busiest. Continue to the end of Avenida Empresa, and then ride straight onto the path that cuts between some buildings. Turn right at the end of the path, 1.3 miles into the ride, onto Live Oak Canyon Trail (paved bike path). Ride across the bridge over CA 241 (freeway) at mile 1.7. At mile 1.95, El Camino Montana (residential road) is immediately adjacent the path. The path veers away from the road at mile 3.0. As the path curves sharply to the right, at mile 3.35, leave the path and cut across the open space on the rudimentary trail. Look for the opening in the railing on the other side of the open space—you are now at Trabuco Canyon Road; turn left here (elevation 1,190 feet). The road plunges into Trabuco Canyon (7.7% grade; you ride up this climb in Ride 20, La Ruta Margarita). Follow the road as it crosses Arroyo Trabuco, then curves to the left to continue a gradual descent.

Enter O'Neill Regional Park where Trabuco Canyon Road curves to the right to become Live Oak Canyon Road (mile 5.0). Note that O'Neill Regional Park can be entered from Trabuco Canyon Road, upstream from the main park entrance. Ride along the loosely marked trail, near the park boundary wall. After crossing the Arroyo Trabuco, enter the road and ride past the main entrance. The map shows this option. Once past the entrance station, make a sharp right onto Live Oak Canyon Trail, which is a paved park road here. The road climbs gradually (3.2%), with Live Oak Canyon Road running parallel on the other side of the stone wall to your right. At the end of the paved road, keep straight onto Hoffman-Homestead Trail (mile 5.8). This dirt trail descends gradually as you truly begin to penetrate O'Neill Regional Park. After a quarter-mile, turn left onto Vista Trail. This is a narrow trail that climbs, in switchbacks, at an average grade of 13.7% to the top of the ridge that towers in the distance. The climbing does not end until you reach the high point of the entire ride (1,491 feet, mile 6.75). Vista Trail continues from here, descending gradually until its junction with Live Oak Canyon Trail. Turn left onto Live Oak Canyon Trail (dirt trail).

Live Oak Canyon descends at a 6.4% grade; stay right at the next two junctions. The grade then increases to 7.5% as you drop back down into the canyon. The trail surface is generally good, although there are some rutted segments. Bear right at the bottom for a short ascent, followed by a final, steep descent (13.4% grade). You are now back in O'Neill Regional Park's central section, where there are restrooms, picnic facilities, water fountains, parking, and sixty-seven campsites. Turn right onto the park road (mile 8.6). Follow it as it loops to the left; look for the Arroyo Trabuco Trail gateway on the right. Turn off of the park road, and ride onto the trail (mile 8.7). This is a speedy, somewhat rocky trail that parallels Arroyo Trabuco, also known as Trabuco Creek. The trail is wide-track, and is gradually downhill. Pass under the CA 241 freeway at mile 8.9, and then Santa Margarita Parkway at mile 9.9. There are intermittent markers along the way, to let you know that you are on Arroyo Trabuco.

Bike Shop

Rock N' Road Cyclery, 27825 Santa Margarita Pkwy., Rancho Santa Margarita, (949) 859-5076, www.rocknroadcyclery.net

There are actually two, parallel trails through here; the other is off to your left. Where the two trails begin to merge, look for the trailhead (mile 11.35) on the left. Turn left here, and ride toward the road. This is the low elevation of the ride (761 feet). Turn left onto Arroyo Vista (mile 11.4), and ride through the Rancho Santa Margarita neighborhood. Arroyo Vista Park appears on your left as you approach Avenida de las Banderas, although the entrance is off of Banderas, after you make the left turn onto that road. The ride ends here.

MILES AND DIRECTIONS

0.0 Start at Arroyo Vista Park in Rancho Santa Margarita. Exit the park and turn left onto Avenida de las Banderas.

0.65 Traffic signal at Avenida Empresa; turn left.

1.2 End of Avenida Empresa; continue onto paved path, between the buildings.

1.3 End of path; turn right onto Live Oak Canyon Trail (paved bike path).

1.7 Bridge over CA 241 freeway.

1.95 El Camino Montana (residential road) is now parallel to path.

3.0 Path veers away from El Camino Montana.

3.35 Leave path as it curves to the right; cut across open space on rudimentary trail.

3.45 Exit open space; turn left onto Trabuco Canyon Road—begin descent.

3.9 Bridge over Trabuco Creek (Arroyo Trabuco).

5.0 Turn left to enter O'Neill Regional Park; turn right after entry, onto Live Oak Canyon Trail (paved park road).

5.8 End of Live Oak Canyon; keep straight onto Hoffman-Homestead Trail (dirt trail).

6.05 Turn left onto Vista Trail; begin steep climb (13.7% grade)—trail is narrow, and features switchbacks.

6.75 High elevation of ride (1,491 feet).

6.9 End of Vista Trail; turn left onto Live Oak Canyon Trail (dirt trail)—begin descent.

6.95 Bear right to remain on Live Oak Canyon Trail.

7.3 Bear right to remain on Live Oak Canyon Trail—descend at 7.5% grade.

8.3 Bottom of descent; bear right to remain on Live Oak Canyon.

8.4 Begin steep descent (13.4% grade).

8.6 End of Live Oak Canyon Trail; turn right onto paved park road.

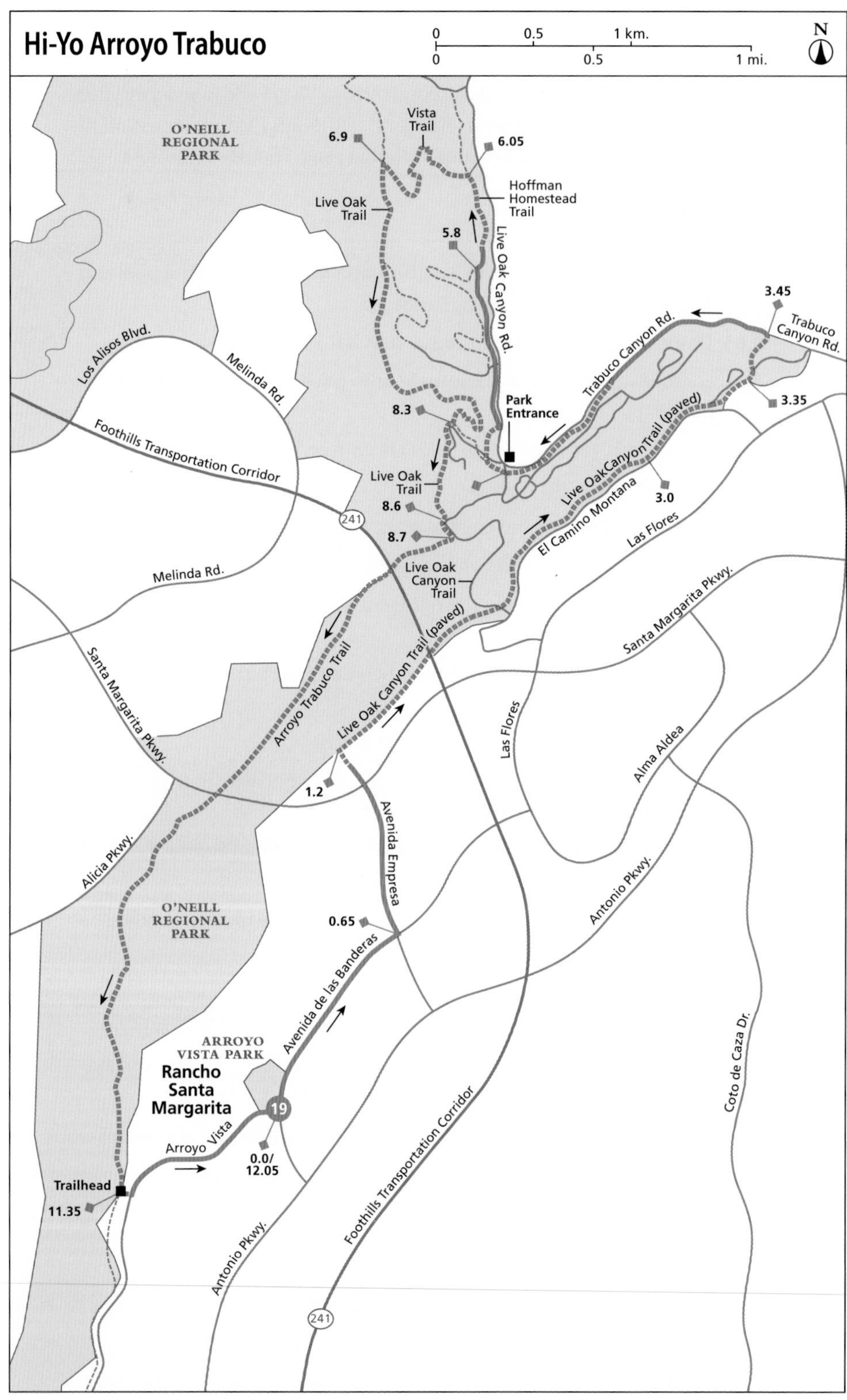
Hi-Yo Arroyo Trabuco
0
0.5
1 km.
0
0.5
1 mi.
N
O'NEILL REGIONAL PARK
Vista Trail
6.9
6.05
Hoffman Homestead Trail
Live Oak Trail
5.8
Live Oak Canyon Rd.
3.45
Trabuco Canyon Rd.
Trabuco Canyon Rd.
Los Alisos Blvd.
Melinda Rd.
8.3
Park Entrance
3.35
Live Oak Canyon Trail (paved)
Foothills Transportation Corridor
Live Oak Trail
3.0
8.6
241
8.7
El Camino Montana
Las Flores
Live Oak Canyon Trail
Melinda Rd.
Santa Margarita Pkwy.
Live Oak Canyon Trail (paved)
Santa Margarita Pkwy.
Arroyo Trabuco Trail
Santa Margarita Pkwy.
Las Flores
Alma Aldea
1.2
Avenida Empresa
Alicia Pkwy.
O'NEILL REGIONAL PARK
Antonio Pkwy.
0.65
Avenida de las Banderas
ARROYO VISTA PARK
Rancho Santa Margarita
19
Coto de Caza Dr.
Foothills Transportation Corridor
Arroyo Vista
0.0/ 12.05
Trailhead
11.35
Antonio Pkwy.
241

A rider slices through the oaks on Arroyo Trabuco Trail, just outside of O'Neill Regional Park.

8.7 Turn left, off of park road, onto Arroyo Trabuco Trail.

8.9 Pass under CA 241 freeway.

9.9 Pass under Santa Margarita Parkway.

11.35 Turn left to leave Arroyo Trabuco Trail and head toward trailhead.

11.4 Turn left onto Arroyo Vista (paved residential street).

12.0 Traffic signal at Avenida de las Banderas; turn left.

12.05 End of ride at Arroyo Vista Park.

La Ruta Margarita

Start: Pinecrest Park, 21310 Pinecrest, Mission Viejo

Length: 12.95 miles (clockwise loop)

Riding time: 40 minutes to 2.5 hours (my time: 50:35)

Terrain and surface: 100% paved roads

Elevations: Low—796 feet at Santa Margarita Parkway and Marguerite Parkway; high—1,439 feet on Live Oak Canyon Road

Traffic and hazards: Santa Margarita Parkway carried up to 56,000 vehicles per day east of Alicia Parkway in 2015. Marguerite Parkway, El Toro Road, and Plano Trabuco Road all carried 15,000 vehicles per day in 2015 on their busiest segments of this route. Trabuco Canyon Road carried 3,400 vehicles per day west of Plano Trabuco Road in 2002.

Map: *The Thomas Guide by Rand McNally—Street Guide: Los Angeles and Orange Counties* (any recent year), page 892

Getting there by car: From central Anaheim, take I-5 south to Lake Forest Drive. Turn left and head northeast on Lake Forest. Turn right at Portola Parkway and head southeast; Portola becomes Santa Margarita Parkway after crossing El Toro Road. Look for Pinecrest after crossing Marguerite Parkway. Turn left on Pinecrest and park along the right side of the street (Pinecrest Park is in the basin below you).

Getting there by public transit: OCTA bus route 82 runs along Santa Margarita Parkway every 50 to 70 minutes on weekdays and every 100 minutes on Saturdays. OCTA bus route 85 runs between Dana Point and Mission Viejo, stopping at Santa Margarita Parkway and Marguerite Parkway, every 30 to 40 minutes on weekdays and every 90 minutes on Saturdays. You can start the ride from the bus stop—head north on Marguerite. OCTA bus route 89 runs between Laguna Beach and Mission Viejo, also stopping at Santa Margarita Parkway and Marguerite Parkway, every 30 to 40 minutes on weekdays and every 70 to 80 minutes on weekends and holidays.

Starting point coordinates: 33.651208°N / 117.639100°W

THE RIDE

La Ruta Margarita is a 12.95-mile loop that visits northern portions of Mission Viejo and Rancho Santa Margarita, as well as unincorporated areas of Orange County, including Live Oak Canyon and Trabuco Canyon. The route features a 643-foot elevation differential, and a total of 773 feet of climbing, making it a reasonably challenging outing, minus any truly long climbs. Roughly half of the ride is suburban, with intermittent traffic signals and busy, wide arterials. The other half of the ride is exurban, on low-volume, two-lane roads in lightly developed areas. The best of both worlds! Start the ride at Pinecrest Park in Mission Viejo. Mission Viejo was the site of the 1984 Summer Olympic Games cycling road races (see Ride 23, Olimpiada Mission Viejo) and is one of the country's largest master-planned communities. Pinecrest Park is to the north of the Olympic route. The park is situated below the road.

Start your timer as you make the right turn from Pinecrest onto Santa Margarita Parkway. Mission Viejo is crisscrossed by a network of four- and six-lane arterials, all with bike lanes. After just 0.3 mile, turn right onto Marguerite Parkway and head north. This is the low elevation of the ride (796 feet). Continue to El Toro Road and turn right, at the ride's 1-mile mark. The Aliso Creek Bikeway parallels El Toro (see Ride 15, Aliso Creek Sneak), on the opposite side of the road. You are welcome to access the bikeway, but El Toro features a bike lane and is suitable for riding. The riding slows here as El Toro climbs steadily from 815 feet at Marguerite to 1,092 feet at the Live Oak Canyon Road junction. El Toro gradually narrows from six to two lanes over this 2.1-mile stretch.

Bike Shop

The Path Bike Shop Live Oak, 30555 Trabuco Canyon Rd., Trabuco Canyon, (949) 589-2800, www.thepathbikeshop.com

Bear right at Live Oak Canyon Road. The junction, also known as Cook's Corner, is a popular takeoff point for motorcyclists and mountain bikers. You are on your road bike today, though, so pedal on past, steadily climbing Live Oak Canyon Road. This is a two-lane road with a narrow shoulder, which is popular among cyclists. The gradient averages 6.8% over the next mile, finally cresting at the high elevation of the ride (1,439 feet). Live Oak Canyon Road then plunges into the namesake canyon, under a canopy of live oak trees. To your right is O'Neill Regional Park (see Ride 19, Hi-Yo Arroyo Trabuco). The road descends 500 feet over the next 2.3 miles. Live Oak Canyon then curves sharply to the left, adjacent the entrance to O'Neill Park (elevation 931 feet), becoming Trabuco Canyon Road. The road gradually climbs from here, with camping areas of O'Neill Park to your right.

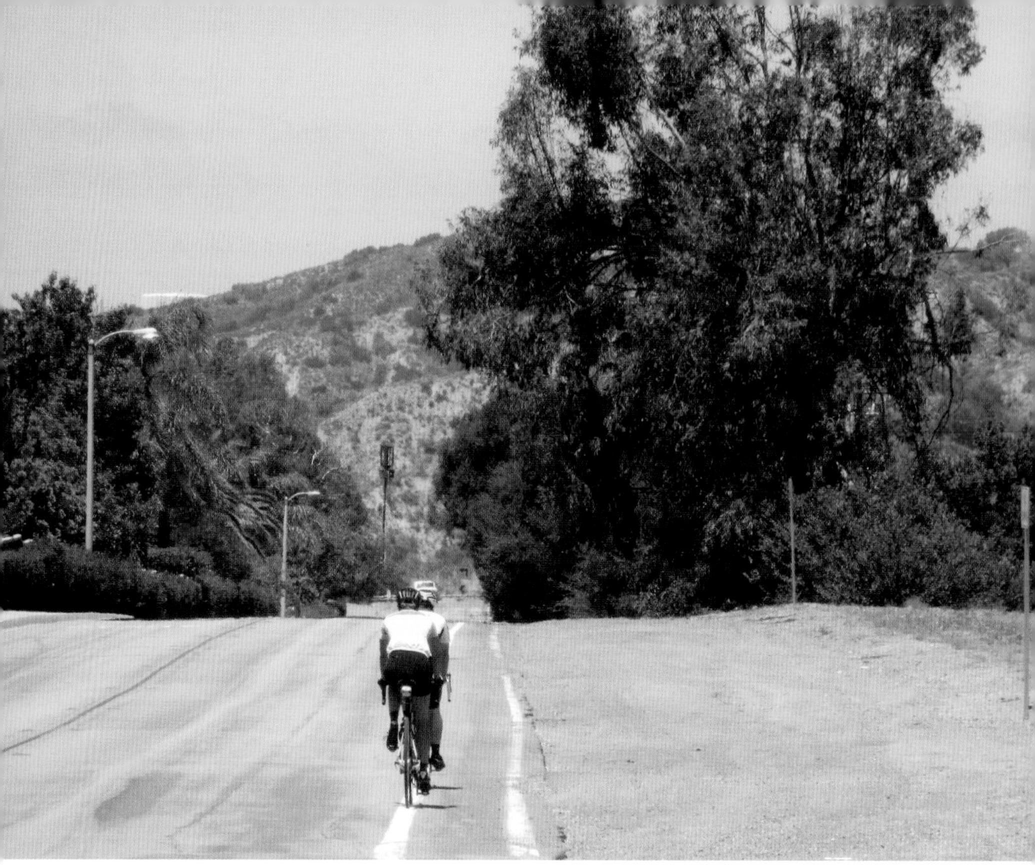

A pair of riders moves in synch along Trabuco Canyon Road, with the Santa Ana Mountains on the horizon.

To your left will be Trabuco Creek Road, the gateway to the small community of Trabuco Canyon. This out-of-the-way place features remnants of an early 20th-century attempt to mine tin here—there are old mining tunnels, foundations, and dams up the canyon. Trabuco is a Spanish word meaning blunderbuss or musket, a type of shotgun. Cross over Trabuco Creek, which is typically dry, at mile 7.4, and then start a stiff climb (8.3% grade) up Trabuco Canyon's back side to the plateau that overlooks the canyons that you just rode. You may envy cyclists speeding down the hill on the other side of the road. Stick with it, as the climb is less than a half-mile in length. At the top, after 0.4 mile of false flat, Trabuco Canyon curves sharply to the right, becoming Plano Trabuco Road (elevation 1,226 feet).

As you are riding along Trabuco Canyon, and then along Plano Trabuco, there is a walled residential community to your right, part of the city of Rancho Santa Margarita. Most of the filming for the TV reality series *The Real Housewives of Orange County* is done in Rancho Santa Margarita. The city and its neighbor, Mission Viejo, are considered to be among the safest in the United States. Suppress your hoodlum tendencies as you ride through.

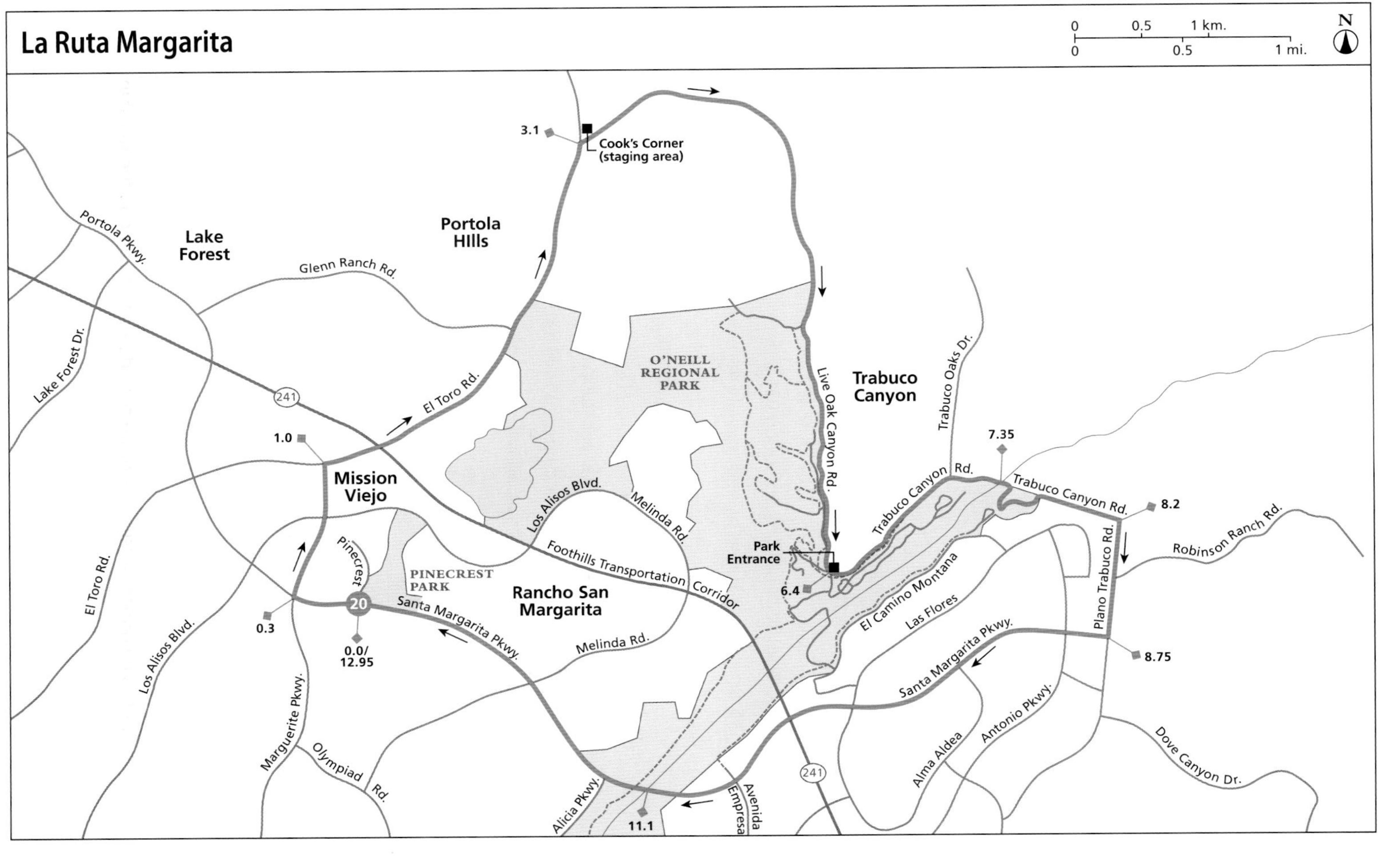
La Ruta Margarita
0
0.5
1 km.
0
0.5
1 mi.
N
3.1
Cook's Corner
(staging area)
Portola Pkwy.
Lake
Forest
Portola
HIlls
Glenn Ranch Rd.
Lake Forest Dr.
241
El Toro Rd.
O'NEILL
REGIONAL
PARK
Live Oak Canyon Rd.
Trabuco
Canyon
Trabuco Oaks Dr.
7.35
1.0
Mission
Viejo
Los Alisos Blvd.
Melinda Rd.
Trabuco Canyon
Rd.
Trabuco Canyon Rd.
8.2
Robinson Ranch Rd.
Plano Trabuco Rd.
Park
Entrance
6.4
Foothills Transportation
Corridor
El Camino Montana
Las Flores
Pinecrest
PINECREST
PARK
Rancho San
Margarita
El Toro Rd.
20
0.3
0.0/
12.95
Santa Margarita Pkwy.
Melinda Rd.
Santa Margarita Pkwy.
8.75
Los Alisos Blvd.
Marguerite Pkwy.
Olympiad
Rd.
Antonio Pkwy.
Alma Aldea
Dove Canyon Dr.
241
Alicia Pkwy.
11.1
Avenida
Empresa

Turn right onto Santa Margarita Parkway; it is 4.2 miles from here to Pinecrest. Santa Margarita gets very busy near CA 241 (toll freeway) and Alicia Parkway. Santa Margarita descends to 854 feet to cross over Trabuco Creek (dry), followed by a climb to 984 feet near Promenade, and then a descent to Pinecrest, back to the original, starting elevation of 823 feet. Turn right onto Pinecrest to conclude the ride.

MILES AND DIRECTIONS

0.0 Start at Pinecrest and Santa Margarita Parkway, adjacent Pinecrest Park, in Mission Viejo. Head west on Santa Margarita Parkway.

0.3 Traffic signal at Marguerite Parkway; turn right (low elevation of ride: 796 feet).

1.0 Traffic signal at El Toro Road; turn right.

3.1 Bear right onto Live Oak Canyon Road at Cook's Corner.

4.1 High elevation of ride (1,439 feet).

6.4 Live Oak Canyon Road curves to the left, adjacent the entrance to O'Neill Regional Park (elevation 931 feet).

7.35 Bridge over Trabuco Creek (usually dry); begin climb at 8.3% grade.

8.2 Trabuco Canyon Road curves to the right, becoming Plano Trabuco Road (elevation 1,226 feet). Enter Rancho Santa Margarita.

8.75 Traffic signal at Santa Margarita Parkway; turn right.

11.1 Bridge over Trabuco Creek (elevation 854 feet).

11.95 Leave Rancho Santa Margarita; enter Mission Viejo (at Melinda Road).

12.95 End of ride at Pinecrest, adjacent Pinecrest Park.

21

Laguna Beach Pageant of the Pedals

Start: Boat Canyon Park, 600-698 Hillcrest Dr., Laguna Beach

Length: 23.6 miles (counterclockwise loop)

Riding time: 1.75 to 4 hours (my time: 2H08:13)

Terrain and surface: 83% paved roads, 17% paved bike path

Elevations: Low—9 feet at Pacific Coast Highway (CA 1) and Broadway in Laguna Beach; high—665 feet on Newport Coast Drive near Ridge Park Road in Irvine

Traffic and hazards: In 2014, CA 1 (Pacific Coast Highway) carried 40,000 vehicles per day in Laguna Beach; CA 133 carried 37,000 vehicles per day near CA 73; Newport Coast Drive carried 22,000 vehicles per day south of CA 73; Bonita Canyon Road carried 20,000 vehicles per day near Newport Coast Drive; Quail Hill Parkway carried 15,000 vehicles per day near Shady Canyon Road; Shady Canyon Road carried 7,000 vehicles per day in Irvine.

Map: *The Thomas Guide by Rand McNally—Street Guide: Los Angeles and Orange Counties* (any recent year), page 950

Getting there by car: From central Anaheim, head south on I-5. Exit to CA 133 (Laguna Freeway) southbound. The freeway becomes a highway in Irvine; continue heading south. Turn right onto CA 1 (Pacific Coast Highway) in Laguna Beach and head northwest. Turn right onto High Drive, entering a Laguna Beach neighborhood, followed by a left turn onto Hillcrest Drive. Boat Canyon Park will be on the right; turn right to enter the park, and park.

Getting there by public transit: OCTA bus route 1 runs along PCH between Long Beach and San Clemente. Exit at High Drive, and follow the above instructions to Boat Canyon Park. Route 1 runs every 35 minutes (from Newport Beach to San Clemente; every 60 minutes from Long Beach) on weekends and every 60 minutes on weekends and holidays.

Starting point coordinates: 33.548136°N / 117.794053°W

THE RIDE

The Laguna Beach Pageant of the Pedals pays homage to Laguna Beach's worldwide reputation as a center for the arts, as well as its sports history. The city was already a tourist destination by the 1880s, and was attracting painters, photographers, filmmakers, and authors by the 1920s (and earlier). The city incorporated in 1927, and quintupled in size between then and the 1960s. Today it receives up to 3 million visitors annually.

The ride is a 23.6-mile, counterclockwise loop that takes you from the coast, into the adjacent hills, and back to the coast. Counterclockwise is the recommended direction, such that the ocean will be on your right as you ride along CA 1, the Pacific Coast Highway. The ride begins at Boat Canyon Park, which is a small community park in Laguna Beach. There is a Boat Canyon Trail that hosts monthly moonlight hikes that leave from the park. The hikes head into Laguna Coast Wilderness Park (please see Ride 17, Crystal Cove Mas Moro). The roads adjacent the park are one-way, so start by circling the park in a clockwise direction. Continue past the park on High Drive, and head to CA 1. Turn left on CA 1, and head into town. Directly opposite Main Beach Park, which seems to be where all of the action is, turn left onto Broadway, which is also CA 133. This is the low elevation of the ride (9 feet). Remaining at the beach may be tempting, but you can return here later. It may be a slow ride through central Laguna Beach on Broadway. As you reach the outskirts of the commercial district, Broadway becomes Laguna Canyon Road. The canyon is an artists' enclave, with studios, residences, and inns to your right and Laguna Coast Wilderness Park and the Laguna College of Art and Design to your left. Laguna Canyon Road can be busy, but there is an adequate shoulder, and bicycling along here is popular.

Keep straight at El Toro Road (mile 4.15) and CA 73 (mile 4.8) as Laguna Canyon Road transitions into a four-lane highway. Leave Laguna Beach at El Toro. To your left, on the hillside, is Stagecoach South Trail, a portion of which is ridden in Crystal Cove Mas Moro, Ride 17. To your right is a sector of Laguna Coast Wilderness Park that is off-limits to bicycles but features several great hiking-running trails. The highway crests at a 400-feet elevation at mile 6.6, then descends gradually. Enter the city of Irvine. After passing Lake Forest Road, prepare to move left for a left turn to continue on Laguna Canyon Road. (The highway becomes a freeway beyond here.) Carefully execute the turn (mile 8.55). Next, navigate the traffic circle, turning left onto Quail Hill Parkway. Quail Hill descends gradually through a

Bike Shop

Laguna Beach Cyclery, 240 Thalia St., Laguna Beach, (949) 494-1522, www.lagunabeachcyclery.com

A solo rider is perfectly balanced on the Pacific Coast Highway's shoulder line, adjacent scenic Crystal Cove.

tree-lined neighborhood, one of several in Irvine's master plan. At Shady Canyon Road, as you leave the Quail Hill community, navigate the traffic circle to turn left onto Shady Canyon (mile 10.15).

Leave Shady Canyon soon after making the turn, veering right onto the adjacent bike path. The path climbs at a 5.4% grade to the entrance to the Shady Canyon subdivision. The path bypasses the entry gate, serving as the only authorized through route for nonresidents. To your right are the Quail Hill Preserve and Strawberry Farms—the latter includes a golf course, as well as some agriculture. Once on the other side of the Shady Canyon community, the path crosses the road to continue. You can also ride in the road along here, as there is an adequate shoulder. Whatever path you choose, both pass by the entrance to Bommer Canyon (mile 12.85—please see Ride 27, San Joaquin Hills Expedition). Turn left onto Bonita Canyon Road at the end of Shady Canyon (mile 14.2), followed by another left turn onto Newport Coast Drive.

While the Shady Canyon climb was a good warm-up, Newport Coast Drive presents a true challenge, climbing from 206 feet at Bonita Canyon Road to a crest at 665 feet, beyond Ridge Park Road, at an average grade of 3.2%. The road crosses over the CA 73 freeway—watch out for rapidly merging vehicles coming from your right, after crossing the freeway. Enter the city of Newport Beach as you cross CA 73. After the crest, Newport Coast descends rapidly to CA 1, at an average grade of 5.6%. With the ocean ahead, resort villas to your left and right, and Pelican Hill Golf Club on either side, you may think that you are descending into paradise. Turn left onto CA 1 (mile 19.2). Reality may set in with the motor vehicle traffic on the highway, but the stunning ocean views to your right are a powerful distraction. To your left and right is Crystal Cove State Park, which ascends into the adjacent hills and extends along the coast for about 3 miles.

Laguna Beach's Arts and Sports History

Laguna Beach became a mecca for artists in the early 20th century, when plein-air painters descended on the community. It was the perfect place for such works, in which the artist paints outdoors, reproducing what he or she sees. Filmmakers also made the trek to Laguna Beach in the 1920s, with the proximity to Hollywood and seaside coves making it a great setting for shooting. A number of notables made Laguna Beach their home during the mid-20th century, including adventurer Richard Halliburton and psychologist / drugs researcher Timothy Leary. The arts community has developed a number of annual events, each of which has become a Laguna Beach staple, including the Pageant of the Masters, Festival of the Arts (juried works by local artists), Sawdust Art Festival (nonjuried arts and crafts), the Art-A-Fair (works by nonlocal artists), and the Plein Air Painting Invitational (a weeklong outdoor public paint-fest). In the Pageant of the Masters, famous artworks are re-created using real persons as models.

A sports community has also developed in the area. The Brooks Street Surfing Classic is the oldest such competition in the world, while the "Vic" Skimboarding World Championship is an annual event. All of the cycling roads and trails in and around Laguna Beach are known around the world, and are meccas for many riders. Laguna Beach incorporated as a city in 1927, at a time when it was somewhat isolated along Orange County's southern coast. The isolation remains even today, with access effectively limited to the Pacific Coast Highway from the north and south, and Laguna Canyon Road from the east. Most "Lagunans," as well as visitors, would agree that the isolation is a key element of the community's appeal.

CA 1 rolls along this stretch, descending to 54 feet above sea level, and then climbing to 112 feet at Crystal Heights Drive. To your right, somewhat hidden, is Crystal Cove Historic District, which is a collection of beachfront cottages built during the 1930s and 1940s. The PCH descends to 16 feet adjacent Crystal Cove—extremely picturesque—and then ascends to 118 feet at Moro Ridge Road, entering the city of Laguna Beach. The highway descends to 45 feet, leaving Laguna Beach and entering the small, unincorporated community of Emerald Bay. Reenter Laguna Beach as the PCH climbs yet again, to 111 feet, before finally descending toward the heart of the city. Turn left at High Drive (mile 23.35) and climb into the neighborhood (6.6% grade). Turn left onto Hillcrest Drive; Boat Canyon Park is on the right, where the ride ends.

MILES AND DIRECTIONS

0.0 Leave Boat Canyon Park in Laguna Beach toward the north (one-way street); loop the park clockwise, and then head south on High Drive.

0.25 Stop sign at CA 1 (Pacific Coast Highway); turn left.

0.75 Low elevation of ride (9 feet), adjacent Main Beach Park in Laguna Beach; turn left onto Broadway (CA 133).

1.1 Leave central district of Laguna Beach; now on Laguna Canyon Road (CA 133).

4.15 Traffic signal at El Toro Road; keep straight—leave Laguna Beach.

4.8 Traffic signals at CA 73 freeway; keep straight.

6.6 Crest in highway (400 feet); enter Irvine—begin gradual descent.

8.55 Turn left to remain on Laguna Canyon Road (CA 133 continues straight, becoming a freeway).

9.05 Traffic circle; turn left onto Quail Hill Parkway.

10.1 Traffic circle; turn left onto Shady Canyon Drive.

10.25 Leave Shady Canyon Drive at Fossil Road; veer right onto adjacent bike path—begin climb at 5.4% grade.

10.8 Crest of climb, adjacent entrance to gated community—bike path is not gated.

12.4 Leave gated community; either cross Shady Canyon Road to continue on bike path or enter road to ride on shoulder. The bike path parallels Shady Canyon Road.

14.2 Traffic signal at Bonita Canyon Road; turn left.

14.7 Traffic signal at Newport Coast Drive; turn left.

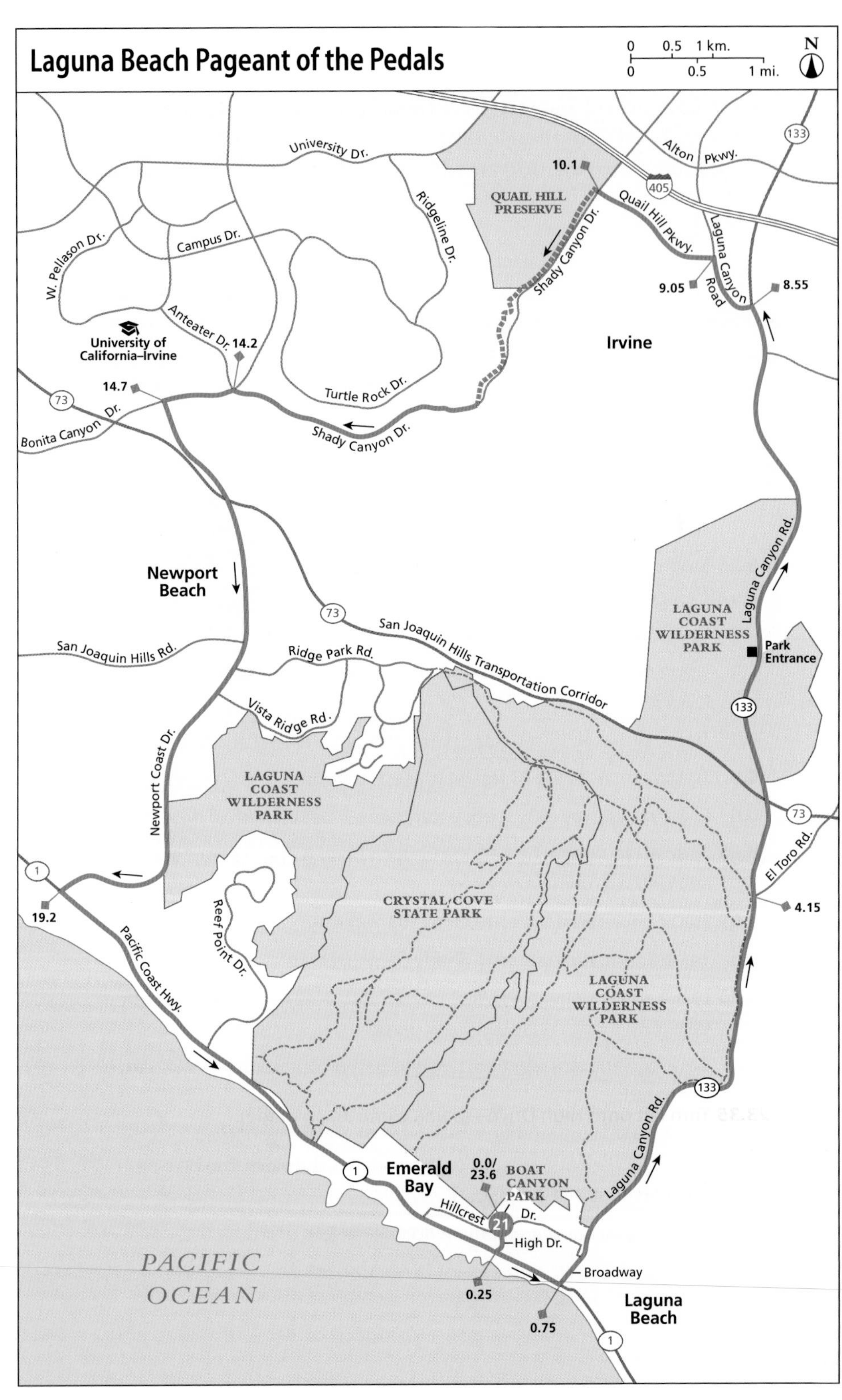

Laguna Beach Pageant of the Pedals
0 0.5 1 km.
0 0.5 1 mi.
N
University Dr.
Alton Pkwy.
133
405
10.1
QUAIL HILL PRESERVE
Quail Hill Pkwy.
Ridgeline Dr.
Shady Canyon Dr.
Laguna Canyon Road
9.05
8.55
Campus Dr.
W. Pellason Dr.
Anteater Dr.
14.2
University of California–Irvine
Irvine
Turtle Rock Dr.
14.7
73
Bonita Canyon Dr.
Shady Canyon Dr.
Newport Beach
Laguna Canyon Rd.
LAGUNA COAST WILDERNESS PARK
Park Entrance
73
San Joaquin Hills Transportation Corridor
San Joaquin Hills Rd.
Ridge Park Rd.
Vista Ridge Rd.
133
Newport Coast Dr.
LAGUNA COAST WILDERNESS PARK
73
El Toro Rd.
1
19.2
CRYSTAL COVE STATE PARK
4.15
Reef Point Dr.
Pacific Coast Hwy.
LAGUNA COAST WILDERNESS PARK
133
Laguna Canyon Rd.
1
Emerald Bay
0.0/ 23.6
BOAT CANYON PARK
Hillcrest Dr.
21
High Dr.
PACIFIC OCEAN
Broadway
0.25
0.75
Laguna Beach
1

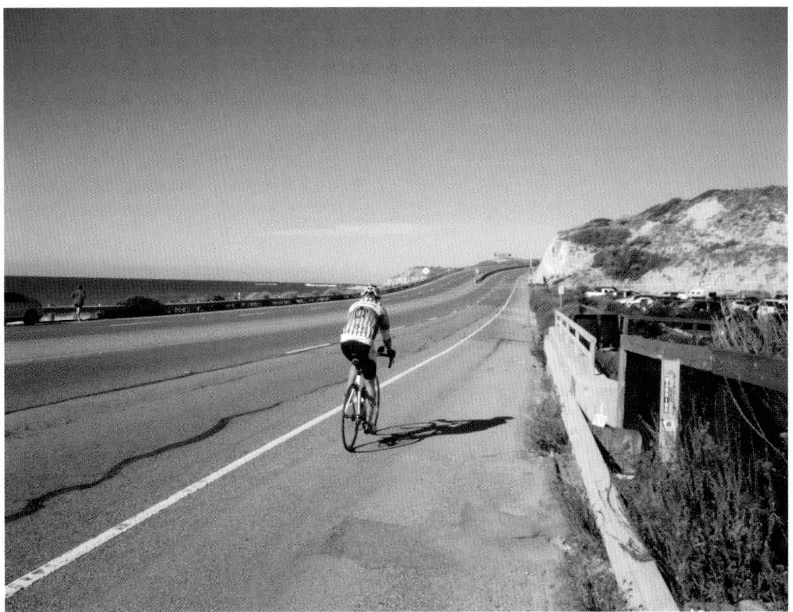

Rolling through Crystal Cove along CA 1: coastal bluffs, unobstructed ocean view, and a wide shoulder.

15.5 Cross over CA 73 freeway; watch for motor vehicles merging from the right—enter city of Newport Beach.

17.4 High elevation of entire ride (665 feet), on Newport Coast Drive beyond Ridge Park Road—begin descent (5.7% grade).

19.2 Traffic signal at CA 1 (Pacific Coast Highway); turn left—Pacific Ocean is on the right.

20.3 Crystal Cove Historic District (collection of cottages) on the right.

21.4 Crystal Cove on the right (highway elevation: 16 feet).

21.8 Enter city of Laguna Beach.

22.4 Leave Laguna Beach; enter community of Emerald Bay.

22.8 Leave Emerald Bay; reenter Laguna Beach.

23.35 Turn left onto High Drive—begin climb (6.6% grade).

23.55 Turn left onto Hillcrest Drive.

23.6 End of ride at Boat Canyon Park.

North San Juan Capistrano Steeplechase

Start: Cook's Park Cordova, 28202 Calle Arroyo, San Juan Capistrano

Length: 12.1 miles (counterclockwise loop)

Riding time: 1 to 3 hours (my time: 1H23:57)

Terrain and surface: 51% dirt trails, 29% paved roads, 17% paved paths, 3% paved walkway

Elevations: Low—58 feet on Trabuco Creek Trail at junction with San Juan Creek Trail in San Juan Capistrano; high—623 feet on Stoneridge Trail between Highland Drive and Monarch Drive

Traffic and hazards: CA 74 (Ortega Highway) carried 28,000 vehicles per day east of La Novia in San Juan Capistrano in 2014.

Map: *The Thomas Guide by Rand McNally—Street Guide: Los Angeles and Orange Counties* (any recent year), page 952

Getting there by car: From central Anaheim, head south on I-5. Exit at CA 74 (Ortega Highway); turn left and head east. Turn right onto Avenida Siega. Follow Siega as it turns to the right, becoming Calle Arroyo. Turn left, just after the curve to the right, to enter Cook's Park Cordova.

Getting there by public transit: Ride OCTA bus route 191 from San Juan Capistrano Train Depot to Ortega Highway (CA 74) and La Novia in San Juan Capistrano. Once on CA 74, head east to Avenida Siega. Turn right and ride to the park.

Starting point coordinates: 33.511764°N / 117.633878°W

THE RIDE

The North San Juan Capistrano Steeplechase rides city-owned trails in the northeastern corner of the city, completing a loop by connecting the trails with a couple of bike paths. The ride is not a pure steeplechase, although there are a few barriers that will require dismounting and hurdling for most riders. It is a 12.1-mile counterclockwise loop that features a few short, steep

Oops—missed a turn; at the three-way junction between Helicopter Hill, Stoneridge, and Malaspina Trails, take Stoneridge!

climbs and some panoramic views of San Juan Capistrano. Most of the trails meander between residences in the city's northeastern hills; it's easy to accidentally wander onto private property in a few locations, so be mindful of staying on the trails.

Start at Cook's Park Cordova (also known as Cook Park, Cook's Park, or Cook's Cordova Park), which is located near the eastern end of the San Juan Creek bike path. The park extends along the path, with different sections—the start-finish for this ride is on the park's far eastern end, which is also used by equestrians. The starting elevation is 141 feet. Exit the parking area and turn right onto the bike path. The path ends after no more than 200 feet; turn left onto Avenida Siega. There is a parallel dirt path for those of you who are game. At CA 74 (Ortega Highway), carefully turn left, watching for motor vehicles. The highway is a bit narrow through here, and gets even narrower up the road. When the walkway appears on the right, I recommend using it. It will be easier to access the upcoming trailhead from the walkway anyway. Look to your right for the entrance to Belford-Marbella Trail, located just past Belford Drive, 1.3 miles into the ride. The trail starts tamely, with an off-camber

segment and plenty of scatter (leaves, dirt, small rocks, and roots) thrown in to get you warmed up for trail riding.

The warm-up is brief, as Belford-Marbella turns upward, to the right, for a 16.3% gradient climb. A few moguls greet you near the top, to let you know that you are not yet out of the woods. The trail turns sharply to the left, cutting between some residential property, as the gradient eases. Cross Calle de la Rosa (mile 1.65) and continue to climb (7.8% grade). The grade eases after crossing Paseo Boveda, and then a service road. Follow the trail as it dips (be careful not to ride into the adjacent house's backyard, as I almost did), curves to the right, and then straightens out. After riding past a couple of residences, the trail begins an extended climb (4.6% grade), taking you up to 571 feet above sea level. After a short downhill, and crossing a service road (mile 2.9), dismount for some steeplechasing—a few logs keep unauthorized users off of the trails. Jump the logs, remount, and continue riding. After a short hill at mile 3.0 (12.8% grade), Belford-Marbella begins to descend. After a steep descent (17.7% grade), cross Golden Ridge Lane, and then curve to the left (steep descent: 16.7% grade). You are now on Helicopter Hill Trail (name origin unknown). The trail continues to descend, passing by the Marbella Country Club.

After another descent (8.9% grade) Helicopter Hill Trail bottoms out in a thick grove of eucalyptus trees (elevation 208 feet), and then climbs, via switchbacks, to the next crest (10.1% grade; elevation 492 feet). This is a three-way junction between Helicopter Hill, Malaspina, and Stoneridge Trails. Turn right onto Stoneridge Trail. This trail descends, climbs, descends, and climbs before curving to the right and crossing Highland Drive (mile 4.8). From here, Stoneridge climbs to the highest elevation of the ride (623 feet) at an average grade of 7.8%. After a steep descent (11.8% grade), Stoneridge Trail comes to an end at Monarch Drive. Next, turn right and ride in the road to the next trailhead, no more than 150 feet away. Turn left onto Trabuco Ridge Trail, and begin a steep climb (9.6% grade). After one more crest (451 feet elevation), Trabuco Ridge descends to the Rancho Viejo Road bike path (mile 6.55). This marks the end of the tour of northeastern San Juan Capistrano's trails system!

Turn right on the path to cross Trabuco Creek, which is usually bone dry, followed by a sharp left onto Trabuco Creek Trail. The latter is paved underneath the I-5 freeway. The pavement ends just beyond the freeway as it dips to cross Trabuco Creek. Stay to the left after crossing the wash. Pass under the railroad bridge at mile 7.5. Curve to the right—you should now be on the perimeter of Saddleback Valley Christian School, separated from the school grounds by a fence. Once past the school, turn sharply to the left to leave the trail, and to pass through a dirt parking lot. Continue onto Oso Road (paved).

Next, turn right onto Avenida de la Vista. This road is ridden in the opposite direction in Ride 31, The South OC BHC. Continue to the end of Avenida de la Vista, past the numerous multi-unit dwellings. Ride onto Trabuco Creek Trail (paved bike path). The path passes under Del Obispo Street, and then connects to San Juan Creek Trail (paved bike path) at mile 9.95. The two paths meet in a V, at the confluence of Trabuco and San Juan Creeks. Curve sharply to the left to ride around the horn of the V, and continue onto San Juan Creek Trail. This is the lowest elevation of the ride (58 feet).

Now on San Juan Creek Trail, pass under Camino Capistrano, and then I-5. The trail then empties onto Paseo Tirador, which is a dead-end street that seems to go nowhere. Do not stray too far from the walkway on your right. Near the end of Paseo Tirador, ride up onto the path; turn right onto Calle Arroyo (actually, stay on the path). After a few awkward driveway crossings, the path crosses La Novia—this is a stop sign–controlled intersection that is also a bit awkward. Once across La Novia, the path curves to the right, and then to the left before continuing eastward. The end of the ride comes as the path reaches the far eastern end of Cook's Park.

Bike Shops

Buy My Bikes, 32302 Camino Capistrano, San Juan Capistrano, (949) 493-5611, http://buymybikes.com

MILES AND DIRECTIONS

0.0 Exit Cook's Park Cordova; turn right onto the San Juan Creek Trail (paved bike path).

0.05 End of path; turn left onto Avenida Siega (paved road).

0.25 Stop sign at CA 74 (Ortega Highway); turn left (caution: narrow highway).

0.7 Ride up onto walkway along CA 74.

1.3 Veer right onto Belford-Marbella Trail.

1.35 Begin steep uphill (16.3% grade).

1.45 Crest of hill—trail has a few moguls.

1.55 Belford-Marbella Trail curves to the left.

1.65 Cross Calle de la Rosa (residential street)—begin 7.8% gradient climb.

1.75 Cross Paseo Bovedo.

1.8 Cross service road.

2.35 Trail curves to the right.

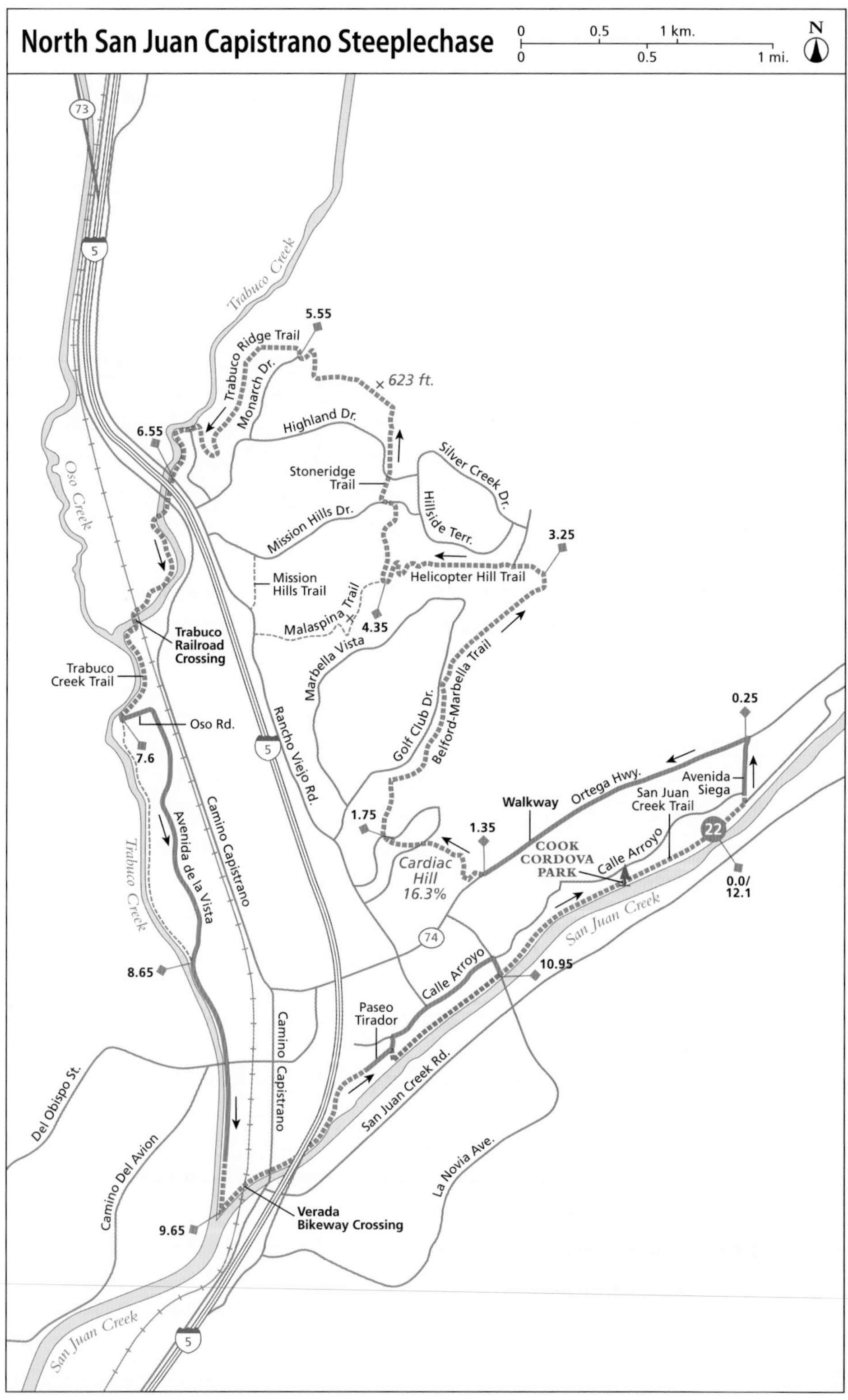
North San Juan Capistrano Steeplechase
0 0.5 1 km.
0 0.5 1 mi.
N
73
5
Trabuco Creek
5.55
Trabuco Ridge Trail
Monarch Dr.
623 ft.
Highland Dr.
6.55
Oso Creek
Stoneridge Trail
Silver Creek Dr.
Hillside Terr.
Mission Hills Dr.
3.25
Mission Hills Trail
Helicopter Hill Trail
Malaspina Trail
4.35
Trabuco Railroad Crossing
Trabuco Creek Trail
Marbella Vista
Belford-Marbella Trail
Golf Club Dr.
Rancho Viejo Rd.
Oso Rd.
7.6
0.25
Ortega Hwy.
Avenida Siega
San Juan Creek Trail
Walkway
1.75
1.35
Avenida de la Vista
Camino Capistrano
Trabuco Creek
Cardiac Hill 16.3%
COOK CORDOVA PARK
Calle Arroyo
22
0.0/ 12.1
San Juan Creek
74
8.65
10.95
Calle Arroyo
Paseo Tirador
Camino Capistrano
Del Obispo St.
San Juan Creek Rd.
La Novia Ave.
Camino Del Avion
9.65
Verada Bikeway Crossing
San Juan Creek

2.45 Keep straight onto trail—begin steady climb (4.6% grade).

2.9 Crest of climb (elevation 571 feet); cross service road—logs mark entry to trail.

3.05 Begin steep descent (17.7% grade).

3.15 Cross Golden Ridge Lane—continue steep descent (16.7% grade).

3.4 Bottom of descent—trail undulates and then bears right—now on Helicopter Hill Trail.

3.65 Begin descent (8.9% grade).

3.85 End of descent (elevation 208 feet); begin climb via switchbacks (10.1% grade).

4.35 Junction between Helicopter Hill, Malaspina and Stoneridge Trails; turn right onto Stoneridge Trail (elevation 492 feet).

4.8 Cross Highland Drive—begin climb (7.8% grade).

5.1 High elevation of entire ride (623 feet); begin steep descent (11.8% grade).

5.55 End of Stoneridge Trail at Monarch Drive; cross street and bear right.

5.6 Bear left onto Trabuco Ridge Trail; begin climb (9.6% grade).

5.75 Begin final descent on trails (6.4% grade).

6.55 End of Trabuco Ridge Trail at Rancho Mission Viejo Road bike path; turn right and cross bridge.

6.6 Turn sharply to the left, onto Trabuco Creek Trail (paved bike path).

6.75 Pass under I-5 freeway—end of pavement.

6.9 Cross Trabuco Creek (i.e., cross wash); curve left.

7.2 Pass under railroad bridge—trail curves to the right; ride along perimeter of school, next to fence.

7.6 Turn sharply to the left and leave trail; ride through dirt parking lot and continue onto Oso Road (paved road).

7.75 Turn right onto Avenida de la Vista (paved road).

8.65 Keep straight onto Trabuco Creek Trail (paved bike path).

9.1 Pass under Del Obispo Street.

9.65 Path curves sharply to the left at the confluence of Trabuco and San Juan Creeks; now on San Juan Creek Trail (paved bike path)—low elevation of ride (58 feet).

9.85 Pass under Camino Capistrano.

10.0 Pass under I-5 freeway.

10.4 Bike path empties onto Paseo Tirador (paved road).

10.55 Turn right, ride on paved walkway, which doubles as San Juan Creek Trail.

10.95 Cross La Novia (stop sign–controlled intersection); continue on bike path.

12.1 End of ride at Cook's Park Cordova.

Capistrano's Zorro

San Juan Capistrano may be most famous for the swallows, which have actually stopped making their famed return to the city, in favor of an inland alternative. In the search for an alternative claim to fame, perhaps the city need go no further than Johnston McCulley's (1883–1958) *The Curse of Capistrano*. Never heard of it? The story, originally published as a serial novel in 1919, was adapted for film in 1920. As the main character of the novel was Don Diego Vega, aka Señor Zorro, the adaptation, starring Douglas Fairbanks Jr., preferred the title *The Mark of Zorro*. Later, the novel adopted the new title, as did film offshoots (*Son of Zorro*, *Zorro Rides Again*), a Disney TV series, and other remakes and spinoffs. In other words, it was a hit! San Juan Capistrano was one of several "mission" towns that served as a setting for Zorro's swashbuckling adventures. The so-called "curse" of Capistrano seemed to be an allusion to general oppression of the general public by the colonial government and wealthy landowners. Corruption, brutality, and villainous actions were all thwarted by Zorro and his sword. As the *Capistrano Dispatch* (author unknown) put it, Zorro left his mark on Mission San Juan Capistrano!

23

Olimpiada Mission Viejo 12/24/2017

Start: Robert A. Curtis Park, 24460 Olympiad Rd., Mission Viejo

Length: 9.8 miles (clockwise loop)

Riding time: 30 to 90 minutes (my time: 37:34)

Terrain and surface: 100% paved roads

Elevations: Low—413 feet on La Paz Road over Oso Creek; high—943 feet at Vista del Lago and Canaveras Ridge Walk Trail (trailhead)

Traffic and hazards: Marguerite Parkway carried 29,100 vehicles per day near La Paz Road, and 19,200 vehicles per day near Olympiad Road; La Paz Road carried 17,000 vehicles per day near Marguerite Parkway; Olympiad Road carried up to 14,500 vehicles per day, all in 2014.

Map: *The Thomas Guide by Rand McNally—Street Guide: Los Angeles and Orange Counties* (any recent year), page 892

Getting there by car: From central Anaheim, head south on I-5. Exit at La Paz Drive and turn left, heading east on La Paz. At Olympiad Road, turn left and head north. Robert A. Curtis Park will be on the right.

Getting there by public transit: OCTA bus route 85 runs between Dana Point and Mission Viejo every 35 minutes on weekdays and every 90 minutes on Saturdays. Route 85 runs along Marguerite Parkway—exit at La Paz Road, and start the ride from there. OCTA bus route 86 runs between Costa Mesa and Mission Viejo every hour on weekdays. Exit the bus at Marguerite Parkway and La Paz Road; start the ride from there. OCTA bus route 87 runs between Laguna Niguel and Mission Viejo every hour Monday through Saturday. Exit the bus at Marguerite Parkway and Alicia Parkway, adjacent Lake Mission Viejo, and start the ride from there.

Starting point coordinates: 33.607861°N / 117.632839°W

THE RIDE

Olimpiada Mission Viejo retraces the route of the 1984 Summer Olympic Games cycling road races. Riding this route offers the rare opportunity to experience, and perhaps even relive, the legendary men's and women's races from the Games. The racers did multiple 9.8-mile laps, with the hills and heat wearing the competitors down. While the winning woman and man averaged 22.5 and 23.6 mph, respectively, the traffic signals, interference from motor vehicles—and perhaps the fact that you are not an Olympic-caliber athlete—prohibit the replication of such speeds today.

While the official Olympic start-finish was at Applegate Park, on the north side of Lake Mission Viejo on Olympiad Road, this ride starts at Robert A. Curtis Park, which is also on Olympiad, but farther south. Robert A. Curtis was a Mission Viejo councilman who, shortly after being elected in 1988, was served with recall papers for supporting the annexation of Aegean Hills. Voters soundly defeated the recall. Curtis served out his term, and then opted to not run for reelection. From the park, head south on Olympiad Road. This road, originally named Felipe Road, was renamed Olympiad between Marguerite Parkway and La Paz Road to commemorate the 1984 Games. Turn right on La Paz and head downhill. This is the fastest part of the route! La Paz speeds past residential areas, Oso Viejo Community Park, and a retail center. Just beyond the retail center, turn right onto Marguerite Parkway. The low elevation point of the ride (413 feet) was reached in crossing Oso Creek, just east of Marguerite. Marguerite climbs at a gradual 2.6% grade to Trabuco Road, then descends gradually, then climbs at 4.0% to Alicia Parkway.

Bike Shops

Rock N' Road Cyclery, 27825 Santa Margarita Pkwy., Mission Viejo, (949) 859-5076, www.rocknroadcyclery.net; Two Wheels One Planet, 24844 Muirlands Blvd., Lake Forest, (949) 581-8900, http://twowheelsoneplanet.com

Once across Alicia Parkway, to your right is scenic Lake Mission Viejo. This man-made, 124-acre lake was built for $10 million from private funds. If it is warm, then curb the desire to get off your bike and jump in the lake—it is private for residents only. As you ride past the lake, nearing Vista del Lago, move to the left lane, watching for motor vehicle traffic. Turn left onto Vista del Lago; I do not recall the left turn signal here being particularly sensitive to bicycles—perhaps a left-turning vehicle will trigger the signal for you. Alternatively, use the pedestrian signals.

Once on Vista del Lago, the reason behind the attrition in the men's Olympic road race becomes clear. The street climbs for a half-mile at a 7.9%

The medalists in the 1984 Olympic women's road race are on display at Lake Mission Viejo.

grade, cresting at the high point of the ride (943 feet) adjacent the Canaveras Ridge Walk trailhead. The descent from here is even steeper, at 11.4%. Grab the brakes and turn right onto Hidalgo, midway down the hill. Hidalgo makes a hard right at the 6-mile mark, becoming Crucero. At the end of Crucero, turn right onto Mustang Run. Next, turn right at the traffic signal onto Marguerite Parkway. Watch the street signs, and prepare to turn left onto Olympiad Road. You can execute this turn from the left-turn lane, or use the pedestrian signal to cross Marguerite. Once on Olympiad, Lake Mission Viejo will be on your right. The view across the lake is very European. Look for the commemorative monuments to the men's and women's Olympic road races on your right—they are easily missed. There are images from the competitions, along with brief stories. On your left, at mile 7.3, is Applegate Park, where the official start-finish of the race was located.

A little farther down Olympiad Road, at mile 7.65, is Florence Joyner Olympiad Park. Although "Flo-Jo" was on the 1984 Olympic team, winning a silver medal in the 200-meter run, it was at the 1988 Olympics in Seoul, South Korea, that she made lasting marks. Flo-Jo won three gold medals and a silver, setting world records during the 1988 season in two events. Flo-Jo died in her sleep, from an epileptic seizure, in 1998, at age 38. From here, Olympiad

1984 Summer Olympic Games Cycling

Although the now-discontinued team time trial of the 1984 Summer Olympic Games was held on the I-110 freeway (which was closed to motor vehicle traffic) right in the heart of L.A., the road races were held in relatively quiet Mission Viejo. In the men's event, 135 cyclists from forty-three nations set out for twelve laps of a 9.8-mile loop. Some 300,000 spectators lined the route. There was plenty of attrition on the hilly course, as only fifty-five riders finished. Among the non-finishers was future five-time Tour de France winner Miguel Indurain of Spain. In the lead heading into the last lap were Steve Bauer of Canada and Alexi Grewal of the United States. Two Norwegians, Dag-Otto Lauritzen and Morten Sæther, were chasing. Grewal had been suspended from the US team for a positive drug test just 10 days before the race. He made a successful appeal, though, and now was in position to medal. Bauer was the better sprinter, and most aficionados gave him the edge. After an apparent sign of weakness on the last lap, Grewal came around Bauer during the final kick for the gold medal. Lauritzen outsprinted his countryman for the bronze medal. Grewal's winning time of 4H59:57 represented an average speed of 23.6 mph.

The women made history, with forty-five riders participating in the first-ever women's Olympic cycling event, in the 49.2-mile road race—five laps of the same 9.8-mile route that the men rode. The men started at 1 p.m. on July 29, while the women started at a cooler 9 a.m. With the earlier start, the women did better than the men, with a 98% completion rate (only one rider did not finish)! A lead group of six broke away from the field. Maria Canins of Italy and Jeannie Longo of France bumped into each other with just 1 kilometer to go, removing them from contention. World champion Rebecca Twigg of the United States was heavily favored at this point, but upstart Connie Carpenter-Phinney would come around in the sprint for the win. Carpenter-Phinney was a former Olympic speed skater who was married to Davis Phinney; he would place fifth in the men's event. Twigg would go on to qualify for two more Olympic teams, although she withdrew from the 1996 team in a dispute over her bicycle. The women's winning time was 2H11:14, representing an average speed of 22.5 mph.

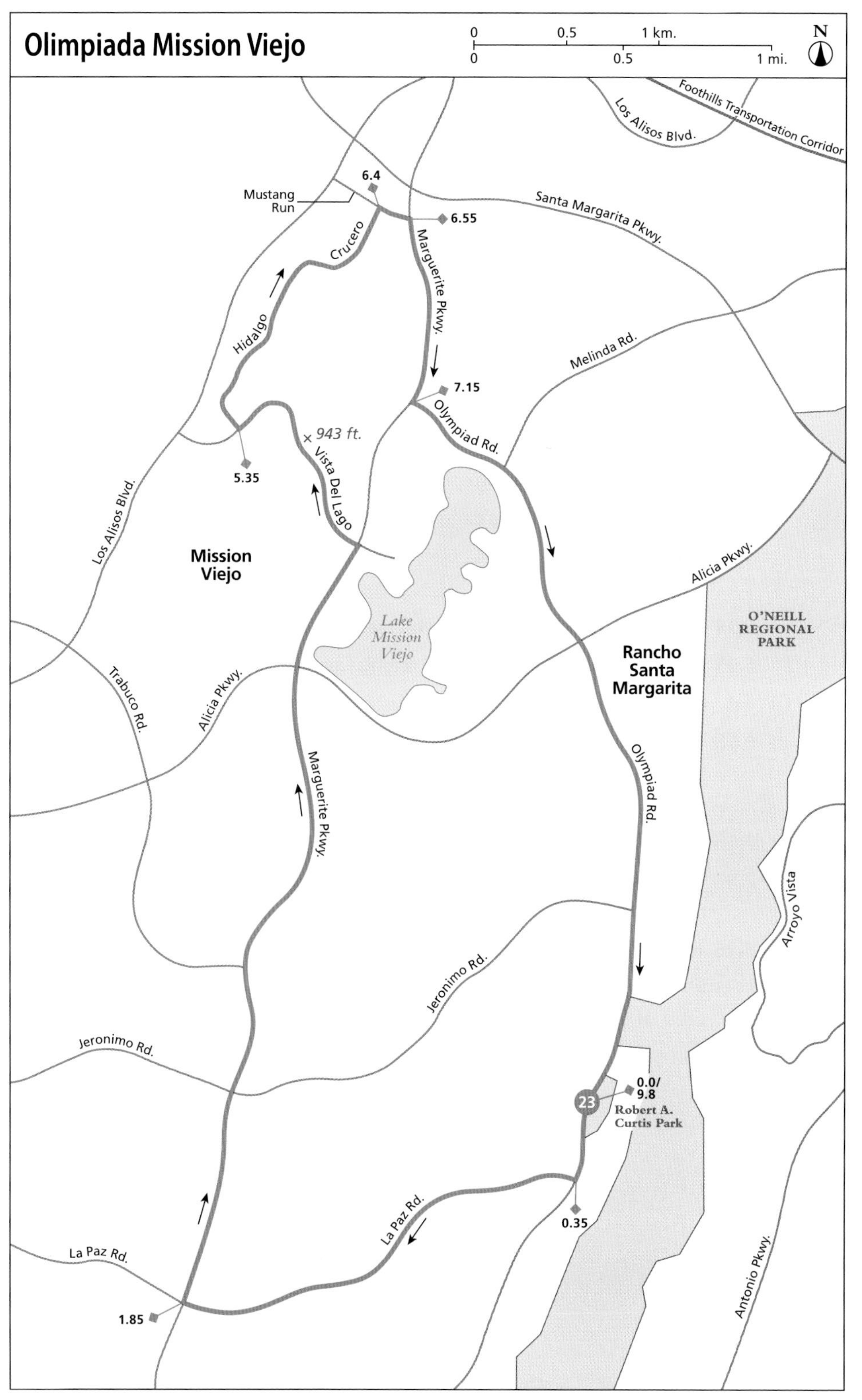

Olimpiada Mission Viejo
0
0.5
1 km.
0
0.5
1 mi.
N
Foothills Transportation Corridor
Los Alisos Blvd.
Santa Margarita Pkwy.
Mustang Run
6.4
6.55
Crucero
Marguerite Pkwy.
Hidalgo
Melinda Rd.
7.15
Olympiad Rd.
943 ft.
Vista Del Lago
5.35
Los Alisos Blvd.
Mission Viejo
Lake Mission Viejo
Alicia Pkwy.
O'NEILL REGIONAL PARK
Rancho Santa Margarita
Trabuco Rd.
Alicia Pkwy.
Marguerite Pkwy.
Olympiad Rd.
Arroyo Vista
Jeronimo Rd.
Jeronimo Rd.
23
0.0/ 9.8
Robert A. Curtis Park
La Paz Rd.
0.35
La Paz Rd.
Antonio Pkwy.
1.85

undulates, climbing to 822 feet at mile 8.0, descending to 795 feet at Alicia Parkway, climbing at a 4.0% grade to 874 feet at mile 8.6 (Stonegate), descending to Jeronimo Road (755 feet), and then climbing gradually to the finish at Robert A. Curtis Park (elevation 796 feet). Although the net elevation change on this route is 530 feet, the total amount of climbing is over 725 feet, making it a challenging ride for any Olympian!

MILES AND DIRECTIONS

0.0 Exit Robert A. Curtis Park (24660 Olympiad Rd., Mission Viejo); turn left and head south on Olympiad Road.

0.35 Traffic signal at La Paz Road; turn right—begin descent.

1.75 Bridge over Oso Creek; low elevation of ride (413 feet).

1.85 Traffic signal at Marguerite Parkway; turn right.

4.6 Traffic signal at Vista del Lago; turn left—begin climb at 7.9% grade.

5.1 High elevation of ride (943 feet) near Canaveras Ridge Walk Trail trailhead.

5.35 Turn right onto Hidalgo and head north.

6.05 Hidalgo curves to the right, becoming Crucero.

6.4 End of Crucero; turn right onto Mustang Run and head east.

6.55 Traffic signal at Marguerite Parkway; turn right and head south. Lake Mission Viejo is on the right, including commemorative Olympic road race plaque and image.

7.15 Traffic signal at Olympiad Road; turn left.

7.3 Applegate Park is on the left (official start-finish point of Olympic road races).

8.25 Traffic signal at Alicia Parkway; keep straight—begin climb at 4.0% grade.

8.6 Crest of climb at Stoneridge.

9.8 End of ride at Robert A. Curtis Park, on your left.

24

Riley Five Miley

Start: Thomas F. Riley Wilderness Park, 30952 Oso Pkwy., Trabuco Canyon

Length: 4.65 miles (counterclockwise loop plus an out-and-back segment)

Riding time: 20 minutes to 1.25 hours (my time: 32:27)

Terrain and surface: 100% dirt trails, walkways and driveways

Elevations: Low—429 feet at southern end of South Wagon Wheel Canyon Trail; high—749 feet at Vista Point along Horned Toad Trail

Traffic and hazards: 100% of the ride is off-road (no motor vehicles). There are four residential street crossings; traffic volumes are low at the crossings.

Map: *The Thomas Guide by Rand McNally—Street Guide: Los Angeles and Orange Counties* (any recent year), page 923

Getting there by car: From central Anaheim, take I-5 southbound to Oso Parkway. Exit and turn left on Oso. Follow Oso to its end, adjacent the (gated) Wagon Wheel and Coto de Caza communities. Turn right into Thomas F. Riley Wilderness Park, just west of South Bend Road. Follow the (dirt) entrance road to the parking area.

Getting there by public transit: Ride OCTA bus route 82 from Saddleback College in Mission Viejo to Oso Parkway and Antonio Parkway. From here, it is a 3-mile ride eastward, along Oso Parkway, to Thomas F. Riley Wilderness Park. The bus was running every 50 to 70 minutes on weekdays and every 100 minutes on Saturdays.

Starting point coordinates: 33.572656°N / 117.592833°W

THE RIDE

The Riley Five Miley is a nifty mountain bike ride that loops through Thomas F. Riley Wilderness Park, with a short (1.3-mile) out-and-back on a trail through the exclusive Coto de Caza community. The ride is an excellent outing for a

Ready to descend Oak Canyon Trail, with a Coto de Caza backdrop, in Riley Wilderness Park

beginner mountain biker, although a few of the route's challenges are suitable for an experienced or expert rider. The challenges include some short, steep climbs, a dry creek crossing, and a steep descent on an eroded trail. The ride is a wee bit short of 5 miles, at 4.65. A speedy and/or fit rider might want to complete the route two or three times.

Riley Wilderness Park covers 544 acres in southeastern Orange County. The terrain features rolling hills of grassland and coastal sage scrub, and groves of Western Sycamore and Coast Live Oak trees. The park is a wildlife sanctuary, so there is some animal life, along with several species of native plant. The area was formerly used for pheasantry. Some old pheasantry "facilities" still exist, as seen in the park, although research has been unable to determine how some of those facilities were used! Thomas F. Riley (1912–1998) was a brigadier general who served in the US Marine Corps for 29 years. He later served for 30 years on the Orange County Board of Supervisors. He was born in Virginia, passed away in Orange County, and was laid to rest in Arlington National Cemetery.

Start the ride in the parking area, and head northeast, toward the trailhead, onto Wagon Wheel Canyon Trail. The starting elevation is 533 feet. This trail parallels Oso Parkway, which is to your right, although you are worlds away from the motor vehicles. The trail climbs gently; there may be some rough sections. Watch the signs for Pheasant Run Trail, at mile 0.35. Bear left here (Wagon Wheel Canyon Trail continues to the right, ultimately ending at Oso Parkway). Please note that during a re-ride of the route, a segment of Pheasant Run was closed, adjacent the trail junction, possibly because of erosion or a failed bridge. To get to Pheasant Run, I rode around the closed-off area counterclockwise, then turned right onto the trail. Follow Pheasant Run Trail as it winds into the grove, across a typically dry creek bed, and up the opposite bank to continue. There may be water in the creek seasonally. Note the pheasantry setup to your left, at mile 0.5. Wording on a nearby sign speculates on how the wooden structure was used. The trail climbs the hillside, across the open grassland, to an elevation of 630 feet before descending to 559 feet, and then climbing again to 622 feet. Turn right onto Mule Deer Trail at mile 1.0. The next stretch of climbing is at an 8.2% grade, taking you up to 717 feet.

At the end of Mule Deer, turn left onto Vista Ridge Trail, and then make an immediate right onto Oak Canyon Trail. This trail begins with a descent that starts gently, and then drops steeply into a narrow canyon. The climb out of the canyon is at a 15.2% grade—the climb is about 150 feet long, so those of you with good momentum (and/or the leg strength) may be able to charge your way to the top. Oak Canyon bends 90 degrees to the left at the crest, and then descends at a 4.5% grade to the next junction, at mile 1.65. Here, turn right onto Horned Toad Trail. This narrow trail climbs to the high point of the ride—Horned Toad Vista Point (elevation 749 feet)—at a gradient of 10.9%. After pausing to take in the view, or catch your breath, Horned Toad descends rapidly (13.1% grade). Most of the descent was eroded when I did this ride, so be careful in choosing a line. Turn right at the bottom of the descent (mile 2.05), back onto Oak Canyon Trail. Enjoy the fast descent, as well as the shaded segment. At the next junction, bear right, onto Sycamore Loop. This trail simply returns to Oak Canyon Trail just a quarter-mile downstream. Once you are back on Oak Canyon, follow it for just over 0.1 mile, and then turn right onto South Wagon Wheel Canyon Trail.

Bike Shops

Performance Bicycle, 2745 El Camino Real (The Market Place), Tustin, (714) 838-0641, www.performancebike.com/bike-shop/store/tustin; The Path Bike Shop Live Oak, 30555 Trabuco Canyon Rd., Trabuco Canyon, (949) 589-2800, www.thepathbikeshop.com

The next portion of the route is out-and-back. Technically, this segment is part of Riley Wilderness Park, although the experience is that of leaving the park, and then returning. The primary message on the signs at the passable gateways along this trail is "stay on the trail," and avoid straying into the adjacent, private community. Cross Sandy Knoll (residential street); follow the crosswalk to remain on the trail. The next street crossing is Vela Court. Beyond here, South Wagon Wheel Canyon continues for 0.3 mile, then comes to an end (fence and gate) adjacent a large retention basin. Turn around here and return to Sandy Knoll. At Sandy Knoll, turn right, and then bear left onto the dirt trail that parallels South Bend Road. This road is one of the main Coto de Caza entrance roads. In fact, you will pass by an entrance station, which is for motor vehicles. Follow the trail to Oso Parkway. Turn left here, remaining on the walkway/trail. After about 200 feet, turn left into Riley Wilderness Park. This was the way you entered the park upon arrival. Return to parking area, where you started, via the dirt entrance road. How do you feel about another lap?

MILES AND DIRECTIONS

0.0 Leave the Riley Wilderness Park parking area, to the north, via Wagon Wheel Canyon Trail (elevation 533 feet).

0.35 Bear left onto Pheasant Run Trail.

0.4 Dry creek crossing (elevation 589 feet).

Coto de Caza Tidbits

The Riley Five Miley skirts the edges of Coto de Caza, which is a gated community in the southeastern Orange County foothills. Orange County is a haven for planned communities, and Coto de Caza, with a population of 14,866 in 2010, is one of the larger ones. Coto de Caza was originally established in 1968 as a hunting resort and lodge, but expanded to include tract housing, custom-built houses, tennis clubs, two golf courses, and extensive roadway and trails networks. Both Coto de Caza and Riley Wilderness Park abut mountain lion habitats, and there have been a few, rare sightings of these animals over the years. The community is probably most known from *The Real Housewives of Orange County*, although filming is done elsewhere. Coto de Caza is in the annals of sports history, having hosted four of the five events of the modern pentathlon during the 1984 Summer Olympic Games. (The modern pentathlon includes horseback riding, fencing, swimming, shooting, and running—only the swimming was not held at Coto de Caza. No bicycling, unfortunately.) Italian athletes won the gold and bronze medals, and easily won the team competition.

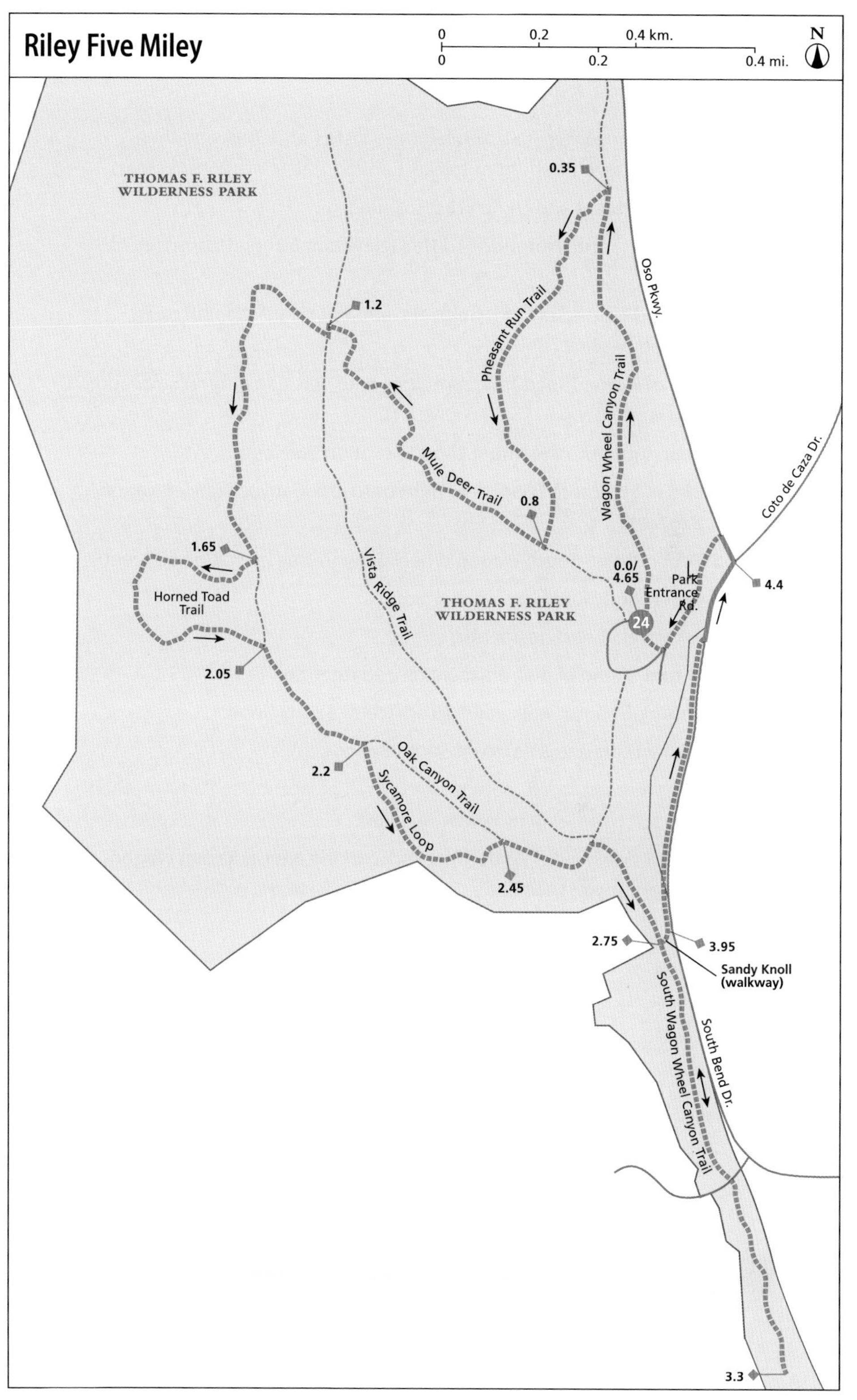
Riley Five Miley
0
0.2
0.4 km.
0
0.2
0.4 mi.
N
THOMAS F. RILEY
WILDERNESS PARK
0.35
1.2
Pheasant Run Trail
Oso Pkwy.
Wagon Wheel Canyon Trail
Mule Deer Trail
0.8
Coto de Caza Dr.
1.65
Horned Toad
Trail
Vista Ridge Trail
THOMAS F. RILEY
WILDERNESS PARK
0.0/
4.65
Park
Entrance
Rd.
24
4.4
2.05
2.2
Oak Canyon Trail
Sycamore Loop
2.45
2.75
3.95
Sandy Knoll
(walkway)
South Wagon Wheel Canyon Trail
South Bend Dr.
3.3

0.8 End of Pheasant Run Trail; turn right onto Mule Deer Trail (elevation 559 feet).

1.2 End of Mule Deer Trail; turn left onto Vista Ridge Trail, and then immediately turn right onto Oak Canyon Trail (elevation 717 feet).

1.25 Steep descent and climb (15.2% grade).

1.65 Turn right onto Horned Toad Trail (elevation 621 feet); climb at 10.9% grade.

1.85 Horned Toad Vista Point (high elevation of ride: 749 feet); steep, eroded descent.

2.05 End of Horned Toad Trail; turn right onto Oak Canyon Trail (elevation 630 feet).

2.2 Bear right onto Sycamore Loop (elevation 568 feet).

2.45 End of Sycamore Loop; bear right onto Oak Canyon Trail (elevation 526 feet).

2.55 Turn right on South Wagon Wheel Canyon Trail (elevation 507 feet).

2.75 Cross Sandy Knoll (residential street).

3.05 Cross Vela Court (residential street).

3.3 U-turn at end of trail, adjacent fenced retention basin.

3.9 Turn right onto (walkway/trail adjacent) Sandy Knoll.

3.95 Bear left onto trail adjacent South Bend Road.

4.4 Continue to the left, onto walkway/trail adjacent Oso Parkway, then turn left to enter Riley Wilderness Park.

4.65 End of ride in Riley Wilderness Park parking area, adjacent Wagon Wheel Canyon trailhead.

25

Ring around San Clemente

Start: San Clemente City Beach, adjacent North El Camino Real and Avenida Pico, San Clemente

Length: 21.05 miles (clockwise loop)

Riding time: 2 to 5 hours (my time: 2H31:25)

Terrain and surface: 70% dirt trails, 26% paved roads, 4% concrete walkway

Elevations: Low—18 feet at San Clemente City Beach; high—733 feet on Forster Ridge Trail

Traffic and hazards: Camino de los Mares carried 17,000 vehicles per day north of Avenida Vaquero in 2014; Avenida Vaquero carried 9,000 vehicles per day north of Camino Capistrano in 2014.

Map: *The Thomas Guide by Rand McNally—Street Guide: Los Angeles and Orange Counties* (any recent year), page 971

Getting there by car: From central Anaheim, head south on I-5. Exit at Avenida Pico in San Clemente. Turn right on Avenida Pico, and travel to the ocean. Park in the area south of the train station.

Getting there by public transit: Ride Metrolink (commuter rail) to San Clemente. The station is at San Clemente City Beach. Service is irregular, though; OCTA bus route 1 runs between Long Beach or Newport Beach and San Clemente along PCH, stopping at Avenida Pico, adjacent the beach. Route 1 runs every 35 minutes (from Newport Beach to San Clemente; every 60 minutes from Long Beach) on weekends and every 60 minutes on weekends and holidays.

Starting point coordinates: 33.432342°N / 117.632972°W

THE RIDE

Most of this ride (70%) is on dirt trails, although the opening portion is on city streets. Start the ride at San Clemente City Beach. While the beach and ocean may be tempting, save them for the end of the ride. Head north on Avenida

Estacion to the traffic signal at El Camino Real; turn left and continue heading north. A bike shop is conveniently located on the corner. After the turn, you have the option of riding on the road's shoulder, on the left side of the Jersey barrier, or on the two-way path on the right side of the barrier. The barrier extends for about a half-mile, and then you are back on the road's shoulder, in a bike lane. Turn right at the second traffic signal, onto Camino Capistrano, followed by another right onto Avenida Vaquero. There is a DMV office on your right, so watch out for brand-new drivers! Continue straight on Avenida Vaquero. The road climbs (3.0% grade) as you head inland. Pass under I-5 at mile 1.85 (no ramps). After one last effort to climb past Shorecliffs Golf Club, turn right onto Camino de los Mares. Use the main road's shoulder rather than the frontage road. Ride Camino de los Mares to its end (mile 4.15); dismount, negotiate the barriers, and continue onto North Los Mares Trail.

You are now on the city trails system, which will take you from the northwest to the northeast side of San Clemente. It is a rude introduction, as North Las Mares climbs at a 11.0% grade to start things off. Turn right onto Forster Ridge Trail (very first trail junction), and head downhill. Cross the dam (short paved segment), and then bear right, back onto the trail. Follow the trail as it makes a hard right; resume climbing. After curving to the left, the climbing becomes steep (13.6% grade) before easing to an average 10% grade. The first crest is at an elevation of 586 feet (mile 5.3), with a great view of the city. Forster Ridge jogs right, and then left, to move away from the Prima Deshecha Landfill perimeter. After a short respite, climbing resumes (10.5% grade), taking you to the highest elevation of the ride (733 feet; mile 5.7). The trails up here are barren, giving you unobstructed views of the hills, the city, and the ocean in the distance. The trail hovers around 700 feet of elevation to mile 6.1, where there is a junction. Stay right to continue on Forster Ridge. As of this writing, the trail heading to the left, Cristianitos, was closed for the construction of La Pata Road.

Forster Ridge descends quickly (9.3% grade) to a saddle before climbing steeply (11.7% grade). At the fork, in the middle of the climb, go either left or right, although the right path may be easier. The two paths merge at mile 6.85; stay to the right at the next split. Next, stay to the left, and then bear left to remain on Forster Ridge. (The right path descends into the adjacent neighborhood.) At the T-junction (mile 7.2), turn right. Forster Ridge Trail hovers around 600 feet of elevation before descending sharply (9.8% grade) to the end of the trail. The end of the trail is the walkway of Avenida Vista Hermosa (paved road). Turn sharply to the left, and ride along the walkway. The walkway passes a Target store, and then descends to an intersection with La Pata Road. You are now at mile 8.8 (elevation 353 feet). Your "target" is the

A rider crests a short climb on San Onofre State Beach singletrack, nowhere near the beach.

diagonally opposite corner, so cross La Pata, and then Vista Hermosa (or vice versa). Once on the opposite corner, head off-road, onto Prima Deshecha Trail.

Prima Deshecha scoots across an undeveloped space before plunging into a canyon. The final descent to the bottom of the canyon is steep (13.0% grade), coming after crossing a paved access road. There is some golf activity down here, as well as a small dam, around which the trail winds. Climb out of the small canyon on the other side (8.4% grade); follow the signs to stay on the trail, and to not venture onto a San Diego Gas & Electric (SDGE) access trail. After passing through a tree-lined stretch, adjacent a San Clemente neighborhood, Prima Deshecha comes to the intersection between Avenida Pico and Avenida Vista Hermosa (mile 10.0). Cross Avenida Pico in the crosswalk, and then turn right to continue on Prima Deshecha. After paralleling the road for a stretch, the trail turns left and heads inland, into the hills. There are numerous spur trails that lead to SDGE facilities. Watch the signs to avoid diverting onto a spur, and watch out for maintenance vehicles. Be sure to stay on the through trail, although some of the spurs appear to be through trails! Your prevailing direction is north. At mile 10.8, after a split, the trail climbs (8.3% grade)—elevation 499 feet. After an undulation, Prima Deshecha descends (9.2% grade), and then curves to the right. You are now at mile 11.85 (elevation 271 feet). Coming out of the curve, you are now heading south and—whoa! The next hill is a steep one (17.2% grade). Grind to the top, and keep straight to the next junction.

At the junction, bear left; you are now leaving Prima Deshecha Trail and are riding onto Ancestors' Trail. Welcome to San Onofre State Beach (SOSB)! Huh? Where's the beach? Well, SOSB is somewhat unusual—for a beach—in that the property extends well inland, to areas nowhere near the ocean. You may occasionally hear the sounds of weaponry and maneuvers coming from Camp Pendleton on the left. There are numerous spur trails within SOSB, making it somewhat of a challenge to stay on the correct trail. A map is posted at the junction—you may want to study it for a while, although spur trails are not shown. In general, from the junction (mile 12.05), Ancestors' Trail descends (8.9% grade) and then climbs (6.9% grade)—stay to the left near the top of the ascent (mile 12.75). Keep straight at the next two junctions. Bear right at the junction at mile 13.25 (elevation 508 feet).

You are now on Peaceful Valley Trail. Keep straight at the next two junctions, and then stay to the right at the next two junctions. You may notice that you want to stay "on the bench" rather than taking any trail that descends for an extended stretch. Keep straight at the next two junctions. At mile 14.35, make a hard right for another steep climb (20.4% grade). You are now on an unnamed firebreak. When this trail descends, stay with it (9.8% grade). The break nears Cristianitos Road. But as you close in on the road, look for the unnamed singletrack trail on the right (mile 15.3—elevation 165 feet). Turn right—there, again, are plenty of spurs. In general, stay parallel to the road, and avoid straying inland (except at one fork, where the left fork clearly heads to the road—stay to the right here). This is a fun, not-too-technical singletrack, but will be challenging for beginners. There is a narrow wooden bridge crossing—put a foot down if you are unsure of your balance and skills. After winding your way along the hillside, with numerous ups and downs, and probably traveling twice as far as you would have had you taken the road, the track widens (mile 15.8). The trail merges with one coming in from the right—keep straight.

Bike Shops

Bicycles San Clemente, 1900 North El Camino Real, San Clemente, (949) 492-5737, http://urbanbicycleoutfitters.com; Cycle Werks, 1421 North El Camino Real, San Clemente, (949) 492-5911, http://cyclewerks.net

The unnamed trail, which is again a firebreak, curves toward the hills, and then makes a couple of left turns to return you to the road. As you near the road, curve left to negotiate a maintenance facility. The trail finally empties out onto Cristianitos Road at mile 16.9. Ride on the shoulder for a quarter-mile.

Look for the guardrail to appear on the right. Head behind the guardrail, onto the unnamed singletrack trail. The trail widens after a short stretch. At the end of the trail, which is marked by some large boulders, jump the curb and continue on the road. San Clemente Golf Club is on the right; you are now on Avenida San Luis Rey (mile 17.45). The road curves to the left, and then crosses El Camino Real (signalized). After crossing the I-5 freeway, and then Avenida del Presidente, ride onto the walkway. Next, enter San Clemente State Beach—there is a pedestrian-bicycle access that is immediately adjacent. Turn right onto Butterfly Trail, which is a short but sweet trail through the facility.

At the end of Butterfly, turn right to continue on the park road. Ride past the entry kiosk, and descend to Avenida Calafia (mile 18.25). Turn left, and head toward the ocean. After taking a counterclockwise half-lap around the

Surfing Capital of the World

While Huntington Beach stakes a claim to "Surf City," San Clemente declares itself to be the "Surfing Capital of the World." In truth, San Clemente has a strong surfing tradition, with Trestles—a collection of well-known surfing spots—located just to the south of the city's border. A number of surfing champions are either natives or residents. Several surfing journals are published in the city, including *Surfing*, *Surfer's Journal*, and *Longboard*. San Clemente High School had won the scholastic National Surfing Championship in six of the previous seven years, as of this writing. There are also a number of surfboard makers and builders in town. I lived in San Clemente for a while, and it seemed as if everyone, except me, surfed.

While surfing may represent San Clemente's character, the city's official slogan is "Spanish Village by the Sea." The name portends a quiet, Mediterranean-style coastal resort town. While President Richard Nixon had roots in Yorba Linda (please see Ride 14, Yorba on Your Bike), he also had significant San Clemente ties during his presidential and post-presidential years. The unofficial "Western White House," also known as Casa Pacifica, was located in San Clemente, very near Trestles. The retreat was visited by numerous world leaders during Mr. Nixon's presidency, including Soviet premier Leonid Brezhnev, Mexican president Gustavo Diaz Ordaz, and Japanese prime minister Eisaku Sato. Following his resignation, Mr. Nixon spent time at Casa Pacifica writing his memoirs. And long before President Nixon entered politics, President Franklin D. Roosevelt spent some time on the property, playing cards with one of his cronies.

parking lot, turn right, and then right again to access San Clemente Beach Trail. The beach and railroad tracks are immediately to your left. The beach trail is heavily used by walkers and joggers, as well as surfers (many of whom sprint across the trail, heading for the waves). Although the trail is mostly flat, and potentially fast, control your speed along here. There are some wooden bridges along the trail, at least one of which required a dismount as of this writing. A dismount is also required in the immediate vicinity of San Clemente Pier (mile 19.85). The trail crosses active railroad tracks at miles 19.45 and 20.05. After the last railroad crossing, it is exactly 1 more mile to the end of the trail, and the end of the ride. Now, how about ditching the bike and heading down to the beach?

MILES AND DIRECTIONS

0.0 From San Clemente City Beach, head north on Avenida Estacion. Starting elevation: 18 feet (lowest elevation of the ride).

0.05 Traffic signal; turn left onto El Camino Real (coastal highway).

0.1 Veer right onto bike path that parallels road (or ride on road's shoulder).

0.55 End of bike path—continue in bike lane along El Camino Real.

0.95 Traffic signal at Camino Capistrano; turn right.

1.05 Traffic signal at Avenida Vaquero; turn right.

1.85 Pass under I-5 freeway.

2.35 Traffic signal at Camino de los Mares; turn right.

4.15 End of Camino de los Mares—continue onto North Los Mares Trail (dirt)—begin climb (11.0% grade).

4.4 Turn right onto Forster Ridge Trail; head downhill (6.8% grade).

4.55 Cross dam; bear right, and then make a hard right.

4.7 Forster Ridge rail curves to the left—begin steep climb (13.0% grade).

4.8 Trail curves to the right—gradient eases slightly (9.7% climb).

5.3 Turn right and then left to continue on Forster Ridge Trail; continue ascent (10.5% grade).

5.7 Highest elevation of ride (733 feet).

6.1 Junction; turn right to continue on Forster Ridge Trail—begin steep descent (9.3% grade).

6.5 End of descent; begin climb (12.3% grade).

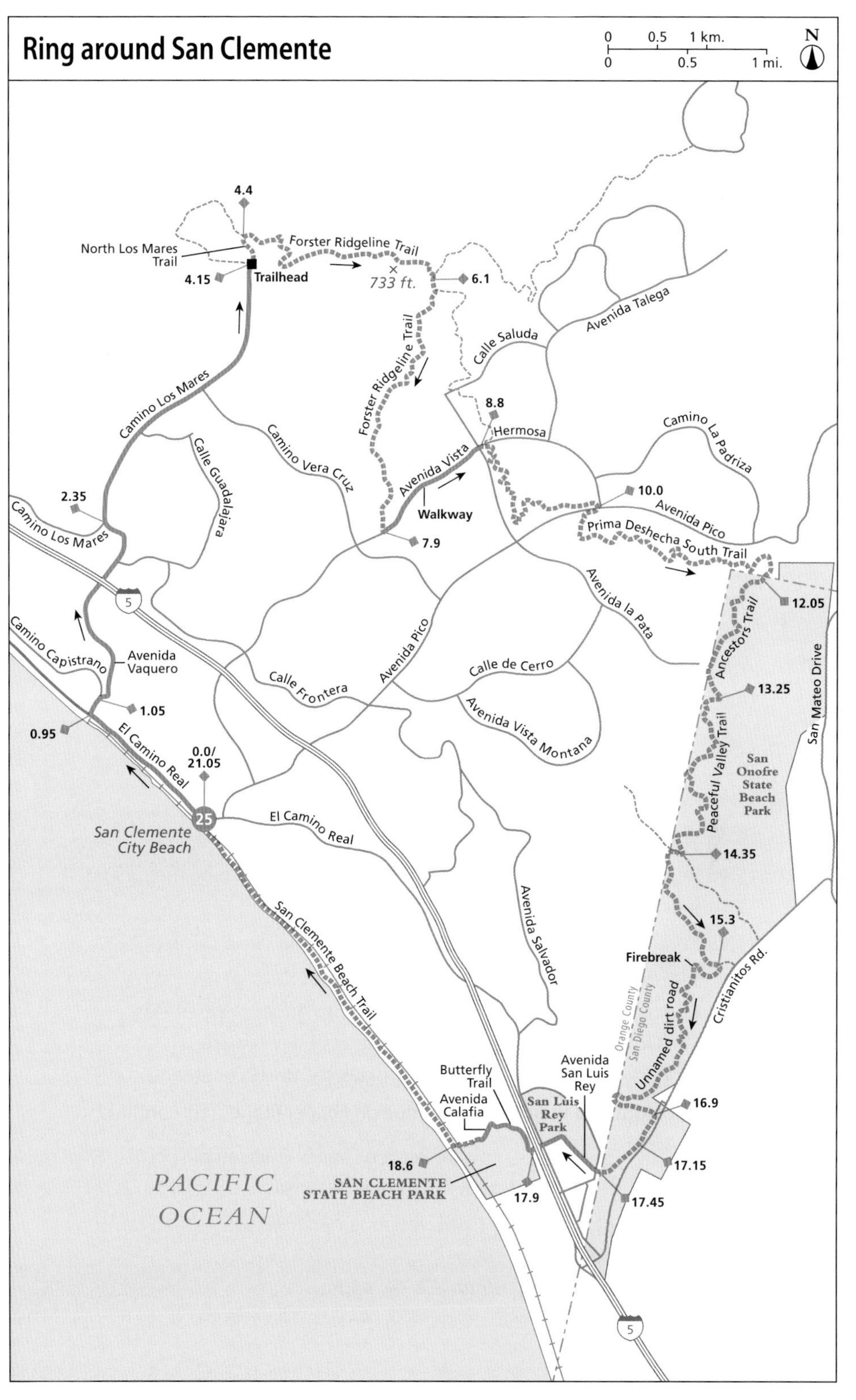

Ring around San Clemente
0
0.5
1 km.
0
0.5
1 mi.
N
4.4
North Los Mares Trail
Forster Ridgeline Trail
4.15
Trailhead
733 ft.
6.1
Avenida Talega
Calle Saluda
Forster Ridgeline Trail
Camino Los Mares
8.8
Hermosa
Camino La Padriza
Calle Guadalajara
Camino Vera Cruz
Avenida Vista
Walkway
10.0
Avenida Pico
Prima Deshecha South Trail
2.35
Camino Los Mares
7.9
5
Avenida la Pata
12.05
Ancestors Trail
Camino Capistrano
Avenida Vaquero
Avenida Pico
Calle de Cerro
San Mateo Drive
Calle Frontera
13.25
1.05
0.95
El Camino Real
Avenida Vista Montana
Peaceful Valley Trail
San Onofre State Beach Park
0.0/ 21.05
25
El Camino Real
San Clemente City Beach
14.35
Avenida Salvador
San Clemente Beach Trail
15.3
Firebreak
Cristianitos Rd.
Orange County
San Diego County
Unnamed dirt road
Butterfly Trail
Avenida Calafia
Avenida San Luis Rey
San Luis Rey Park
16.9
18.6
17.15
PACIFIC OCEAN
SAN CLEMENTE STATE BEACH PARK
17.9
17.45
5

6.6 Fork in trail—stay to the right; continue climbing (11.2% grade).

6.85 Begin series of junctions: Stay right, then left, then left, and then right, to remain on Forster Ridge Trail.

7.4 T-junction; turn right to continue on Forster Ridge.

7.55 Begin downhill on 9.8% grade.

7.9 End of Forster Ridge Trail; turn sharply to the right to ride along walkway adjacent Avenida Vista Hermosa.

8.05 Begin downhill (3.3% grade).

8.5 Target store on the left.

8.8 End of walkway path at signalized intersection between La Pata Road and Avenida Vista Hermosa. Cross both streets (one and then the other); once on diagonally opposite corner, continue onto Prima Deshecha Trail—begin descent into canyon.

9.1 Cross road used to access golfing facility—keep straight; steep descent to bottom of canyon (13.0% grade).

9.2 Bottom of canyon; wind around dam, and then climb out of canyon (8.4% grade).

9.6 Stay to the left at split in trail.

10.0 Traffic signal at Avenida Pico; cross road, and then turn right to continue on Prima Deshecha.

10.3 Trail curves to the left; stay right and then left at upcoming splits in trail.

10.8 Stay right at split in trail; begin climb (8.3% grade).

11.45 Begin descent (9.2% grade)—keep straight at upcoming merge and junction.

11.85 Prima Deshecha Trail curves to the right; begin steep climb (17.2% grade).

12.05 End of Prima Deshecha Trail; bear left onto Ancestors' Trail—enter San Onofre State Beach, and begin descent (8.9% grade).

12.3 End of descent; begin climb (6.9% grade).

12.75 Gradient eases; stay to the left.

13.25 Junction; stay right—now on Peaceful Valley Trail; remain on "bench"—avoid taking spur trails that descend.

14.35 Turn sharply to the right; now on unnamed firebreak—steep climb (20.4% grade).

14.45 Crest of climb; begin descent (9.8% grade).

15.3 Turn right onto unnamed singletrack trail, near end of firebreak.

15.85 End of singletrack—trail widens; now on unnamed firebreak.

16.35 Stay left, and then left again to head toward road.

16.6 Turn left to negotiate maintenance facility.

16.9 End of fire break at Cristianitos Road; turn right to ride along road's shoulder.

17.15 Leave road to the right, head behind guardrail onto unnamed singletrack trail.

17.25 Trail widens.

17.45 End of trail; jump curb and enter roadway (Avenida San Luis Rey)—keep straight.

17.75 Avenida San Luis Rey curves to the left, adjacent golf course.

17.85 Traffic signal at El Camino Real.

17.9 Stop sign at Avenida del Presidente; keep straight and ride onto walkway—then enter San Clemente State Beach (camping area).

17.95 Bear right onto Butterfly Trail (dirt).

18.05 End of trail; turn right onto park road.

18.25 Stop sign at Avenida Calafia; turn left.

18.4 Enter San Clemente State Beach parking area; stay right to loop the lot.

18.6 Leave parking area by turning right onto path toward beach, and then right again onto San Clemente Beach Trail (dirt).

18.8 Wooden bridge (dismount).

19.45 Cross railroad tracks.

19.85 San Clemente Pier area (dismount).

20.05 Cross railroad tracks.

20.35 Long wooden bridge (OK to ride).

21.05 End of ride at end of trail, at San Clemente City Beach.

26

Ronald Caspers Wild Ride

Start: Ronald Caspers Wilderness Park, 33401 Ortega Hwy. (CA 74), San Juan Capistrano (Orange County)

Length: 11.95 miles (counterclockwise loop)

Riding time: 1.5 to 4 hours (my time: 1H51:59)

Terrain and surface: 90% dirt trails, 10% paved park roads

Elevations: Low—382 feet on Caspers Park Road; high—1,622 feet on North Bell Spur

Traffic and hazards: 100% of the ride is within a park, with 90% on dirt trails (no motor vehicles).

Map: *The Thomas Guide by Rand McNally—Street Guide: Los Angeles and Orange Counties* (any recent year), page 924

Getting there by car: From central Anaheim, head south on I-5. Exit at CA 74 (Ortega Highway), and turn left. Continue past Antonio Parkway. Watch for the signing for Ronald Caspers Wilderness Park. Turn left and enter the park (fee); park in the first available lot, just off of Caspers Park Road.

Getting there by public transit: There is no public transportation service to Ronald Caspers Wilderness Park. Riding to the park on CA 74 is not recommended. The only bicycle access to the park is from the north, via trails.

Starting point coordinates: 33.537267°N / 117.550225°W

THE RIDE

The aptly titled Ronald Caspers Wild Ride is entirely within Ronald Caspers Wilderness Park. Once the massive climb to the high elevation of the route is conquered, the ride truly does get wild, with a long descent on rugged terrain, followed by a gradual descent on a rock-strewn trail. Both of these segments—in fact, the entire route—will find you dodging mini trail hazards and searching for the best line. It is a great route for someone with some mountain

A rider races along Bell Canyon Trail in Ronald Caspers Wilderness Park—yes, he actually is racing, Expert Class, in a local competition.

biking experience—the ride may be a bit too gnarly and challenging for a beginner.

Start from the parking area nearest the entrance to Ronald Caspers Wilderness Park; that is, to the right as one enters the park. Head for the trailhead at the end of the lot, which puts you on San Juan Creek Trail. From a starting elevation of 391 feet, the trail climbs gradually. The trail parallels CA 74 (Ortega Highway), which is to your right. San Juan Creek Trail crosses a couple of rock-strewn washes (San Juan Creek, which is normally dry) at miles 0.95 and 2.75. The rocks and general trail erosion are thick in a few places, adding to the challenges of this ride. After the second wash, the trail climbs at an 8.3% incline for about a quarter-mile. From the crest, the trail descends slightly to the junction with Oso Trail.

Turn left onto Oso Trail, now at an elevation of 625 feet (mile 3.7), and start the long climb to the crest that you see well off in the distance. The climb is relentless, and rugged, with an average grade of 9.4%. You have reached an elevation of 1,559 feet at the junction with Cold Springs Trail (mile 5.55); keep straight on Oso Trail. The trail continues to climb, then eases for about a half-mile before kicking up again. The last kick is a doozy, with a gradient of 18.7%, taking you to the highest elevation of the ride (1,622 feet). You can almost see forever up here, but chances are your eyes will be glued to the trail. The trail starts to descend immediately (7.8% grade, then increasing to 11.5%).

Hold onto those handlebars! This is why it is a "wild" ride. You can pick your way down the hill, being ever selective of your line (like me), or you can just let it go, like a downhill skier—whatever suits your comfort and skills. Bear right at mile 8.05 to remain on Oso Trail, as the descent continues (5.1% grade). The trail starts to bottom out at mile 8.7, although your reward for survival is a rock-strewn wash crossing. Choose your line carefully! Oso Trail ends at mile 8.75. Turn left here, onto Bell Canyon Trail. This trail has a net descent of about 130 feet in just over 2 miles, with a few undulations thrown in along the way. You can sustain a good speed on this trail by pedaling the short uphills, and selecting a line that avoids rocks and other hazards. The chatter of your

Ronald W. Caspers

Ronald Caspers was the chair of the Orange County Board of Supervisors during a mid-1970s term. He was instrumental in purchasing 5,500 acres of the former Starr Ranch for use as a public recreation facility, on the present-day site of the park. The land served as a prosperous cattle ranch from the 1900s until the 1960s. With the death of ranch owner Eugene Starr in 1966, the ranch entered a period of inactivity. By 1970, a corporation expressed interest in turning the ranch into a commercial amusement facility. Perhaps a new theme park, to bring some Knott's Berry Farm and Disneyland action to southern Orange County?

Conservation and preservation prevailed during the 1970s, however, when the northern part of the ranch was deeded to the National Audubon Society. The southern part of the ranch, under Caspers's direction, became Starr Viejo Regional Park in 1974. Within 2 months of the park's dedication, Mr. Caspers, members of his family, and some friends were all lost at sea when their vessel sank off the coast of Baja California. The circumstances of the incident have never been fully resolved. There have even been allegations that the incident was masterminded. In any case, it took just 2 months for Starr Viejo to be renamed Ronald W. Caspers Wilderness Park, in honor of its champion. Later, additional acreage was added, bringing the park's present-day total to about 8,000. In a strange, sad coincidence, Mr. Caspers's first wife also lost her life at sea 20 years earlier, in 1954. Mr. Caspers survived that incident.

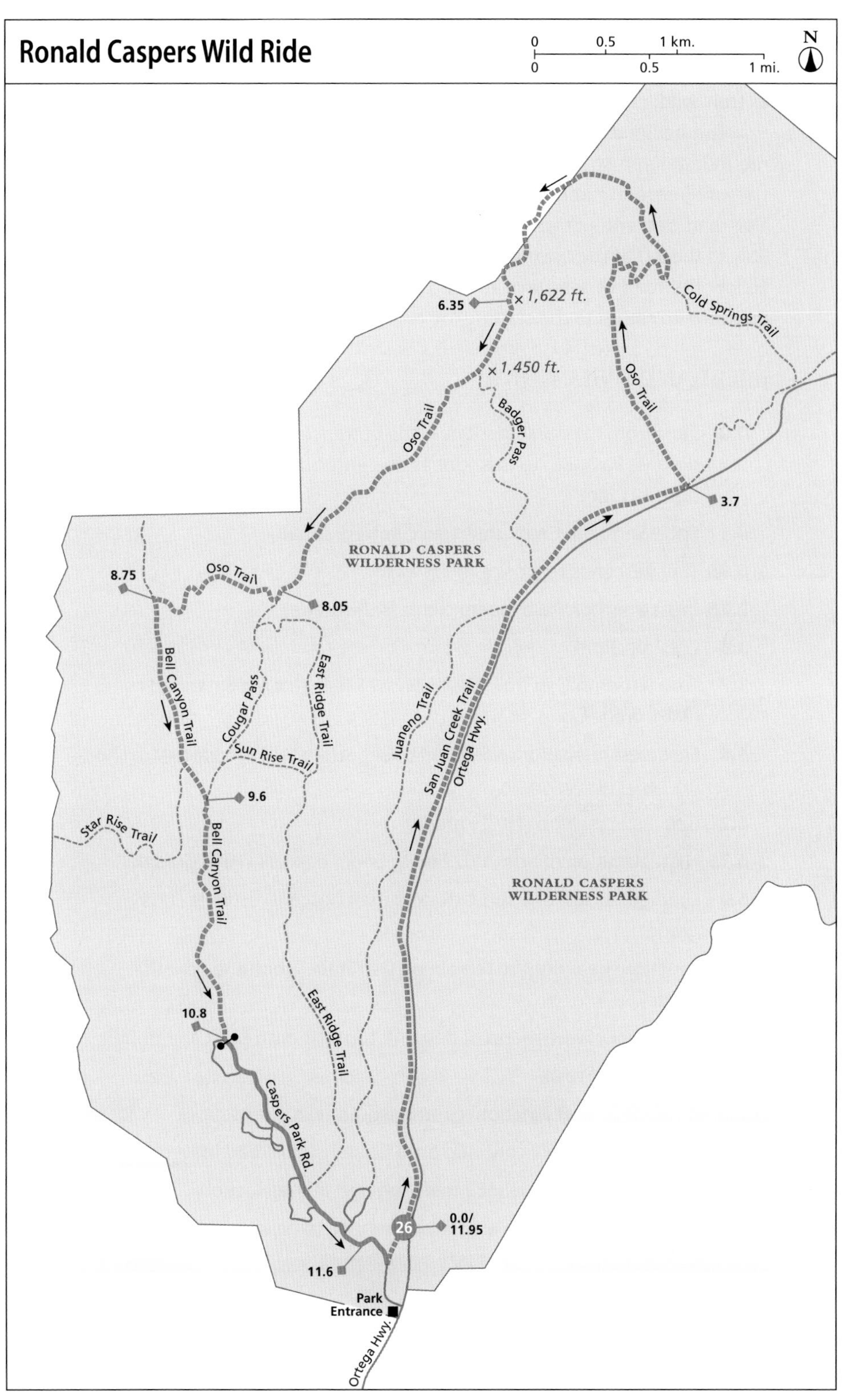
Ronald Caspers Wild Ride
0
0.5
1 km.
0
0.5
1 mi.
N
6.35
1,622 ft.
1,450 ft.
Cold Springs Trail
Oso Trail
Badger Pass
Oso Trail
3.7
RONALD CASPERS
WILDERNESS PARK
8.75
Oso Trail
8.05
East Ridge Trail
Bell Canyon Trail
Cougar Pass
Sun Rise Trail
Juaneno Trail
San Juan Creek Trail
Ortega Hwy.
9.6
Star Rise Trail
Bell Canyon Trail
RONALD CASPERS
WILDERNESS PARK
10.8
East Ridge Trail
Caspers Park Rd.
26
0.0/
11.95
11.6
Park
Entrance
Ortega Hwy.

wheels, and the occasional opportunity to catch some air, all cement this one as truly wild!

The trail ends at a gate (mile 10.8), which can be navigated without dismounting. Keep straight onto Caspers Park Road, which is paved. The road passes by several campsites, as well as a restroom with water for rehydration. The road descends gradually to the lowest elevation of the ride (382 feet). Stay to the left at the upcoming intersection to remain on Caspers Park Road. Follow the road as it returns to the park entrance. Turn left, just before the entrance, to return to the starting lot, and to conclude the ride.

MILES AND DIRECTIONS

0.0 Start from the parking lot near the entrance to Ronald Caspers Wilderness Park (i.e., to the right as one enters the park). Starting elevation: 391 feet.

0.1 Enter San Juan Creek Trail; trail climbs gradually.

0.95 Trail descends to cross a rocky wash.

2.75 Cross another wash; begin climb (8.3% grade).

3.0 Crest of climb.

3.7 Turn left onto Oso Trail; elevation: 625 feet—begin extended climb (9.4% grade).

5.6 First crest (elevation: 1,559 feet); keep straight at junction—trail hovers near this elevation.

6.2 Begin steep climb (18.7% grade).

6.35 High elevation of ride (1,622 feet); begin descent (7.8% grade).

6.9 Gradient eases for a short stretch; then descent resumes (11.5% grade).

8.05 Junction; bear right to remain on Oso Trail—continue downhill (5.1% grade).

8.75 Cross rocky wash—end of descent; turn left onto Bell Canyon Trail.

9.15 Cross rocky wash.

9.6 Keep straight at junction; continue gradual descent.

10.8 Gate—end of trail; continue onto Caspers Park Road (paved).

11.6 Low elevation of ride (382 feet); turn left at intersection.

11.95 End of ride at parking area near entrance to park.

San Joaquin Hills Expedition

Start: Bommer Canyon Trailhead, 6400 Shady Canyon Dr., Irvine

Length: 7.45 miles (clockwise loop)

Riding time: 40 minutes to 2 hours (my time: 50:13)

Terrain and surface: 90% dirt trails, 6% paved bike paths, 4% paved roads

Elevations: Low—287 feet at Shady Canyon Trail and Bommer Canyon Road; high—1,048 feet at West Fork and Turtle Ridge Trails junction

Traffic and hazards: Summit Park Drive was carrying 1,420 daily vehicles as of 2011.

Map: *The Thomas Guide by Rand McNally—Street Guide: Los Angeles and Orange Counties* (any recent year), page 890

Getting there by car: From central Anaheim, head south on I-5. Exit to CA 55 southbound, and then to I-405 southbound. Exit at Culver Drive and turn right onto Culver Drive southbound. Turn left onto Shady Canyon Drive and head east. Look for Bommer Canyon Road, providing access to Bommer Canyon trailhead. Drive to the trailhead and park in the small lot.

Getting there by public transit: There is no transit service to Bommer Canyon; the closest transit stop is at Culver and Campus Drives, located 2.5 miles from the trailhead. OCTA bus routes 79 and 175 both serve this stop. Route 79 runs between Tustin, Irvine, and Newport Beach every 30 to 45 minutes on weekdays and every hour on weekends and holidays. Route 175 runs between central Irvine and University Center, near the University of California–Irvine, every 40 to 70 minutes on weekdays.

Starting point coordinates: 33.628489°N / 117.806083°W

THE RIDE

CA 73 is a toll freeway connecting I-405 and I-5 between Costa Mesa and Laguna Niguel in Orange County. The middle part of the drive along this freeway is surprisingly scenic, cutting across the lightly developed, and mostly

Having done a zig, a rider prepares for a zag along Bommer Meadow Trail in Bommer Canyon.

preserved, San Joaquin Hills. To the north and south are protected lands, nearly all of it owned by the Irvine Company. The trails that cut through these open spaces are a mixture of ones that are open to the public and ones that are open for scheduled programs only, such as ranger-led nature hikes. The Irvine Company grew out of Irvine Ranch, which was established in 1864 through a merger of three adjoining Mexican land grants. The ranch covered 185 square miles, and has since grown into the sprawling city of Irvine (see Ride 32, Tour of the Master Plan: Irvine Ranch), plus portions of the neighboring cities of Anaheim, Laguna Beach, Newport Beach, Orange, and Tustin. (The cattle ranch, from which Irvine Ranch gets its name, ceased operations during the 1970s.) Chairman Donald Bren was considered by *Forbes* to be the wealthiest landowner in the United States, with the value of his property estimated at $14 *billion*.

Just over 50% of Irvine Ranch has been set aside for protection through a collection of wilderness parks and recreational preserves. About 80% of these lands were federally designated as a National Natural Landmark (NNL) in 2006. A number of the rides in this book take advantage of trails within the NNL, including this one. Start the San Joaquin Hills Expedition at the Bommer

Canyon trailhead, located off Shady Canyon Drive in Irvine. Although the address is on Shady Canyon Drive, the trailhead is somewhat inland, away from Shady Canyon Drive, along Bommer Canyon Road. This is a 7.45-mile (exactly 12 kilometers in metric parlance) mountain bike ride that travels through Bommer Meadow, ascends to Turtle Ridge, and then descends to Shady Canyon to close the loop. Although there are plenty of other trails that can be accessed from Bommer Meadow, most of them are not open to general use.

Leave the trailhead via Bommer Meadow Trail, the portal to which may be a little hard to see, just beyond the restroom facility. The trail gradually ascends as it twists and winds its way through and across the meadow. Two thumbs up to the trail designer for turning what could have been a blasé path straight across the meadow into a sinewy, rather artistic traverse. At the end of Bommer Meadow Trail, make a sharp right onto Nature Loop Trail. Bommer Canyon Road, not accessible to bikes, is just to your left. Nature Loop Trail effectively continues the ride across Bommer Meadow, with plenty of curves and twists and a gradual climb. The trail makes a couple of hard switchbacks near its end, as you arrive at Bommer Canyon Cattle Camp. The camp is a historical preservation, on the actual site, of the former Irvine Ranch Cattle Camp. The camp operated from the 1860s until the 1970s; some of the original facilities are still in their original setting. Today, the camp is used for campouts, company picnics, and other private events. The trail system is designed to circumnavigate the camp. Follow the signs and ride along the border of the camp, continuing onto Bommer Pass Trail. This trail ascends part of the way up the adjacent hillside, using a few switchbacks, and then descending to bring you down to the opposite side of the camp!

Once beyond the camp, bear left onto Bommer Canyon Trail. After just 0.1 mile, bear right at the junction onto West Fork Trail. If you look up, you will see West Fork working its way up the mountain ahead in a series of switchbacks. That is where you are headed. The trail ascends from 468 feet at its base to 1,048 feet at the crest, at an average grade of 13.9%. Settle into a rhythm, and you should be able to negotiate most of the climb. The climb is steepest near the ridge; here, the trail narrows and becomes technical, with exposed rock, perhaps requiring a dismount for all but the most skillful and fit riders. Stick with it as the trail twists its way through the coastal sage scrub. Bear right at the crest onto Turtle Ridge Trail. This is the high elevation of the ride (1,048 feet), atop Turtle Hill, which is the highest point in the San Joaquin Hills. From here, the trail begins a descent, with a commanding view of Irvine Valley and hillside communities within

Bike Shop

Bike Religion (repair shop), 405 West Peltason Dr., Irvine, (949) 824-3123, www.bikereligion.com

Irvine. In fact, you are aiming for one of those communities right now: Turtle Ridge. As you descend along the outskirts of a Turtle Ridge subdivision, the trail makes a sharp right-hand bend—this is a "wipeout" turn, so use caution when negotiating it. Shortly after the turn—did you wipe out?—Turtle Ridge Trail turns to the left. Keep straight here, 5.95 miles into the ride, onto the unnamed community trail. At the street crossing (Summit Park Drive), continue to the other side with caution, turn right onto the walkway, and then bear left to continue on the community trail.

About 0.1 mile after crossing Summit Park Drive, the community trail begins a steep descent (14% grade). The trail features intermittent stairways, designed especially for hikers, but not necessarily for bikers. Skilled cyclists may be able to ride these, but many riders may feel most comfortable taking these on foot. The stairways continue for about a quarter-mile, during which the trail drops from 592 feet to 400 feet elevation. At the bottom, cross over Summit Park Drive—use the opening in the median—turn left, and descend Summit Park in the road. It is a short segment (just 0.2 mile) shared with a light volume of motor vehicles. Turn right at Shady Canyon Drive onto Shady Canyon Trail. The trail parallels the road for one-third of a mile before veering off to the right. At the intersection with Bommer Canyon Road, which is merely an access road, with brightly colored pavement, turn right. This is the low

National Natural Landmarks

With national parks, monuments, recreation areas, conservation areas, forests, wildlife refuges, and historic places all on the US preservation system's menu, one might wonder what a National Natural Landmark (NNL) is, and where it fits into the overall preservation scheme. Unlike the other components of the system, the NNL includes biological and geological features that may be either publicly or privately owned. The owners are, therefore, responsible for upkeep. It is also the owner's decision regarding access to the landmark. An owner may decide, for example, that a landmark not be publicly accessible—such a decision need not affect the NNL designation. There were 592 NNLs as of 2012. Some of the more well-known NNLs include Diamond Head and Mauna Kea in Hawaii, and Emerald Bay at Lake Tahoe, the La Brea Tar Pits in Los Angeles, and the San Andreas Fault, all in California. The Irvine Ranch NNLs are unique in that the features range in age from the late Cretaceous Period (80 million years ago) to the present. There are twenty-two Irvine Ranch NNLs, including Bommer Canyon.

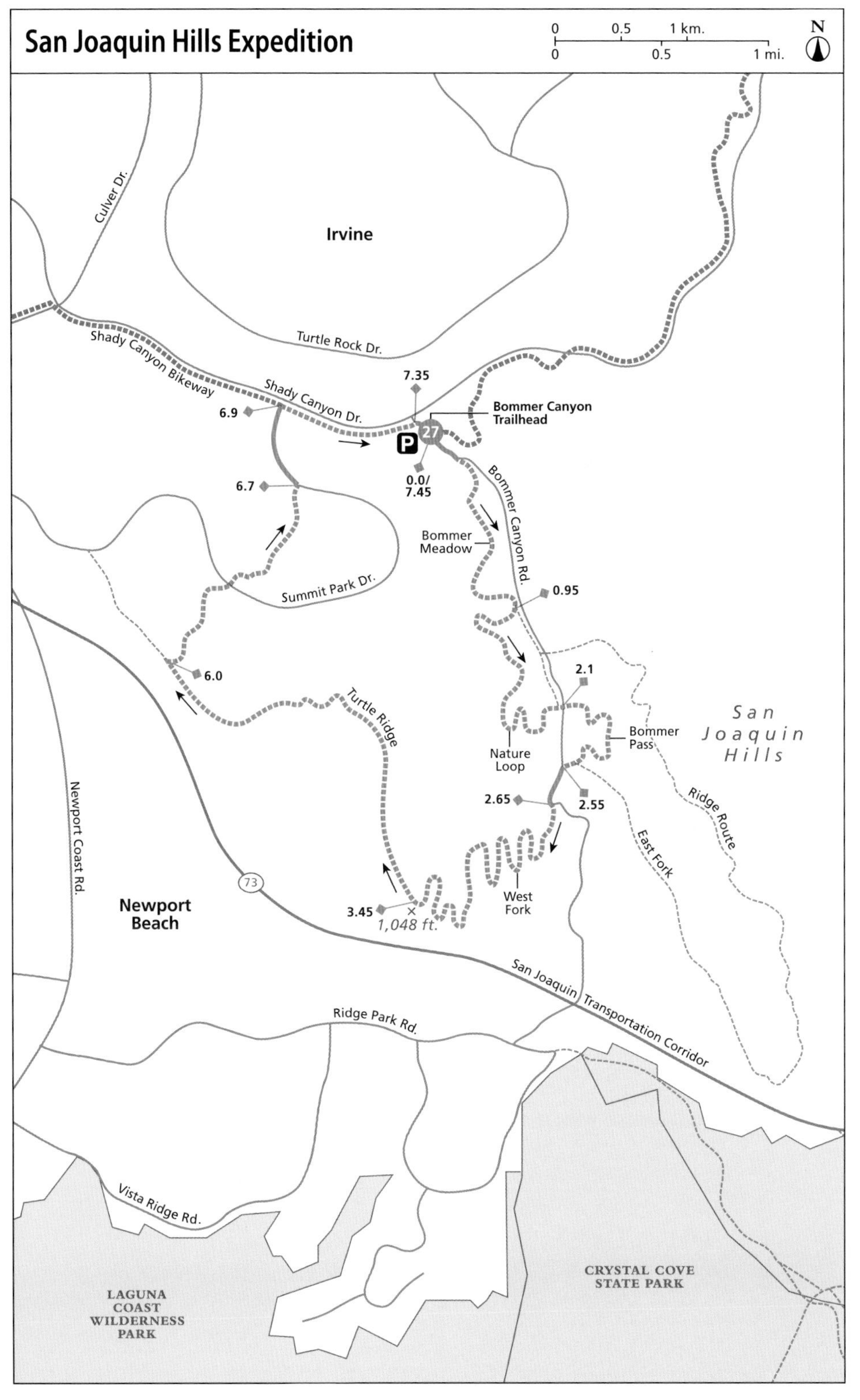

San Joaquin Hills Expedition
0
0.5
1 km.
0
0.5
1 mi.
N
Culver Dr.
Irvine
Turtle Rock Dr.
Shady Canyon Bikeway
Shady Canyon Dr.
7.35
6.9
Bommer Canyon
Trailhead
27
P
0.0/
7.45
6.7
Bommer Canyon Rd.
Bommer
Meadow
Summit Park Dr.
0.95
6.0
2.1
Turtle Ridge
San
Joaquin
Hills
Bommer
Pass
Nature
Loop
2.65
2.55
Ridge Route
East Fork
Newport Coast Rd.
73
West
Fork
3.45
1,048 ft.
Newport
Beach
San Joaquin Transportation Corridor
Ridge Park Rd.
Vista Ridge Rd.
CRYSTAL COVE
STATE PARK
LAGUNA
COAST
WILDERNESS
PARK

elevation point of the ride, at 287 feet. Ride on Bommer Canyon Road for 0.1 mile to the Bommer Canyon trailhead to conclude the ride. Note that motor vehicles can use Bommer Canyon Road to access parking at the trailhead.

MILES AND DIRECTIONS

0.0 Leave Bommer Canyon trailhead via Bommer Meadow Trail, heading southward.

0.95 End of Bommer Canyon Trail; turn right to continue on Nature Loop Trail.

2.1 End of Nature Loop Trail, adjacent Bommer Canyon Cattle Camp; follow signs to continue onto Bommer Pass Trail.

2.55 End of Bommer Pass Trail; turn left onto Bommer Canyon Trail.

2.65 Bear right at the fork onto West Fork Trail; begin climb of Turtle Hill via switchbacks (13.9% grade).

3.45 End of West Fork Trail atop Turtle Hill (elevation 1,048 feet); now on Turtle Ridge Trail.

6.0 Keep straight onto unnamed community trail, where Turtle Ridge Trail turns to the left.

6.35 Cross Summit Park Drive; turn right onto walkway, then bear left onto dirt trail.

6.45 Begin 14% downgrade; trail features intermittent stairways for hikers—riders may prefer to dismount and walk.

6.7 End of trail; cross Summit Park Drive through opening in median, turn left, and head downhill in road.

6.9 Turn right onto Shady Canyon Trail (paved bike path parallel to Shady Canyon Drive).

7.35 Turn right onto Bommer Canyon Road (access road to Bommer Canyon Trailhead, shared with motor vehicles—low elevation of ride, at 287 feet).

7.45 End of ride at Bommer Canyon trailhead.

28 San Juan Hills Grind

Start: Acu Canyon Park, 27999 Camino Las Ramblas, San Juan Capistrano

Length: 9.85 miles (counterclockwise loop)

Riding time: 1 to 3 hours (my time: 1H15:52)

Terrain and surface: 59% of the ride is on dirt trails, 25% is on paved roads, 16% is on paved paths (no motor vehicles), and less than 1% is on a concrete walkway.

Elevations: Low—88 feet on San Juan Creek Road at the McCracken View Trail trailhead; high—774 feet on Patriot Trail

Traffic and hazards: In 2012, San Juan Creek Road was carrying 9,500 vehicles per day west of La Novia Road; Camino Las Ramblas was carrying 4,300 vehicles per day toward the Las Ramblas trailhead.

Map: *The Thomas Guide by Rand McNally—Street Guide: Los Angeles and Orange Counties* (any recent year), page 972

Getting there by car: From central Anaheim, head south on I-5. In San Juan Capistrano, exit at Camino Las Ramblas and turn left. Climb Camino Las Ramblas to Acu Canyon Park, which will be on the left. Park on the street.

Getting there by public transit: Ride OCTA bus route 1 along PCH, or route 187 from Laguna Hills, to PCH and Doheny Park Road. It is 2.1 miles to Acu Canyon Park from here. Head north on Doheny Park Road; turn right on Camino Capistrano. After passing under I-5, turn left onto Via Canon (climb the hill). Next, turn right onto Via Fortuna, followed by a left turn onto Via California. Pass over I-5, descend the hill, and then turn right onto Camino Las Ramblas. The park will be on the left after a short climb.

Starting point coordinates: 33.469983°N / 117.657300°W

THE RIDE

The San Juan Hills Grind is a challenging, enjoyable mountain bike ride with good pacing. Within a little less than 10 miles, this ride hands the rider a little bit of everything: wide dirt trails, narrow singletrack trails, gradual and steep climbs and descents; some mud, mulch, hiking, and road riding; a few unnamed-trail segments; and even a few jump-able barriers. I have admittedly set out to attack this course, thinking of it as reasonably short, and always finished it depleted. One reason is that the route's lowest elevation of 88 feet, and its highest elevation of 774 feet, are separated by just 1.3 miles, coming toward the end of the counterclockwise loop, perhaps hitting the rider when he or she is most fatigued.

Start the ride at Acu Canyon Park in San Juan Capistrano (SJC). The route takes advantage of a portion of SJC's nifty trails system that penetrates the San Juan Hills. The Hills' maximum elevation is 883 feet. SJC's famous swallows have not come back since 2009. The theory is that extensive urban development has lessened the mission's prominence among tall buildings—the building's height of 85 feet was an attractive stopover for the birds on their migratory route from Argentina. The swallows still come back, but were nesting at a new location in Chino Hills, about 45 miles directly to the north, as of this writing. SJC city officials were planning to meet with the leaders of the cliff swallows to provide incentives for their return (kidding). Although the romance of the returning cliff swallows may have been lost, the city retains its charm and historical interest.

Leave Acu Canyon Park (elevation 319 feet), and head toward the San Juan Hills! Climb Camino Las Ramblas to its end, which is 0.8 mile away (5.8% grade). Continue past the (jump-able!) log barriers onto Las Ramblas Trail. Some maps show Camino Las Ramblas continuing as a paved road here, but don't you believe it. Once on the trail, the climb continues for another 0.1 mile (elevation 587 feet) before a short descent. The climbing then continues (6.2% grade), taking you up to 652 feet. Bear right to reach the junction with Prima Deshecha Trail at mile 1.5—the one with the steep hill looming in front of you. Work your way to the top of this short, steep climb, and then prepare for a steep, rollercoaster descent and climb. At the three-way split at mile 1.95, and although the trails to your left and right may seem more attractive, keep straight onto the steep hill, remaining on Prima Deshecha. It is a 16.1% grind to the top of the hill (elevation 614 feet), followed by a descent, and then another climb (11.4% grade) and descent.

Bear right at the next junction onto Whispering Hills Trail: Main. Some maps were showing this as a "proposed" trail; apparently, the proposal was accepted! After another rapid descent (11.7% grade), the trail climbs gradually.

On the Prima Deshecha Trail, with the San Juan Hills Estates to the left and a landfill to the right

At mile 3.05, stay left to remain on the main trail. At mile 3.15, bear right onto Whispering Hills Trail: East (also "proposed"). Descend the somewhat rough trail to an elevation of 438 feet (mile 3.6), followed by a short climb (7.8% grade). From here, the trail descends precipitously toward the developed valley below. There are a couple of switchbacks as you drop down to 204 feet above sea level. The trail levels and comes to an end—you can practice your cyclocross skills by hurdling the log barriers. From here, cross the quiet, residential street and continue onto La Cougue. This is a mulch equestrian trail that can be ridden, although bike control on the soft, uneven surface may be a challenge. The downgrade aids in retaining some speed.

Cross Calle Posado (residential street), and continue on La Cougue. There were no curb cuts at the crossing. After another short segment, La Cougue comes to an end at San Juan Creek Road. Cross the street (no curb cut), and access the Las Vaqueras Trail on the opposite side. Turn left and head southwest on Las Vaqueras (paved path). To your right is a series of equestrian properties (stables and plenty of horses). Signing discourages riders (equestrians) from using the bike path, so you should not experience any conflicts. The path ends as you approach Harold Ambuehl Elementary School. Just before you arrive at the school, at mile 5.75, bear right onto the unnamed dirt trail that circumnavigates the perimeter of the school property. This is a singletrack trail that runs along the school's fence, with the school to your left. The trail makes a sharp left at a corner in the fence to remain adjacent the school. You may find an unusually muddy patch along this trail, on the back side of the school, probably from irrigation. Dismount and use the neatly placed bypass trail, or ride through it. After passing the school, the trail widens and descends to a low area (elevation 102 feet). Bear left here, climbing slightly, to return to San Juan Creek Road. Turn right and ride along the walkway. The walkway ends at La Novia Road.

Carefully cross La Novia, and turn left. Next, turn right at the signal to continue riding along the shoulder of San Juan Creek Road. After 1 mile of speedy riding, with the San Juan Hills Golf Club to your right, look for the McCracken View Trail trailhead to your left. It is an unnamed, "unofficial" trailhead at the base of the bluff. This is the low elevation of the ride (88 feet), at mile 7.15. Carefully cross San Juan Creek Road, and head onto the trail. The trail is steep and narrow at the onset, climbing to 172 feet in just 0.1 mile (17.7% grade, with some steeper segments). I admittedly had to walk most of this. The narrow trail levels, and then climbs gradually to 217 feet—including a tricky crossing of a protruding tree root—before descending to La Novia Road. Carefully cross La Novia, turn left, and then bear right to continue on the trail. There are no markers out here, but you are still on McCracken View Trail. Navigate the gate at mile 7.5—you will probably have to dismount—and continue climbing. Follow the trail as it traverses a large open space. There are some sections of old pavement out here, relics of the space's former life as the Forster Canyon Landfill. Avoid veering off to the right; that is, stay toward the left edge of the space. After climbing at 7.4% for a little over a half-mile, turn right, and then curve right to head toward the base of the massive hill in front of you. From mile 8.05 (elevation 436 feet), the trail switches back—you are now on Forster Canyon Trail—and climbs at a 20.0% grade(!) to a junction (elevation 679 feet). Yes, this one is steep, exacerbated by the off-camber cross-section and the gritty surface.

Bike Shop

Buy My Bikes, 32302 Camino Capistrano, San Juan Capistrano, (949) 493-5611, http://buymybikes.com

When you finally reach the crest, possibly out of breath, take the second left and continue climbing(!), now on Patriot Trail. This trail is so named because, up the hill behind you, the summit features a US flag. Patriot, in your direction, climbs at the "navigable" grade of 11.2% to the high elevation of the entire ride, 774 feet. Stay left at the next junction to remain on the main, wide trail. Beyond the crest, look for the unnamed, narrow trail on your right. Take this, and head toward the large water tank. The trail bears right prior to the tank and descends to Delgado Canyon Trail. This "trail" is actually a paved access road for the water tank. Enjoy the descent, losing nearly 300 feet over the next 0.6 mile (8.9% grade). At the bottom, Delgado Canyon curves to the left, and then ends at a gateway to the Meredith Canyon residential community. Dismount and hurdle the log barriers, and continue onto the paved Calle Delgado (quiet residential cul-de-sac). Turn left onto Calle Miramar. Ready for one more climb? This one is paved, at a "gentle" 5.9% grade. Some of San Juan Capistrano's nicest houses are in this upscale neighborhood. Once over the summit, the road descends; the name changes to Avenida Pescador after a couple of curves as you enter the Alto Capistrano community. Avenida Pescador ends at Camino Las Ramblas, with Acu Canyon Park off to your left, to conclude the ride.

MILES AND DIRECTIONS

0.0 Head uphill on Camino Las Ramblas from Avenida Pescador, adjacent Acu Canyon Park.

0.8 End of road; continue onto Las Ramblas Trail (dismount to enter trail).

1.5 Bear right onto Prima Deshecha Trail—begin series of climbs and descents.

1.95 Split in trail; keep straight, remaining on Prima Deshecha: 16.1% uphill, followed by a descent and climb.

2.5 Bear right at split in trail onto Whispering Hills Trail: Main. Trail descends (11.7% grade) and then climbs (7.3% grade).

3.05 Stay left at split in trail (i.e., stay on main trail).

3.15 Bear right at split onto Whispering Hills Trail: East. Trail descends (6.4% grade), followed by a short climb (7.8%), and then descends steeply (8.6%).

4.25 End of Whispering Hills Trail: East. Cross the log barriers; bear left and cross the street, and then continue on La Cougue (equestrian trail—mulch surface; gradual downhill).

4.55 Cross Calle Posada (residential street—no curb cuts)—continue on La Cougue.

4.6 End of La Cougue; cross San Juan Creek Road (no curb cuts on La Cougue side), and turn left onto Las Vaqueras Trail (paved bike path).

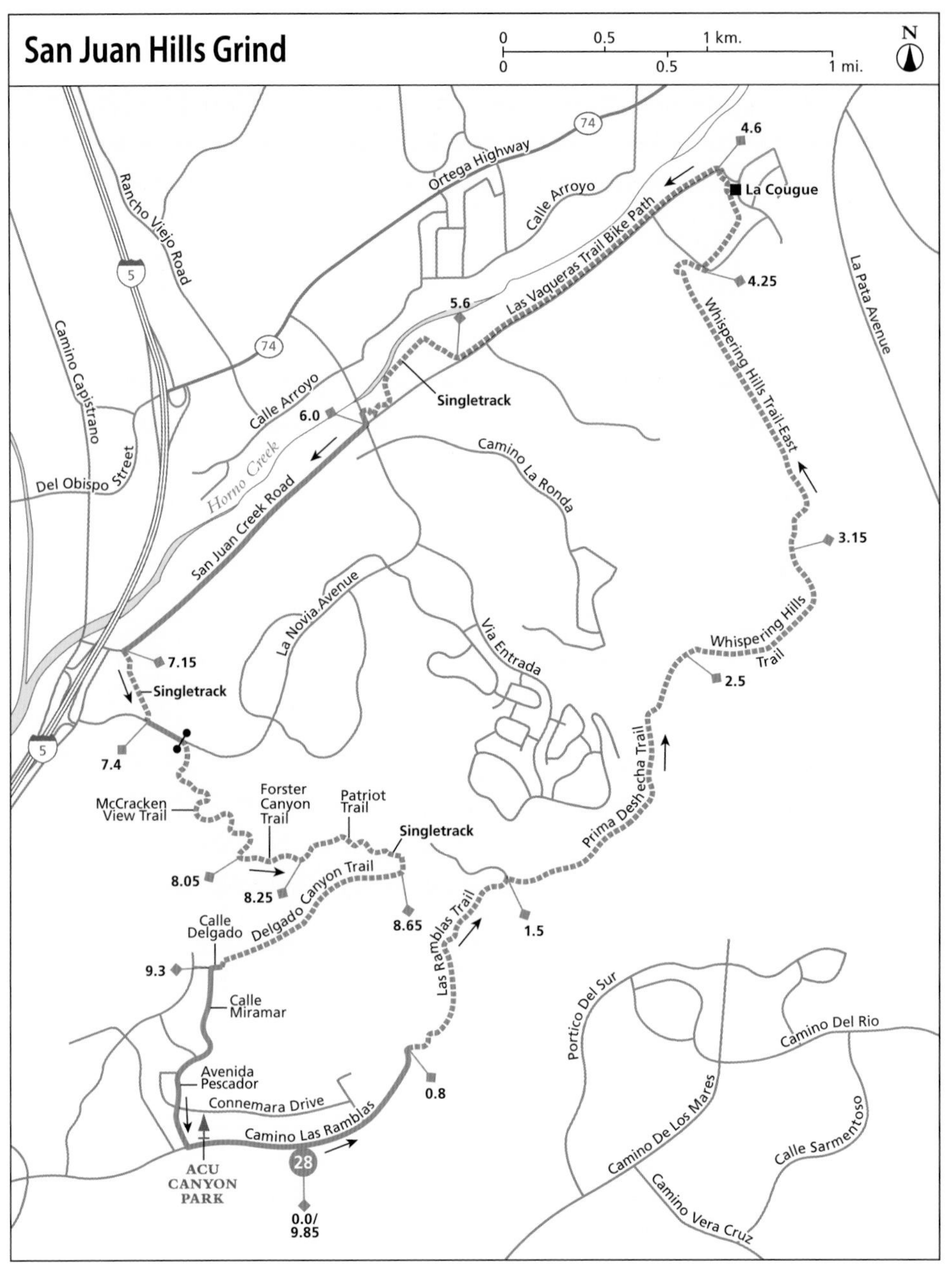
San Juan Hills Grind
0
0.5
1 km.
0
0.5
1 mi.
N
74
Ortega Highway
Rancho Viejo Road
5
Calle Arroyo
La Cougue
4.6
Las Vaqueras Trail Bike Path
4.25
La Pata Avenue
Camino Capistrano
5.6
Whispering Hills Trail-East
Singletrack
Calle Arroyo
6.0
Del Obispo Street
Horno Creek
Camino La Ronda
San Juan Creek Road
3.15
La Novia Avenue
Via Entrada
Whispering Hills Trail
7.15
Singletrack
2.5
5
7.4
Prima Deshecha Trail
McCracken View Trail
Forster Canyon Trail
Patriot Trail
Singletrack
8.05
8.25
Delgado Canyon Trail
8.65
1.5
Las Ramblas Trail
Calle Delgado
9.3
Calle Miramar
Portico Del Sur
Camino Del Rio
Avenida Pescador
Connemara Drive
0.8
Camino Las Ramblas
Camino De Los Mares
Calle Sarmentoso
28
ACU CANYON PARK
Camino Vera Cruz
0.0/ 9.85

5.6 Near the end of Las Vaqueras Trail, veer right, off of the path, onto the unnamed dirt trail that continues along the perimeter of the adjacent Harold Ambuehl Elementary School.

5.75 90-degree bend to the left to continue along unnamed trail adjacent school fence.

5.9 After descending to a low area, turn left and ascend to San Juan Creek Road walkway.

6.0 Turn right and continue along San Juan Creek Road walkway.

6.05 End of walkway at La Novia Road; cross road, and then turn left to ride along road.

6.1 Traffic signal at San Juan Creek Road; turn right. Ride along shoulder.

7.15 Cross San Juan Creek Road to base of adjacent bluff—continue onto steep uphill trail (McCracken View Trail). Low elevation of ride (88 feet).

7.4 Gate at La Novia Road; cross road and turn left.

7.45 Bear right off of road and onto trail to continue on McCracken View; go around gate to continue on trail.

7.65 Stay left to continue on McCracken View; trail curves to the left.

8.05 Turn right, followed by a 180-degree bend to the left; now on Forster Canyon Trail—climb at 20.0% grade.

8.25 Trail junction at false crest; take the second left, onto Patriot Trail—continue climbing.

8.4 High elevation of ride (774 feet).

8.5 Bear right onto narrow, unnamed trail. Follow trail as it descends past water tank.

8.65 Turn right onto Delgado Canyon Trail (paved access road). Road descends at 8.9% grade.

9.25 After curving to the left, Delgado Canyon Trail ends at gateway to Meredith Canyon community. Cross the log barriers, and continue on Calle Delgado (paved street).

9.3 Turn left onto Calle Miramar—climb and then descend through neighborhood.

9.55 Now on Avenida Pescador, in Alta Capistrano community.

9.85 End of ride at Camino Las Ramblas, adjacent Acu Canyon Park.

Soft and Hard Tails of Aliso-Wood

Start: Aliso and Wood Canyons Regional Park

Length: 11.55 miles (out-and-back portion plus a counterclockwise loop)

Riding time: 1.5 to 4 hours (my time: 1H58:19)

Terrain and surface: 91% dirt trails; 9% paved roads

Elevations: Low elevation—87 feet at Meadows Trail and Wood Canyon Trail in Aliso and Wood Canyons Regional Park; high—1,008 feet at Alta Laguna Boulevard and Zeil Drive in Laguna Beach

Traffic and hazards: The only paved road on the route is residential Alta Laguna Boulevard in Laguna Beach. Portions of Meadows Trail are steep and technical.

Map: *The Thomas Guide by Rand McNally—Street Guide: Los Angeles and Orange Counties* (any recent year), page 951

Getting there by car: From central Anaheim, head south on I-5. Exit at Alicia Parkway; turn right and head southwest. Look for the entrance to Aliso and Wood Canyons Regional Park just past Aliso Creek Road, at Awma Road, in Laguna Niguel. Pull off the road, on the left, and park in the dirt lot.

Getting there by public transit: OCTA bus route 87 runs from Laguna Hills Mall to Alicia Parkway in Laguna Niguel every hour on weekdays and Saturdays. Exit at Awma Road and enter the park.

Starting point coordinates: 33.551053°N / 117.719675°W

THE RIDE

Soft and Hard Tails of Aliso-Wood, as the title suggests, is a mountain bike ride through Aliso and Wood Canyons Regional Park in Laguna Niguel and Laguna Beach. Whether you ride a soft or hard tail, you will probably find this ride to be particularly challenging. The opening portion of the ride is easy, however. Begin by heading southward into Aliso Canyon on Aliso Canyon Trail. Turn left at mile 0.1 to continue on the trail, which is wide enough for maintenance

A typical scene on Wood Canyon Trail: Two riders and a runner hone their fitness while sharing the dirt.

vehicle access. The trail crosses the paved Aliso Canyon Road at mile 0.75, and then turns left to continue, parallel to the road. The trail narrows, and has a few technical spots. Aliso Canyon is one of the features of this ride, with majestic hills towering to either side of you. You are also treated to this canyon, on the parallel road, in Ride 15, Aliso Creek Sneak. The trail ends at mile 1.5, at the junction with Wood Canyon Trail. Turn right here, and head up the canyon (elevation 95 feet).

Wood Canyon Trail climbs gradually through the canyon (average 2.3% grade). There are a number of connecting trails to your left and right (mostly to your left), including Dripping Cave, Mathis Canyon, Alwut, Coyote Run, and Wood Creek. There are a couple of creek crossings along the way—one features a wooden bridge, while with the other you are on your own. If there is water in the creek, then give your tires a bath! By the time you reach Cholla Trail, which is a popular connector for mountain bikers, you are at an elevation of 447 feet, 4.5 miles into the ride. You could ride Cholla up to the ridge on your left. My route, though, takes you out of the park, through the gate, and then up the boundary trail on the left. This is the short, steep (17.3% grade)

way to the top of the ridge. Once at the crest, at mile 4.9, turn left to reenter the park.

You are now on West Ridge Trail. Keep straight at the junction with Lynx Trail at mile 5.1, and begin a climb (6.3% grade). The climb ends at the junction with Stairsteps Trail (mile 5.3)—keep straight here, and begin a short descent. At the junction with Rock-It Trail (mile 5.45), keep straight, and head into the next climb. After the second junction with Rock-It, the trail descends (8.9% grade) to a false junction (the connector leads nowhere); keep straight here. Stay left at the split in the trail at mile 6.15, and begin another climb (5.8% grade). This climb continues to the end of West Ridge Trail (mile 7.1). Keep straight at the end of the trail, onto the paved Alta Laguna Boulevard. There will probably be others up here, whether by bike or by car, enjoying the view. You are now in the Top of the World neighborhood of Laguna Beach. No—you cannot afford to live here, but you can certainly ride through. After hovering around the 1,000-foot-elevation mark, Alta Laguna reaches the highest altitude of the ride, 1,008 feet, at Zeil Drive. Alta Laguna starts to descend from here, with the road narrowing at mile 8.05. Just when you think that you made an unauthorized entry into an exclusive community, turn right onto the unnamed, rugged trail.

Bike Shops

Jax Bicycle Center, 27190 Alicia Pkwy., Laguna Niguel, (949) 364-5771, www.jaxbicycles.com; Rock N' Road Cyclery, Plaza de la Paz, 27281 La Paz Rd., Laguna Niguel, (949) 360-8045, www.rocknroadcyclery.net

The unnamed trail's initial descent is steep (19.6% grade) and rugged, so hang on. The trail effectively circumvents that exclusive community that you were entering, coming out on the other side, at mile 8.25. Turn right here to continue on the paved road. The road's opening descent is steep as well (17.8% grade). The gradient eases at mile 8.2. Despite the two steep drops, you are still at an elevation of 855 feet. Aliso Canyon is to your left, and you may be stunned at how high above the canyon floor you are. You are going down there in a moment, with a left turn onto Meadows Trail (mile 8.5). This trail is not for beginners, although there are a few, intermittent segments that can easily be ridden. Most of the trail is steep (13.2% average grade), and rugged in places. Put your foot down when needed (maybe both feet), and stay with it. Meadows finally reaches the canyon floor after a little over 1 mile, now at an elevation of a mere 92 feet. The trail curves sharply to the left at mile 9.55 to parallel the paved Aliso Canyon Road. After dropping to the lowest elevation of the ride (87 feet), Meadows Trail ends at Wood Canyon Road (mile 10.0). Turn right here, and then make an immediate left onto Aliso Canyon Trail. You are now riding in the reverse direction of the opening outbound

segment. Follow the trail as it crosses Aliso Canyon Road to continue heading northward on the other side. At mile 11.45, turn right to return to the parking area. The ride ends after the short ride back to the lot.

MILES AND DIRECTIONS

0.0 Start at the trailhead to Aliso Canyon, leaving from the parking area at Aliso and Wood Canyons Regional Park, just off of Awma Road; head south on Aliso Canyon.

0.1 Bear left to continue on Aliso Canyon Road (dirt road).

0.75 Cross paved road, continue onto dirt trail—bear left and head south.

1.5 End of trail at junction with Wood Canyon Trail (dirt); turn right and head into canyon (elevation: 95 feet)—begin gradual climb (average 2.3% grade).

2.2 Keep straight at junction with Dripping Cave Trail.

2.55 Keep straight at junction with Mathis Canyon Trail.

2.95 Keep straight at junction with Alwut Trail.

3.45 Keep straight at junction with Five Oaks Trail.

3.6 Merge with Coyote Run Trail.

4.05 Keep straight at junction with Wood Creek Trail—creek crossing.

4.15 Stay right at Lynx Trail.

4.5 Keep straight at junction with Cholla Trail.

4.55 Gate: Leave Aliso and Wood Canyons Regional Park—keep straight on trail.

4.6 Bear left onto boundary trail—begin steep climb (17.3% grade).

4.9 Crest of climb (elevation 718 feet); turn left and reenter Aliso and Wood Canyons Regional Park—now on West Ridge Trail.

5.1 Keep straight at junction with Lynx Trail; begin climb (6.3% grade).

5.3 Keep straight at junction with Stairsteps Trail—crest of climb; begin descent.

5.45 Keep straight at junction with Rock-It Trail—end of descent.

5.7 Keep straight at "false" junction.

6.15 Split in West Ridge Trail; stay left—begin climb (5.8% grade).

6.5 Stay to the right—continue climb.

7.1 End of West Ridge Trail—continue onto road (Alta Laguna Boulevard).

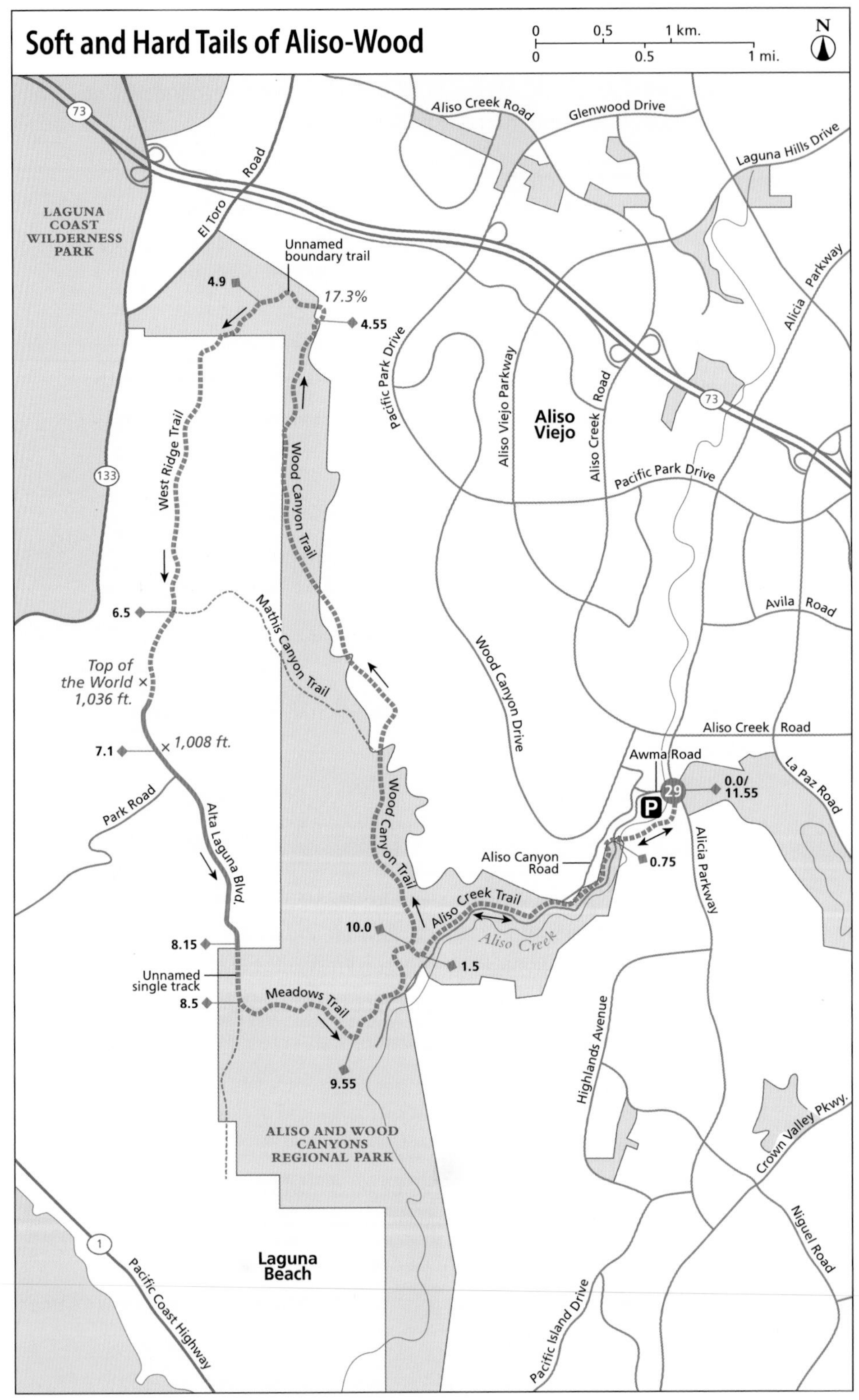
Soft and Hard Tails of Aliso-Wood
0 0.5 1 km.
0 0.5 1 mi.
N
73
Aliso Creek Road
Glenwood Drive
Laguna Hills Drive
El Toro Road
LAGUNA COAST WILDERNESS PARK
Unnamed boundary trail
4.9
17.3%
4.55
Alicia Parkway
Pacific Park Drive
Aliso Viejo Parkway
Aliso Creek Road
Aliso Viejo
73
133
West Ridge Trail
Wood Canyon Trail
Pacific Park Drive
Avila Road
6.5
Mathis Canyon Trail
Top of the World × 1,036 ft.
Wood Canyon Drive
Aliso Creek Road
7.1
× 1,008 ft.
Awma Road
29
0.0/ 11.55
La Paz Road
Park Road
Wood Canyon Trail
Alta Laguna Blvd.
Aliso Canyon Road
0.75
Alicia Parkway
Aliso Creek Trail
10.0
Aliso Creek
8.15
1.5
Unnamed single track
8.5
Meadows Trail
9.55
Highlands Avenue
Crown Valley Pkwy.
ALISO AND WOOD CANYONS REGIONAL PARK
Niguel Road
1
Laguna Beach
Pacific Coast Highway
Pacific Island Drive

7.65 Highest elevation of ride (1,008 feet), at Zeil Drive.

8.05 Alta Laguna Boulevard narrows.

8.15 Leave road; turn right onto rugged, unnamed trail—steep descent initially (19.6% grade).

8.25 Turn right onto paved road—steep descent (17.8% grade).

8.35 End of descent; road climbs gradually.

8.5 Leave paved road; turn left onto Meadows Trail—begin steep descent (13.2% grade) on intermittently technical surface.

9.55 End of steep descent; Meadows Trail curves to the left.

9.65 Low elevation of ride (87 feet).

10.0 End of Meadows Trail; turn right onto Wood Canyon Trail.

10.05 Turn left onto Aliso Canyon Trail (parallel to Aliso Canyon Road).

10.8 Cross road and continue on trail.

11.45 Turn right to return to parking area.

11.55 End of ride at Aliso and Wood Canyons Regional Park parking area.

South Laguna Summit-to-Sea

Start: Laguna Niguel Regional Park, 28241 La Paz Rd., Laguna Niguel

Length: 21.8 miles (clockwise loop)

Riding time: 1.25 to 3.5 hours (my time: 1H35:06)

Terrain and surface: 100% paved roads

Elevations: Low—9 feet at CA 1 and Broadway in Laguna Beach; high—889 feet at Pacific Island Drive and Talavera Drive in Laguna Niguel

Traffic and hazards: The heaviest traffic volumes in 2014 were on CA 1 (37,000 vehicles per day north of Crown Valley Parkway), Laguna Canyon Road (36,000 vehicles per day), El Toro Road (34,000 vehicles per day north of CA 73), Aliso Creek Road (33,000 vehicles per day at Alicia Parkway), and Alicia Parkway (35,000 vehicles per day south of Aliso Creek Road). The lightest traffic volumes were on Aliso Viejo Parkway between Pacific Park Drive and Aliso Creek Road (9,000 vehicles per day), Highlands Avenue (7,000 vehicles per day), and Pacific Island Drive (6,000 vehicles per day). Only portions of CA 1 and CA 133 (both in central Laguna Beach) did not have bike lanes.

Map: *The Thomas Guide by Rand McNally—Street Guide: Los Angeles and Orange Counties* (any recent year), page 951

Getting there by car: From central Anaheim, head south on I-5. Exit at La Paz Road in Laguna Hills; turn right and head south. Enter Laguna Niguel south of Oso Parkway. Once south of Aliso Creek Road, look for the entrance to Laguna Niguel Regional Park on the right. Enter the park (fee), and park in a lot that is near the entrance.

Getting there by public transit: OCTA bus route 187 runs from Laguna Hills Mall to Laguna Niguel Regional Park (via La Paz Parkway) eight times every weekday (morning and evening). There is no midday or weekend service.

Starting point coordinates: 33.552422°N / 117.709992°W

THE RIDE

Although most of this ride is busy with motor vehicles, there are bike lanes along nearly the entire route. Thus, bicycles and motor vehicles can coexist—well, not always in harmony—through some of southern Orange County's most favored scenery. The ride is hillier than Ride 21, Laguna Beach Pageant of the Pedals, which is this ride's companion, making this the more challenging option. The climbs are strenuous, but the descents are rewarding, and there are some great ocean views. The recommended direction for this ride is clockwise, to take advantage of right turns.

Start the ride at Laguna Niguel Regional Park. The main entrance is from La Paz Road in Laguna Niguel; park in a lot near the entrance. Start the ride with a jaunt through the park, heading toward its west side. Access from the west is closed to motor vehicles, but not to bicycles. There are a few speed humps along the park road. At the western end, once past the gate, turn left onto Alicia Parkway, a half-mile into the ride. Look for a safe place to cross the road—you may have to ride on the walkway to the next intersection. Once you are riding on the right side of Alicia Parkway, look for Highlands Avenue; turn right here, and start the ride's first climb (7.4% grade). The crest comes at Niguel Road (mile 2.0; elevation 577 feet). Descend from here (4.1% grade), to the end of Highlands Avenue. At the end of the road, turn right onto Pacific Island Drive. This is the toughest climb of the ride—a 9.1% grade that takes you to the highest elevation of the route (889 feet, at Talaveras Drive).

From the crest, Pacific Island descends rapidly (8.2% grade), losing all of the altitude that you just gained, and then some, to the road's terminus at Crown Valley Parkway (elevation 201 feet; mile 5.4). You are now in South Laguna, which is a district within Laguna Niguel. Turn right here, and head toward the ocean. Crown Valley begins with a climb (3.2% grade), followed by a brisk descent (6.2% grade). At CA 1 (Pacific Coast Highway), now at an elevation of 157 feet, turn right and head northwest. Although this is the coastal highway, you cannot see much of the ocean, because of oceanfront development. It is admittedly not as scenic as CA 1 north of Laguna Beach, but there is a buzz of energy along the road, under the aura of the nearby ocean. Enter Laguna Beach at Vista de la Luna. CA 1 rolls through here, climbing, descending, climbing, and then descending to Aliso Beach—which is technically the mouth of Aliso Canyon. The highway drops to just 20 feet above sea level, with the beach and ocean immediately to your left.

Next, CA 1 climbs (3.8% grade) toward central Laguna Beach. After cresting near Terry Road (142 feet above sea level), the highway makes a gradual descent into Laguna Beach's commercial district. You may have to brake for

A group of riders—clearly in for the long haul—chill on the shoulder of the Pacific Coast Highway in Laguna Niguel.

slow-moving motor vehicles through here. Also, watch out for on-street parking activity, including pedestrians entering and exiting vehicles and crossing the highway. In the center of town, at Broadway, turn right (mile 11.4). This is the lowest elevation of the ride (9 feet), immediately adjacent Main Beach. Keep it slow to savor the experience, and for safety. Once on Broadway, which is CA 133, you are heading away from the coast. This segment is also ridden in Ride 21, Laguna Beach Pageant of the Pedals. Enter Laguna Canyon as you leave the city's commercial district.

Pass the Willow Canyon trailhead (please see Ride 17, Crystal Cove Mas Moro), on the left, at mile 14.65. Just downstream of the trailhead, turn right onto El Toro Road. The road climbs gradually (1.7% grade) as it leaves Laguna Canyon. Pass under the CA 73 freeway at mile 15.6, entering Aliso Viejo. After a few signalized intersections, turn right onto Aliso Creek Road and start a climb (6.3% grade). After the crest, which is at an elevation of 630 feet, descend (5.7% grade) to Glenwood Drive. Turn right here; Glenwood is on the edge of Aliso Viejo's core area, wherein all of the city's industrial and retail development is concentrated. The city's plan was to locate all residences within 1.5

miles of the core area, to thereby reduce commuting and shopping distances. Certainly a great idea for those who work locally, but perhaps not having much of an impact on those who live here but work elsewhere. Glenwood Drive becomes Pacific Park Drive after crossing over CA 73 (mile 17.9).

After one more crest (elevation 672 feet), Pacific Park Drive begins to descend (5.0% grade). Turn right onto Aliso Viejo Parkway, also referred to as Laguna Hills Drive, and then turn right again onto Aliso Creek Road. At busy Alicia Parkway, turn right and enter Laguna Niguel. The end of the ride is nigh, as Laguna Niguel Regional Park is immediately to your left. As you approach the park from its western side—you may recall that there is no motor vehicle access from here—you will notice that there is no left turn lane from Alicia. There is a signalized pedestrian crossing of Alicia adjacent the entrance, however. The safest strategy would to be to use the signal and cross Alicia in the crosswalk. Once inside the park, head eastward, to the park's other side, to conclude the ride.

Bike Shops

Jax Bicycle Center, 27190 Alicia Pkwy., Laguna Niguel, (949) 364-5771, www.jaxbicycles.com; Rock N' Road Cyclery, Plaza de la Paz, 27281 La Paz Rd., Laguna Niguel, (949) 360-8045, www.rocknroadcyclery.net

MILES AND DIRECTIONS

0.0 Start from Laguna Niguel Regional Park in Laguna Niguel. Park near the entrance, on the east side, and ride westerly, through the park, to the west side.

0.15 Turn left, inside the park, to continue heading west on park road.

0.5 Exit park; turn left onto walkway, or cross Alicia Parkway, turn left, and head south.

1.15 Traffic signal at Highlands Avenue; turn right and begin climb (7.4% grade).

2.0 Crest of climb at Niguel Road; begin descent (4.1% grade).

2.8 Traffic signal at Pacific Island Drive; turn right—begin climb (9.1% grade).

3.85 Crest of climb at highest elevation of ride (889 feet), at Talaveras Drive; begin descent (8.2% grade).

5.4 Traffic signal at Crown Valley Parkway; turn right—begin climb (3.2% grade). Enter Laguna Beach.

5.9 Crest of climb; begin descent (6.2% grade).

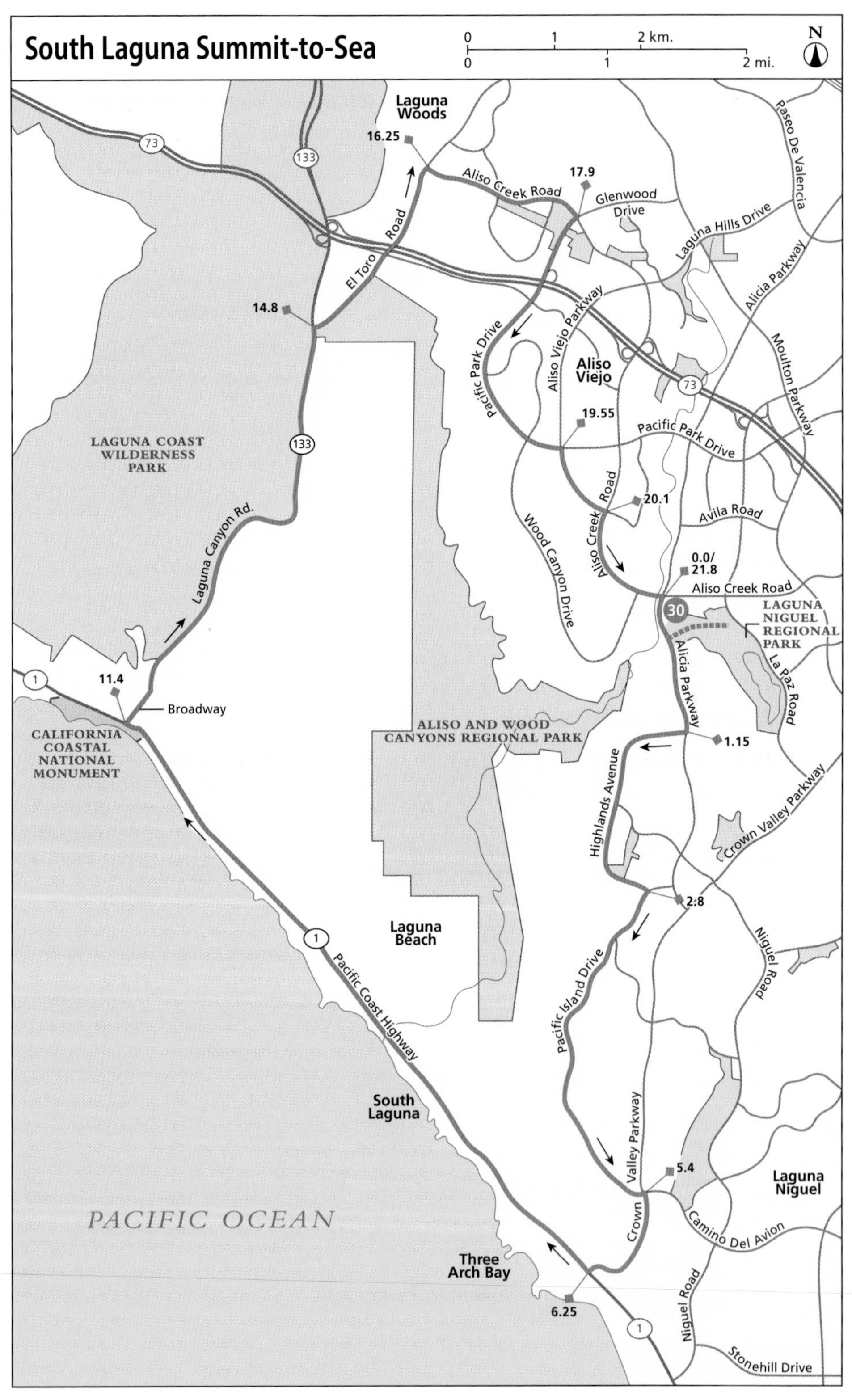

South Laguna Summit-to-Sea
0
1
2 km.
0
1
2 mi.
N
Laguna Woods
16.25
17.9
14.8
19.55
20.1
0.0/ 21.8
11.4
1.15
2.8
5.4
6.25
73
133
1
30
Aliso Creek Road
Glenwood Drive
Laguna Hills Drive
Paseo De Valencia
Alicia Parkway
El Toro Road
Aliso Viejo Parkway
Pacific Park Drive
Aliso Viejo
Moulton Parkway
LAGUNA COAST WILDERNESS PARK
Wood Canyon Drive
Avila Road
Laguna Canyon Rd.
LAGUNA NIGUEL REGIONAL PARK
La Paz Road
Broadway
CALIFORNIA COASTAL NATIONAL MONUMENT
ALISO AND WOOD CANYONS REGIONAL PARK
Highlands Avenue
Crown Valley Parkway
Laguna Beach
Pacific Coast Highway
Pacific Island Drive
Niguel Road
South Laguna
Laguna Niguel
PACIFIC OCEAN
Three Arch Bay
Camino Del Avion
Stonehill Drive

6.25 Traffic signal at CA 1; turn right—highway ascends, then descends.

8.45 Aliso Beach on the left (elevation 20 feet)—begin climb (3.6% grade).

9.3 Crest of climb at Terry Road; begin gradual descent into Laguna Beach.

11.4 Traffic signal at Broadway (CA 133); turn right—lowest elevation of the ride (9 feet). Main Beach is immediately to the left.

11.75 Leave central district of Laguna Beach; now on Laguna Canyon Road (CA 133).

14.8 Traffic signal at El Toro Road; turn right.

15.6 Pass under CA 73 freeway; enter city of Aliso Viejo.

16.25 Traffic signal at Aliso Creek Road; turn right—begin climb (6.3% grade).

17.05 Crest of climb; begin descent (5.7% grade).

17.4 Traffic signal at Glenwood Drive; turn right—begin gradual climb.

17.9 Cross over CA 73 freeway; now on Pacific Park Drive.

18.7 Elevation 672 feet; begin descent (5.0% grade).

19.55 Traffic signal at Aliso Viejo Parkway (Laguna Hills Drive); turn right.

20.1 Traffic signal at Aliso Creek Road; turn right.

20.95 Traffic signal at Alicia Parkway; turn right.

21.3 Cross Alicia Parkway at signalized pedestrian crossing adjacent Laguna Niguel Regional Park; enter park.

21.65 Bear right to continue through park.

21.8 End of ride, near main entrance to Laguna Niguel Regional Park.

The South OC BHC

Start: Capistrano Beach Park, 35005 Beach Rd., Capistrano Beach (Dana Point)

Length: 28.1 miles (figure eight shape, but with a big top loop and small bottom loop)

Riding time: 1.25 to 3.5 hours (my time: 1H40:05)

Terrain and surface: 65% of the ride is paved roads; 32% is on paved paths; 3% is on park roads with limited motor vehicle access.

Elevations: Low—4 feet on Island Way in Dana Point Harbor; high—608 feet on Golden Lantern Street at Dunes Street in Laguna Niguel

Traffic and hazards: The heaviest traffic volumes in 2014 were on Golden Lantern Street (39,000 vehicles per day south of Paseo de Colinas), Paseo de Colinas (24,000 vehicles per day), CA 1 (28,000 vehicles per day west of Dana Point's commercial district), Pacific Coast Highway (16,000 vehicles per day adjacent Doheny State Beach), Camino Capistrano (14,000 vehicles per day south of Junipero Serra Road), and Dana Point Harbor Drive (13,000 vehicles per day east of Golden Lantern Street).

Map: *The Thomas Guide by Rand McNally—Street Guide: Los Angeles and Orange Counties* (any recent year), page 972

Getting there by car: From central Anaheim, head south on I-5. Exit at Pacific Coast Highway (CA 1) in Dana Point; turn right. Exit at Pacific Coast Highway–Doheny Park Road. Turn left onto Doheny Park Road and pass under the highway. After curving to the left, Doheny Park becomes Pacific Coast Highway. Turn right at Palisades Drive and enter Capistrano Beach Park; park here.

Getting there by public transit: OCTA bus route 1 runs along PCH. Exit at Doheny State Beach. Also, Route 91 runs between Laguna Hills Mall and San Clemente, serving the beach, every 35 minutes on weekdays and every 45 minutes on weekends and holidays.

Starting point coordinates: 33.455264°N / 117.668281°W

THE RIDE

The South OC BHC—the South Orange County Beaches, Harbor, and Creeks—may be the consummate urban beach cities ride. The ride starts in Dana Point (Capistrano Beach district), and passes through San Clemente, San Juan Capistrano, Laguna Niguel, and other Dana Point districts. About two-thirds of the ride is on public roads, while the rest is on bike paths and roads through park areas which have restricted motor vehicle access. Segments of the ride, particularly along Doheny State Beach, Capistrano Beach, and Dana Point Harbor, are great for family riding. The San Juan Creek, Trabuco Creek, and Salt Creek bike paths are also fine for young riders.

Start the ride at Capistrano (Capo) Beach Park, at Palisades Drive and the Pacific Coast Highway (PCH) in Capo Beach. Note that PCH in this area is not CA 1; the official CA 1 ends at I-5, after passing through Dana Point, just north of here. The ride begins with the first of three challenging climbs along this route. Leave the park, head straight across PCH and onto Palisades Drive. It is a quarter-mile climb (8.2% grade) to the top of the Capistrano Bluffs. Turn right at the top, onto Camino Capistrano. This road winds and undulates its way along the top of the bluffs, through some pleasant ocean-view neighborhoods. Those who cannot see the ocean from where they live can at least hear it. Follow Camino Capistrano as it descends (5.9% grade) from the bluff and curves to the right, eventually intersecting with PCH just opposite Poche Beach. Turn right here and ride along the highway. It is an uninterrupted stretch for the next 1.65 miles—you have the option of riding along the highway's shoulder or on the opposite side of the Jersey barrier on your left, where there is a protected bike lane.

At the traffic signal, returning to Palisades Drive, turn left into Capo Beach Park, where you started. Is the ride over? No—that was just the warm-up. You are now 4 miles into the ride. After crossing the railroad tracks, turn right onto the connecting path. Go slow through here, as the path is frequented by walkers, runners, and drifting sand. Keep straight into Doheny State Beach. Well, not the sandy beach, but the long, linear parking area that parallels the beach. Pick up some speed along here, as there should be plenty of room, except on very busy beach days. Near the end of the parking area, the pavement narrows to a two-lane road. Follow the road to its end at Park Lantern Street. Turn left here, cross the bridge over San Juan Creek, and then make an immediate left onto the path. At the end of the path, curve sharply to the left, onto the San Juan Creek Bike Path (mile 5.2).

The path takes you under Park Lantern Street, eventually leaving Dana Point and entering San Juan Capistrano. Pass under Stonehill Drive at mile 6.1. After making a long sweeping curve along the usually dry creek, the path

A rider wearing a "soft-shell" helmet pedals along the San Juan Creek Bike Path in San Juan Capistrano.

makes a sharp right turn across a bumpy wooden bridge (mile 7.6). At the end of the bridge, turn left onto the Trabuco Creek Bike Path (which is ridden in the opposite direction in Ride 22, North San Juan Capistrano Steeplechase). Pass under Del Obispo Street at mile 8.1.

The Trabuco Creek Bike Path ends at mile 8.55, emptying out onto Avenida de la Vista. Continue heading northward, now in the road. At the end of de la Vista, turn right onto Oso Road, and cross over the railroad tracks. Next, turn left onto Camino Capistrano. Note that Mission San Juan Capistrano is to your right, about a half-mile away, along Camino Capistrano. The route makes a left turn here, now at mile 9.5—there can be a long delay, depending on train activity. Once on Camino Capistrano, head north—the road eventually becomes part of a corridor, with the railroad to your left and I-5 to your right. Camino Capistrano enters Laguna Niguel as you near a CA 73 freeway underpass. The next segment of the ride can be busy with motor vehicle activity, as the road passes several fast-food establishments and mini-marts, as well as Avery Parkway, which provides direct access to I-5. After crossing Avery, turn right onto Paseo de Colinas (mile 11.95). The road curls around to the right and climbs, passing over Camino Capistrano. After passing under CA 73, Paseo de Colinas climbs steeply (7.3% grade) to El Sur before easing. After reaching an elevation of 479 feet, Paseo de Colinas descends to intersect with Golden Lantern Street.

You need to make a left turn onto Golden Lantern; there is a dual left-turn lane from Paseo de Colinas. Use caution when making the turn. Golden Lantern is the busiest road of the ride, but there is a bike lane. Now at mile 13.25, Golden Lantern climbs at a 7.8% grade. After reaching a crest at Dunes Street (elevation 608 feet), Golden Lantern rolls southbound through Laguna Niguel. Look for the Salt Creek Bike Path after passing the Sardina–St. Christopher intersection. Leave Golden Lantern, veering right onto the Salt Creek path. The path curves its way downhill into Chapparosa Park. The path is part of Salt Creek Corridor Regional Park. Once in the park, temporarily leave the path, turning left onto Chapparosa Park Road. At the end of the road, 16.5 miles into the ride, continue straight onto the Salt Creek Bike Path. The path makes a sharp right; then, at the junction, turn left to continue heading toward the ocean. After bearing left to pass under Niguel Road, and then coming out the other side, the path turns sharply to the left, and then climbs steeply (12.3% grade) for about 500 feet.

After one more undulation (5.7% gradient climb), the Salt Creek Bike Path makes a steady descent to the ocean. The path passes under Camino del Avion, entering Dana Point, and then PCH—you may be sharing the path with a few golf carts, as you are adjacent the Monarch Bay Golf Club. After passing under PCH (mile 19.7), the path curves to the left. This is a beautiful stretch, with the Ritz Carlton Laguna Niguel on the left and Salt Creek Beach on the right. Slow down along here to share the path with other users. At the end of the path, turn left onto the access road (maintenance vehicles only), and climb away from the beach (9.1% grade). This is the last serious climb of the ride. After passing under Ritz Carlton Drive, the access road empties into a large parking lot. Turn right, and then right again to get to the lot's exit ramp. At the end of the ramp, turn left onto Ritz Carlton Drive—watch for traffic, as sight distance is poor. At the traffic signal, turn right onto CA 1, and head toward Dana Point's commercial district.

Bike Shops

Buy My Bikes, 32302 Camino Capistrano, San Juan Capistrano, (949) 493-5611, http://buymybikes.com; Bicycles San Clemente, 1900 North El Camino Real, San Clemente, (949) 492-5737, http://urbanbicycleoutfitters.com; Cycle Werks, 1421 North El Camino Real, San Clemente, (949) 492-5911, http://cyclewerks.net

As CA 1 curves to the left, climbing gradually, the road splits, with Del Prado Avenue veering to the right. Take Del Prado, as the "business" alternative to CA 1. Del Prado descends through Dana Point's commercial district, barely giving you time to notice the local shops and restaurants. Many of the streets have a "lantern" attachment, such as Golden Lantern Street. Speaking of Golden Lantern, turn right here and descend (6.7% grade) to Dana Point Harbor Drive. Turn right here for a tour of the harbor's roads, now at mile 22.45. You can bypass the tour by turning left onto Dana Point Harbor, but why not take the tour? While all of southern Orange County's beachfront

Dana Point's Lanterns and Harbor

Nearly any story about Dana Point begins with author Richard Henry Dana, who visited the area in 1835, and later wrote about it in *Two Years Before the Mast*. The city, which incorporated in 1989, was named for Dana Point, which is the prominent bluff at the southwestern edge of the city, overlooking the ocean. The point had been named for Mr. Dana, who referred to the area as the most beautiful spot on the California coast, and "the only romantic spot" on the coast. Despite his praise, Mr. Dana was critical of Dana Point's anchorage, which he described as poor.

Mr. Dana's assessment of the anchorage came long before the construction of the harbor, which was dedicated in 1971. The harbor is home to a marina, shops, restaurants, and beach, along with the Ocean Institute, which is an educational and research facility for the marine environment. The institute owns *The Pilgrim*, which is a replica of the original *Pilgrim* that Richard Henry Dana sailed during the early 19th century. On the downside, perhaps for surfers, is that Dana Point Harbor "killed" Killer Dana, which was the name of a renowned surf break just off the coast of Dana Point. With the construction of a breakwater to tame the waves, for the harbor, Killer Dana ceased to exist. Fortunately, there is still good surf at Doheny State Beach, just to the southeast of the harbor.

Dana Point is also known for its Lantern Village, which is a community of about 12,000 residents located just to the north of the commercial district. The lanterns concept arose from the historical use, some 200 years ago, of colored lanterns by ships that moored in the harbor. The colors advertised the ships' wares. In tribute to that era, there is a series of "lantern" streets: Street of the Blue Lantern, Street of the Violet Lantern, and also Amber, Green, Park, and Ruby. The most famous may be the Street of the Golden Lantern, which is used in this ride.

cities have beach access, only Dana Point has a harbor. The next harbor to the north is in Newport Beach. Ride Dana Point Harbor Drive all the way to its end, adjacent the Ocean Institute. You will probably notice the vintage ship to your left—*The Pilgrim*, a replica of Richard Henry Dana's vessel. Return via Dana Point Harbor Drive; at Island Way, turn right and cross the bridge for an island tour. You are just 4 feet above sea level on the island, the lowest elevation of the ride. Turn right onto Dana Drive and head to one end of the island, then turn around and head to the other end. Turn around again, and return to Island Way via Dana Drive, and then cross Island Way to return to Dana Point Harbor Drive. The island tour is 2.1 miles in length, including the bridge.

Back at Dana Point Harbor Drive (mile 25.95), turn right to leave the harbor area. Turn right at Park Lantern Street and ride on into Doheny State Beach. Continue on Park Lantern, over San Juan Creek (you were here earlier), keeping straight, under the railroad tracks, and then turning right onto PCH. Doheny State Beach and the railroad tracks are now on your right. Folks heading for the beach who do not want to pay the state fee park along here, and then walk across the pedestrian bridge that you see up ahead. Ride under the bridge; at Palisades Drive, turn right to enter Capo Beach Park and conclude the ride.

MILES AND DIRECTIONS

0.0 Start at Capistrano Beach Park in Dana Point. Leave the park, and head toward the Pacific Coast Highway (PCH), crossing the railroad tracks.

0.05 Traffic signal at PCH; keep straight onto Palisades Drive—begin climb (8.2% grade).

0.3 Stop sign at Camino Capistrano; turn right.

1.9 Camino Capistrano curves to the right and heads downhill (5.9% grade).

2.35 Traffic signal at PCH; turn right—option to cross PCH and ride in the protected bike lane.

3.95 Traffic signal at Palisades Drive; turn left and enter Capistrano Beach Park.

4.0 Turn right onto paved path, then keep straight into Doheny State Beach parking area (long, linear paved lot).

4.7 Leave the parking area—keep straight onto park road.

4.95 Stop sign at Park Lantern Street; turn left.

5.05 Bridge over San Juan Creek.

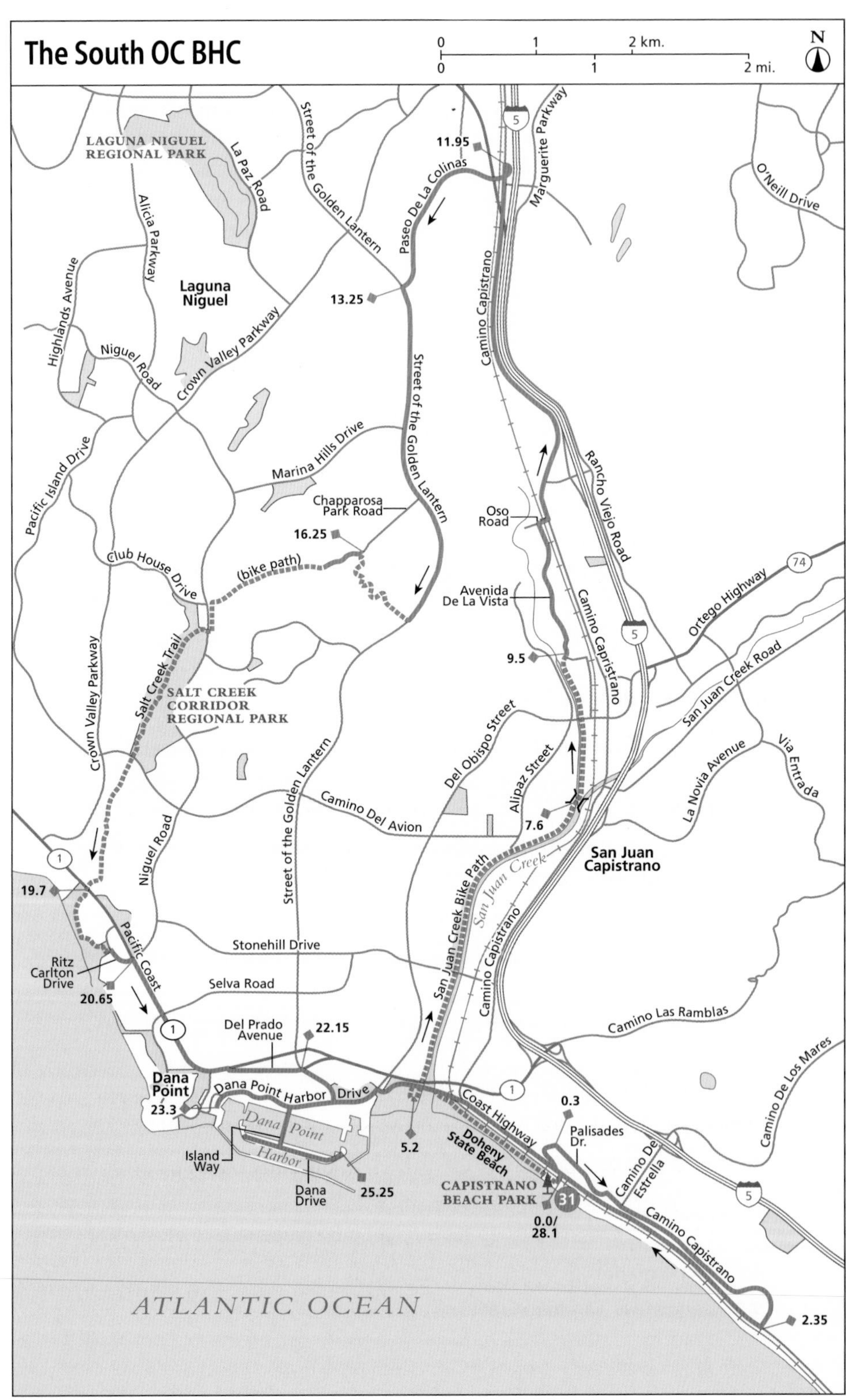

The South OC BHC
0
1
2 km.
0
1
2 mi.
N
LAGUNA NIGUEL
REGIONAL PARK
La Paz Road
Street of the Golden Lantern
Paseo De La Colinas
11.95
5
Marguerite Parkway
O'Neill Drive
Alicia Parkway
Highlands Avenue
Laguna
Niguel
13.25
Camino Capistrano
Niguel Road
Crown Valley Parkway
Street of the Golden Lantern
Marina Hills Drive
Pacific Island Drive
Rancho Viejo Road
Chapparosa
Park Road
Oso
Road
16.25
Club House Drive
(bike path)
74
Ortego Highway
Avenida
De La Vista
Camino Capistrano
5
Crown Valley Parkway
Salt Creek Trail
9.5
SALT CREEK
CORRIDOR
REGIONAL PARK
San Juan Creek Road
Del Obispo Street
La Novia Avenue
Via Entrada
Street of the Golden Lantern
Alipaz Street
Camino Del Avion
7.6
Niguel Road
San Juan
Capistrano
1
San Juan Creek Bike Path
San Juan Creek
19.7
Camino Capistrano
Pacific Coast
Stonehill Drive
Ritz
Carlton
Drive
Selva Road
20.65
Camino Las Ramblas
1
Del Prado
Avenue
22.15
Camino De Los Mares
Dana
Point
Dana Point Harbor
Drive
1
23.3
Coast Highway
0.3
Dana Point
Harbor
Island
Way
5.2
Doheny
State Beach
Palisades
Dr.
Camino De
Estrella
Dana
Drive
25.25
CAPISTRANO
BEACH PARK
31
0.0/
28.1
5
Camino Capistrano
ATLANTIC OCEAN
2.35

5.1 Turn left onto paved path.

5.2 Turn sharply to the left (180 degrees) and continue onto San Juan Creek Bike Path.

6.1 Pass under Stonehill Road; enter San Juan Capistrano to the north of Stonehill.

7.6 Turn right to cross bridge over San Juan Creek, then turn left, at end of bridge, to continue on Trabuco Creek Bike Path.

8.1 Pass under Del Obispo Street.

8.55 End of bike path; continue onto Avenida de la Vista.

9.45 Stop sign at Oso Road; turn right.

9.5 Traffic signal at Camino Capistrano; turn left.

10.9 Short bridge over Trabuco Creek; enter Laguna Niguel.

11.6 Pass under CA 73 freeway.

11.85 Pass under Paseo de Colinas.

11.95 Traffic signal at Paseo de Colinas; turn right.

12.1 Pass under CA 73 freeway again; begin climb (7.3% grade).

12.55 Gradient of climb eases at El Sur.

13.0 Crest of climb at Del Cerro; begin descent.

13.25 Traffic signal at Golden Lantern Street; turn left—begin climb (7.8% grade).

13.65 Crest of climb at Dunes Street (elevation 608 feet); begin rolling segment.

15.5 Leave Golden Lantern, bearing right onto Salt Creek Bike Path.

16.25 End of path; turn left onto Chapparosa Park Road; enter Chapparosa Park.

16.5 End of road; keep straight onto Salt Creek Bike Path.

17.35 Turn left at junction.

17.55 Pass under Niguel Road, then bear left to continue on Salt Creek path; steep climb (12.3% grade).

17.75 Crest of climb; after one more climb, path begins to descend.

18.7 Turn right and pass under Camino del Avion; enter Dana Point.

19.7 Pass under PCH; path curves to the left.

20.3 End of path; Salt Creek Beach is on the right—turn left and climb hill (9.1% grade).

20.4 Pass under Ritz Carlton Drive; enter parking lot.

20.45 Turn right, and then right again to access parking lot exit ramp.

20.5 Turn left onto Ritz Carlton Drive (poor sight distance).

20.65 Traffic signal at CA 1 (PCH); turn right.

21.65 Bear right onto Del Prado Avenue; descend through commercial district.

22.15 Traffic signal at Golden Lantern Street; turn right—descend 6.7% grade.

22.45 Traffic signal at Dana Point Harbor Drive; turn right.

23.3 End of Dana Point Harbor Drive; turn around and return.

23.85 Turn right onto Island Way, and cross bridge.

24.1 Turn right on island (Dana Drive); ride to the road's end, then turn around & return.

25.25 At other end of island, turn around and return on Dana Drive.

25.7 Turn right onto Island Way; cross bridge.

25.95 Turn right onto Dana Point Harbor Drive.

26.55 Traffic signal at Park Lantern Street; turn right.

26.85 Bridge over San Juan Creek.

27.05 Pass under railroad tracks.

27.1 Turn right onto PCH.

28.05 Traffic signal at Palisades Drive; turn right.

28.1 End of ride at Capistrano Beach Park.

32

Tour of the Master Plan: Irvine Ranch

Start: Mike Ward Community Park, 20 Lake Rd., Irvine

Length: 22.85 miles (two intersecting loops)

Riding time: 1.5 to 3.5 hours (my time: 1H43:05)

Terrain and surface: 77% paved paths, 23% paved roads

Elevations: Low—26 feet in William R. Mason Regional Park; high—248 feet at Yale Avenue and Hicks Canyon Trail

Traffic and hazards: Yale Avenue carried 12,000 vehicles per day north of Irvine Center Drive in 2014; Harvard Avenue carried 14,000 vehicles per day north of Barranca Parkway in 2014.

Map: *The Thomas Guide by Rand McNally—Street Guide: Los Angeles and Orange Counties* (any recent year), page 860

Getting there by car: From central Anaheim, head south on I-5. Exit at Culver Drive and turn right. Turn left at Alton Parkway, then turn left onto Lake Road. Mike Ward Community Park is on the right; enter the park, and park.

Getting there by public transit: OCTA bus route 86 runs along Alton Parkway in Irvine, operating between Costa Mesa (South Coast Plaza) and Mission Viejo every hour on weekdays. The bus stops at Lake Road, adjacent the park. Also, route 175 runs north–south in Irvine, between Northwood Village and UC–Irvine, every 70 minutes on weekdays. The bus stops on Lake Road, at the park.

Starting point coordinates: 33.676533°N / 117.574931°W

THE RIDE

The Tour of the Master Plan: Irvine Ranch takes the rider on a mini-excursion through the city of Irvine, predominantly on bike paths. Any shortened version of the ride would be suitable for families. Outside of the University of California complex, the city features two commercial districts: Irvine Business Complex in the west and Irvine Spectrum in the east. The Tour of the Master

Plan stays within the central part of Irvine, never straying west of the Business Complex, east of the Spectrum, or south of the university.

Start the ride in Mike Ward Community Park, just off of Lake Road, north of Alton Parkway, in central Irvine. The lakes in the park were part of an original, circular plan for the city which lost its footing when it proved impossible to locate UC–Irvine in the center. You will tour the lakes later in the ride. For now, start by heading toward the north side of the park, crossing the bridge over San Diego Creek, and then turning right onto San Diego Creek Trail (paved bikeway). After crossing Creek Road at grade (mile 0.25), and passing under Jeffrey Road (mile 1.0), the path curves to the left and deposits you onto Jeffrey Road's walkway. Never fear—make a sharp left to ride along the walkway, crossing over San Diego Creek. Next, turn left to continue on the bikeway. Although the path continues, leave the bikeway at Sand Canyon Avenue; turn right and ride along the roadway. After crossing Alton Parkway, ride up onto the walkway, and onto Freeway Trail (paved bikeway). The path curves to the right to parallel the I-405 freeway.

Next, take the Jeffrey Open Space Trail (bridge) over I-405, and resume riding on the University Trail (paved bikeway) on the other side, continuing in the same direction that you were riding before crossing. Follow the bikeway as it curves to the left to parallel University Drive. After crossing Strawberry Farm Road and Ridgeline Drive, turn left onto Ridgeline (walkway), and then bear right to enter William R. Mason Regional Park (mile 4.9). To your left, beyond the boundary of the park, is Concordia University, a private Christian institution founded in 1973. Olympic beach volleyball gold medalist Misty May-Treanor is one of Concordia's accomplished graduates.

Follow the path as it curves to the right, and then to the left. The path is downhill through here, so watch your speed rounding those curves! At the split (mile 5.7), stay to the right to remain on University Trail; stay to the left at the next split (mile 5.8). The trail splits again at mile 6.15; stay to the right here, and head for the intersection of Culver Drive and University Drive. Cross Culver Drive at the intersection, in the crosswalk, and then bear left and then right to continue riding through Mason Regional Park. Stay on the path, near

Bike Shops

ARB Cyclery, 17985 Sky Park Circle, Suite E, Irvine, (949) 752-2080, www.arbcyclery.com; Irvine Bicycles, 6616 Irvine Center Dr., (949) 453-9999, www.irvinebicycles.com; Jax Bicycle Center, Heritage Plaza, 14210 Culver Dr., Irvine, (949) 733-1212, http://jaxbicycles.com; Rock N' Road Cyclery, Woodbury Town Center, 6282 Irvine Blvd., Irvine, (949) 733-2453, www.rocknroadcyclery.net

A rider cruises along Peters Canyon Trail in Irvine, adjacent heavily vegetated Peters Canyon Wash, with Loma Ridge in the distance.

the park's north side as it crosses a park road and then enters a fun chicane. If there are no other path users around, then you can test your bike handling skills by swerving through the curves. University Trail reaches the lowest elevation of the ride (26 feet) near the park's western end (mile 7.0).

Turn right onto the park road, and head toward the exit; next, turn left onto the University Drive walkway, and ride to the Harvard Avenue intersection. Cross University Drive here, and then cross Harvard to continue on the path. Look for the connecting path, on your right, to take you to San Diego Creek. Turn right onto San Diego Creek Trail (mile 7.25; paved bikeway), watching for other trail users, and head north, toward central Irvine. San Diego Creek Trail is a speedy bike path; follow it as it curves to the left, passing under Michelson Drive (mile 8.25), and then I-405 (mile 8.45). Once on other side of the freeway, turn right onto Freeway Trail (paved bikeway). Pass under Harvard Avenue at mile 8.75, and then cross Culver Drive (at-grade crossing—wait for the traffic signal). Leave Freeway Trail at Yale Avenue by turning left onto the connector path, and then emerging adjacent Yale. Cross over to the other side of Yale when it is safe, and ride along the road's shoulder. After

Outcomes of the Master Plan

Irvine was famously planned by architect William Pereira and Irvine Company visionary Raymond Watson. The city's current layout is based on strings of villages or townships that are separated by six-lane surface streets. There are two parallel main streets (Culver Drive and Jeffrey Road–University Drive) that cross the city, eventually meeting at the "pendant," which is the University of California–Irvine, in the city's south. The city of Irvine has grown rapidly, from sketches on a planner's vellum in the early 1960s to nearly full buildout, with a population of over 250,000 in 2015. Prior to the development of the Master Plan, James Irvine was busy, during the late 19th century, acquiring property from the owners of Spanish/Mexican land grants. By the time Mr. Irvine died, in 1886, his 110,000 acres stretched from the Santa Ana River to the Pacific Ocean. His son, James Irvine Jr., incorporated the land into the Irvine Company, and shifted its interests from ranching to crops, including olives and citrus fruits. By 1914, a town named Irvine was growing around a local Santa Fe Railroad station. When James Irvine Jr. died in 1947, his son Myford assumed leadership of The Irvine Company and began opening the doors to urban development. The rest, as they say, is history.

Along the way, the city has won numerous awards, such as a ranking by *Business Week* as the fifth-best city in the United States in 2011, as well as America's "best-run city" by *24/7 Wall Street* in 2014. Several major businesses are headquartered in Irvine, including Ford Motor Company's West Coast operations, In-N-Out Burger, Quicksilver Software, Ruby's Diner, Tilly's, and Taco Bell (owned by China's Yum! Brands, Inc.). The city's largest employer is the University of California–Irvine, which has thrived despite not being located in the heart of the city, as according to William Pereira's original plan. UC–Irvine has attracted top-notch faculty and graduated such notables as actor-comedian Jon Lovitz, author Alice Sebold, Olympic gold medalists Brad Alan Lewis (rowing) and Greg Louganis (diving), and Internet pioneer Roy Fielding, among many others. Not much seems to have gone wrong in Irvine's development, although the city fought for a while to obtain the former Marine Corps Air Station El Toro property. Also, the former Lion Country Safari—an outdoor, drive-through zoo—went bankrupt in 1984 and was replaced by Wild Rivers. The waterpark also shut down, in 2011, along with the adjacent Camp James, and was dormant as of this writing, with the exception of seasonal cyclocross and running events.

crossing East Yale Loop (a looping road), ride up onto the walkway. Bear right, and then bear left to ride along the edge of South Lake. Stay to the right at the split to move away from the lake (mile 10.7). Stay to the left, to the right, and then to the right at the next three junctions. Cross Clearlake (residential street), and then follow the path as it curves to the left, and then to the right. Cross the bridge over Alton Parkway (mile 11.1) and keep straight. You are now back at Mike Ward Community Park—but the ride is not over! You can stop here, but the ride is only half over, and you will miss the awesome tour of the northern parts of the city! So turn right to cross the bridge over San Diego Creek (the same one that you crossed at the beginning of the ride). Once across the bridge, keep straight.

The path enters a small retail center—follow the signs as they guide you through the parking area and onto another bridge—this one crossing Barranca Parkway. Touchdown on the other side of the bridge places you on the shore of North Lake (mile 11.65), South Lake's companion. Ride along the shore path, on the west side of the lake—slowing down for other path users—until the path veers away from the lake at mile 12.05. Follow the path as it enters Irvine's Woodbridge Village. The path curves to the right, and then to the left to skim Lemongrass Park. After another curve to the right, the path returns to the shoreline of North Lake. From here, ride to the far north end of the lake (mile 12.4), at West Yale Loop.

Next, cross West Yale Loop, and then continue northward on Yale Avenue (note that you may have to cross West Yale and then Yale, in succession). You are now riding northward on Yale's shoulder, still in Woodbridge Village. Yale crosses over Como Channel and Walnut Trail (paved bikeway—another great riding option) at mile 13.05. Yale crosses over I-5 at mile 13.8, and enters Irvine's Northwood Village. The road continues a very gradual climb through the village. At mile 15.85, look for Hicks Canyon Trail (paved bikeway) on the left. Turn left here, now at the highest elevation of the ride (248 feet). After a pleasant stretch along which the trail is parallel to a dirt path, Hicks Canyon passes under Culver Drive. The path reverts to a walkway on the other side, crossing Central Park Avenue at grade at mile 16.95, and then curving to the left to join Peters Canyon Trail (paved bikeway) at mile 17.25.

You are now heading southward on Peters Canyon Trail. Pass under Irvine Boulevard at mile 17.5, under Bryan Avenue at mile 18.05, under El Camino Real at mile 18.25, and I-5 at mile 18.5. The trail is gradually downhill along this entire stretch. After passing under Harvard Avenue (mile 19.0) and Walnut Avenue (19.1), the path curves sharply to the left, and then ends at Harvard Avenue (mile 19.75). At Harvard Avenue, the path continues as Walnut Trail (paved bikeway) or, by crossing Harvard and turning to the right, as Harvard Trail. This route uses neither of these options, though, preferring to simply

ride on the shoulder of Harvard Avenue. Continue to Barranca Parkway (mile 21.3); cross here, ride up onto the walkway, turn right, and then turn sharply to the left to access San Diego Creek Trail once again.

Follow San Diego Creek Trail as it passes under Harvard, Paseo Westpark (mile 21.75), Culver Drive (mile 22.1), and Yale Loop (mile 22.25). Cross Lake Street at grade (sorry; no underpass here) and continue to the bridge on your right. Turn right and cross over San Diego Creek—this is the third time that you have crossed this bridge! Continue into Mike Ward Community Park to conclude the ride.

MILES AND DIRECTIONS

0.0 From Mike Ward Community Park in Irvine, start by crossing the bridge over San Diego Creek on the north side of the park.

0.05 Turn right onto San Diego Creek Trail (paved bikeway).

0.25 Cross Creek Road at grade.

0.8 Pass under Yale Loop.

1.0 Pass under Jeffrey Road, and then turn sharply to the left, onto Jeffrey Road's walkway.

1.1 Turn left to resume riding on San Diego Creek Trail.

1.25 Pass under Valley Oak Drive.

2.35 Exit the path at Sand Canyon Avenue; turn right on Sand Canyon—OK to ride in the road.

2.65 Cross Alton Parkway (traffic signal), and ride up onto the walkway—veer right onto Freeway Trail (paved bikeway).

3.6 Turn left to cross over I-405 on Jeffrey Open Space Trail (bridge).

3.7 Merge onto University Trail (paved bikeway) heading west, then curving left to head southwest.

4.45 At-grade crossing of Strawberry Farm Road (traffic signal); keep straight.

4.8 At-grade crossing of Ridgeline Drive (traffic signal); cross street and then turn left onto walkway.

4.9 Bear right onto University Trail; enter William R. Mason Regional Park.

5.7 Stay right at junction to remain on University Trail.

5.8 Stay left at split in trail to remain on University Trail.

6.15 Bear right at split in trail to remain on University Trail.

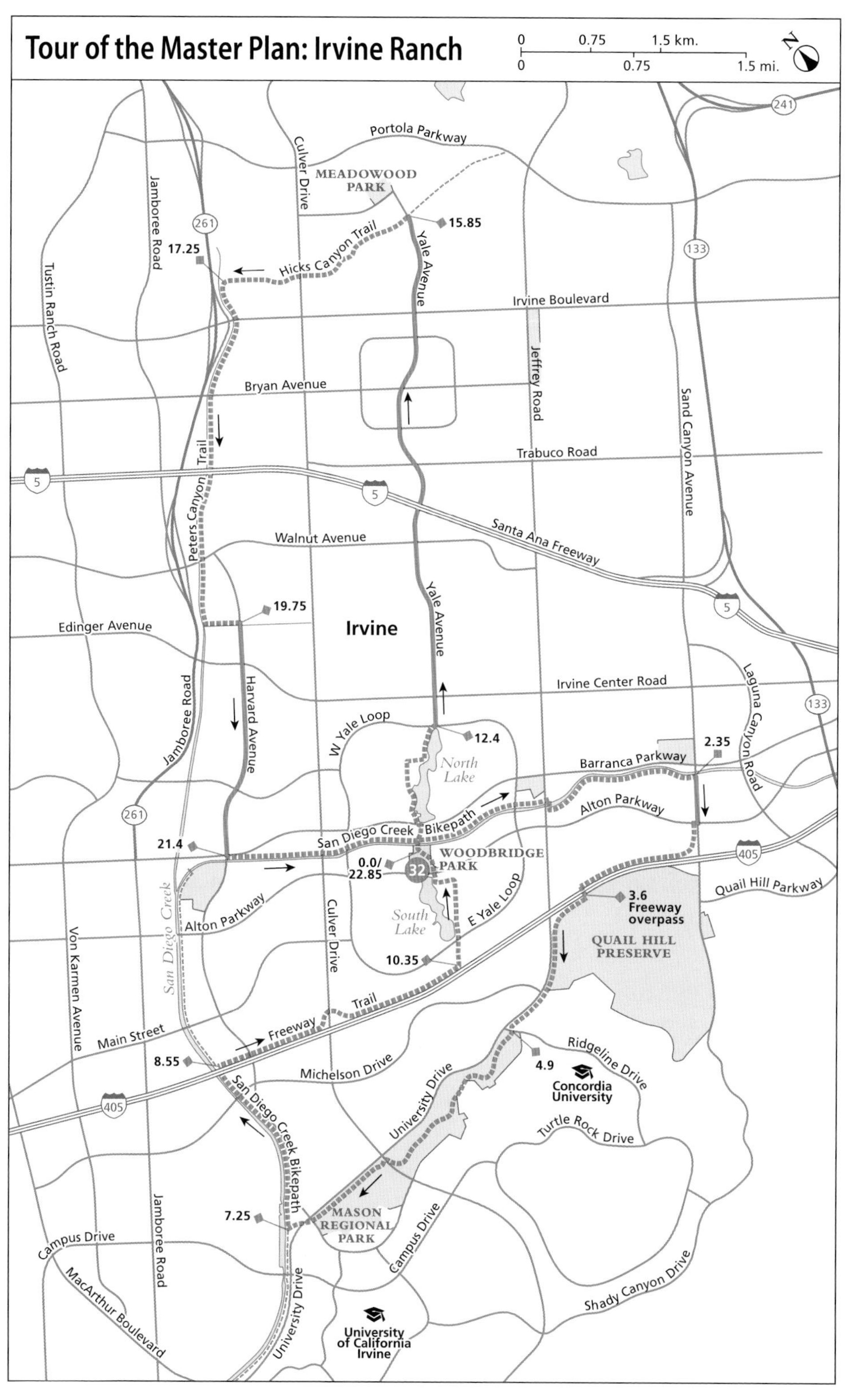

Tour of the Master Plan: Irvine Ranch
0 0.75 1.5 km.
0 0.75 1.5 mi.
N
Portola Parkway
MEADOWOOD PARK
Culver Drive
Jamboree Road
Tustin Ranch Road
261
17.25
15.85
Hicks Canyon Trail
Yale Avenue
133
241
Irvine Boulevard
Jeffrey Road
Bryan Avenue
Trabuco Road
Sand Canyon Avenue
Peters Canyon Trail
5
Santa Ana Freeway
Walnut Avenue
19.75
Irvine
Edinger Avenue
Irvine Center Road
Laguna Canyon Road
Harvard Avenue
W Yale Loop
12.4
North Lake
2.35
Barranca Parkway
Alton Parkway
San Diego Creek Bikepath
21.4
0.0/ 22.85
32
WOODBRIDGE PARK
405
Quail Hill Parkway
3.6 Freeway overpass
South Lake
E Yale Loop
QUAIL HILL PRESERVE
San Diego Creek
Von Karmen Avenue
10.35
Freeway Trail
Main Street
Ridgeline Drive
8.55
Michelson Drive
4.9
Concordia University
University Drive
Turtle Rock Drive
San Diego Creek Bikepath
7.25
MASON REGIONAL PARK
Campus Drive
MacArthur Boulevard
Shady Canyon Drive
University of California Irvine

6.3 Cross Culver Drive at traffic signal; turn left after crossing, and then veer right to continue on University Trail, through Mason Regional Park.

6.6 At-grade crossing of park road.

7.0 Lowest elevation of ride (26 feet); turn right onto park road.

7.05 End of park road; turn left onto University Drive, and then cross both Harvard Avenue and University Drive to continue on University Trail on the opposite side of the road.

7.15 Turn right onto connector path.

7.25 End of connector path; turn right onto San Diego Creek Trail (paved bikeway)—watch for other path users.

8.1 Bear left to remain on San Diego Creek Trail.

8.25 Pass under Michelson Drive and then under I-405.

8.55 Turn right onto Freeway Trail (paved bikeway).

8.75 Pass under Harvard Avenue.

9.4 At-grade crossing of Culver Drive and I-405 freeway ramp (traffic signal); keep straight.

10.35 Turn left onto connector path.

10.5 Merge onto Yale Avenue—cross over to the other side when safe, and head north.

10.55 Stop sign at East Yale Loop; ride across and up onto walkway, then turn right onto lakeside path.

10.7 Stay to the right, moving away from South Lake.

10.75 Stay left, then right, and then right again at the next three trail junctions.

10.9 Cross Clearlake (residential street) at grade.

11.0 Path curves to the left, and then to the right to cross bridge over Alton Parkway.

11.1 Enter Mike Ward Community Park; keep straight, on path.

11.4 Turn right to cross bridge over San Diego Creek (same bridge as at the start).

11.45 Keep straight at junction; enter parking area of retail center—follow signs to remain on path.

11.55 Bridge over Barranca Parkway.

11.65 Path is now along the western shore of North Lake; remain lakeside.

11.9 Path veers to the left, away from lake—enter Woodbridge Village.

11.95 Cross Crosscreek (residential street) at grade; keep straight.

12.05 Path curves to the right, then to the left, and then to the right, returning to lakeside.

12.4 End of path at West Yale Loop; cross street and head north on Yale Avenue. You may need to cross Yale Loop, and then Yale Avenue to be positioned on the right side of Yale.

13.05 Cross over Walnut Trail (paved bikeway) and Como Channel.

13.8 Cross over I-5.

15.85 Turn left onto Hicks Canyon Trail (paved bikeway); highest elevation of ride (248 feet).

16.7 Pass under Culver Drive.

16.95 Cross Central Park Avenue at grade (traffic signal); keep straight.

17.25 Path curves left; merge with Peters Canyon Trail (paved bikeway).

17.5 Pass under Irvine Boulevard, Bryan Avenue, El Camino Real, I-5, Harvard Avenue, and Walnut Avenue over the next 1.6 miles.

19.55 Path curves sharply to the left.

19.75 End of path at Harvard Avenue; turn right onto Harvard—ride in roadway.

21.3 Cross Barranca Parkway (traffic signal); ride up onto walkway and turn right, and then sharply to the right, onto San Diego Creek Trail (paved bikeway).

21.4 Pass under Harvard Avenue, Paseo Westpark, Culver Drive, and Yale Loop over the next 0.85 mile.

22.65 At-grade crossing of Lake Street; keep straight.

22.75 Turn right to cross bridge over San Diego Creek.

22.85 Enter Mike Ward Community Park; end of ride.

Whiting Ranch Wilderness Excursion

Start: Whiting Ranch Wilderness Park, Borrego parking lot (small parking fee), 26701 Portola Pkwy., Foothill Ranch

Length: 5.4 miles (clockwise loop)

Riding time: 30 minutes to 2 hours (my time: 42:53)

Terrain and surface: 82% dirt trails, 18% paved roads

Elevations: Low—800 feet at Portola Parkway and Lake Forest Drive; high—1,462 feet at Four Corners (junction between Mustard Road, Whiting Ranch Trail, and other trails) in Whiting Ranch Wilderness Park

Traffic and hazards: Portola Parkway carried 35,000 vehicles per day east of Lake Forest Drive in 2014; traffic volumes were lighter west of Lake Forest Drive. Motor vehicles were absent on the trails of Whiting Ranch Wilderness Park.

Map: *The Thomas Guide by Rand McNally—Street Guide: Los Angeles and Orange Counties* (any recent year), page 862

Getting there by car: From central Anaheim, head south on I-5. Exit at Bake Parkway; turn left and head northeast on Bake. Turn left at Portola Parkway, in the Foothill Ranch community of Lake Forest. Turn right onto Market Place Court, and then make an immediate left to enter the Borrego parking lot.

Getting there by public transit: OCTA bus route 82 runs between Saddleback College in Mission Viejo and Foothill Marketplace, opposite the Borrego parking lot, every 30 to 65 minutes on weekdays and every 100 minutes on Saturdays. Route 177 runs between Laguna Hills and Foothill Marketplace every 45 minutes on weekdays, every 100 minutes on Saturdays, and every 80 minutes on Sundays and holidays.

Starting point coordinates: 33.681017°N / 117.664494°W

THE RIDE

The Whiting Ranch Wilderness Excursion is a nifty 5.4-mile mountain bike ride through the namesake park, on the fringes of Lake Forest's Foothill Ranch. Whiting Ranch Wilderness Park is a 2,500-acre expanse of riparian and oak woodland canyons, with rolling hills of grassland, and some steep slopes covered with coastal sage scrub and chaparral. The park is known for its scenic rock formations, including Red Rock Canyon. Red Rock is not accessible by bike, but the half-mile-long Red Rock Canyon Trail can be accessed on foot from Mustard Road, which is along the route described here. While the park is peaceful most of the time, it has had its share of notoriety. On January 8, 2004, Mark Reynolds was attacked and killed by a mountain lion while mountain biking through Whiting Ranch—this was the last known mountain lion–initiated fatality in California. In October and November of 2007, the Santiago Fire burned 90% of Whiting Ranch, threatening nearby homes in Foothill Ranch. The fire was started by an arsonist, burned for 31 days, involved up to 1,100 firefighters, sixteen of whom were injured, burned 28,445 acres, and caused $21.6 million worth of damage. The park continues to recover from the scars. In 2012, the park was closed for a while because of mountain lion sightings. In 2014, ten years after the fatality, a mountain lion was observed to be stalking a family out for a hike. The animal was scared off by an onlooker who threw rocks, and was later shot and killed (the mountain lion, not the hiker) by park officials. Wild indeed!

Presuming that the preceding news has not dissuaded you from riding here, leave the Borrego parking lot (be sure to pay the parking fee), and access Borrego Canyon Trail, the entrance to which is located at the northwest end of the lot. And, what an entrance! The trail immediately descends into the canyon—the descent is actually quite short, but it can catch an unsuspecting biker (like me) off guard. Welcome to the wild! Note that Borrego Canyon Trail is one-way all the way to the Mustard Road junction, so you should not see anyone riding in the opposite direction. There were segments of loose sand along the way when I rode this, as well as a couple of technical spots, so be prepared for some tough hauling. It is a net climb up Borrego Canyon, from a starting elevation of 812 feet to the junction with Mustard Road, which is actually a wide dirt trail, at 1,060 feet.

Bike Shops

Twohubs Cycling Boutique, 27231 Burbank #201, Foothill Ranch (Lake Forest), (877) 480-2453, www.twohubs.com; The Bike Company, 21098 Bake Pkwy. #112, Lake Forest, (949) 470-1099, www.bikeco.com

A cyclist dismounts for a technical segment along Borrego Canyon Trail, in a valley of oaks.

Turn right onto Mustard and continue climbing, steeply at times (9.5% average grade). Aim for that high ridge up ahead. The steep bluffs lined with coastal sage scrub and chaparral, for which Whiting Ranch is known, are in view along this stretch. The climb finally ends at Four Corners, which is a catchy name for the junction between Cactus Hill Trail, Mustard Road, Water Tank Road, Whiting Spur Road, and Whiting Road, all of which are dirt trails. There is a signboard and water here. Although the choices of trails can be confusing, be sure to take the second right, onto Whiting Road. To get to Whiting, turn left at Four Corners, ride a short distance, and then turn right. (An immediate right puts you on Water Tank Road.) This is the high point of the ride, at 1,462 feet. Stay to the right at the Y to remain on Whiting Road (the left fork puts you on Cactus Hill Trail). Whiting Road remains nearly level for about a quarter-mile before widening and dropping precipitously into Upper Serrano Canyon. The descent is at a 12.4% gradient. Near the end of Whiting Road, bear left at the Edison Road junction. Whiting Road ends after another 150 feet; turn right here, onto Line Shack Road (wide dirt trail), and begin the descent of Upper Serrano Canyon. It is not a steep descent, but nonetheless a fast one, as you lose about 250 feet of elevation over the next 1.5 miles.

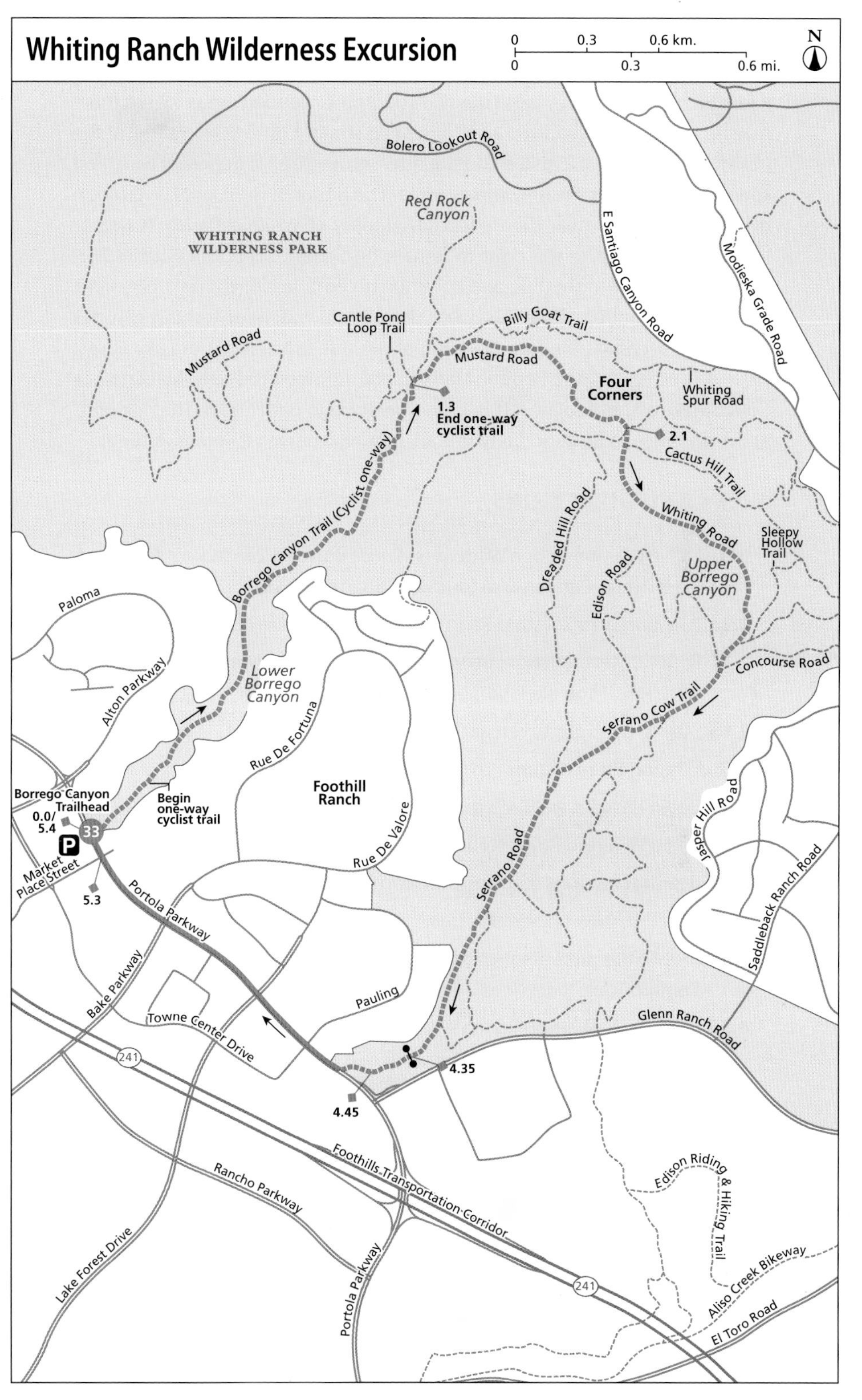
Whiting Ranch Wilderness Excursion
0
0.3
0.6 km.
0
0.3
0.6 mi.
N
Bolero Lookout Road
Red Rock Canyon
WHITING RANCH WILDERNESS PARK
E Santiago Canyon Road
Modjeska Grade Road
Cantle Pond Loop Trail
Billy Goat Trail
Mustard Road
Mustard Road
Four Corners
Whiting Spur Road
1.3
End one-way cyclist trail
2.1
Cactus Hill Trail
Borrego Canyon Trail (Cyclist one-way)
Dreaded Hill Road
Whiting Road
Sleepy Hollow Trail
Edison Road
Upper Borrego Canyon
Paloma
Alton Parkway
Lower Borrego Canyon
Concourse Road
Serrano Cow Trail
Rue De Fortuna
Foothill Ranch
Jasper Hill Road
Borrego Canyon Trailhead
0.0/ 5.4
33
P
Begin one-way cyclist trail
Rue De Valore
Serrano Road
Saddleback Ranch Road
Market Place Street
5.3
Portola Parkway
Bake Parkway
Towne Center Drive
Pauling
Glenn Ranch Road
241
4.35
4.45
Foothills Transportation Corridor
Rancho Parkway
Edison Riding & Hiking Trail
Lake Forest Drive
Portola Parkway
Aliso Creek Bikeway
241
El Toro Road

Junction to Serrano Cow Trail at the next fork—stay to the right. There are a few technical sections, particularly through the wooded areas where there may be a mixture of shadows and light. Keep straight onto Serrano Trail at the next junction, now 3.55 miles into the ride. Serrano Trail is generally wide and speedy. Stay right at the next fork to remain on Serrano. The roar of civilization gets louder as you near the (fenced) boundary of Whiting Ranch. Navigate the gate, and keep to the right to remain on Serrano. The trail ends at Portola Parkway. Turn right here and continue on Portola, which has a bike lane. There are a number of traffic signals along here; watch for turning vehicles at the intersections. The low elevation of the ride (800 feet) is at Lake Forest Drive. Keep straight past Foothill Marketplace, turning right onto Marketplace Court. Make an immediate left to enter the Borrego parking lot. The ride ends at the entrance to Borrego Canyon Trail. Take another lap if you have time!

MILES AND DIRECTIONS

0.0 Leave Whiting Ranch Wilderness Park's Borrego Canyon parking lot via Borrego Canyon Trail (one-way up the canyon).

1.3 Junction with Mustard Road (wide dirt trail); turn right.

2.1 Four Corners junction; bear left, and then right onto Whiting Road (dirt trail). High elevation of ride (1,462 feet).

2.15 Stay to the right to remain on Whiting Road.

2.3 Whiting Road widens.

2.4 Begin descent at 12.4% grade.

2.95 End of Whiting Road; turn right on Line Shack Road (dirt trail).

3.15 Bear right at junction, onto Serrano Cow Trail.

3.55 Bear left; now on Serrano Trail.

4.15 Stay to the right at junction with Raptor Road (dirt trail) to remain on Serrano Trail.

4.35 Gate; leave Whiting Ranch Wilderness Park—stay right at the next junction to remain on Serrano Trail.

4.45 End of Serrano Trail; turn right onto Portola Parkway (paved road).

4.55 Traffic signal at Lake Forest Drive (low elevation of ride: 800 feet); keep straight.

5.3 Traffic signal at Market Place Court; turn right.

5.35 Turn left to enter Borrego parking lot.

5.4 End of ride at entrance to Borrego Canyon Trail.

Best Edge of Orange County Rides

To get a full tour of Orange County's roads and trails, entering Los Angeles, Riverside, and San Bernardino Counties cannot be completely avoided. For example, to get to the east face of the Santa Ana Mountains, it is easier to enter from the east side (Riverside County) than the west. This chapter includes a few edge rides, including some that start and finish outside of Orange County, but that enter and leave it along the way. These edge rides explore the southern and eastern sections of Chino Hills State Park, the Santa Ana Mountains, the Puente Hills, the Prado Dam area, and US Marine Corps Base Camp Pendleton. The rides provide opportunities to see cities and communities that act as gateways from Orange County into Los Angeles County, and the adjacent Inland Empire, including Chino, Chino Hills, Corona, Hacienda Heights, La Habra Heights, Lake Elsinore, Rowland Heights, Temescal Valley, and Whittier. Given that San Juan Capistrano's swallows seem to have found a new home in Chino Hills, it is arguably appropriate that cyclists also establish a link to Orange County's edge. There are nine rides on the edge, five of which are for mountain bikes.

Chino Hills Ridges Challenge

Start: Quarter Horse Drive trailhead, on Quarter Horse Drive just past Winners Circle, Yorba Linda

Length: 23.6 miles (clockwise loop)

Riding time: 2.5 to 6.5 hours (my time: 3H06:58)

Terrain and surface: 71% of the ride is on dirt trails; 27% is on paved public roads, and 2% is on a paved park road.

Elevations: Low—391 feet at Esperanza Road and New River Road in Yorba Linda; high—1,711 feet on South Ridge Trail near the Orange County–San Bernardino County line

Traffic and hazards: Although most of the ride is in Chino Hills State Park, the return portion is on city streets in Yorba Linda. In 2014, Yorba Linda Boulevard was the busiest, carrying 24,000 vehicles per day; Village Center Drive carried 12,000 vehicles per day north of Yorba Linda Boulevard, and Fairmont Drive carried 8,000 vehicles per day near Quarter Horse Drive.

Map: *The Thomas Guide by Rand McNally—Street Guide: Los Angeles and Orange Counties* (any recent year), page 740

Getting there by car: From central Anaheim, head north on CA 57, and then junction to CA 91 heading east. Exit at Imperial Highway; turn left and head north. Exit at Kellogg Drive and turn right. At Yorba Linda Boulevard, turn right, followed by a left turn onto Fairmont Drive. Near the crest of the climb, turn left onto Quarter Horse Drive. Look for the trailhead (paved parking area) on the right, just past Winners Circle (which will be on the left).

Getting there by public transit: Ride OCTA bus route 26 from central Fullerton to the end of the line at Fairmont Drive and Bastanchury Road in Yorba Linda. From here, it is an uphill half-mile ride via Fairmont (northbound), and a left turn onto Quarter Horse Drive, to the trailhead. Route 26 runs every hour on weekdays and every 45 minutes on weekends and holidays.

Starting point coordinates: 33.904783°N / 117.785339°W

THE RIDE

The Chino Hills Ridges Challenge is exactly as titled. As the companion ride to Ride 4, Chino Hills Trails Trek, the Challenge takes on a longer route that explores the central and southeastern sectors of the park. Although the high-low elevation differential is "just" 1,320 feet, there are four challenging climbs along the way, such that the total elevation gain exceeds 2,700 feet. No water is available for a long stretch, so be sure to bring plenty of fluids. Also, be prepared for a microclimate in the Chino Hills that might be warmer than in the surrounding areas.

Start from the trailhead off of Quarter Horse Drive in the hills of Yorba Linda. There is a paved parking area that directly accesses a connecting trail that takes you into Chino Hills State Park (no barriers, no fees). The trail offers the first challenge of the ride, as it climbs from 781 feet at the trailhead to 1,106 feet at South Ridge Trail (12.1% grade). If you are walking already, then do not be dismayed, but this is actually a taste of what is to come. Turn right onto South Ridge Trail (mile 0.5) and head east. The trail opens with a descent (10.8% grade) to another trailhead, followed by a climb (11.2% grade). While South Ridge Trail undulates, similarly to other ridge trails, the prevailing direction is up. There are short climbs of 9.4%, 10.4%, and 11.4% gradients, interspersed with short descents, over the next mile. Be careful not to "overcook" yourself this early on in the ride, as you will be exhausted by the time you reach the climbs that come later. Keep straight at the junction with Rim Trail at mile 2.05. South Ridge Trail climbs steeply (12.9% grade) beyond here. After a short break, the climbing resumes (9.1% grade). At mile 2.6, a 12.4% grade takes you up to an elevation of 1,572 feet.

Bike Shop

Jax Bicycle Center, 17593 Yorba Linda Blvd., Yorba Linda, (714) 996-9093, http://jaxbicycles.com

After hovering at this elevation for about 0.3 mile, the climbing resumes (7.6% grade), ultimately reaching 1,711 feet at mile 3.65, the highest elevation of the ride. Enter San Bernardino County shortly beyond the crest, and then start a long descent into the canyon (9.8% grade to the merge with Telegraph Spur, and then a 6.4% grade into the canyon). South Ridge Trail ends at Telegraph Canyon Road at mile 6.15, at an elevation of 703 feet, which is lower than the elevation at which you started! Turn right onto Telegraph Canyon Road, which is paved, and negotiate the short climb and descent over the transition between Telegraph Canyon, Bane Canyon, and Lower Aliso Canyon. Note that this area is the heart of the state park. Although you bypassed it at the last turn, just up the road is the Rolling M

A rider stops to soak in the view of Yorba Linda and beyond from a crest along South Ridge Trail in Chino Hills State Park.

Ranch, which features a campground and some historical sites. Turn right onto Bane Canyon Road, which was an overgrown dirt road when I rode it, and head south. At the junction, turn left onto Aliso Canyon Trail (dirt), and head south into Lower Aliso Canyon. To your left is Water Canyon Natural Preserve, which is a "biological corridor" intended for use by certain species of animals.

Continue as Aliso Canyon Trail makes a generally downhill run through the canyon. The trail is rocky in places, and is consistently rough and rugged. Enter Riverside County at mile 10.25. The trail comes to an end at a gate at mile 10.3. Go through the gate, and then turn right onto the Santa Ana River Trail (SART). This is the same SART that is ridden in other routes in this book, although in this area, the SART is a dirt trail, and is not adjacent the river. After another gate, the trail reenters San Bernardino County (mile 10.4). You may see a few horses out here. Notice the huge alluvial plain to your right. At mile 11.0, make a hard right onto Scully Ridge Trail. Reenter Chino Hills State Park, and start climbing (11.6% grade). Within less than 1 mile, the trail climbs from 433 feet at the bottom to 1,029 feet. You can gauge your climb according to how high above the CA 91 freeway you are. As the freeway noises become faint, Scully Ridge Trail continues to escape to the quiet and ruggedness of the Chino Hills. As for that microclimate, mentioned earlier, this is where you might truly feel it.

After a brisk descent (8.2% grade), stay to the left at the junction with Scully Hills Trail to remain on Scully Ridge (mile 12.3). Climb away from the junction (6.6% grade); Water Canyon Natural Preserve is now to your immediate left. The preserve provides habitat for bobcats and mountain lions; hopefully, they will all find what they need inside the preserve, and have no reason to venture out onto the trails. After climbing up to 1,108 feet, Scully Ridge Trail descends (10.0% grade) to a junction with Brush Canyon Trail (mile 13.3). Keep straight here. At mile 13.65, Scully Ridge enters a series of climbs and descents, with gradients ranging from 7 to 9%. Scully Ridge merges with a spur trail at mile 15.0. At the junction with Bobcat Loop Trail (mile 15.05), turn right to remain on Scully Ridge. The trail finally comes to an end at Bobcat Ridge Trail; turn left (mile 15.15).

Bobcat Ridge Trail begins with a long climb (average grade 6.3%) that eventually takes you up to 1,539 feet (mile 16.5). Be sure to keep straight at the junction with Bobcat Loop Trail. After crossing the Orange County line, the trail starts to descend (6.2% grade). After curving to the left, Bobcat Ridge empties out onto a paved access road. The end of the access road is the gateway to civilization as you leave Chino Hills State Park and reenter Yorba Linda. You are now on Hidden Hills Road, in a hillside neighborhood. Hidden Hills descends quickly (10.4% grade)—control your speed. Turn right at mile 18.4 to continue descending on Hidden Hills Drive. Hidden Hills curves to the right at mile 19.4, now at an elevation of 392 feet, becoming Esperanza Road. After all of the steep climbs and descents, Esperanza should be a relaxing transition, as the road is effectively flat. Turn right onto New River Road at the lowest elevation of the entire ride (391 feet). If your legs are exhausted, then unfortunately, it is essentially all uphill from here to the finish.

Turn right onto New River Road (mile 19.7), followed by a right turn onto Avenida Adobe, followed by a right turn onto Yorba Linda Boulevard. The latter is busy, but beautifully tree-lined along this stretch. After reaching a crest at mile 20.9, the boulevard starts to roll. Turn right at Village Center Drive, and start another climb (4.1% grade). At the end of Village Center (mile 21.7), turn left onto Fairmont Drive—it is a fairly steep climb (7.0% grade) to Forest Avenue, where Fairmont starts to descend (4.8% grade). As you are building up speed, turn right onto Quarter Horse Drive for the final segment of the ride. It is a climb (6.9% grade) to the trailhead to conclude the ride. Congratulations for surviving the challenge!

MILES AND DIRECTIONS

0.0 From the Quarter Horse Drive trailhead just off of Fairmont Drive in Yorba Linda (starting elevation: 781 feet). Head up the connector trail (12.1% grade); enter Chino Hills State Park.

0.5 End of trail; turn right onto South Ridge Trail—begin descent (10.8% grade).

0.75 End of descent at junction; keep straight—begin climb (11.2% grade).

1.05 End of climb—enter rolling segment.

1.3 Climb (9.4% grade), followed by a descent (9.5% grade).

1.6 Climb (10.4% grade), followed by a descent (7.4% grade) and a climb (11.4% grade).

1.8 End of climb—trail continues to descend and climb.

2.05 Keep straight at junction with Rim Trail; begin climb (12.9% grade).

2.3 Gradient eases, then continues (9.1% grade), and then eases.

2.6 Steep climb (12.4% grade).

2.85 Gradient eases.

3.15 Begin climb (7.6% grade).

3.65 Highest elevation of ride (1,711 feet).

3.75 Enter San Bernardino County; begin descent (9.8% grade).

4.75 Merge with Telegraph Spur Trail; descent continues (6.4% grade).

6.15 End of South Ridge Trail; turn right onto Telegraph Canyon Road (paved)—elevation 703 feet.

6.55 Turn right onto Bane Canyon Road (dirt)—begin gradual descent.

7.25 End of Bane Canyon Road; turn right onto Aliso Canyon Trail (dirt). Trail continues gradual descent.

10.25 Enter Riverside County—end of Aliso Canyon Trail at gate; go around gate and turn right onto Santa Ana River Trail (dirt).

10.4 Gate; keep straight—reenter San Bernardino County (elevation 447 feet).

11.0 Turn sharply to the right onto Scully Ridge Trail (dirt)—begin climb (11.6% grade).

12.05 Crest of climb (elevation 1,064 feet); begin descent (8.2% grade).

12.3 Keep straight at junction with Scully Hill Trail—begin climb (6.6% grade).

Chino Hills Ridges Challenge

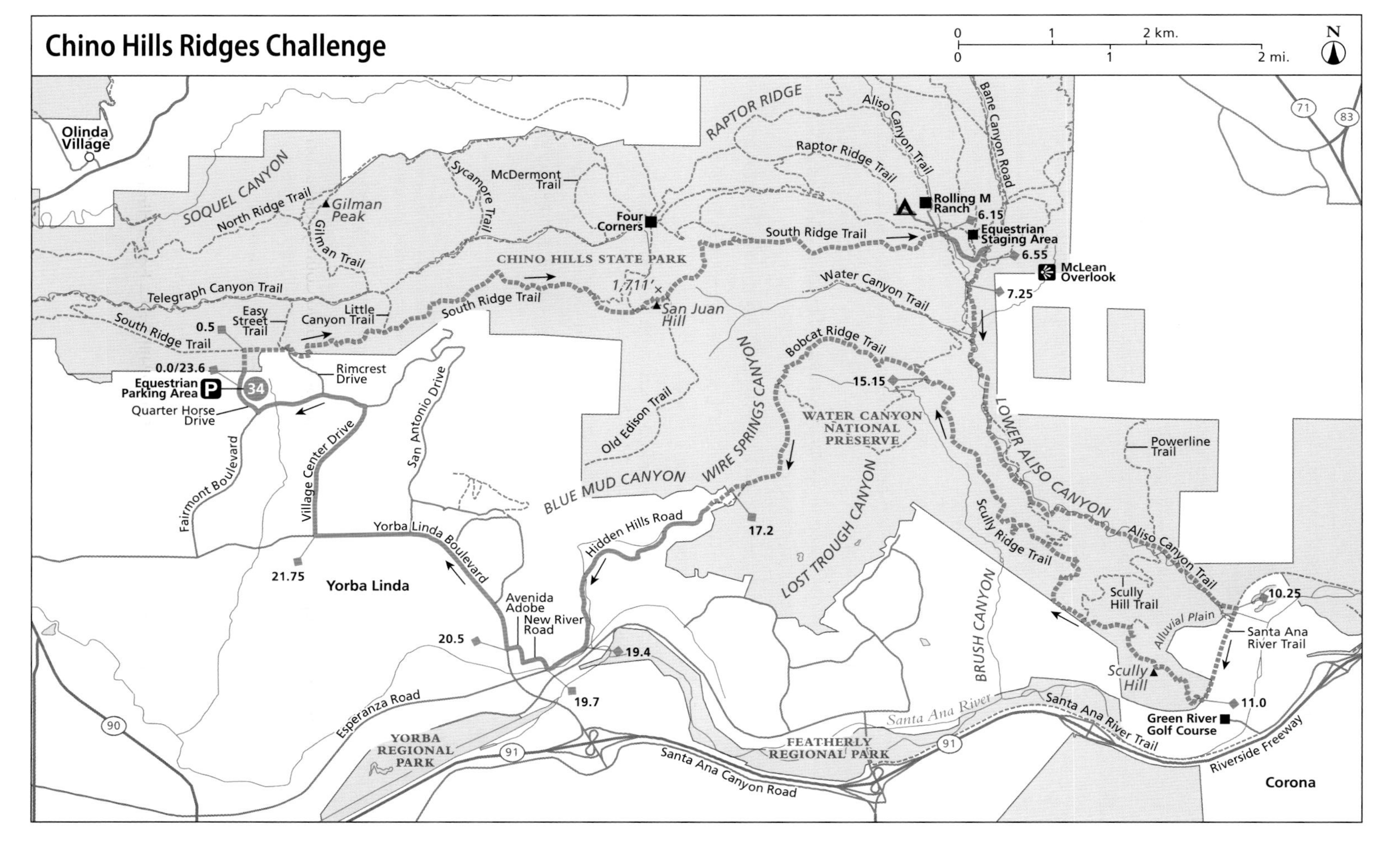

12.55 Gradient eases, then continues.

12.85 Crest of climb (elevation 1,108 feet); begin descent (10.0% grade).

13.3 Keep straight at merge with Brush Canyon Trail—end of descent.

13.65 Begin series of climbs and descents at 7% to 9% grades.

15.0 Stay to the right at merge with unnamed trail.

15.05 Turn right at junction with Bobcat Loop Trail to remain on Scully Ridge Trail.

15.15 End of Scully Ridge Trail; turn left onto Bobcat Ridge Trail—begin climb (8.5% grade).

16.35 Keep straight at junction with Bobcat Loop Trail.

16.5 Enter Orange County.

16.75 Crest of climb (elevation 1,539 feet); begin descent (6.2% grade).

17.2 Trail curves to the left and empties out onto paved access road; leave Chino Hills State Park.

17.55 Enter residential community in Yorba Linda—now on Hidden Hills Drive; begin steep road descent (10.4% grade).

18.4 Turn right to continue on Hidden Hills Drive; downhill continues.

19.4 Hidden Hills curves to the right, becoming Esperanza Drive. End of descent (elevation 392 feet).

19.7 Traffic signal at New River Road; turn right (lowest elevation of the ride: 391 feet).

19.8 Traffic signal at Avenida Adobe; turn right—climb at 3.2% grade.

20.15 Traffic signal at Yorba Linda Boulevard; turn right—climb at 2.6% grade.

20.9 Gradient of climb eases—begin rolling segment.

21.75 Traffic signal at Village Center Drive; turn right—climb at 4.1% grade.

22.75 Stop sign at Fairmont Drive; turn left—begin climb (7.0% grade).

23.05 Crest of climb at Forest Avenue; begin descent (4.8% grade).

23.45 Turn right onto Quarter Horse Drive; begin climb (6.9% grade).

23.6 End of ride at entrance to parking area for trailhead.

35

Circuito Chiquito Ortega

Start: San Juan Loop trailhead, 34950 Ortega Hwy. (CA 74), Cleveland National Forest

Length: 12.85 miles (clockwise loop)

Riding time: 2 to 5.5 hours (my time: 3H30:45)

Terrain and surface: 58% of the ride is on dirt trails, 38% is on paved roads, and 4% is on paved park roads.

Elevations: Low—1,679 feet at San Juan Loop Trail and Chiquito Trail; high—3,393 feet on Long Canyon Road

Traffic and hazards: CA 74 (Ortega Highway) was carrying 10,500 vehicles per day in the vicinity of the San Juan Loop trailhead in 2014. The Ortega Highway is a narrow, high-speed two-lane road that should be ridden with caution. The route includes 2.4 miles of riding on the highway in the westbound direction, which is downhill. Note that the predominant direction of traffic flow is eastbound in the afternoons and westbound in the mornings (on weekdays).

Map: *The Thomas Guide by Rand McNally—Street Guide: Los Angeles and Orange Counties* (any recent year), page 864; or *The Thomas Guide by Rand McNally—Street Guide: Riverside County* (any recent year), page 895

Getting there by car: From central Anaheim, head south on I-5. Exit at CA 74 (Ortega Highway) in San Juan Capistrano; turn left and head east. It is about 20 miles to the San Juan Loop trailhead, in Cleveland National Forest, within the Santa Ana Mountains.

Getting there by public transit: There is no public transportation service to the staging area in Cleveland National Forest. Riding to the trailhead, from any direction, is not recommended.

Starting point coordinates: 33.613108°N / 117.426644°W

THE RIDE

Circuito Chiquito Ortega is a challenging mountain bike ride that is short enough for intermediate riders (like me), but can probably be ridden straight through only by expert, experienced riders (unlike me). I had a difficult time with the technical aspects of the San Juan Loop Trail and Chiquito Trail; hence the slow time for the route. In other words, I did a lot of hiking! It is possible to complete the ride in a much faster time. The rider should be forewarned that the closing 2.4 miles of the ride are along CA 74 (Ortega Highway) in Cleveland National Forest. This is a narrow, high-speed, two-lane highway that is not popular among cyclists, except for the downhill direction. The portion of the highway that I have chosen for this route is downhill, and can be completed quickly. I chose a weekday afternoon starting time for the ride, meaning that the predominant direction of traffic was eastbound, while I was heading westbound. I was passed by a total of five vehicles on the highway. Weekend traffic varies; you might see heavy usage by motorcyclists, though most of them are not thrill-seekers.

Start the ride from the San Juan Loop trailhead, located along CA 74 in Cleveland National Forest, in the Santa Ana Mountains. The trailhead is directly across from Ortega Oaks Candy Store, which is a well-known stop in these parts. Be sure to have a National Forest Adventure Pass displayed in the window of your motor vehicle. Head onto San Juan Loop Trail (east side of the parking area). The trail is quite rideable at first, but soon enters sections of exposed rock. These require technical skills to navigate; if you are unsure, then dismount and walk through. From a starting elevation of 1,970 feet, the trail climbs (5.8% grade) to 2,013 feet, and then descends into the canyon. The descent is steep initially (9.8% grade), and then eases (5.6% grade). After what might seem like more than 1.15 miles, turn right onto Chiquito Trail (now at an elevation of 1,679 feet, the lowest of the ride).

Chiquito is a narrow-track trail along which the terrain varies from rideable dirt to challenging, rocky sections. In either case, the trail's prevailing direction is up, as in up the mountain. Begin by crossing San Juan Creek (dry except during and after rain), and then heading up a long canyon. The canyon climb is gradual (4.0% grade), and may have you thinking that this is a piece of cake. At mile 1.85, at an elevation of 1,832 feet, Chiquito Trail curves to the left to begin a climb out of the canyon, and across the adjacent mountainside. Portions of the trail are either very narrow, quite rugged, or both. An expert rider should be able to navigate the challenges, while the rest of us might prefer to hike. The average grade is 9.5% along this segment. The ride began in Riverside County; enter Orange County at mile 3.4 (elevation 2,610 feet). The gradient eases for the next mile, even heading downhill for a while

Heading into Cleveland National Forest on the rocky San Juan Loop Trail, in the Santa Ana Mountains

(3.8% grade). The climbing resumes at mile 4.4, at a reasonable 4.6% gradient. Where the trail curves to the left, at mile 6.15, the grade kicks up to 7.4%.

While you are working your way up Chiquito Trail, you may take some time to appreciate the horticultural variety of the forest. Along the way, you may see white sage, foothill ash, parish goldenbush, chamise, toyon, laurel sumac, chaparral yucca, just plain old chaparral, sycamore trees, oracle and coast live oak trees, Coulter and knobcone pine trees, and other varieties of plant and tree life. Although, you may at times be focused on the sizes of those boulders! Chiquito Trail meets San Juan Trail at mile 6.55 (elevation 2,987 feet). Turn right onto San Juan. After a respite from climbing, the trail digs in, with a steep segment (16.9% grade) taking you up to 3,216 feet. Keep straight at the junction, where the grade eases to 5.0%. With the exception of the steepness, note that San Juan Trail is quite a bit more manageable than Chiquito Trail, in terms of the surface texture. The trail somewhat unceremoniously empties out into Blue Jay Campground at mile 7.5, right next to a lavatory.

Turn right onto the paved park road, and ride through the campground. The climbing continues. At Long Canyon Road, turn right—it is a short climb to the highest elevation of the ride (3,393 feet, at mile 8.0). From here, the

road descends on poor pavement—better for a mountain bike than a road bike—at a 7.4% grade. At the intersection with the road having the smooth-looking pavement (mile 8.75), turn left—you are still on Long Canyon Road, descending an 8.8% grade. Merge with US Forest Route 6S05 at mile 10.1; the gradient eases here, to 4.1%. Enter Riverside County just beyond the merge. The road ends at CA 74 at mile 10.5, now at an elevation of 2,387 feet.

The next 2.4 miles are on CA 74—hug the shoulder, and be wary of motor vehicle traffic. The highway is downhill (3.9% grade) for 2.2 miles. After passing a scenic overlook of Decker Canyon, CA 74 enters a sweeping S-turn. Once out of the turn, the highway descends to a low point near the trailhead for the Tenaja Truck Trail, on the left. Keep straight; after descending to 1,945 feet, CA 74 climbs gradually for the next quarter-mile, to the end of the ride at the San Juan Loop trailhead, on the right. And, yes, it is not a mirage: The Ortega Oaks Candy Store is directly across the highway!

Bike Shop

Vincent's Bicycle Shop, 29400 3rd St., Lake Elsinore, (951) 796-4197, http://vincents bicycleshop.weebly.com

Cleveland National Forest

Cleveland National Forest is spread over 460,000 acres and three districts in Southern California. Most of the Santa Ana Mountains are included in the Trabuco Ranger District. The forest was established in 1908 by President Theodore Roosevelt, and was named in honor of former president Grover Cleveland. Some of the infrastructure in the forest, particularly cut-stone masonry structures, was built during the 1930s by President Franklin D. Roosevelt's Civilian Conservation Corps.

Most of the forestation in Trabuco is California chaparral and woodlands. This ecoregion features extensive quantities of chaparral, scrub biome, scrub oak, oak savannas, coastal sage, grasslands, and a variety of plant species. Tall trees are found at the higher elevations, and include several varieties of pine, oak, and sycamore, and a few rare species such as cypress. The plant life in the forest is naturally fire resilient, generally having a dry, crackly feel and look. Whereas small brush fires may be common, major fires are rare, but do occur. The Santiago Fire, mentioned earlier in this book, burned 28,445 acres in October and November of 2007. The larger Santiago Canyon Fire, which burned in September of 1889, singed an estimated 300,000 acres, and was the most epic wildfire in California history. In both events, the notorious Santa Ana Winds contributed to fanning the flames.

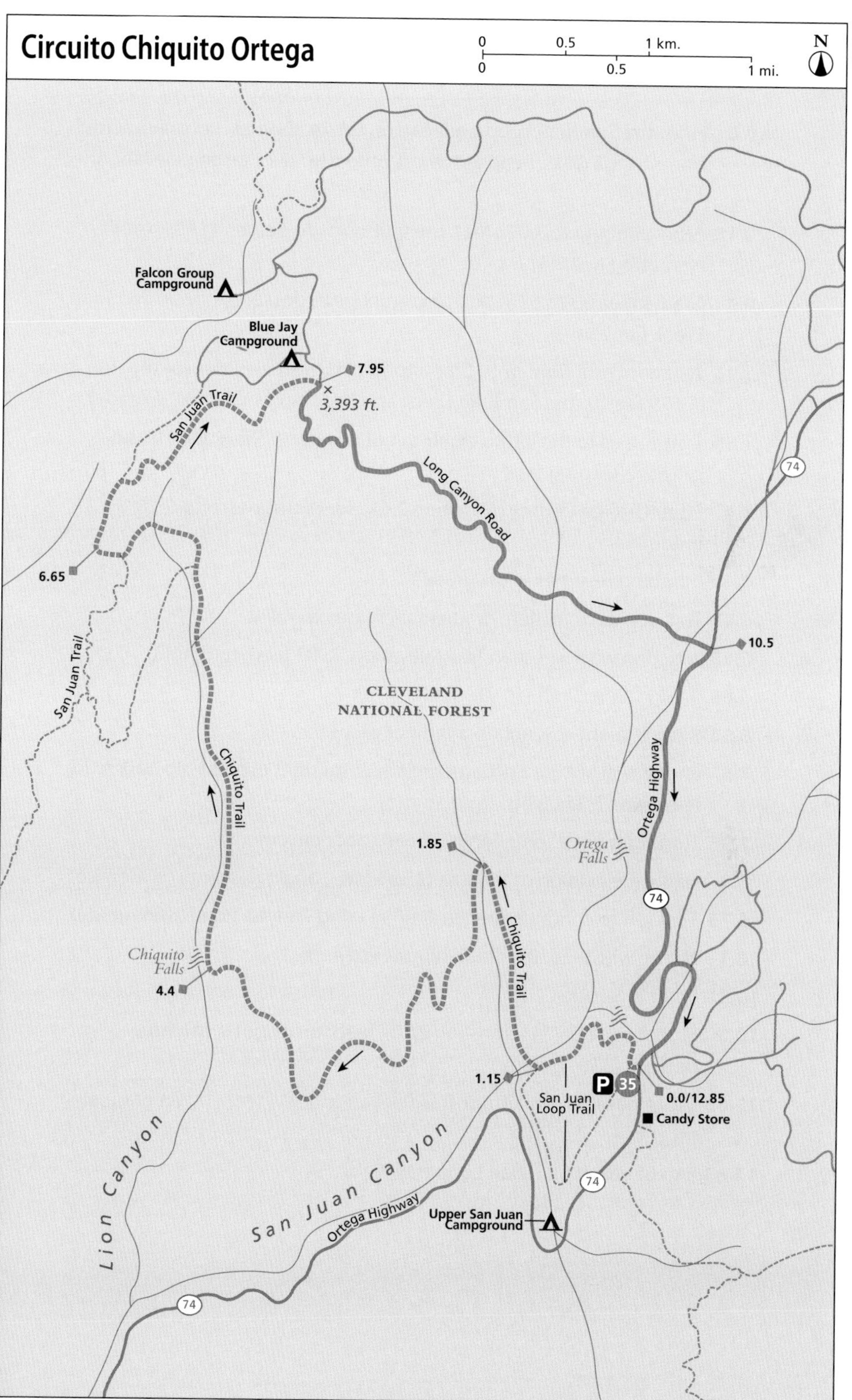

Circuito Chiquito Ortega
0
0.5
1 km.
0
0.5
1 mi.
N
Falcon Group Campground
Blue Jay Campground
7.95
3,393 ft.
San Juan Trail
Long Canyon Road
74
6.65
10.5
San Juan Trail
CLEVELAND NATIONAL FOREST
Chiquito Trail
Ortega Highway
Ortega Falls
1.85
74
Chiquito Trail
Chiquito Falls
4.4
1.15
P
35
0.0/12.85
San Juan Loop Trail
Candy Store
Lion Canyon
San Juan Canyon
Ortega Highway
74
Upper San Juan Campground
74

MILES AND DIRECTIONS

0.0 From the San Juan Loop trailhead on CA 74 (Ortega Highway), across from Ortega Oaks, head eastward, onto the trail. Starting elevation: 1,970 feet.

0.15 After climbing to 2,013 feet, the trail starts to descend (7.2% grade, increasing to 9.8%).

0.4 Gradient eases to 5.6% as trail continues to descend, now in San Juan Creek Canyon.

1.15 Junction; turn right onto Chiquito Trail. Lowest elevation of the ride (1,679 feet); cross San Juan Creek and head up canyon (4.0% grade).

1.85 Trail curves to the left to climb out of canyon (9.5% grade); technically challenging trail.

3.4 Enter Orange County (elevation 2,610 feet); trail descends (3.8% grade).

4.4 Climbing resumes (4.6% grade).

6.15 Trail curves to the left; gradient increases to 7.4%.

6.55 Junction with San Juan Trail (elevation 2,987 feet); turn right.

6.65 Begin steep climb (16.9% grade).

6.95 Keep straight at junction; gradient eases to 5.0%.

7.5 End of trail at Blue Jay Campground; turn right onto paved park road (elevation 3,362 feet).

7.95 Turn right onto Long Canyon Road (poor pavement).

8.0 Highest elevation of the ride (3,393 feet); begin descent (7.4% grade).

8.75 Turn left to continue descending on Long Canyon Road (8.8% grade).

10.1 Merge with FR 6S05; gradient eases to 4.1%.

10.3 Enter Riverside County.

10.5 Stop sign at CA 74 (elevation 2,387 feet); turn right—continue descent (3.9% grade).

12.65 CA 74 passes Tenaja Truck Trail (elevation 1,945 feet); begin gradual ascent.

12.85 End of ride at San Juan Loop trailhead.

36

El Cariso–Trabuco Peak Epic

Start: Deleo Regional Sports Park, 25655 Santiago Canyon Rd., Temescal Valley (Riverside County)

Length: 32.8 miles (clockwise loop)

Riding time: 3.5 to 8 hours (my time: 5H33:15)

Terrain and surface: 58% of the ride is on dirt roads and "truck trails," and 42% is on paved roads.

Elevations: Low—1,149 feet at Indian Truck Trail and Temescal Canyon Road; high—4,474 feet on Main Divide Road North, adjacent Trabuco Peak in the Santa Ana Mountains

Traffic and hazards: Indian Truck Trail carried 10,230 vehicles per day at I-15 in 2013; De Palma Road carried 9,335 vehicles per day south of Indian Truck Trail in 2012. Year 2005 traffic volumes in Lake Elsinore, potentially having increased by 22% since then, according to the city, were 6,500 vehicles per day on Temescal Canyon Road north of Lake Street, 18,300 vehicles per day on Lake Street, and 6,600 vehicles per day on Grand Avenue near the El Cariso Road trailhead.

Map: *The Thomas Guide by Rand McNally—Street Guide: Riverside County* (any recent year), page 834

Getting there by car: From central Anaheim, head north on CA 57. Exit to CA 91 eastbound. Once in Corona, junction to I-15 southbound. Exit at Indian Truck Trail (paved road) and turn right. Turn left onto De Palma Road, followed by a right turn onto Santiago Canyon Road. Follow Santiago Canyon as it climbs into the neighborhood. Look for Deleo Regional Sports Park on the left, after Santiago Canyon curves to the right.

Getting there by public transit: There was no public transit service to the Sycamore Creek community.

Starting point coordinates: 33.744936°N / 117.463906°W

THE RIDE

The El Cariso–Trabuco Peak Epic is indeed that. Give yourself plenty of time to complete this 32.8-mile clockwise loop that travels from Temescal Valley into the Santa Ana Mountains, and back down. The ride opens on the road, then goes off-road to head up into the mountains, and to descend, and then finishes with a short road segment. The net elevation difference of 3,325 feet is the greatest of any in this book. The high elevation of 4,474 feet is reached as Main Divide Road North passes by Trabuco Peak, which is the third highest in the Santa Ana Mountains. Epic! It took me just over 5.5 hours to complete the ride, although it seemed as though I picked a day, or perhaps a season, during which warm temperatures and dry conditions had reduced the traction on sandy dirt roads. Portions of Main Divide Road North were unrideable—or perhaps I was just tired—with plentiful soft dirt, and spinning wheels. Note that once you leave the roads, there is no water along the route. Be sure to bring plenty of fluids for the long off-road portion of the ride.

Start the ride in the comfort of Deleo Regional Sports Park (starting elevation: 1,314 feet), located in the Sycamore Creek community of Temescal Valley, south of Corona. Note that the ride starts in Riverside County, on the east side of the Santa Ana Mountains. About one-third of the ride is in Orange County, though, along Main Divide North in the mountains. Stock up on water at the park. Leave by turning right onto Santiago Canyon Road and heading downhill. The trailhead for Indian Truck Trail, where you will be returning later, is at mile 0.35. Santiago Canyon makes a short climb, and then descends to De Palma Road. Turn left here, and then turn right onto Indian Truck Trail (paved road). Pass under I-15, and then turn right onto Temescal Valley Road. This is the lowest elevation of the ride (1,149 feet).

Once sleepy Temescal Valley has transformed into a string of urban communities, located along the I-15 corridor, south of the city of Corona. Sycamore Creek is just one of those new communities. Traffic volumes on two-lane Temescal Valley Road remain light and suitable for riding, though, since I-15 is a parallel, faster alternative. Soon after making the turn, Corona Lake is on the left, which is usually stocked with trout, catfish, and tilapia. The lake was closed as of this writing, however, because of low water resulting from an ongoing Southern California drought. Next, Temescal Canyon Road passes along the outskirts of the Horsethief Canyon Ranch community. After passing under I-15 (mile 3.75), the road enters the community of Alberhill. This unincorporated town was founded in the 1890s on the mining of coal and clay,

Bike Shop

Citrus Cyclery, 90222 Pulsar Ct., Suite C, Corona, (951) 444-7353, www.citruscyclery.com

Wow—spectacular early-evening view of Temescal Valley from Indian Truck Trail, descending from the Santa Ana Mountains

both of which were readily found in the area. The Alberhill post office closed in 1969, after mining and mining-related activities ceased.

Turn right onto Lake Street (mile 5.0), and enter the growing city of Lake Elsinore. From here, it is a steady, gradual climb from 1,235 to 1,452 feet over the next few miles. After passing Lakeshore Drive, you are now on Grand Avenue, riding through the northwestern corner of the city. Look for McVicker Canyon Park Road on the right at mile 8.3. The adjacent McVicker Park is the last chance to replenish water before the route heads off-road. Just beyond Toft Drive, look for the trailhead for El Cariso Road (aka El Cariso Truck Trail; aka FR 6S05) on the right. There is very little fanfare at the trailhead—no signing, no markers. Yet it is here that you enter Cleveland National Forest. The climb starts off steeply (8.6% grade), and gets steeper farther up the mountain (10.2% grade). It is a 2.9-mile, steady climb; the first half was more eroded than the second half when I rode it. Halfway up the climb, keep straight at the junction. The left fork takes you to the Bethel Retreat Center, which is an out-of-the-way religious facility.

After merging with the access road from the Bethel Center, the climb gets a bit steeper (11.0% grade). After curving to the right, the grade on El Cariso Road eases to 7.1%, and then is finally flat (elevation 2,630 feet) as you near

CA 74. El Cariso Road does not quite get to the highway, though, as the road ends at Main Divide Road North, just east of the intersection. Turn right onto Main Divide, now 12.25 miles into the ride. You are now on the outskirts of El Cariso Village, a small community nestled in the nearby woods. The village is entirely within Cleveland National Forest, and is purported to have harbored a few outlaws. Main Divide Road North puts you back on pavement for the next few miles, climbing above the 3,000-foot mark. There are some great views up here, and very little motor vehicle traffic. The road straddles the line between Riverside and Orange Counties for a stretch, before entering Orange County for good. At mile 16.65, the road splits, with Long Canyon Road (paved) heading off to the left, toward Blue Jay Campground (please see Ride 35, Circuito Chiquito Ortega), and Main Divide Road North (unpaved) heading off to the right.

Take the more ominous-looking Main Divide Road North. You are now at 3,404 feet. The choice "rewards" you by immediately kicking into a steep climb (9.1% average grade) that continues for the next 1.65 miles. There are plenty of spectacular views along the way. At the crest (4,201 feet), bear right at the junction to continue on Main Divide Road North. From here, for the next 3 miles, the dirt road undulates, with an elevation hovering around 4,100 feet, but dropping as low as 3,900 feet. Gradients continue to be steep, reaching 9% along selected stretches (up and down). The terrain tends to range from

Trabuco Peak

Trabuco Peak is the third-highest in the Santa Ana Mountains, at 4,607 feet. The two higher peaks—Santiago (5,687 feet) and Modjeska (5,342 feet)—are to the northwest. Trabuco means "musket," in reference to an early type of firearm. The story is that a soldier with the 1769 Gaspar de Portola expedition lost his musket in nearby Trabuco Canyon. Thereafter, perhaps as a reminder to the soldier of his slippery fingers, several sites were named "Trabuco." Trabuco's summit is blanketed with a thick covering of manzanita and chaparral; hence, views from the summit are obscured. Thus, unlike some of the Santa Anas' other peaks, there is no infrastructure on Trabuco. As for the "devilish" Santa Ana winds, note that they do not originate in the Santa Ana Mountains. Rather, they are generated in southwestern deserts, primarily the Great Basin, and then blow westward, passing through mountain passes, such as those in the Santa Ana Mountains. In passing through mountains, some currents may accelerate, while others may pick up loose debris or smoke—should there be a fire—and blow it all westward, to the Pacific Ocean. The winds are characterized by warmth, dryness, and speed (40 mph or more).

rocky to sandy, with rideable, graded segments in between. At this elevation, you will certainly notice that the trees are taller than at the lower elevations. There is a high-country feel as you pass by cedar, fir, oak, and pine trees.

At mile 21.15, Main Divide Road North starts a steady and steep (11.9% grade) climb to the highest elevation of the ride, Trabuco Peak. The road does not quite reach the summit, which is at 4,607 feet, but passes near it, maxing out at 4,474 feet (mile 22.25). Trabuco Peak is the third-highest peak in the Santa Ana Mountains (Santiago Peak is the highest, at 5,687 feet). You can see Santiago to the northwest of here. Santiago and the second-highest peak, Modjeska, form a "saddleback" that is clearly visible from down below; there is little evidence of it up here.

Presumably you are ready for some downhill? Here it comes—Main Divide Road North is predominantly downhill from Trabuco Peak, with an average 6.5% grade (increasing to 9% after entering Riverside County). Turn right at Indian Truck Trail (FR 5S01)—there should be a marker—at mile 24.15, now at an elevation of 3,781 feet. Indian Truck Trail is a nearly steady 8.3-mile descent from the mountains. You can pick up a lot of speed on the descent, although the average grade (5.7%) is low enough to keep matters under control. There are some wonderful views of Temescal Valley (please see photo) as the trail lowers you into the canyon. There is evidence of civilization during the final mile or so of the trail, as you pass by a large, wooded compound, perhaps wondering if you are still on a public dirt road. I wondered if the facilities were part of the Glen Eden Nudist Resort, which is located just down the canyon to your right; but I was unable to tell by peeking through the trees. Kidding about peeking, but you are still on Indian Truck Trail, approaching the Sycamore Creek community. The trail intersects with Santiago Canyon Road at mile 32.45. One favorable aspect of the route design is that you are nearly done with the ride. Turn left onto Santiago Canyon, and ride the short climb back to Deleo Regional Sports Park, where the ride ends. Please note that further development of the Sycamore Creek community may affect the location of the Indian Truck Trail trailhead.

MILES AND DIRECTIONS

0.0 From Deleo Regional Sports Park in the Sycamore Creek community of Temescal Valley, turn right onto Santiago Canyon Road. Starting elevation: 1,314 feet.

0.35 Indian Truck Trail trailhead on the right; keep straight.

0.85 Traffic signal at De Palma Road; turn left.

1.0 Traffic signal at Indian Truck Trail (paved road); turn right.

1.2 Pass under I-15 freeway.

1.3 Traffic signal at Temescal Valley Road; turn right. Lowest elevation of the ride (1,149 feet).

3.75 Pass under I-15 freeway; enter Alberhill community.

5.0 Traffic signal at Lake Street (end of Temescal Valley Road); turn right—enter city of Lake Elsinore. Begin gradual climb.

7.6 Traffic signal at Lakeshore Drive; keep straight—now on Grand Avenue (elevation 1,452 feet). Enter segment of rolling hills.

8.3 McVicker Park on the right (off of McVicker Canyon Park Road); last chance to replenish water before going off-road.

9.35 Trailhead for El Cariso Road (aka El Cariso Truck Trail and FR 6S05); leave the road and enter the trail (elevation 1,407 feet). Enter Cleveland National Forest and begin climbing (8.6% grade).

10.85 Junction—keep straight; gradient increases to 10.2%.

11.1 Trail merges with trail from Bethel Retreat Center; gradient increases to 11.0%.

11.25 Trail curves to the right; grade eases to 7.1%.

12.1 Merge with side trail; trail is now flat (elevation 2,630 feet).

12.25 End of El Cariso Road; turn right onto Main Divide Road North (paved; FR 3S04)—continue climbing (average grade 3.5%).

12.8 Enter Orange County (road reenters Riverside County, then Orange County, then Riverside County, and then finally Orange County over the next mile).

16.45 Bear right to continue on Main Divide Road North (unpaved); paved road continues as Long Canyon Road to the left. Steep climb (9.1% average grade).

18.1 Los Pinos Trail junction; bear right to remain on Main Divide Road. Elevation: 4,201 feet; begin descent (6.8% grade).

18.9 End of descent; begin climb (9.0% grade).

19.2 Junction with unnamed trail; keep straight. From here, Main Divide Road North makes numerous undulations, generally hovering around 4,100 feet of elevation.

20.85 Begin descent (5.7% grade).

21.15 End of descent; begin steady climb toward Trabuco Peak (11.9% grade).

22.25 Highest elevation of ride, adjacent Trabuco Peak (4,474 feet); begin descent (6.5% grade).

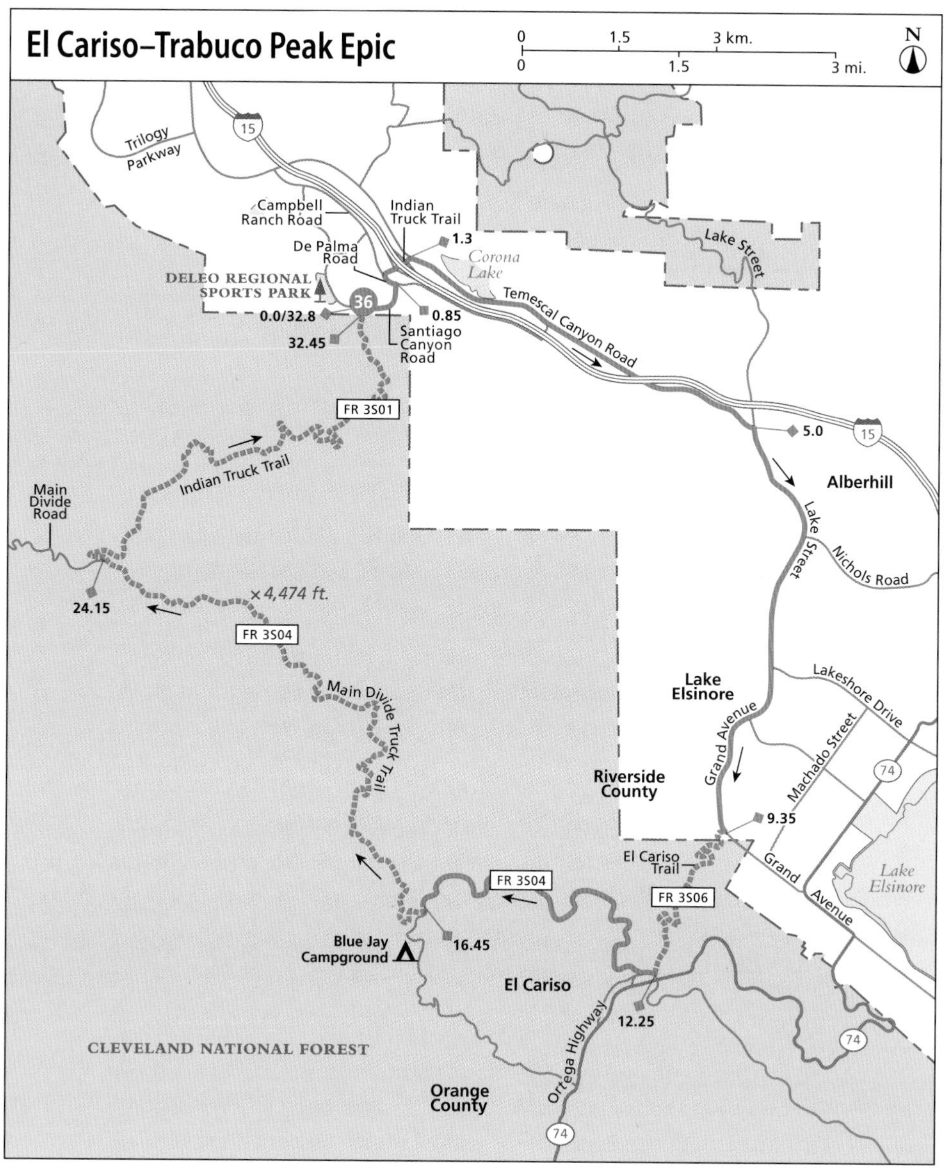

23.8 Leave Orange County; enter Riverside County (elevation 3,947 feet)—continue descent (9.0% grade).

24.15 Turn right onto Indian Truck Trail (FR 5S01); elevation 3,781 feet—begin long descent (average grade 5.7%).

32.45 Intersection with Santiago Canyon Road; turn left.

32.8 End of ride at Deleo Regional Sports Park.

Elsinore Mountains Divide Ride

Start: El Cariso South Picnic Site and Wildland Firefighter Memorial, CA 74 and South Main Divide Road, El Cariso Village (Cleveland National Forest)

Length: 45.85 miles (clockwise loop)

Riding time: 3 to 7 hours (my time: 3H32:49)

Terrain and surface: 100% of the ride is on paved roads.

Elevations: Low—1,212 feet at Grand Avenue and Clinton Keith Road in Wildomar; high—3,332 feet on South Main Divide Road adjacent Elsinore Peak

Traffic and hazards: CA 74 (Ortega Highway) carried 10,500 vehicles per day between Cleveland National Forest and the Elsinore Trough in 2014; Grand Avenue carried 24,020 vehicles per day west of Corydon Road in 2013; Clinton Keith Road carried 6,430 vehicles per day north of Avenida La Cresta in 2010; Tenaja Road carried 1,840 vehicles per day west of Clinton Keith Road in 2012. The opening portion of the ride descends CA 74, which is a narrow, two-lane highway with shoulders. Use extra caution on the descent.

Map: *The Thomas Guide by Rand McNally—Street Guide: Riverside County* (any recent year), page 895

Getting there by car: From central Anaheim, head south on I-5. Exit at CA 74 (Ortega Highway) in San Juan Capistrano; turn left and head east. Continue into the Santa Ana Mountains. Just beyond El Cariso Village, look for Main Divide Road South, just before the descent into Lake Elsinore. Turn right onto Main Divide Road South, and then make an immediate left at the El Cariso South Picnic Site and Wildland Firefighter Memorial.

Getting there by public transit: There is no public transportation service to El Cariso. Riding to the El Cariso South Picnic Site on CA 74 is not recommended.

Starting point coordinates: 33.651561°N / 117.408639°W

THE RIDE

The Elsinore Mountains Divide Ride is a 45.85-mile clockwise loop that starts high in the Santa Ana Mountains, descends rapidly into the Elsinore Trough, climbs up onto the Santa Rosa Ecological Plateau, and then continues to climb up into the Elsinore Mountains to return. The recommended direction is clockwise, such that the ride on CA 74 (Ortega Highway) is in the downhill direction. Please note that CA 74 is a two-lane highway with shoulders. The shoulders are generally wide enough, although they are often littered with small rocks that tumble down from the hillside. CA 74 has a speed limit of 45 mph; the majority of motorists cannot exceed this given the winding nature of the highway, which is a cliffhanger in places. I descended the highway at 30 to 35 mph, and was not passed by any motorist until reaching the very bottom of the descent. I was unable to hold the shoulder the whole way, preferring to cut a few corners to save speed, and to avoid shoulder debris. My hope is that you, too, will have a similar experience with forgiving motorists!

The route of the Elsinore Mountains Divide Ride is entirely within Riverside County, although the start-finish is exactly 0.5 mile, as the crow flies, from the Orange County line. The latter part of the ride is in the Elsinore Mountains, which form a ridge on the southeastern edge of the Santa Ana Mountains. Start the ride at the El Cariso South Picnic Site, which is also home to the California Wildland Firefighter Memorial, located on South Main Divide Road just south of CA 74. The road is just east of the El Cariso Fire Station, and intersects with CA 74 just before the highway starts its descent. Start the ride by heading north on South Main Divide Road. Turn right onto CA 74; the highway climbs gradually for 0.2 mile. As you pass through the gap, Lake Elsinore, in the valley below, comes into view. From here, in exactly 5 miles, CA 74 loses 1,360 feet (average 5.2% grade). Hug the shoulder, and be alert to the motorists behind and in front of you. The highway winds through numerous curves as it makes its way down the side of the mountain. There are plenty of breathtaking views, although one's eyes tend to be glued to the road.

The Lookout Roadhouse is on the left in the opening stages of the descent. This is a popular hangout for motorcyclists. You may also see small packs of motorcyclists on the highway. While there are numerous curves on the descent, note that one of them, as you near the bottom, rotates through about 270 degrees! The highway widens as you near the bottom. Touchdown is at the intersection with Grand Avenue, just downstream of the Lake Elsinore city limit. Lake Elsinore (the lake), which you could see clearly from above, is not visible at this elevation because of lakeside development. Turn right onto Grand Avenue, now 5.25 miles into the ride (elevation 1,314 feet). It is a long and straight 9.2 miles on Grand Avenue from here. You are now in the Elsinore

Trough, which is a large rift valley between the Santa Ana Mountains in the west, and the Temescal Mountains, and other mountains and valleys, in the east and south. Grand Avenue makes a net descent of just over 100 feet along the way, although there are several false flats, and a couple of short climbs and descents. The stay in Lake Elsinore is short, as Grand Avenue leaves that city and enters the unincorporated community of Lakeland Village. Enter the city of Wildomar at Corydon Road at mile 10.75.

At mile 14.45, at the end of Grand Avenue, turn right onto Clinton Keith Road. This is the lowest elevation of the ride (1,212 feet). Leave Wildomar and enter the city of Murrieta. The ride leaves Murrieta as Clinton Keith climbs away from the developed areas, toward the Santa Rosa Ecological Plateau. Clinton Keith climbs gradually to Calle del Oro Oso (mile 15.15), where the grade increases. The gradient continues to increase, particularly after passing the fire station on the left. The average grade from here is 5.0%, although there is a steeper stretch before the road finally crests. At the aptly named Avenida La Cresta, Clinton Keith is at an elevation of 1,780 feet, now 17.35 miles into the ride. Keep straight here as the road enters the Santa Rosa Plateau Ecological Reserve. This 9,000-acre reserve is at the southern end of the Santa Ana Mountains, and hosts a number of ecosystems that provide habitat for a mixture of plant and animal life.

Clinton Keith Road bends to the right at mile 18.55, becoming Tenaja Road. Tenaja curves and winds its way across the plateau, easily disorienting the traveler. Your best bet is to follow the signs and stay on Tenaja, and not worry too much about which direction you are heading. Tenaja turns to the right at Via Volcan (mile 20.3). The elevation here is 1,992 feet, reflecting a gradual climb since the junction with Clinton Keith. Enter the community of La Cresta, which is on the plateau. La Cresta is known for its estates, ranches, idyllic scenery, and general affluence. The grade increases past Oak Trail Court, to 8.6%, followed by a short downhill, and then another climb (6.0% grade) to Camino Bon Aire (elevation 2,234 feet). Tenaja's grade is generally downhill for the next 1.65 miles, with a few rollers, and plenty of curves. Tenaja is a two-lane road with narrow shoulders, but the traffic volume of 1,840 vehicles per day near Clinton Keith diminishes as you move across the plateau.

Bike Shop

Vincent's Bicycle Shop, 29400 3rd St., Lake Elsinore, (951) 796-4197, http://vincentsbicycleshop.weebly.com

The Tenaja Valley Airport, which is a small facility with a single, gravel runway, is on your right at mile 22.8 (elevation 2,114 feet). Tenaja climbs from here, including a short, steep segment, to Corta Colinga at mile 23.65 (elevation 2,245 feet). Tenaja descends from here—look for the entrance to

The Wildomar Truck Trail slices through a gap in Cleveland National Forest, at an elevation of about 3,000 feet.

Cleveland National Forest, via Cleveland National Forest Road (FR 7S02), on the right at 24.5. Turn right here (elevation 2,037 feet) and begin a gradual descent. There are restrooms on the left just downstream of the turn. The road narrows beyond here—the road is lightly used, but be sure to stay to the right, in case of oncoming vehicles. At mile 27.3 the road begins to descend in earnest (5.2% grade). It is a strange effect, since you have entered the mountains, and may have been expecting to go up. The road twists its way down into the canyon, finally reaching the bottom at mile 29.65, at an elevation of 1,340 feet.

At the fork, bear right onto the Los Alamos Truck Trail (paved road). Los Alamos is a narrow uphill road (3.4% average grade). As the road winds its way up into the mountains, you can catch glimpses of the La Cresta community below, to your right. By the time you reach the Wildomar Off-Highway Vehicle Recreation Area, you will have covered just under 8 miles of steady uphill, now at an elevation of 2,775 feet. Go around the gate—you are now on Wildomar Truck Trail. Some of the finest roadside scenery is along this segment of the route, as the road cuts its way through the landscape. The average grade of this climb is 4.8%. As the road makes a 90-degree bend to the right, now at an elevation of 3,108 feet, you are now on South Main Divide Road. The road continues to climb until it is adjacent Elsinore Peak (mile 39.85), reaching the highest elevation of the ride (3,332 feet). Elsinore Peak is the second-tallest in the Elsinore Mountains, with a summit at 3,575 feet. There are a number of communications towers at the peak.

Beyond Elsinore Peak, South Main Divide Road descends. Enter a small mountain community at mile 41.15. The road continues to descend through and beyond the community, with a few undulations, to mile 43.85 (elevation 2,813 feet). The final climb of the ride starts here (3.5% grade), and continues to the right of the knob in the foreground. With an open vista of the Elsinore Trough to the right, here you have an excellent view of Lake Elsinore. The final descent begins at mile 44.65. It is a thriller as the road makes a sweeping, high-speed S-curve to return you to the El Cariso South Picnic Site, and the end of the ride.

The California Wildland Firefighter Memorial

The ride fittingly begins and ends at the California Wildland Firefighter Memorial, one of a number of such memorials in the United States. This one in particular is dedicated to California firefighters, with specific, local reference to the Decker Fire of August 1959. Six firefighters were killed in the blaze, and dozens more were burned. The El Cariso South Picnic site of the memorial is not to be confused with the El Cariso Hotshots memorial, which commemorates twelve firefighter fatalities in the 1966 Loop Fire in the Angeles National Forest (located in Sylmar, city of Los Angeles).

MILES AND DIRECTIONS

0.0 Start the ride at the El Cariso South Picnic Site and Wildland Firefighter Memorial in Cleveland National Forest; turn right onto South Main Divide Road (elevation 2,620 feet).

0.05 Stop sign at CA 74 (Ortega Highway); turn right.

0.25 Elevation 2,674 feet; begin 5.0-mile descent at 5.2% grade. Caution: two-lane, winding, twisting highway with adequate shoulders.

5.25 Traffic signal at Grand Avenue; turn right. Now in Lake Elsinore (elevation 1,314 feet).

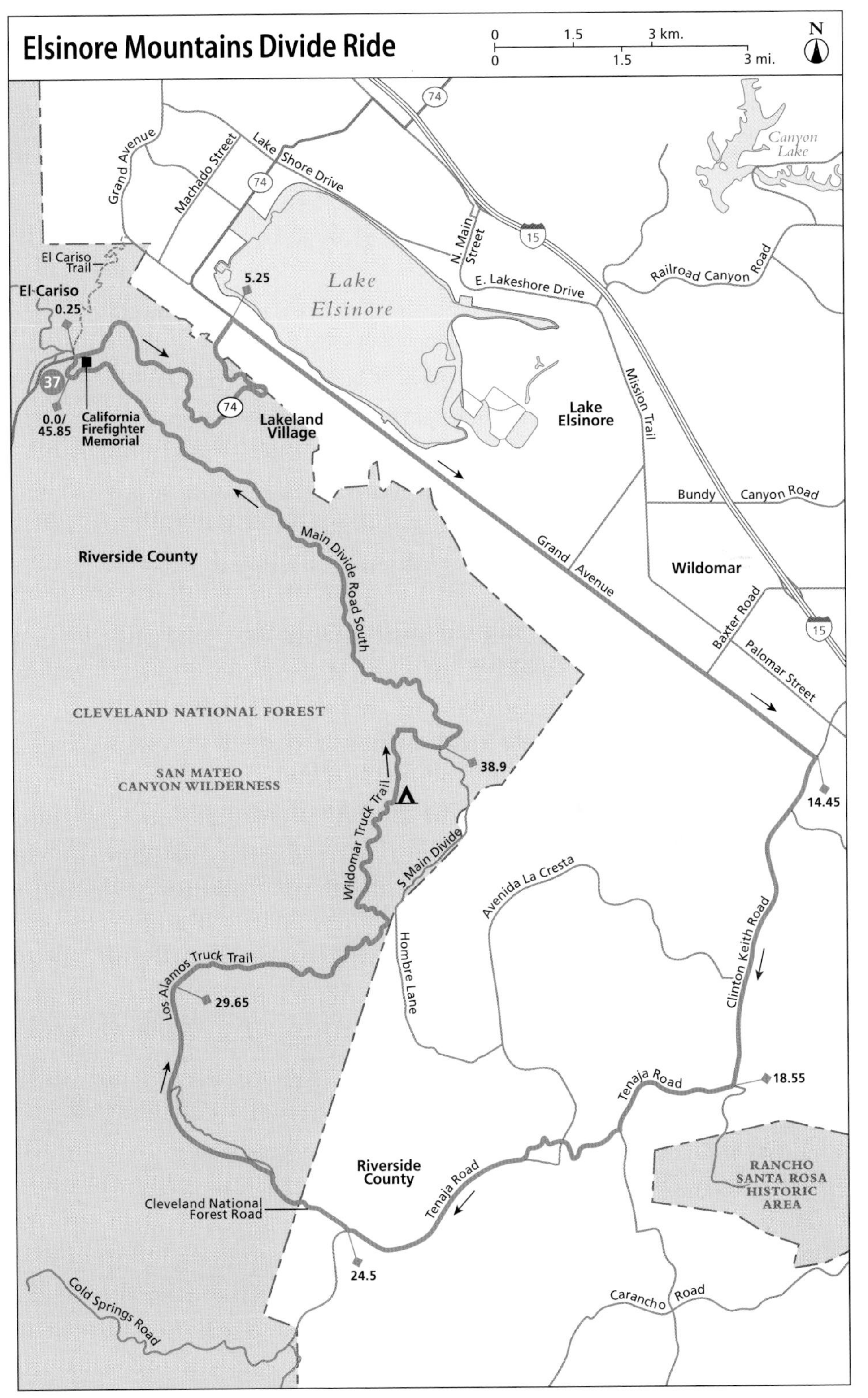

Elsinore Mountains Divide Ride
0
1.5
3 km.
0
1.5
3 mi.
N
74
Canyon Lake
Grand Avenue
Machado Street
Lake Shore Drive
74
15
N. Main Street
Railroad Canyon Road
El Cariso Trail
El Cariso
5.25
Lake Elsinore
E. Lakeshore Drive
0.25
37
0.0/ 45.85
California Firefighter Memorial
74
Lakeland Village
Lake Elsinore
Mission Trail
Bundy Canyon Road
Main Divide Road South
Riverside County
Grand Avenue
Wildomar
Baxter Road
15
Palomar Street
CLEVELAND NATIONAL FOREST
38.9
SAN MATEO CANYON WILDERNESS
Wildomar Truck Trail
14.45
S Main Divide
Avenida La Cresta
Hombre Lane
Clinton Keith Road
Los Alamos Truck Trail
29.65
Tenaja Road
18.55
Riverside County
RANCHO SANTA ROSA HISTORIC AREA
Tenaja Road
Cleveland National Forest Road
24.5
Cold Springs Road
Carancho Road

5.45 Keep straight at Bonnie Lea Drive; leave Lake Elsinore—enter community of Lakeland Village.

10.75 Traffic signal at Corydon Road; keep straight—enter city of Wildomar.

14.45 Traffic signal at Clinton Keith Road; turn right—enter city of Murrieta—lowest elevation of ride (1,212 feet).

15.15 Grade of climb increases to 5.0%, with steeper inclines toward the crest.

17.35 Stop sign at Avenida la Cresta (elevation 1,780 feet); keep straight—enter Santa Rosa Plateau Ecological Reserve.

18.55 Clinton Keith Road turns to the right, becoming Tenaja Road.

20.3 Stop sign at Via Volcan; turn right to continue on Tenaja Road.

20.55 Begin climb (8.6% grade).

20.95 Gradient of climb eases; short downhill, then continue climbing (6.0% grade).

21.15 Crest of climb at Camino Bon Aire (elevation 2,234 feet); begin net descent.

22.8 Tenaja Road passes Meadows Lake Airport; net climb from here, including one steep pitch.

23.65 Crest of climb at Corta Colinga (elevation 2,245 feet); begin descent.

24.5 Turn right onto Cleveland National Forest Road (FR 7S02); enter Cleveland National Forest (elevation 2,037 feet).

27.3 Begin long descent on twisting, winding road (5.2% grade).

29.65 End of descent (elevation 1,340 feet); bear right onto Los Alamos Truck Trail—begin long climb (3.4% average grade).

37.55 Keep straight onto Wildomar Truck Trail, adjacent Wildomar Off-Highway Vehicle Recreation Area (elevation 2,775 feet)—continue climbing (4.8% grade).

38.9 Wildomar Truck Trail curves to the right; now on South Main Divide Road—continue climbing (4.4% grade).

39.85 Crest of climb at highest elevation of ride (3,332 feet), adjacent Elsinore Peak—begin descent (3.8% grade).

41.15 Enter small mountain community—descent continues.

43.85 End of descent (elevation 2,813 feet); begin climb (3.5% grade).

44.65 Crest of climb (elevation 2,962 feet); begin final descent.

45.85 End of ride at El Cariso South Picnic Site.

38

Partial Pendleton Perimeter Ride

Start: Upper Trestles parking lot (fee), next to Carl's Jr. (3929 South El Camino Real), San Clemente

Length: 25.15 miles (two out-and-back segments)

Riding time: 1.25 to 3 hours (my time: 1H30:00)

Terrain and surface: 52% of the ride is on paved public roads and paths; 26% of the ride is on roads within Camp Pendleton; 22% of the ride is on a paved park road.

Elevations: Low—17 feet on Old US Highway 101 at access path to Trestles; high—190 feet on Cristianitos Road half a mile north of El Camino Real in San Clemente

Traffic and hazards: Traffic volumes are generally light.

Map: *The Thomas Guide by Rand McNally—Street Guide: Los Angeles and Orange Counties* (any recent year), page 993

Getting there by car: From central Anaheim, head south on I-5. Exit at Cristianitos Road in San Clemente, and turn left. Turn left again onto South El Camino Real. Make an immediate right into the Upper Trestles parking lot.

Getting there by public transit: Ride OCTA bus route 1 along PCH, from as far north as Long Beach, to the end of the line in San Clemente, at South El Camino Real and Cristianitos Road, adjacent the Trestles parking lot. Route 1 runs every 35 minutes (from Newport Beach to San Clemente; every 60 minutes from Long Beach) on weekends, and every 60 minutes on weekends and holidays.

Starting point coordinates: 33.396800°N / 117.592611°W

THE RIDE

The Partial Pendleton Perimeter Ride skirts the northwestern and western edges of US Marine Corps Base Camp Pendleton, entering the base's property for a (legal) stretch before turning around and returning. Most of the

A peloton of riders approaches critical mass through Camp Pendleton, nearing Las Pulgas Road, with I-5 in the distance.

ride is in San Diego County, although the staging area is in Orange County. Camp Pendleton's property stretches from Oceanside in the south to San Clemente in the north, for a distance of about 18 miles. Other than I-5, which passes through the base alongside the Pacific Ocean, there is no through motor vehicle access. Through bicycle access is allowed, however, on certain roads, although bicycle access can be disrupted by construction or military exercises. In fact, following the September 11, 2001, terrorist attacks, bicycle access was suspended completely for 3.5 years, finally reopening in February 2005. Bicycling through Camp Pendleton is popular (please see photo), and you are bound to see plenty of other riders making the transit. This ride takes you about halfway through the base, before turning around and returning to Orange County.

The net high-low elevation differential of this ride is just 173 feet. Portions of the ride are suitable for families, particularly stretches of Old US Highway 101 in Camp Pendleton and within San Onofre State Beach. Start the ride by leaving the Upper Trestles parking lot and turning left onto South El Camino Real. Plenty of surfers park here, and on the adjacent roads (free parking), preparing to head down to Trestles. If you are not a surfer, then avoid feigning surfer lingo—just prep your bike and go about your business. Turn left at Cristianitos Road and head north. Most riders bypass Cristianitos, aiming for San Onofre and Camp Pendleton. But Cristianitos is a fine road for riding, with an uninterrupted 2.55-mile stretch of undulations. The only traffic hazard may be military personnel speeding to get either on or off base. After a gradual climb to the high point of the entire ride (190 feet) at mile 0.5, Cristianitos undulates to the turnaround at a secured, gated entrance to the base. Note that the entrance to San Mateo Campground is on the right at mile 1, well before the base entrance.

Turn around at the Cristianitos entry and return. You are 5.2 miles into the ride at South El Camino Real, returning to where you started. Continue across I-5, and make an immediate left onto the connector path. Be watchful of other path users, which may include surfers carrying longboards. Beyond the access path to Trestles, the path widens; the road is part of Old US Highway 101, which was the main route through here long before I-5 was constructed. The old highway was decommissioned in 1964. After a short climb, stay to the left onto a paved path; the wider road to the right continues to a dead end. After passing through an open gateway, merge onto the continuation of Old US 101, now at mile 6.45. There is a short downhill from here; the next small hill is at a railroad overpass, at mile 7.6. The artistic-sounding SONGS (San Onofre Nuclear Generating Station) is on the right at mile 8.25. Although the two prominent domes of the nuclear reactor are quite visible, the plant was actually decommissioned in 2013. The station operated from 1968 until 2012, when premature wear was found inside tubes within steam generators that had only recently been replaced. The plant was shut down as a precaution.

Bike Shop

San Clemente Cyclery, 2801 South El Camino Real, San Clemente, (949) 492-8890, http://sccyclery.com

You may be searching for some of your own nuclear power as you pedal past the old plant. Enter San Onofre State Beach (SOSB) at mile 9.1. This is an official entrance to SOSB, but Trestles, the entire stretches of beach to the north and south of SONGS, as well as the wilderness adjacent Cristianitos Road, are all part of SOSB. Please see Ride 25, Ring around San Clemente, for some riding on SOSB's trails. The next stretch of 2.75 miles passes by campgrounds that are adjacent the beach. At the far end of the road (mile 11.85), there is a gate; access beyond the gate is restricted to bicycles. This marks the boundary of Camp Pendleton. Keep riding on through—there are parallel paths for a while, with the one on your right probably being the smoothest. There are some great, open views of the ocean through here. The road curves to the right, and

Camp Pendleton

Marine Corps Base Camp Pendleton was established in 1942, during World War II. It is named for Major General Joseph Henry Pendleton (1860–1942), who was a longtime advocate of setting up a Marine Corps training base on the West Coast of the United States. It became the home of the 1st Marine Division, and later broadened to become the home of the 1st Marine Expeditionary Force. One of the most notable periods in the base's history was during the mid-1970s, when it was a temporary home for some 50,000 Vietnamese refugees. Today, the base is associated with some 42,000 active military personnel, with another 77,000 retired military living within a 50-mile radius. Various operating forces and commands train here. Although the base is heavily secured, bicycle access has been consistently supported. Also, civilians can participate in a yearlong series of sporting events, including bike and running races, duathlons, mud runs, and other competitions.

then curves left to swoop under I-5 through a dark tunnel (mile 13.6). Signs indicate that access through the tunnel can be restricted at times.

Once out of the tunnel, stay to the right to continue on Old US Highway 101. The road heads gradually downhill as it nears Las Pulgas Road. Turn around at Las Pulgas for the ride back. The bike route through the base continues with a turn to the left at Las Pulgas, for those who are interested. On the return ride, the tunnel under I-5 comes at mile 16.65, and the entrance to SOSB comes at 18.45. Leave SOSB at mile 21.2, passing by SONGS and then crossing over the railroad tracks. After a short but brisk climb, leave the road by turning left and heading toward the fence and gateway, and onto the path. The path descends, and then merges with Old US 101. After crossing over San Mateo Creek, continue straight onto the path. After another short but brisk climb, turn right onto Cristianitos Road. Cross over I-5, and then turn left onto South El Camino Real. The ride ends at the Upper Trestles parking area, which is on the right.

MILES AND DIRECTIONS

0.0 Start from Upper Trestles parking lot on South El Camino Real, near Cristianitos Road and I-5, in San Clemente. Head south on South El Camino Real.

0.05 Stop sign at Cristianitos Road; turn left.

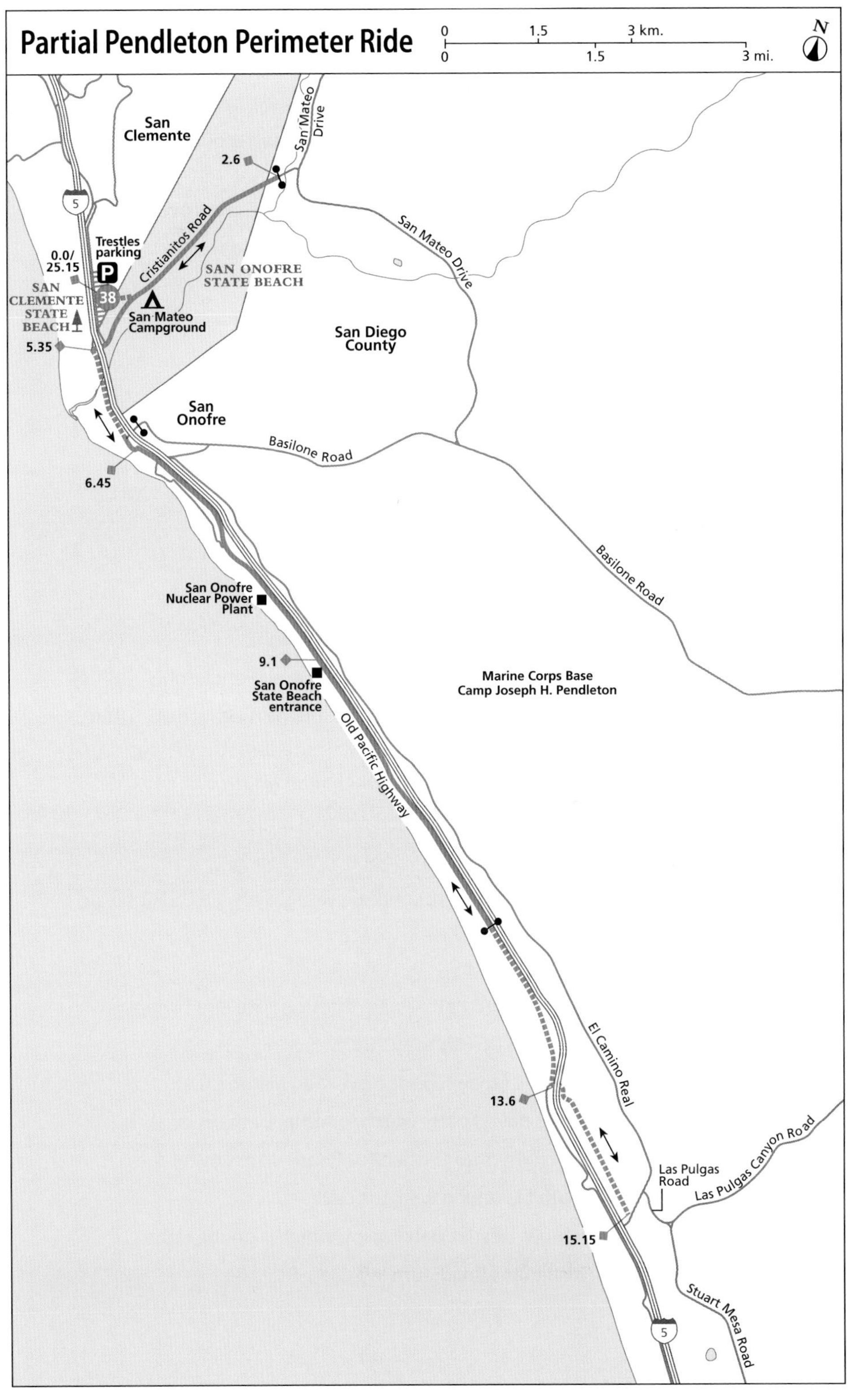

Partial Pendleton Perimeter Ride
0
1.5
3 km.
0
1.5
3 mi.
N
San Clemente
San Mateo Drive
2.6
5
Cristianitos Road
Trestles parking
0.0/ 25.15
P
38
SAN ONOFRE STATE BEACH
SAN CLEMENTE STATE BEACH
San Mateo Campground
San Mateo Drive
San Diego County
5.35
San Onofre
Basilone Road
6.45
Basilone Road
San Onofre Nuclear Power Plant
9.1
San Onofre State Beach entrance
Marine Corps Base Camp Joseph H. Pendleton
Old Pacific Highway
El Camino Real
13.6
Las Pulgas Road
Las Pulgas Canyon Road
15.15
Stuart Mesa Road
5

0.5 High elevation of ride (190 feet). Road undulates from here.

1.0 Entrance to San Mateo Campground on the right; keep straight.

2.6 Secured, gated entrance to Camp Pendleton; turn around here and return.

5.2 Stop sign at South El Camino Real; keep straight—cross over I-5.

5.35 Turn left onto path, adjacent freeway—begin descent. Watch for other path users.

5.6 Access path to Trestles surfing spot on the right; keep straight—now on Old US Highway 101.

5.95 Bridge across San Mateo Creek; lowest elevation of ride (17 feet)—begin climb.

6.35 Bear left onto paved path.

6.45 Ride through opening in fence and continue onto roadway (Old US Highway 101).

7.6 Bridge over railroad tracks.

8.25 San Onofre Nuclear Generating Station on the right.

9.1 Entrance to San Onofre State Beach; keep straight.

11.85 Gate at end of state beach property; enter Camp Pendleton.

13.6 Road curves to the right, and then to the left, passing under I-5 (tunnel); stay to the right on the other side.

15.15 Stop sign at Las Pulgas Road; turn around and return.

16.65 Old road curves to the left and enters tunnel under I-5.

18.45 Gate marking entrance into San Onofre State Beach.

21.2 Leave San Onofre State Beach; continue straight on Old US Highway 101.

22.65 Bridge over railroad tracks.

23.85 Turn left, off of road, onto path—pass through gate and continue.

23.95 Path merges with Old US Highway 101.

24.45 Low elevation of ride (again); bridge over San Mateo Creek.

24.7 Keep straight onto paved path; watch for other path users.

24.95 End of path; turn right onto Cristianitos Road—cross over I-5.

25.1 Stop sign at South El Camino Real; turn left.

25.15 End of ride at Upper Trestles parking lot, which is on the right.

39

Puente Hills Ridge Cycle

Start: Pathfinder County Park, 18150 Pathfinder Rd., Rowland Heights (Los Angeles County)

Length: 15.0 miles (clockwise loop with a short out-and-back segment)

Riding time: 1.5 to 4 hours (my time: 2H04:11)

Terrain and surface: 58% of the ride is on dirt roads and trails, 37% is on paved roads, and 5% is on a concrete walkway.

Elevations: Low—552 feet just east of Colima Road in Whittier, on singletrack trail; high—1,360 feet at Skyline Drive and Radio Road in the Puente Hills

Traffic and hazards: Colima Road was carrying 36,880 vehicles per day south of Camino del Sur in Hacienda Heights in 2010.

Map: *The Thomas Guide by Rand McNally—Street Guide: Los Angeles and Orange Counties* (any recent year), pages 678 and 708

Getting there by car: From central Anaheim, head north on Harbor Boulevard. Enter Los Angeles County. Turn right onto Pathfinder Road in Rowland Heights, and then look for the entrance to Pathfinder County Park. Turn right, and then right again, and drive up the hill into the park.

Getting there by public transit: There was no public transportation service from Orange County to Pathfinder County Park. One alternative would be to ride from central Fullerton to the park by heading northbound via Harbor Boulevard, and then eastbound via Pathfinder Road (7.5 miles). Note that the ride involves a climb and descent of the Coyote Hills, followed by a climb into the Puente Hills, all along Harbor.

Starting point coordinates: 33.966928°N / 117.913933°W

THE RIDE

The Puente Hills Ridge Cycle is a compact loop around and across the Puente Hills, north of Orange County. Note that the ride is in Los Angeles County, very near the Orange County border. In fact, most of the route is within the

city of La Habra Heights, which is in Los Angeles County; the city of La Habra, immediately to the south, is in Orange County. The ride also visits Whittier and Rowland Heights, as well as a corner of Hacienda Heights. The terrain is a mixture of dirt roads and trails and residential roads, although there is one stretch along busy Colima Road in Whittier. It is a reasonably challenging ridge ride, with climbs and descents, some of which are quite steep. The trails do not travel through any designated parks, but are nonetheless open to public access.

Start the ride at Pathfinder County Park in Rowland Heights. The park is nestled in the foothills at the top of an access road off of Pathfinder Road, just east of Harbor Boulevard. The starting elevation is 680 feet. Leave the park by descending the park road; turn left at the bottom, onto the dirt trail that parallels Pathfinder Road. As the path nears Harbor, it bears left, descends, and then curves to the right to pass under Harbor through a tunnel. On the other side of the tunnel, the path curves to the right. At the top, turn sharply to the right to ride along Harbor Boulevard's walkway. Follow the walkway as it curves to the right at Fullerton Road. Enter the city of La Habra Heights.

At the trailhead, turn right onto the trail, and then turn left onto Black Walnut Trail. The trail immediately begins a steep climb (15.7% grade). Relief is ahead as you bear left onto Nogales Trail just a little under 400 feet up. The turn begins a clockwise loop, which you will close later in the ride. Nogales is a bit technical as it drops down the hillside, at times off-camber, into Powder Canyon. There is a gate at mile 1.0; you may need to dismount to negotiate it. Resume riding, now on Powder Canyon Trail. The trail climbs gradually (2.5% grade) to Gray Squirrel Trail. Turn left here; this is a steep climb (9.3% grade). Gray Squirrel ends at Fullerton Road (paved; mile 1.6); turn right here, and then make an immediate right onto paved East Road. East Road provides part of the primary east–west access through La Habra Heights. The road is mainly downhill through here, with a few curves, particularly as it passes alongside Hacienda Golf Club. At the end of East Road, turn right onto busy Hacienda Road, followed by an immediate left onto Encanada Drive. Use caution when turning onto and off of Hacienda Road, because sight distance is poor to upstream and downstream curves in the road. You are now 4.05 miles into the ride.

Bike Shop

Giant Cycling World, Puente Hills Mall, 17400 Colima Rd., Rowland Heights, (626) 810-0108, www.giantrowlandheights.com

Encanada Drive passes by Hacienda Park, also known as "The Park," as it heads into one of the city's rustic neighborhoods. The park is the staging area for Ride 41, Vamanos Alturas La Habra. After a short descent, Encanada

Overgrowth on the unnamed, singletrack trail that parallels Hacienda Road in La Habra Heights nearly smothers this bicycle.

climbs gradually (4.5% grade) to a crest at Virazon Drive (740 feet) before descending to Subtropic Drive. Turn right here and continue descending. Turn right onto Las Palomas Drive (mile 5.25) and resume climbing (6.2% grade). Stay left at Lupin Hill Road to remain on Las Palomas. There seems to be a small private zoo to your left, as you can hear animals that do not sound like your basic cats and dogs. Las Palomas continues to climb; as you near the end of the road, look to the right for the Arroyo San Miguel trailhead. Leave the road here (mile 5.7), and ride onto Arroyo San Miguel Trail. The trail opens with a brisk descent into the canyon. You are now in the city of Whittier. You will see plenty of coyote bush and laurel sumac as you descend the trail.

As the trail nears Colima Road (there is an underpass ahead), bear left onto the singletrack trail (mile 7.15). (The underpass is off-limits to bicycles.) The trail descends to the lowest elevation of the ride (552 feet) before climbing up steeply (19.6% grade) to Colima Road. Next, turn right onto Colima Road and make the climb up to its crest. Colima is busy, but there is a wide shoulder. The grade of the climb is 5.9%. The crest is at mile 8.0 (elevation 791 feet). The descent of Colima begins right away; avoid picking up too much speed though, because you will leave the road at mile 8.4, turning right onto Skyline Drive. (The road's dirt portions are also referred to as Skyline Fire Road.) Skyline is a dirt fire road; there is no curb cut at the trailhead. You will have to dismount anyway, as the gate to Skyline is narrow and somewhat tricky to navigate. Skyline starts to climb immediately (9.6% grade), through a dense collection of trees. You are now on a segment of the Juan Bautista de Anza National Historic Trail, which is a 1,210-mile-long route stretching from Nogales, Arizona, to San Francisco, California. Bear left at the crest (mile 8.95—elevation 970 feet) onto Draper Road (dirt; no sign), and take on the steep descent (11.8% grade). The trail was eroded when I rode it; use caution.

At the bottom of the hill, just when it appears as if you are about to be emptied onto Hacienda Road, the trail makes a sharp turn to the right, where you will encounter a tunnel. The trail then curves to the left to pass under Hacienda. Fo Guang Shan Hsi Lai Temple is across the street. The Buddhist temple was completed in 1991 after encountering some local resistance. The temple went "mainstream" in 2011, when it served as the starting point for TV's *The Amazing Race*. On the other side of the tunnel, the trail narrows to singletrack, immediately adjacent Hacienda Road. The trail was not well maintained and was a bit gnarly in segments, with overgrowth and plenty of fragments (i.e., wood chips, broken roots, rocks, uneven dirt). The trail was nonetheless rideable (6.8% average grade; please see photo). After a ride through some occasionally dense vegetation, sandwiched between residences on the left

La Habra

Although the city of La Habra is referred to as the companion or partner of La Habra Heights, it bears little resemblance to its neighbor to the north. The two cities are in different counties (Orange vs. Los Angeles), and the population of La Habra (60,239) in 2010 was nearly twelve times that of La Habra Heights. While the latter has resisted commercial development, La Habra has welcomed it, including the expansive La Habra Marketplace and La Habra Westridge Plaza. While La Habra Heights acquired fame because of a single avocado tree (the Hass Avocado Mother Tree, planted in the 1920s by Rudolph Hass), La Habra has invested in retail. In fact, the city's largest employers are retailers such as CVS Pharmacy, Costco, Target, and Walmart. La Habra's most famous residents have included 1976 Olympic basketball silver medalist Ann Meyers and singer Norma "The Champagne Lady" Zimmer, who was named the honorary mayor of the city in 1975.

and Hacienda Road on the right, turn left onto Skyline Drive at mile 10.1. You are now at 902 feet, ready to head toward this ride's highest elevations.

Skyline begins to climb immediately, at an 8.7% grade, first cresting at 1,034 feet, then descending briefly, before climbing again. The second climb is steeper (9.3% grade), and takes you a little higher (1,214 feet). This would seem to be the high point, but it is not; turn right to continue on Skyline. The fire road descends steeply from here (13.3% grade), and then climbing resumes, first at a 7.8% grade, and then a very steep 17.7%. The third crest is at 1,303 feet, and is followed by a short descent. Turn right at mile 11.45 to continue on Skyline Drive. Leave the Juan Bautista de Anza National Historic Trail, which bears to the left at this point. This next climb is at a 10.9% grade, finally leading to the highest elevation of the ride, 1,360 feet, at Radio Road. As suggested, there is some telecommunications equipment up here. Keep straight as Skyline starts to descend.

At mile 12.4, Skyline turns to the right—keep straight here; you are now on Purple Sage Trail. Purple Sage descends rapidly (9.7% grade) into the valley below. Note that Purple Sage is ridden in the opposite direction in Schabarum Scramble, in *Best Bike Rides Los Angeles*. At the end of Purple Sage, turn right onto Powder Canyon Trail to continue the descent. At the second trail junction, which is Black Walnut Trail, turn left to begin the last long climb of the ride (mile 13.1). You are now at an elevation of 775 feet, heading once again for the 1,000-foot mark. The climb is at an average grade of 7.8%. Beyond the crest, Black Walnut descends steeply (13.2% grade), passing the junction with Nogales Trail, and closing the loop that you began early on in the ride. Beyond Nogales, turn right and aim for the trailhead. You are now riding in the reverse direction of the opening segment.

Turn left onto Fullerton Road's walkway, which curves to the left at Harbor Boulevard. Turn sharply to the left onto the trail, off of Harbor, and reverse direction to access the tunnel under Harbor. The trail curves to the left on the other side of the tunnel, and then to the right at Pathfinder Road. Follow the trail adjacent Pathfinder to the entrance to Pathfinder County Park. Turn right at the entrance, and then turn right again onto the park road. It is a short climb (5.0% grade) back to the parking area, where the ride ends.

MILES AND DIRECTIONS

0.0 Start at Pathfinder County Park in Rowland Heights. Starting elevation: 680 feet. Start by descending the park road, to Pathfinder Road.

0.15 Turn left onto the dirt trail parallel to Pathfinder Road.

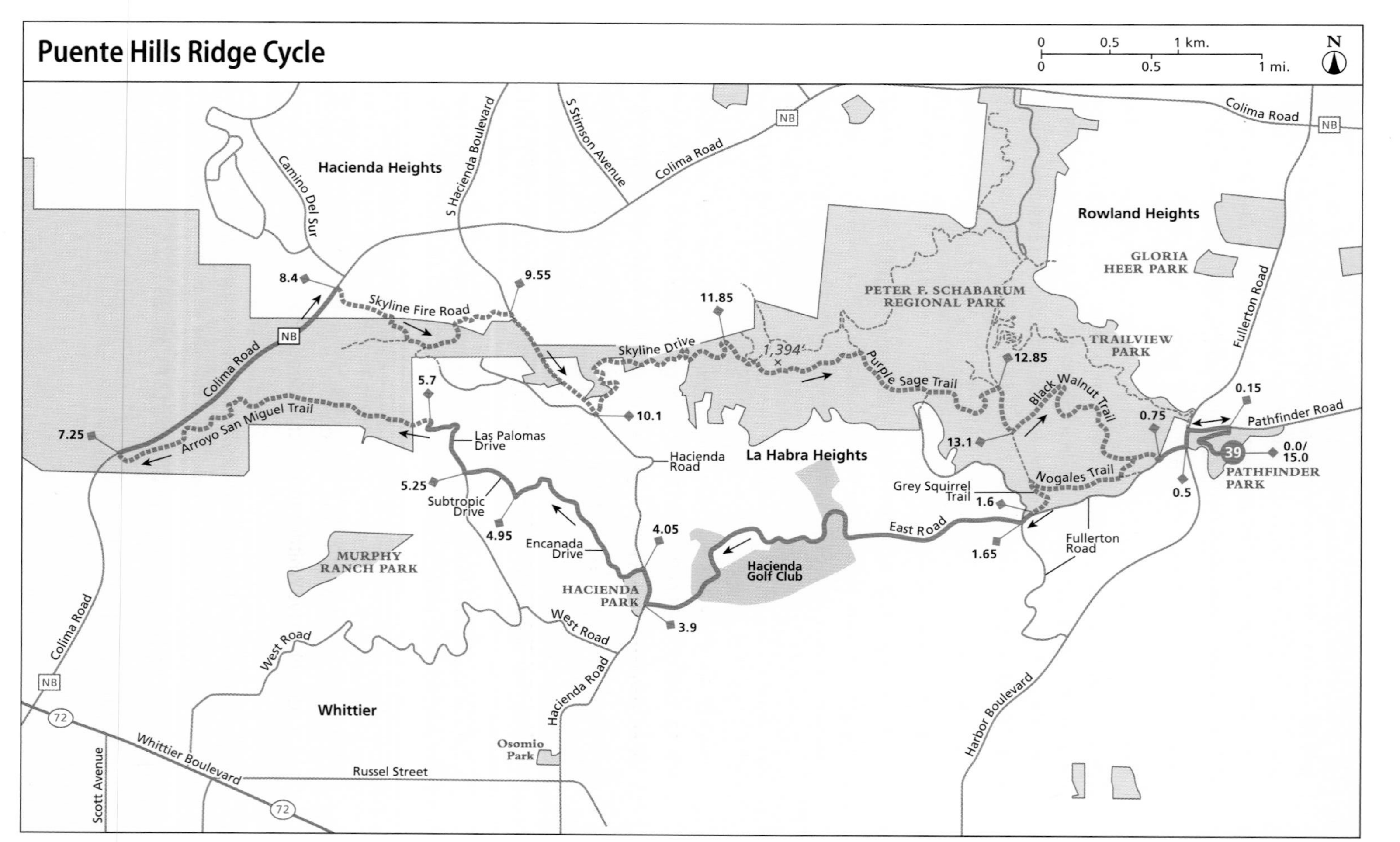
Puente Hills Ridge Cycle
0
0.5
1 km.
0
0.5
1 mi.
N
Colima Road
NB
Hacienda Heights
Camino Del Sur
S Hacienda Boulevard
S Stimson Avenue
Colima Road
NB
Rowland Heights
GLORIA HEER PARK
Fullerton Road
PETER F. SCHABARUM REGIONAL PARK
TRAILVIEW PARK
8.4
9.55
11.85
Skyline Fire Road
Skyline Drive
1,394'
Purple Sage Trail
12.85
Black Walnut Trail
0.15
Pathfinder Road
0.75
0.0/ 15.0
39
PATHFINDER PARK
0.5
NB
Colima Road
5.7
10.1
Arroyo San Miguel Trail
7.25
Las Palomas Drive
Hacienda Road
La Habra Heights
13.1
Nogales Trail
Grey Squirrel Trail
1.6
5.25
Subtropic Drive
4.95
Encanada Drive
4.05
East Road
1.65
Fullerton Road
Hacienda Golf Club
MURPHY RANCH PARK
HACIENDA PARK
3.9
West Road
West Road
Colima Road
NB
Whittier
Hacienda Road
Harbor Boulevard
72
Whittier Boulevard
72
Scott Avenue
Osomio Park
Russel Street

0.35 Trail bears left at Harbor Boulevard, and then curves right and enters tunnel under Harbor.

0.45 Trail curves to the right upon exiting tunnel.

0.5 Turn sharply to the right onto Harbor Boulevard walkway, and then right again at Fullerton Road.

0.7 Leave walkway and Fullerton Road; bear right onto trail—enter city of La Habra Heights.

0.75 Turn left onto Black Walnut Trail; begin steep climb (15.7% grade).

0.85 Turn left onto Nogales Trail; descend hillside, into Powder Canyon.

1.0 Gate; keep straight onto Powder Canyon Trail.

1.35 Turn left onto Gray Squirrel Trail; begin climb (9.3% grade).

1.6 End of trail at Fullerton Road (paved); turn right, and then right again onto East Road; begin gradual descent.

3.9 Traffic signal at Hacienda Road; turn right.

4.05 Turn left onto Encanada Drive; Hacienda Park is on the left.

4.15 After a short downhill, begin gradual climb (4.5% grade).

4.85 Crest of climb at Virazon Drive (elevation 740 feet); begin downhill.

4.95 Stop sign at Subtropic Drive; turn right—continue downhill.

5.25 Stop sign at Las Palomas Drive; turn right—begin climb (6.2% grade).

5.45 Stay left at Lupin Hill Drive to remain on Las Palomas; continue climb.

5.7 Leave road; turn right onto Arroyo San Miguel Trail (elevation 801 feet)—begin descent. Enter city of Whittier.

7.15 Turn left onto unnamed singletrack trail, just upstream of tunnel under Colima Road.

7.2 Lowest elevation of ride (552 feet); begin short steep climb (19.6% grade) to Colima Road.

7.25 Turn right onto Colima Road. Ride on road's shoulder; climb 5.9% grade.

8.0 Crest of climb on Colima (elevation 791 feet); begin downhill (4.4% grade). Leave Whittier and enter Hacienda Heights.

8.4 Leave Colima Road; turn right onto Skyline Drive (dirt fire road)—dismount to negotiate curb and gate. Begin climb (9.6% grade).

8.95 Crest of climb (elevation 970 feet); bear left onto Draper Road (dirt; no sign) and begin steep descent (11.8% grade).

9.45 Bottom of hill; trail curves to the right, and then left to pass under Hacienda Road in tunnel.

9.55 Singletrack trail continues on other side of tunnel, parallel to Hacienda Road. Begin climb (6.8% grade).

10.1 Turn left onto Skyline Drive (dirt fire road); climb continues (8.7% grade).

10.45 Skyline Drive reaches a false crest (elevation 1,034 feet); after a break, climbing resumes (9.3% grade).

10.95 Bear right to continue on Skyline Drive (elevation 1,214 feet); begin steep descent (13.2% grade).

11.05 Climbing resumes, initially at a 7.8% grade, then more steeply (17.7% grade).

11.25 Crest of climb (elevation 1,303 feet); begin short downhill.

11.45 Turn right to continue on Skyline Drive—begin steep climb (10.9% grade).

11.85 High elevation of ride (1,360 feet) at Radio Road; keep straight and begin downhill (9.7% grade).

12.4 Keep straight at junction; Skyline Drive turns right—now on Purple Sage Trail.

12.85 End of Purple Sage Trail (elevation 870 feet); turn right onto Powder Canyon Trail—continue downhill (7.8% grade).

13.1 Turn left onto Black Walnut Trail; begin climb (7.5% grade).

13.75 Crest of climb (elevation 1,007 feet).

13.85 Begin steep descent (13.2% grade).

14.2 Turn right onto "exiting" trail—head for trailhead, then bear left onto walkway adjacent Fullerton Road.

14.4 Walkway curves to the left at Harbor Boulevard.

14.45 Turn sharply to the left onto trail—descend to tunnel; pass through tunnel under Harbor Boulevard.

14.55 Trail curves to the left on other side of tunnel, then to the right at Pathfinder Road.

14.8 Turn right at entrance to Pathfinder County Park; turn right onto park road—climb 5.05% grade.

15.0 End of ride at Pathfinder County Park parking area.

40

Sierra Peak Enduro

Start: Mountain Gate Community Park, 3100 South Main St., Corona

Length: 24.5 miles (clockwise loop)

Riding time: 2.5 to 6 hours (my time: 3H06:58)

Terrain and surface: 44% dirt roads, 41% paved roads, and 15% paved bike paths

Elevations: Low—414 feet on the Santa Ana River Trail at the Coal Canyon Trail junction; high—3,019 feet on Main Divide Road North adjacent Sierra Peak

Traffic and hazards: Green River Road carried 21,200 vehicles per day west of Palisades Drive in 2013; Paseo Grande carried 11,700 vehicles per day in 2011; Ontario Avenue carried 28,100 vehicles per day west of Main Street in 2013; Main Street carried 17,000 vehicles per day south of Magnolia Avenue in 2013; Mountain Gate Drive carried 3,900 vehicles per day in 2013; Lincoln Avenue carried 6,800 vehicles per day north of Mountain Gate Drive in 2013; Foothill Parkway carried 4,600 vehicles per day west of Lincoln Avenue in 2011.

Map: *The Thomas Guide by Rand McNally—Street Guide: Riverside County* (any recent year), page 773

Getting there by car: From central Anaheim, head north on CA 57. Exit to CA 91 eastbound. In Corona, exit at Main Street; turn right and head south. Turn right at Magnolia Avenue to remain on Main Street. At the end of Main, turn right onto Mountain Gate Drive. The entrance to Mountain Gate Community Park will be on your left. Park here.

Getting there by public transit: Riverside Transit bus route 216 runs from Orange (The Village shopping center) to central Corona on weekdays (nine trips: four in the morning and five in the evening) and weekends (every 4 hours). Exit at the Corona Transit Center, and ride southward on Main Street to Mountain Gate park (3.1 miles).

Starting point coordinates: 33.842769°N / 117.574931°W

THE RIDE

Sierra Peak Enduro is a challenging, mountainous mountain bike ride featuring a mixture of dirt roads, paved roads, and a paved bike path. The ride starts and ends in the city of Corona, in Riverside County, but passes through Orange County when in the Santa Ana Mountains. The high-low elevation difference of 2,605 feet makes this ride one of the most epic and rewarding in the book. The recommendation direction for the loop is clockwise, as the climb up Skyline Drive is less steep than the climb up Coal Canyon (speaking from experience). An "enduro" is a route that features a series of timed downhills connected by a series of untimed transfer legs, which may be uphill. This route is sort of like that, except that there is only one long downhill, and the entire ride should be timed. This route may be viewed as a companion to Ride 36, El Cariso–Trabuco Peak Epic, which covers a southern portion of the Santa Ana Mountains, using roads to complete a loop. This ride covers a northern portion of the Santa Anas, and also uses roads to complete a loop.

The ride starts in the city of Corona, at Mountain Gate Community Park. Corona began as a small, predominantly agricultural community, but has grown into a city of more than 150,000. Among Corona's most famous residents were Cuban-American bandleader and actor Desi Arnaz (1917–1986) and regional Mexican singer-songwriter Jenni Rivera (1969–2012). Exit the park and turn left onto Mountain Gate Drive (starting elevation: 1,098 feet). At the traffic signal at Lincoln Avenue, turn right. At the traffic signal at Foothill Parkway, turn left (mile 1.1). After crossing the bridge over Hagador Canyon, turn left onto Skyline Drive. The opening segment of Skyline Drive is paved, passing behind upscale houses in a South Corona neighborhood. Skyline curves to the right at mile 2.1, veering away from Hagador Canyon, and then crosses Elker Road. After crossing Burrero Way (mile 2.3), Skyline becomes a dirt road and enters Cleveland National Forest (elevation 1,185 feet). Skyline climbs gradually (4.2% grade) to a hairpin turn.

After the hairpin turn, Skyline begins to climb in earnest, at an average grade of 7.1%. The road executes a number of switchbacks, and there are several pullouts enabling one to check out some expansive views. Skyline is, in fact, popular with riders, hikers, and even a few motorists who have access, so always be alert to other trail users. Enter Orange County at mile 6.55, at an elevation of 2,695 feet. At the junction with Main Divide Road North (unpaved fire road; FR 3S04, also known as Leonard Road), which is just up the road, turn right. This junction is the turnaround point for Ride 1, Black Star Canyon Adventure. Main Divide Road North travels along a pastoral stretch, adjacent a communications facility to your left. Beyond here, over the next mile, the road executes a number of climbs and descents, with the steepest climb at

Majestic view of Santa Ana Mountain lands from Main Divide Road North, with the barely visible towers of an easement in the foreground (in the canyon)

a 10.9% grade. After reentering Riverside County (mile 7.9, elevation 2,858 feet), the road climbs to over 2,900 feet for the first time. The climb gets steep at mile 8.3 (10.4% grade), as the road comes within 3 feet of 3,000. Another descent takes you below 2,900 feet again; stay to the left at the split at mile 8.65—the right fork continues to an old water collection basin. The climbing resumes at mile 8.8, on a 10.0% grade that takes you to the highest elevation of the ride (3,019 feet).

Stay to the left at the junction (mile 9.05) at the crest; the right fork continues to the summit of Sierra Peak, which is adjacent. This is the first Santa Ana Mountains summit when moving from the north to the south. The elevation at the peak is 3,045 feet, and there is a large collection of communications equipment there. There are great views of the San Gabriel Valley, Los Angeles, and even the Pacific Ocean to the west, as well as the San Gabriel Mountains to the north. Ready for some downhill? You will have to reenter Orange County for that, which occurs just beyond the peak, at mile 9.15. It is a steady downhill into Santa Ana River Canyon way down below, with the exception of a short climb where the road passes under an easement. Stay

to the left as the road curves past a junction at mile 9.5. The average grade is 6.1% to mile 11.3, where several trails converge at rocky Moab Peak. Make a hard right here, onto Coal Canyon Trail (elevation 2,213 feet).

Coal Canyon Trail descends rapidly, at an 11.4% grade, for the next 1.4 miles. The trailside scenery, which includes Tecate cypress and a bounty of chaparral, may be a blur as you coast down the hill. At mile 12.7, now at an elevation of 1,372 feet, the trail curves to the left and enters the Coal Canyon Ecological Reserve. The reserve is a 956-acre unit on the north flanks of the Santa Ana Mountains. The reserve features grasslands, sage scrub and chaparral, and habitats for lizards, rabbits, raptors, and rodents. The reserve also provides passage for deer migration. Coal Canyon Trail continues its quick descent, although the gradient eases to 7.6%. After a few sweeping switchbacks, the trail sweeps down into the canyon, leaving Coal Canyon, the reserve, and the forest, and entering the Santa Ana River canyon corridor. Pass through a gate at mile 14.9 (elevation 489 feet), and continue under the CA 91 freeway. On the other side of the underpass, turn right onto the Santa Ana River Trail (SART; paved bike path).

The dirt riding is over, and it is all pavement for the final 9.45 miles of the trip. The next 1.2 miles are on the SART, which is featured in several other rides in this book. Enter Riverside County at mile 15.85, where the path begins a gradual climb. The lowest elevation of the ride (414 feet) is just before the county line. The path ends at mile 16.25; continue onto Green River Road. Green River climbs (5.9% grade) to an interchange with CA 91; watch out for motor vehicles entering and exiting the freeway, as well as those visiting adjacent convenience stores, fast-food restaurants, and gas stations. You may want to stop to refresh at one of these. Once across CA 91, Green River heads slightly downhill, and then climbs slightly to the intersection with Palisades Drive (mile 18.05). Although you did a lot of climbing to reach Sierra Peak, the descent took you to a lower elevation than where you started. Thus, it is a net climb back to the starting point. A significant portion of that climb comes after passing Palisades Drive, where the road turns upward (5.0% grade) for a nearly 300-foot climb. After a brief respite at Serfas Club Drive, the climbing resumes (3.2% grade), all the way to the end of Green River.

Bike Shops

Jenson USA Bicycles, 2410 Wardlow Rd., Corona, (951) 736-0700, www.jensonusa.com; Nad's Bicycles, 1441 West 6th St. #10C, Corona, (951) 808-8889

As Corona grows, Green River Road will continue eastward as a through street. For now, though, the road bears to the left, becoming Paseo Grande. The road narrows, and you may find yourself passing stopped motor vehicles, even on the uphills. Paseo Grande briefly enters the unincorporated enclave of Coronita, which has resisted annexation by the city of Corona. Turn right onto Ontario Avenue, now back in Corona, and start another climb (5.5% grade). Beyond the crest of the climb, at Border Avenue (elevation 961 feet), Ontario is gradually downhill, and then gradually uphill, over the next 2.25 miles. Turn right onto Main Street to begin the final climb (3.5% grade) of the ride. Turn right at Magnolia Avenue to remain on Main Street. Turn right at Mountain Gate Drive, and then turn left to enter Mountain Gate Community Park to conclude the ride.

MILES AND DIRECTIONS

0.0 Start at Mountain Gate Community Park in Corona, located adjacent Main Street and Mountain Gate Drive. Starting elevation: 1,098 feet. Exit the park and turn left onto Mountain Gate Drive.

0.7 Traffic signal at Lincoln Avenue and Upper Drive; turn right onto Lincoln Avenue.

1.1 Traffic signal at Foothill Parkway; turn left.

1.75 Turn left onto Skyline Drive (paved path) after crossing bridge over Hagador Canyon.

2.1 Skyline Drive curves to the right—cross Elker Road at grade; keep straight.

2.3 Cross Burrero Way at grade; keep straight—enter Cleveland National Forest. Skyline Drive is now a dirt fire road. Elevation 1,185 feet—begin climb (4.2% grade).

2.8 Skyline Drive makes a hairpin turn; climb gets steeper (7.1% average grade).

6.55 Enter Orange County; elevation 2,695 feet.

6.65 Junction; bear right onto Main Divide Road North (FR 3S04; elevation 2,704 feet)—begin sequence of climbs and descents.

7.9 Enter Riverside County (elevation 2,858 feet).

8.2 Crest of climb (elevation 2,945 feet); begin short descent, then continue climb at 10.4% grade.

8.45 Elevation 2,997 feet; begin descent (6.0% grade).

8.8 End of descent; resume climbing (10.0% grade).

9.05 Highest elevation of ride (3,019 feet), adjacent Sierra Peak; stay left at junction—begin descent.

9.15 Enter Orange County (elevation 2,972 feet).

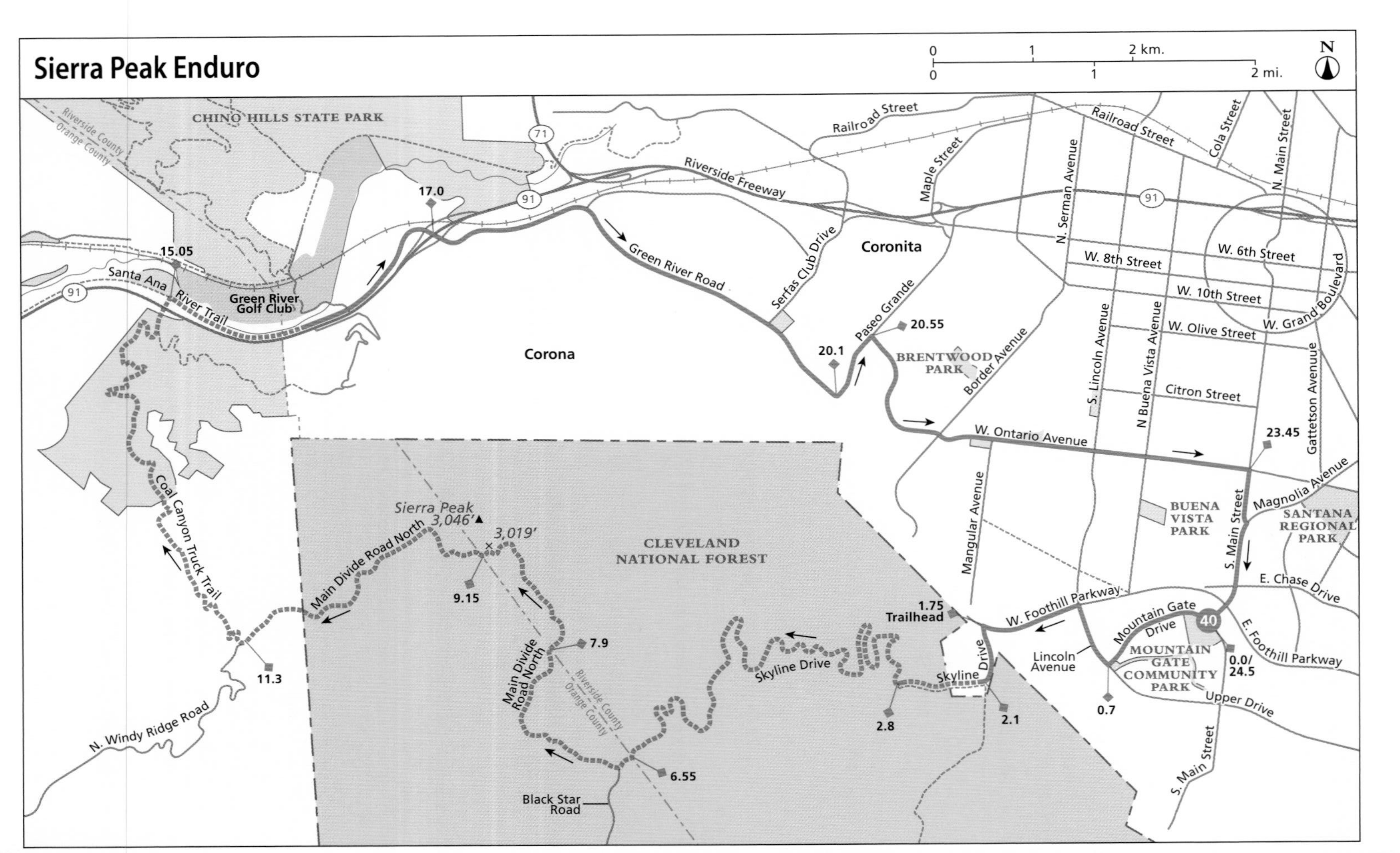

Sierra Peak Enduro
0
1
2 km.
0
1
2 mi.
N
CHINO HILLS STATE PARK
Riverside County
Orange County
71
91
17.0
15.05
Santa Ana River Trail
Green River Golf Club
Riverside Freeway
Green River Road
Railroad Street
Maple Street
Serfas Club Drive
Coronita
Corona
Paseo Grande
20.55
20.1
BRENTWOOD PARK
Border Avenue
N. Serman Avenue
W. 8th Street
W. 6th Street
W. 10th Street
W. Olive Street
W. Grand Boulevard
Cola Street
N. Main Street
S. Lincoln Avenue
N Buena Vista Avenue
Citron Street
Gattetson Avenuue
W. Ontario Avenue
23.45
Magnolia Avenue
SANTANA REGIONAL PARK
BUENA VISTA PARK
Mangular Avenue
S. Main Street
E. Chase Drive
CLEVELAND NATIONAL FOREST
Sierra Peak 3,046′
3,019′
Main Divide Road North
9.15
7.9
6.55
Black Star Road
Coal Canyon Truck Trail
11.3
N. Windy Ridge Road
Skyline Drive
2.8
2.1
1.75 Trailhead
W. Foothill Parkway
Lincoln Avenue
Mountain Gate Drive
40
MOUNTAIN GATE COMMUNITY PARK
0.0/ 24.5
E. Foothill Parkway
Upper Drive
0.7

9.5 Stay left at junction (elevation 2,798 feet).

11.3 Junction at Moab Peak; turn sharply to the right onto Coal Canyon Trail (elevation 2,213 feet)—begin steep descent (11.4% grade).

12.7 Trail curves to the left; enter Coal Canyon Ecological Reserve (elevation 1,372 feet)—continue descent (7.6% grade).

14.9 Leave Coal Canyon and Cleveland National Forest; gate.

15.05 Road passes under CA 91 freeway.

15.15 Turn right onto Santa Ana River Trail (SART; paved bicycle path).

15.7 Lowest elevation of ride (414 feet).

15.85 Enter Riverside County.

16.25 End of SART; continue onto Green River Road (paved road).

16.6 Begin climb (5.9% grade).

17.0 Cross over CA 91 freeway; watch for entering and exiting motor vehicles.

18.05 Traffic signal at Palisades Drive (elevation 537 feet); keep straight—begin climb (5.0% grade).

19.2 Crest of climb at Ridgeline Drive (elevation 831 feet); begin short descent.

19.45 Climbing resumes at Serfas Club Drive (3.2% grade).

20.1 Green River Road curves to the left, becoming Paseo Grande—road narrows.

20.55 Stop sign at Ontario Avenue; turn right—begin climb (5.5% grade).

21.3 Crest of climb at Border Avenue (elevation 961 feet); begin gradual downhill, followed by gradual uphill.

23.45 Traffic signal at Main Street; turn right—begin climb (3.5% grade).

23.75 Traffic signal at Magnolia Avenue; turn right to continue on Main Street.

24.45 Stop sign at Mountain Gate Drive; turn right.

24.5 Enter Mountain Gate Community Park on the left to conclude the ride.

Vamanos Alturas La Habra

Start: Hacienda Park (also known as "The Park"), 1885 Hacienda Rd., La Habra Heights

Length: 29.2 miles (clockwise loop)

Riding time: 1.5 to 4 hours (my time: 1H56:06)

Terrain and surface: 100% paved roads

Elevations: Low elevation—270 feet at La Sierra Drive and Janine Drive in Whittier; high—934 feet on Pathfinder Road at South Hillrise Drive in Rowland Heights

Traffic and hazards: Colima Road carried 36,685 vehicles per day south of Camino del Sur in Hacienda Heights in 2010; Fullerton Road carried 27,905 vehicles per north of Pathfinder Road in Rowland Heights in 2012; Pathfinder Road carried 15,475 west of Hillrise Drive in Rowland Heights in 2011; Brea Canyon Cutoff carried 17,735 vehicles per day south of Pathfinder Road in 2010; Brea Canyon Road carried 18,680 vehicles per day at the Orange County–Los Angeles County line in 2015. Also, in 2014, Central Avenue carried 33,000 vehicles per day west of Brea Boulevard in Brea; Harbor Boulevard carried 31,000 vehicles per day north of Whittier Boulevard in La Habra.

Map: *The Thomas Guide by Rand McNally—Street Guide: Los Angeles and Orange Counties* (any recent year), page 708

Getting there by car: From central Anaheim, head north on Harbor Boulevard. In La Habra, turn left on Whittier Boulevard and head west. Next, turn right on Hacienda Road and head north, into La Habra Heights. At Encanada Drive, turn left; the park is on the left.

Getting there by public transit: There is no direct public transit service from Orange County to La Habra Heights. But OCTA bus route 143 runs from Fullerton Metrolink station to Harbor Boulevard and Whittier Boulevard in La Habra every 75 minutes on weekdays and every 65 minutes on weekends and holidays. Start the ride by heading north on Harbor from Whittier.

Starting point coordinates: 33.958292°N / 117.550225°W

THE RIDE

Vamanos Alturas La Habra is the road companion to Ride 39, Puente Hills Ridge Cycle. While the latter is a mountain bike tour of the Puente Hills, the former makes a loop around and through the hills on roads. The ride starts and finishes in La Habra Heights, in Los Angeles County, and visits Whittier, Hacienda Heights, Rowland Heights, and Diamond Bar, all in L.A. County, along with Brea and La Habra, which are in Orange County. Always be alert to motor vehicles along the way, as this is truly an urban ride. All of the roads have adequate shoulders, except for East Road and West Road in La Habra Heights, both of which are lightly traveled, and Fullerton Road south of Colima Road in Hacienda Heights (use caution here).

Start the ride at Hacienda Park, also known as "The Park," in La Habra Heights. The starting elevation is 609 feet. Leave the park by turning right onto Encanada Drive, followed by another right onto Hacienda Road. Be careful here, because sight distance is poor, the road is narrow, and motor vehicles are heading downhill! Turn right onto West Road. After the opening downhill on Hacienda (4.8% grade), West Road is flat for a while, then climbs at a 3.3% grade. Now at mile 1.4, the road descends, twisting and winding through La Habra Heights. Enter the city of Whittier as West Road makes one final turn to the left, becoming Santa Gertrudes Avenue (mile 3.25).

As Santa Gertrudes approaches busy Whittier Boulevard, turn right onto Janine Drive, which is a quieter, parallel alternative. At La Sierra Drive, turn left, and then right to continue on Janine. This is the lowest elevation of the ride, at 270 feet. Whittier Hospital and Medical Center is on the right, so things may occasionally be frenetic. At the end of the road, turn right onto Colima Road. Now at mile 4.2, the next couple of miles are all uphill (average 4.6% grade, steeper near the crest). Enter a stretch of open space after passing Lodosa Drive. Access to the Arroyo San Miguel Trail is on the right at mile 5.5; Ride 39, Puente Hills Ridge Cycle, shares Colima Road with this ride from here to the Skyline Drive trailhead. Colima crests at mile 6.35 (791 feet), then descends rapidly (5.4% grade). The Skyline Drive trailhead is on the right at mile 6.7. Enter the community of Hacienda Heights.

After reaching the bottom of the hill, just west of Hacienda Road (mile 7.2, elevation 549 feet), Colima Road is heading generally eastward, entering a long stretch of gradual elevation changes. There is plenty of commercial activity along Colima, particularly east of Azusa Avenue, with Puente Hills Mall on the left and strip retail on the right (and left). The entrance to Schabarum Regional Park is on the right, directly across from the mall (try the Schabarum Scramble, described in *Best Bike Rides L.A.*). Beyond the park, Colima enters the unincorporated community of Rowland Heights. Turn right onto Fullerton

A rider claims his space along the shoulder of Brea Canyon Road on the edge of the Puente Hills, in Los Angeles County.

Road (mile 11.45, elevation 480 feet) and head south. Use caution here, as Fullerton was lacking a shoulder from Colima Road to Galatina Street for about two-thirds of a mile. Fullerton has two lanes in each direction, so drivers will (hopefully) have the wherewithal to use the other lane when passing. There is a frontage road beginning at Galatina.

At Pathfinder Road, turn left and head east (mile 13.0). Pathfinder County Park (starting point for Ride 39, Puente Hills Ridge Cycle) is on the right at mile 13.15; keep straight. Pathfinder Road rolls until mile 14.95, where it begins a climb (4.4% grade) to the highest elevation of the ride, at Hillrise Drive (mile 16.35, elevation 934 feet). Pathfinder descends from here. Turn right at Brea Canyon Cutoff (mile 16.6), and continue the descent (4.7% grade). Pass under the CA 57 freeway, entering the city of Diamond Bar, and then turn right onto Brea Canyon Road. This road is ridden in the opposite direction in Ride 2, Brea-Carbon (Free) Canyons Loop. Brea Canyon Road is a net downhill, now heading southward. Leave Diamond Bar and pass under the CA 57 freeway again, at mile 18.5. Enter Orange County at mile 19.6—you are now on Brea Boulevard. The road narrows to cross Brea Creek—be alert to motorists encroaching upon your shoulder space. Enter the city of Brea at mile 21.2. Turn right at Central Avenue (mile 21.5, elevation 382 feet) and head west.

Central Avenue is busy, so let's get off of it by turning right onto Berry Street (mile 22.2), entering a Brea neighborhood. It is a 3.3% grade climb on Berry. The circulation pattern has you turning left onto Northwood Avenue, left onto Puente Street, and then right onto Whittier Boulevard. There are a few undulations along the way, including a downhill on Puente (4.5% grade). On Whittier Boulevard, enter the city of La Habra at mile 24.05. Turn right at Harbor Boulevard (mile 24.75, elevation 397 feet), and start the climb up to La Habra Heights, in the Puente Hills. The uphill grade on Harbor Boulevard is 4.9%. Enter La Habra Heights at mile 25.25. At Fullerton Road, carefully cross the road and turn left (elevation 700 feet; mile 25.95). After a short, easy stretch, Fullerton Road cranks upward for the steepest climb of the ride (9.4% grade).

After twisting and winding your way up, Fullerton Road reaches a crest at Kanola Road (mile 26.5; elevation 894 feet). It is a slight downhill to East Road; turn left here. The rest of the ride duplicates a portion of Ride 39, Puente Hills Ridge Cycle. East Road is 2.2 miles long, mostly downhill, with a few curves through the Hacienda Golf Club, as you make your way past La Habra Heights residences. At Hacienda Road, turn right (narrow road with poor sight distance) and ride the short distance to Encanada Drive. Use caution when turning left onto Encanada. Hacienda Park is on the left, where the ride ends.

MILES AND DIRECTIONS

0.0 Start at Hacienda Park (The Park) at Encanada Drive and Hacienda Road in La Habra Heights. Turn right on Hacienda Road and head downhill, to the south. Starting elevation: 609 feet.

0.15 Traffic signal at West Road; turn right. Road undulates, and then is generally downhill.

3.25 West Road curves to the left, becoming Santa Gertrudes Road. Enter the city of Whittier.

3.5 Stop sign at Janine Drive; turn right.

3.95 Stop sign at La Sierra Drive; turn left. Lowest elevation of the ride (270 feet).

4.0 Turn right onto Janine Drive.

4.2 Stop sign at Colima Road; turn right (elevation 276 feet)—begin climb (4.6% average grade).

5.5 Climb gets steeper at Arroyo San Miguel Trail access (5.9% grade).

6.35 Crest of climb (elevation 791 feet); begin descent (5.4% grade)—leave Whittier and enter Hacienda Heights.

Bike Shops

La Habra Cyclery, 451 North Harbor Blvd., La Habra, (562) 691-7118, http://lahabracyclery.com; Whittier Cyclery, Inc., 10316 Santa Gertrudes Ave., Whittier, (562) 947-1214, http://whittiercyclery.net

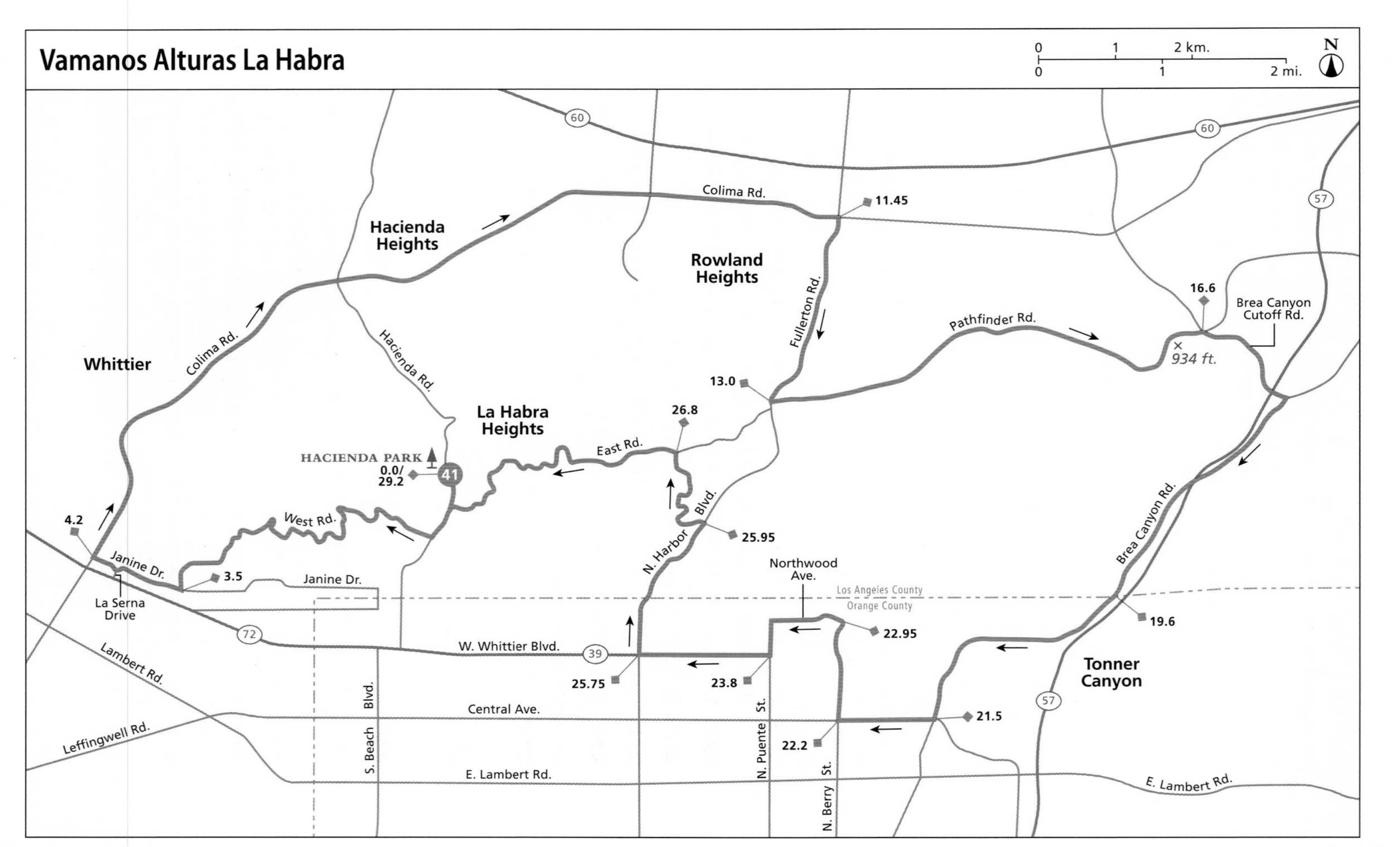
Vamanos Alturas La Habra
0
1
2 km.
0
1
2 mi.
N
60
Colima Rd.
11.45
57
Hacienda
Heights
Rowland
Heights
Fullerton Rd.
16.6
Brea Canyon
Cutoff Rd.
Pathfinder Rd.
934 ft.
Whittier
Colima Rd.
Hacienda Rd.
13.0
La Habra
Heights
26.8
East Rd.
HACIENDA PARK
0.0/
29.2
41
4.2
West Rd.
Blvd.
25.95
Brea Canyon Rd.
Janine Dr.
3.5
Janine Dr.
N. Harbor
Northwood
Ave.
Los Angeles County
Orange County
La Serna
Drive
19.6
72
22.95
W. Whittier Blvd.
39
Tonner
Canyon
Lambert Rd.
25.75
23.8
S. Beach Blvd.
Central Ave.
N. Puente St.
21.5
Leffingwell Rd.
22.2
E. Lambert Rd.
N. Berry St.
E. Lambert Rd.

7.2 End of downhill, just west of Hacienda Road; begin series of false flats and descents.

10.0 Puente Hills Mall is on the left and Schabarum Regional Park is on the right; enter community of Rowland Heights.

11.45 Traffic signal at Fullerton Road; turn right. Note: There is little to no shoulder on Fullerton for about two-thirds of a mile.

13.0 Traffic signal at Pathfinder Road; turn left.

14.95 Begin climb at 4.3% grade.

16.35 Highest elevation of ride (934 feet), at Hillrise Drive; begin descent.

16.6 Traffic signal at Brea Canyon Cutoff; turn right—continue downhill.

17.4 Pass under CA 57 freeway; enter city of Diamond Bar.

17.5 Traffic signal at Brea Canyon Road; turn right.

18.5 Leave Diamond Bar; pass under CA 57 freeway again.

19.6 Enter Orange County.

21.2 Enter city of Brea.

21.5 Traffic signal at Central Avenue and State College Boulevard; turn right onto Central Avenue (elevation 382 feet).

22.2 Traffic signal at Berry Street; turn right—begin climb (3.3% grade).

22.95 Stop sign at Northwood Avenue; turn left.

23.5 Stop sign at Puente Street; turn left—begin downhill (4.1% grade).

23.8 Stop sign at Whittier Boulevard; turn right.

24.05 Enter city of La Habra.

24.75 Traffic signal at Harbor Boulevard; turn right (elevation 397 feet)—begin climb (4.9% grade).

25.25 Enter city of La Habra Heights and Los Angeles County.

25.95 Turn left onto Fullerton Road (elevation 700 feet).

26.1 Begin steep climb (9.4% grade).

26.5 Crest of climb at Kanola Road (elevation 894 feet); begin slight downhill.

26.8 Turn left onto East Road; begin gradual downhill.

29.0 Traffic signal at Hacienda Road; turn right—narrow road with poor sight distance.

29.2 Turn left at Encanada Drive—use caution when making turn. End of ride (Hacienda Park is on the left).

Yorba–Prado Dam Pronto

Start: Jessamyn West Park, 19115 Yorba Linda Blvd., Yorba Linda

Length: 46.8 miles (clockwise loop)

Riding time: 2.25 to 6 hours (my time: 2H49:30)

Terrain and surface: 90% paved roads, 10% paved bike paths

Elevations: Low—349 feet along Santa Ana River Trail west of Gypsum Canyon Road in Yorba Linda; high—1,157 feet on Carbon Canyon Road, east of Olinda

Traffic and hazards: The heaviest traffic volumes in 2014 were on Imperial Highway (46,000 vehicles per day north of Bastanchury Road in Yorba Linda), CA 83 (30,000 vehicles per day north of CA 71 in Chino), Yorba Linda Boulevard (25,000 vehicles per day east of Imperial Highway in Yorba Linda), La Palma Avenue (22,000 vehicles per day east of Yorba Linda Boulevard in Yorba Linda); and Green River Road (21,300 vehicles per day west of Palisades Drive in Corona in 2013).

Map: *The Thomas Guide by Rand McNally—Street Guide: Los Angeles and Orange Counties* (any recent year), page 740

Getting there by car: From central Anaheim, head north on CA 57. Junction to CA 91 eastbound. Exit at Lakeview Avenue; turn left onto Santa Ana Canyon Road, and then left again onto Lakeview Avenue. In Yorba Linda, turn right onto Yorba Linda Boulevard. Look for Jessamyn West Park on the left, directly opposite Club Terrace Drive. Turn left to enter the park.

Getting there by public transit: Ride OCTA bus route 26 from central Fullerton to the end of the line at Fairmont Drive and Bastanchury Road in Yorba Linda. Exit on Yorba Linda Boulevard, adjacent Jessamyn West Park. Route 26 runs every hour on weekdays and every 45 minutes on weekends and holidays.

Starting point coordinates: 33.897208°N / 117.8000214°W

THE RIDE

Saving the best for last? Well, Yorba-Prado Dam Pronto is the longest ride in the book by just under a mile, at 46.8 miles. The route is a giant, clockwise loop that passes through three counties (Orange, San Bernardino, and Riverside) and six cities (Yorba Linda, Brea, Chino Hills, Chino, Norco, and Corona). The route is the shortest way to loop the Chino Hills and Prado Dam by bicycle, where there are no shortcuts.

Start the ride at Jessamyn West Park in Yorba Linda. My first reaction, "Is there a Jessamyn East Park?" was retracted upon learning that Jessamyn West (1902–1984) was an author of short stories and novels, the most well known of which was *The Friendly Persuasion* (1945). She lived in Yorba Linda during the 1920s. Leave the park by turning right onto busy Yorba Linda Boulevard. The starting elevation is 396 feet. At mile 0.75, turn right onto even busier Imperial Highway and head northwest. At Rose Drive, at mile 2.75, turn right and head north. Enter the city of Brea at Blake Road (mile 3.15). Turn right at Valencia Avenue (mile 3.85), which climbs at a 3.2% grade. At the next signal (mile 4.2), turn right onto Carbon Canyon Road (CA 142) to start the long trek up Carbon Canyon. The elevation at the turn is 519 feet.

CA 142 descends gradually, passing Carbon Canyon Regional Park on the right (mile 4.9), and then leveling to pass an entrance to Chino Hills State Park on the right. The highway actually enters the park, too. Begin the gradual canyon climb here (elevation 472 feet). Leave the park and enter the community of Olinda, which is within the city of Brea, at mile 6.5. After a short downhill, the climb resumes (2.5% grade). Enter San Bernardino County and the city of Chino Hills at mile 8.6. After an extended but gradual climb, CA 142 crests at 1,157 feet (mile 10.5), the highest elevation of the ride. From here, the highway plummets down a steep 7.8% grade, including a couple of switchbacks. Avoid crossing the center line and, better yet, hug the right shoulder. The highway straightens and the gradient eases as you leave the canyon and the hills. At Chino Hills Parkway, turn right and head east, still on CA 142. Just as you are approaching the CA 71 freeway, turn right onto Pipeline Avenue and head south, entering a Chino Hills neighborhood. At Woodview Avenue, Pipeline climbs (3.4% grade) to an intersection with Soquel Canyon Parkway, passing the Los Serranos Country Club on the left.

Turn left onto Soquel Canyon Parkway (mile 15.7); the elevation at the turn is 772 feet. That was the last climb of the ride until the very end, so enjoy the gentle terrain. Turn right onto Butterfield Ranch Road and head south. Chino Hills State Park is in the hills to your right, although there is no park access from here. Cross over the CA 71 freeway at mile 20.15, leaving Chino Hills and entering the city of Chino. Home to two state prisons, Chino—particularly the

Riders light up the Santa Ana River Trail in Yorba Linda, heading toward Gypsum Canyon Road (you'll be heading the other way).

prisons—has been referenced many times in songs, TV shows, and films. In crossing over CA 71, the road turns northward, becoming CA 83 (Euclid Avenue). The Prado Olympic Shooting Park is on the left, and the main entrance to Prado Regional Park is on the right. At the traffic signal at Pine Avenue, turn right to head east, followed by a right turn at Chino Corona Road to head south.

Chino Corona Road passes by one of the aforementioned prisons—the California Institution for Women, at mile 23.5. Chino Corona curves to the left to head east just beyond the prison. New construction and a new alignment for the road has it curving to the left again, at mile 24.45, to become Legacy Park Road. Legacy Park then turns sharply to the right to head eastward. Construction in this area was in progress as of this writing, so there may be further alignment shifts. At Hellman Avenue, also subject to construction, turn right and head south. Hellman curves to the left at mile 26.65, entering Riverside County. At Archibald Avenue, turn right to continue on River Road—enter the city of Norco (short for North Corona). Prado Basin Park, to your right, was closed when I visited it.

River Road crosses over the Santa Ana River at mile 27.8. Next, turn right onto Corydon Avenue, leaving Norco and entering the city of Corona. The road briefly enters the Prado Dam Flood Control Basin, curving to the left to become Rincon Street. At Smith Avenue, turn right and enter an industrial area. Turn right again at Railroad Street and head west. Among the many businesses along here is Fender Musical Instruments, a well-known guitar maker. Railroad Street curves sharply to the left at mile 32.35 and elevates, to cross over railroad tracks and become Auto Center Drive. Things get busy through here, particularly with truck traffic, as you pass under the CA 91 freeway. On the other side of the underpass, you are on Serfas Club Drive, entering the unincorporated enclave of Coronita. Turn right at Palisades Drive, still in Coronita, to head westward. Palisades heads gradually downhill, leaving Coronita and reentering Corona. After a pastoral stretch, Palisades ends at Green River Road. Turn right to continue heading west (mile 34.95).

The next segment is ridden in the opposite direction in Ride 40, Sierra Peak Enduro (on a mountain bike). On Green River Road, you may be able to catch glimpses of Prado Dam's giant bicentennial mural on the right, although the best way to see the mural is from the freeway, heading eastbound on CA 91 or northbound on CA 71. Cross over CA 91 at mile 36.0—use caution here, watching for motor vehicles entering and exiting the freeway. After passing a few mini-marts and fast-food eateries, Green River Road descends (5.9% grade). The Green River Golf Club is on the right. At the bottom of the hill the road narrows and then ends. Continue onto the Santa Ana River Trail (SART), bearing right, and then curving to the left. Enter Orange County at mile 37.15, and then the city of Yorba Linda, adjacent the access road to Coal Canyon, at mile 37.85. With the exception of CA 91 roaring to your left, somewhat out of view, this is a peaceful stretch. As you enter Featherly Regional Park, with campsites to your right, the SART curves to the right to pass under Gypsum Canyon Road.

Bike Shops

Jax Bicycle Center, 17593 Yorba Linda Blvd., Yorba Linda, (714) 996-9093, http://jaxbicycles.com

On the other side of the underpass, the SART curves to the left and right, and then left again to head up to the road. There is a water fountain on the left. After the short climb up to Gypsum Canyon Road, continue across the Santa Ana River; the SART is along the bridge's walkway. On the opposite side, turn left to continue on the SART. The Santa Ana River is now on your left. The lowest elevation of the entire ride (349 feet) is along here. After a little over 2 miles, stay to the right to climb the short hill to an at-grade crossing of the entrance to a retail center. It is time to leave the path so, very cautiously, cross the adjacent road, which is La Palma Avenue, and continue heading

westward. Continue on La Palma to Yorba Linda Boulevard. Turn right here (mile 42.8), and begin a gradual climb (2.1% grade). After reaching a crest at Yorba Ranch Road, it is another couple of miles, generally downhill, to Jessamyn West Park, where the ride ends.

MILES AND DIRECTIONS

0.0 Start at Jessamyn West Park in Yorba Linda. Exit the park and turn right onto Yorba Linda Boulevard.

0.75 Traffic signal at Imperial Highway; turn right.

2.75 Traffic signal at Rose Drive; turn right.

3.15 Enter city of Brea at Blake Road.

3.85 Traffic signal at Valencia Avenue (CA 142); turn right.

4.2 Traffic signal at Lambert Road and Carbon Canyon Road (CA 142); turn right onto CA 142.

4.9 Carbon Canyon Regional Park on the right; keep straight.

5.4 Chino Hills State Park on the right; keep straight—begin climb up canyon (average 2.4% grade). Highway enters Chino Hills State Park.

6.5 Leave state park; enter community of Olinda; short downhill, and then climb continues.

8.6 Enter San Bernardino County and city of Chino Hills.

10.5 Crest of climb; highest elevation of ride (1,157 feet); begin steep, winding descent (7.8% grade).

11.35 Highway straightens and gradient eases.

12.5 Traffic signal at Chino Hills Parkway; turn right (elevation 757 feet).

14.05 Traffic signal at Pipeline Avenue; turn right.

15.2 Begin climb at Woodview Avenue (3.4% grade).

15.7 Stop sign at Soquel Canyon Parkway; turn left—begin gradual descent.

17.0 Traffic signal at Butterfield Ranch Road; turn right—begin rolling terrain.

20.15 Cross over CA 71 freeway; road curves to the left and heads north—now on CA 83 (Euclid Avenue) in the city of Chino.

20.7 Prado Olympic Shooting Park on the left.

21.4 Main entrance to Prado Regional Park on the right.

21.9 Traffic signal at Pine Avenue; turn right.

22.95 Traffic signal at Chino Corona Road; turn right.

23.5 California Institution for Women (prison) on the right.

23.75 Chino Corona Road curves to the left.

24.45 Road curves to the left, becoming Legacy Park Road.

25.0 Turn right to continue heading eastward on Legacy Park Road.

25.25 Traffic signal at Hellman Avenue; turn right.

Shooting at Prado Dam

Prado Dam may be one of the most visible in Southern California, as it can be clearly seen from the CA 71 and CA 91 freeways, on the western edge of the city of Corona, in Riverside County. A giant mural on the face of the dam, painted by Corona High School students in 1976 to honor the US bicentennial, makes it even more prominent. The US Army Corps of Engineers was set to remove the mural in 2015 because of deterioration, vandalism, and lead paint, but a conservancy won a federal order against its removal, under the Visual Artists Rights Act. The dam's primary function is flood control of the Santa Ana River. A large flood control basin surrounds the dam, providing water storage for groundwater recharge, as needed. The dam is earth-filled, making it vulnerable during extremely heavy rains. In fact, a leak in the dam after heavy storms in 2005 forced the evacuation of about 3,000 downstream residents. Work continues on improving the dam's downstream channel flow capacity.

Immediately to the north of Prado Dam is Prado Regional Park, which in 1984 hosted the Summer Olympic Games shooting competitions. Shooting competitions are not necessarily crowd spectacles, but the eyes of the world were on the men's Free Pistol event, as it awarded the very first gold medal of the Games, on July 29th. Xu Haifeng got his fame as the winner of the Games' and China's first (ever) gold medal in the sport. The silver medal went to Sweden's 50-year-old Ragnar Skanåker, who had won the gold medal in 1972, and who would go on to win two more medals, with the last one coming at age 58! The "lazy" French team observed that the shooting venue was too far from the Olympic Village, which was 50 miles away at the University of Southern California. They elected to camp nearby in rented motorhomes, using fishing equipment and crossbows to catch their food. The strategy worked for 21-year-old Philippe Héberlé, who won gold in the air rifle. Note that in the air rifle, the competitors just pretend to shoot, and are scored on their rifle sounds and perceived precision (kidding).

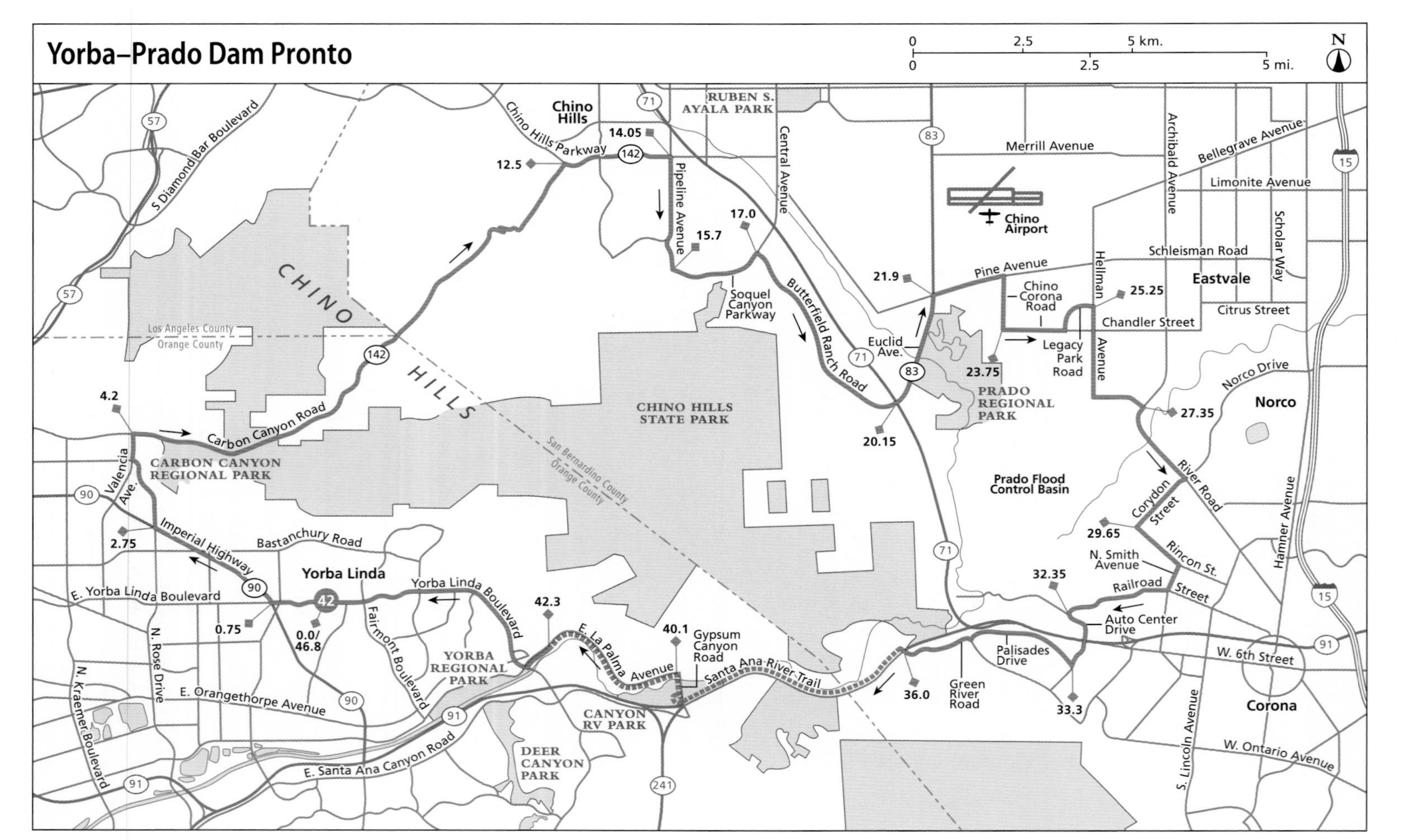
Yorba–Prado Dam Pronto
0
2.5
5 km.
0
2.5
5 mi.
N
Chino Hills
Chino Hills Parkway
S Diamond Bar Boulevard
Los Angeles County
Orange County
CHINO HILLS
RUBEN S. AYALA PARK
Central Avenue
Pipeline Avenue
Soquel Canyon Parkway
Butterfield Ranch Road
Merrill Avenue
Chino Airport
Archibald Avenue
Bellegrave Avenue
Limonite Avenue
Scholar Way
Schleisman Road
Eastvale
Citrus Street
Chandler Street
Hellman Avenue
Pine Avenue
Chino Corona Road
Legacy Park Road
Euclid Ave.
PRADO REGIONAL PARK
Norco Drive
Norco
Prado Flood Control Basin
River Road
Corydon Street
Rincon St.
N. Smith Avenue
Railroad Street
Auto Center Drive
Hamner Avenue
Palisades Drive
Green River Road
W. 6th Street
Corona
S. Lincoln Avenue
W. Ontario Avenue
CHINO HILLS STATE PARK
San Bernardino County
Orange County
Carbon Canyon Road
CARBON CANYON REGIONAL PARK
Valencia Ave.
Imperial Highway
Bastanchury Road
Yorba Linda
Yorba Linda Boulevard
E. Yorba Linda Boulevard
N. Rose Drive
Fairmont Boulevard
YORBA REGIONAL PARK
E. La Palma Avenue
Gypsum Canyon Road
Santa Ana River Trail
CANYON RV PARK
DEER CANYON PARK
E. Orangethorpe Avenue
N. Kraemer Boulevard
E. Santa Ana Canyon Road
57
71
83
142
15
91
90
241
42
0.0/ 46.8
0.75
2.75
4.2
12.5
14.05
15.7
17.0
20.15
21.9
23.75
25.25
27.35
29.65
32.35
33.3
36.0
40.1
42.3

26.65 Hellman Avenue curves to the left, becoming River Road. Enter Riverside County.

27.35 Stop sign at Archibald Avenue; turn right to continue on River Road—enter city of Norco.

27.8 Bridge over Santa Ana River.

28.65 Traffic signal at Corydon Avenue; turn right—leave Norco and enter city of Corona.

29.65 Corydon Avenue curves to the left, becoming Rincon Street.

30.45 Stop sign at Smith Avenue; turn right.

30.85 Traffic signal at Railroad Street; turn right.

32.35 Railroad Street curves sharply to the left, becoming Auto Center Drive—road elevates to cross over railroad tracks.

32.85 Pass under CA 91 freeway; now on Serfas Club Drive.

33.3 Stop sign at Palisades Drive; turn right—begin gradual downhill.

34.95 Traffic signal at Green River Road; turn right.

36.0 Cross over CA 91 freeway; watch for motor vehicles entering and exiting the freeway—begin downhill (5.9% grade).

36.4 End of downhill—road narrows.

36.75 End of Green River Road—bear right onto Santa Ana River Trail (SART, paved bike path).

37.15 Enter Orange County.

37.85 Access to Coal Canyon on the left; keep straight—enter city of Yorba Linda.

39.45 SART curves to the right to pass under Gypsum Canyon Road.

39.55 Bear left onto connector path to access Gypsum Canyon Road.

39.65 SART crosses over Santa Ana River on Gypsum Canyon Road bridge.

40.1 Turn left to continue on SART, now on other side of Santa Ana River.

42.3 SART climbs slightly to cross retail center entrance at grade—leave path here and cross La Palma Avenue (use caution); continue heading westward on La Palma.

42.8 Traffic signal at Yorba Linda Boulevard; turn right (elevation 358 feet)—begin climb (2.1% grade).

43.4 Bridge over Esperanza Road and railroad tracks.

44.65 Crest of climb at Yorba Ranch Road (elevation 543 feet); keep straight—begin gradual downhill.

46.8 End of ride at Jessamyn West Park, which is on the right.

Oh my—East Ridge View Trail in Peters Canyon Regional Park is steeper than it looks in the photo. Here we go!

References

BOOKS, PERIODICALS, AND REPORTS

Ambrose, Stephen E. *Nixon: The Education of a Politician 1913–1962*. New York: Simon & Schuster, 1987.

Arlington Cemetery. "Thomas F. Riley." www.arlingtoncemetery.net/tfriley.htm.

Beene, Richard. "300,000 Watch in Horror as Fighter Crashes—Spectators Say F/A-18 Jet Appeared to Stall as Pilot was Making a Loop." *Los Angeles Times: Orange County Edition*, April 25, 1988, 1.

Bell, Ellen, and the Irvine Historical Society. *Images of America: Irvine*. Charleston, SC: Arcadia Publishing, 2011.

Bermudez, Enrique. "The Swallows of Goya—Flight Plan of a Fantastic Flight." *Para Todos*, April-May 1996.

Burnett, Claudine E., and Paul Burnett. *Surfing Newport Beach: The Glory Days of Corona Del Mar*. Charleston, SC: The History Press, 2013.

Butterfield, Sherri. "Creating Lake Mission Viejo Was No Easy Task." *Mission Viejo Patch*, June 3, 2011. http://patch.com/california/missionviejo/creating-lake-mission-viejo-was-no-easy-task.

California Avocado Society. "Mother Hass Tree." http://californiaavocadosociety.org/mother-hass-tree.html.

California Department of Forestry and Fire Protection (CAL FIRE). *California Fire Siege 2007: An Overview*. Undated report.

California Department of Transportation. *2014 Traffic Volumes on the California State Highway System*. Division of Traffic Operations, California State Transportation Agency, State of California, Sacramento, 2015.

California Missions Resource Center. "Movies and the Missions: How Hollywood Helped Romanticize the Mission Era," authors and date unknown, http://missionscalifornia.com/stories/movies=missions.html.

Carlberg, David. *Bolsa Chica: Its History from Prehistoric Times to the Present*. Garden Grove, CA: Printmedia Books, 2009.

Carlson, Carole C. *Corrie ten Boom, Her Life, Her Faith: A Biography*. Old Tappan, NJ: F. H. Revell, Co., 1983.

Cassidy, Jon. "Wild Rivers Closes After 25 Years." *Orange County Register*, September 25, 2011.

Chambers, Bruce. "'This Way' to Orange County's Redwood Forest." *Orange County Register*, March 11, 2013.

"Chino's Days of Olympic Excitement: 1984 Olympic Shooting Events Were Held Near Prado Park." www.chinohills.com/news-articles-details/Chinos_Days_of_Olympic_Excitement-2361.

City of Irvine, California. *Summit at Turtle Ridge Community Traffic Calming Review*. Prepared by RK Engineering, Inc., Newport Beach, CA, November 29, 2011.

Coleman, Marion Moore. *Fair Rosalind: The American Career of Helena Modjeska*. New Lenox, IL: Cherry Hill Books, 1969.

Collins, Mabel. *The Story of Helena Modjeska: Madame Chlapowska* (Classic Reprint). London: Forgotten Books, 2015 (originally published in 1883).

Cowan, Jill. "Final Pieces of Irvine Ranch Complete 'Open-Space Puzzle' in O.C." *Los Angeles Times*, October 6, 2014. www.latimes.com/local/orange county/la-me-irvine-ranch-20141006-story.html.

Dana, Richard Henry. *Two Years Before the Mast*. Harper and Brothers, 1840 (original publication—reproductions are available).

Deering, Susan. *Images of America: Silverado Canyon*. Charleston, SC: Arcadia Publishing, 2008.

Delaney, Jeff. *Images of America: Newport's Balboa and Balboa Island*. Charleston, SC: Arcadia Publishing, 2007.

Delaney, Jeff. *Newport Beach: Then & Now*. Charleston, SC: Arcadia Publishing, 2011.

Drew, Elizabeth. *Richard M. Nixon: The American Presidents Series*. New York: Times Books, 2007.

Environmental and GIS Services, LLC. *Initial Study and Environmental Checklist for Aliso Creek Recovery, Reuse, and Conservation Project: Laguna Beach, California*. Laguna Niguel, CA, July 2008.

Epting, Chris. *Huntington Beach Chronicles: The Heart of Surf City*. Charleston, SC: History Press, 2014.

Esquivel, Ramon. "Another Year Without Swallows: Festival Goes on Without Birds at Historic Mission." *Los Angeles Times*, March 25, 2009.

French, Sally. "Happy Trails in Fullerton." *Orange County Register*, September 4, 2013. www.ocregister.com/articles/trails-524133-trail-city.html.

Glomb, Jozef. *A Man Who Spanned Two Eras: The Story of Bridge Engineer Ralph Modjeski*. Philadelphia: Kosciuskzo Foundation, 2002.

Halsey, Richard W. *Fire, Chaparral, and Survival in Southern California*. San Diego, CA: Sunbelt Publications, 2005.

Hoover, Mildred Brooke, Hero Eugene Rensch, Ether Grace Rensch, and William N. Abeloe. *Historic Spots in California*, 5th edition. Stanford, CA: Stanford University Press, 2002.

"Hope Seen for Lost Boatmen." *Desert Sun,* Palm Springs, CA, June 18, 1974, A2.

James, Elysse. "Officials Kill Aggressive Mountain Lion in Whiting Ranch Park." *Orange County Register*, March 31, 2014. www.ocregister.com/articles/lion-607742-mountain-hughan.html.

Jordan, Carol. *Tustin: An Illustrated History*. Tustin, CA: Tustin Historical Society, 2010.

Leneman, Mike. "Devil Winds: Santa Ana Winds Explained by One of Us." *Mariner*, Issue 153, November 2015, 8–9.

McCulley, Johnston. *The Curse of Capistrano* (retitled *The Mark of Zorro*). New York: Grosser & Dunlap, 1924.

Meadows, Don. *Historic Place Names in Orange County*. Balboa Island (Newport Beach), CA: Paisano Press, 1966.

Meier, Gisela. "Jessamyn West Is City's Other Famous Resident." *Yorba Linda Star*, January 6, 1979, 2.

Messina, Frank. "Mission Viejo Council Names Park After Robert Curtis." *Los Angeles Times*, April 30, 1993. http://articles.latimes.com/1993-04-30/local/me-29544_1_mission-viejo.

Miller, Michael, and Britney Barnes. "Harriett M. Wieder Dies: She Was the First Woman on the Orange County Board of Supervisors." *Daily Pilot*: Article Collections, January 12, 2010, http://articles.dailypilot.com/2010-01-12/news/dpt-wieder01132010.art_1_national-advisory-environmental-health-bolsa-chica-conservancy-harriett-m-wieder.

Miranda, Carolina A. "Court Order Halts Destruction of Prado Dam Bicentennial Mural in Corona." *Los Angeles Times*, June 10, 2015.

Mitchell, Patrick. *Santa Ana Mountains History, Habitat and Hikes*. Charleston, SC: Natural History Press, 2013.

Molina, Alejandra. "Irvine Surpasses 250,000 Population Mark." *Orange County Register*, May 6, 2015.

Newland, James D. *Images of America: Cleveland National Forest*. Charleston, SC: Arcadia Publishing, 2008.

O'Hara, Thomas. *Images of America: Marine Corps Air Station El Toro*. Charleston, SC: Arcadia Publishing, 1999.

O'Neill, Stephen, and Nancy H. Evans. "Notes on Historical Juaneño Villages and Geographical Features." *Journal of California and Great Basin Anthropology*, Vol. 2, 1980.

Reed, Roberta A., and the Santa Ana Historical Preservation Society. *Images of America: Santa Ana 1940–2007*. Charleston, SC: Arcadia Publishing, 2008.

Robinson, Mark. "Olympic Moments: 1984—Grewal Edges Bauer in Thriller." *Cycling News*, May 30, 2012. www.cyclingnews.com/features/olympic-moments-1984-grewal-edges-bauer-in-thriller/.

Schad, Jerry, and David Money Harris. *Afoot and Afield Orange County: A Comprehensive Hiking Guide*, 4th edition. Birmingham, AL: Wilderness Press, 2015.

Schlom, Corey. *The Unseen O.C.: The Untold History, Stories and Legends of the Unseen Orange County*. Philadelphia: JPS Publishing, 2010.

Stephenson, Terry E. *Shadows of Old Saddleback: Tales of the Santa Ana Mountains*. Orange, CA: The Rasmussen Press, 1974.

Strawther, Larry. *A Brief History of Los Alamitos & Rossmoor*. Charleston, SC: The History Press, 2012.

Strawther, Larry. *Seal Beach: A Brief History*. Charleston, SC: The History Press, 2014.

Testa, Stephen M. "The History of Oil Along the Newport-Inglewood Structural Zone—Los Angeles County, California." *Oil-Industry History*, Vol. 8, No. 1, 2007, 9–35.

Thomas, Henry W. *Walter Johnson: Baseball's Big Train*. Lincoln: University of Nebraska Press / Bison Books, 1995.

Vogel, Claire Marie. *Images of America: Laguna Beach*. Charleston, SC: Arcadia Publishing, 2009.

Vogel, Randy, and Larry Kuechlin. *Mountain Biking Orange County, California*. Guilford, CT: Morris Book Publishing, 1996.

Walker, Doris I. *Images of America: Dana Point*. Charleston, SC: Arcadia Publishing, 2007.

Wallechinsky, David, and Jaime Loucky. *The Complete Book of the Olympics: 2008 Edition*. London: Aurum Press Ltd., 2008.

Warshaw, Matt. *The Encyclopedia of Surfing*. Orlando, FL: Harcourt, Inc., 2005.

Whiting, David. "The Mystery Above Black Star Canyon." *Orange County Register*, February 3, 2009.

Womack, David. *Mountain Bike! Orange County: A Wide-Grin Ride Guide*. Birmingham, AL: Menasha Ridge Press, 2008.

Wood, Alex. "Trabuco Peak." www.summitpost.org/trabuco-peak/507606.

Yi, Daniel. "Irvine Wins Bid to Annex El Toro Site." *Los Angeles Times*, November 13, 2003.

"Zorro Left Mark on Mission San Juan," author unknown, *Capistrano Dispatch*, June 11, 2010.

WEBSITES

Back Bay Loop Trail, www.newportbeach.ca.gov/how-do-i-/view/things-to-do/back-bay-loop-trail.

California Wildland Firefighter Memorial, http://cwfm.info.

Chino Hills State Park, www.parks.ca.gov/?page_id=648.

City of Chino Hills Traffic Counts, www.chinohill.org/DocumentView.asp?DID=1137.

City of Corona: Existing Traffic Control with Average Daily Traffic Volumes, www.discovercorona.com/CityOfCorona/media/Media/Public%20Works%20/Documents/Traffic%20Engineering/ADT-20140106.pdf.

City of Diamond Bar, Traffic Counts—Streets, http://cityofdiamondbar.com/index.aspx?page=429.

City of Whittier, Bike Route Map, www.cityofwhittier.org/civicax/fileblank/blobdloadaspx?blobid=6425.

Cleveland National Forest, http://fs.usda.gov/cleveland.

Coal Canyon Ecological Reserve, California Department of Fish and Wildlife, www.wildlife.ca.gov/Lands/Places-to-Visit/Coal-Canyon-ER.

County of Los Angeles, Department of Public Works, Traffic Volume Counts, http://dpw.lacounty.gov/tnl/trafficcounts.

County of Riverside Transportation Department, Transportation and Land Management Agency, Traffic Counts—2014, http://rctlma.org/Portals/7/documents/WEB%20COUNTS.pdf.

Crystal Cove State Park, www.parks.ca.gov/?page_id=644.

Huntington Beach Surf and Sport (surfing statistics and data), www.hsssurf.com.

International Surfing Museum, www.surfingmuseum.org.

Irvine Ranch Conservancy, www.irconservancy.org.

Juan Bautista de Anza National Historic Trail, US National Park Service, www.nps.gov/juba; also www.anzahistorictrail.org.

Marine Corps Base Camp Pendleton, www.pendleton.marines.mil.

Mariposa Reserve, www.wildlandsconservancy.org/preserve_mariposa.html.

Midway City History, www.midwaycity.com/mchistory.htm.

Newport Dunes Resort, www.newportdunes.com.

Orange County Model Engineers, www.ocmetrains.org.

Orange County Public Works, "Coyote Creek—Metals TMDL," OC Watersheds, http://ocwatersheds.com/programs/waterways/tmdl/coyotecreek.

Orange County Regional Parks, http://ocparks.com. Articles on Aliso and Wood Canyons Regional Park, Carbon Canyon Regional Park, Craig Regional Park, Harriett M. Wieder Regional Park, Laguna Coast Wilderness Park, Peters Canyon Regional Park, Talbert Regional Park, Thomas F. Riley Wilderness Park, Upper Newport Bay Nature Preserve, Whiting Ranch Wilderness Park.

Orange County Transportation Authority, 2013/2014 Traffic Flow Map; System Map (buses); Bikeways Map; www.octa.net/pdf/2013trafficflow.pdf; www.octa.net/Bus/Roues-and-Schedules/System-Map; www.octa.net/pdf/BikewaysMap_2013-0504.pdf.

Puente Hills Habitat Preservation Authority, www.habitatauthority.org.

San Juan Capistrano information, www.sanjuancapistrano.org.

Traffic volumes on California State Highways, www.dot.ca.gov/hq/traffops/census/2014all.

Wikipedia articles on Aliso Canyon, Aliso Viejo, American cliff swallow, Anaheim, Auto Club Raceway at Pomona, Black Star Canyon, Bommer Canyon, Brea, Brea-Olinda Oil Field, Cañada Gobernadora, Chino, Chino Hills, Cities in Orange County, Cleveland National Forest, Coto de Caza, Coyote Creek (San Gabriel River), *The Curse of Capistrano*, Cycling at the 1984 Summer Olympics, Dana Point, Diamond Bar, Elsinore Mountains, Elsinore Peak, Elsinore Trough, Enduro (mountain biking), Fountain Valley, Fullerton, Hawaiian Gardens, Hsi Lai Temple, Huntington Beach, Irvine, Irvine Company, Irvine National Natural Landmarks, La Habra, La Habra Heights, La Palma, Laguna Beach, Laguna Hills, Lake Elsinore, Lake Forest, Lake Mission Viejo, Lion Country Safari, List of famous residents of Newport Beach, List of largest California cities by population, List of people from Irvine, California, List of University of California, Irvine people, Los Alamitos, Marine Corps Air Station El Toro, Marine Corps Base Camp Pendleton, Midway City, Modjeska Canyon, National Natural Landmarks, Newport Beach, Norco, Orange, Orange County, Placentia, Prado Dam, Puente Hills, San Joaquin Hills, Santa Ana, Santa Ana Mountains, Santa Ana River, Santa Ana Winds, Santiago Canyon Fire, Santiago Fire, Seal Beach, Silverado, Silverado Canyon, The Tyra Banks Show, Trabuco Peak, Tustin, US Open of Surfing, Upper Newport Bay, Walter Johnson, Wild Rivers (Water Park), Yorba Linda.

Wildland Firefighters' Monument and Memorial Sites, www.wildlandfire.com/docs/memorials.htm.

Ride Index

About the Author

Wayne D. Cottrell is a civil engineering educator specializing in transportation, and a researcher, author, runner, and cyclist. He is a member of the Transportation Research Board's Bicycle Transportation Committee, and has been an active cyclist and member of USA Cycling for 25 years. His bicycle racing résumé includes occasional road and mountain bike wins. He won an award for his writing from the National Research Council in 1999. Wayne grew up in the Bay Area, in Oakland. He bicycled to college, then occasionally to work after graduating, and then for recreation and competition, becoming familiar with biking routes throughout California. Wayne is the author of *Road Biking Utah*, a FalconGuide published in 2010; seventeen articles on transportation in refereed technical journals; thirty technical articles in conference proceedings; and a number of transportation research reports. He earned a PhD in transportation engineering from the University of Utah in 1997, and is a registered traffic engineer in California. Wayne is a licensed Category 3 and Masters cyclist with USA Cycling. He currently resides in Crestline, California.